THE ROCKEFELLER MILLIONS

Also by Jules Abels:

OUT OF THE JAWS OF VICTORY

THE TRUMAN SCANDALS

THE WELFARE STATE

THE ROCKEFELLER MILLIONS

THE STORY OF THE WORLD'S
MOST STUPENDOUS FORTUNE

Jules Abels

FREDERICK MULLER

First published in Great Britain in 1967
by Frederick Muller Ltd., Fleet Street, London, E.C.4

I am grateful to Mr. Laurance S. Rockefeller for granting me an interview, thus subjecting himself to a battery of my questions. I also want to thank Mr. Steven V. David, a representative of the Rockefeller family, who has been most helpful in supplying me with information. My thanks also to Peter Smith for permission to quote from the *History of the Standard Oil Company* by Ida Tarbell, published by Peter Smith, 20 Railroad Avenue, Gloucester, Massachusetts.

Printed in Great Britain by offset Litho at
Taylor Garnett Evans & Co. Ltd
Watford, Herts

CONTENTS

CONTENTS

BOOK FOUR: THE AGE OF PHILANTHROPY

ILLUSTRATIONS

INTRODUCTION
From Villainy to Sainthood

IN March 1905 the Congregationalist Board of Foreign Missions in Boston announced with "joyous surprise" that it had received a gift of $100,000 from John D. Rockefeller, president of the Standard Oil Company and a devout Baptist. The announcement of this "unexpected" bounty from the oil king set off a sensational controversy throughout the nation.

A group of thirty Congregational ministers meeting in Boston urged that the gift be returned: "This company stands before the public under repeated and formidable indictments for methods which are morally iniquitous and socially destructive." The leader in the fight to reject the gift was a longtime foe of Rockefeller, Dr. Washington Gladden, of Columbus, Ohio, who was moderator of the National Council of Congregational Churches. It was he who first used the phrase "tainted money." In a sermon he said: "The money does not rightfully belong to the man who gives it. It has been flagitiously acquired and all the world knows it. Shall the young men and women of the missionary colleges be taught to regard Mr. Rockefeller as a great benefactor? The colleges might better be permanently closed."

"Tainted Money." As Rockefeller's aide, Frederick Gates, later wrote, "Literature had been enriched with a deathless phrase." The whole nation now debated the propriety of a church's acceptance of "tainted money." Everyone had an opinion. The vaudevillians had a new gag: "It's tainted, all right. 'T aint yours and 't aint mine."

Though church periodicals were disturbed about Mr. Rockefeller, they were also understandably disturbed about the loss of such gifts. The inference in many editorials was that even though the old reprobate was undoubtedly headed for damnation, his money wasn't doomed; and in any event it would be magnanimous on the part of the church to undertake his salvation. The Boston

Congregationalist said, "Even Mr. Rockefeller deserves Christian treatment." The *Missionary Review* said: "If the gift is refused, every dollar thrown in the plate must be scrutinized and its pedigree searched out. . . . The source of the gift did not disturb Him but the niggardliness of the giver did. He rebuked the shortsightedness which could not see that publicans and sinners are worth saving and are not proper subjects for a boycott declared by the subjects of God." Rationalizations of all kinds appeared. "Tens of thousands think business is war." To refuse "singles out one illustrious example of the pernicious system and leaves the system itself unrebuked."

Newspapers injected a good deal of cynicism into a debate of high moral principle. The New York *Sun's* comment was to be repeated many times thereafter: "Gifts of millions deodorize themselves." The New York *Messenger* asked, "Do they fear the gift of ten thousand dollars perhaps to a school in Turkey or Ceylon will corrupt its teachers so that they will not properly instruct Armenians or Singhalese in the atrocities of the American trusts?" The Chicago *Chronicle* said, "When Christian ministers get to be holier than Jesus Christ they ought to watch sedulously against translation [to heaven]."

The interesting thing about this debate was that everybody assumed that the money was tainted. Although Rockefeller was the target of many charges, he had been convicted of no crime. The condemnation was therefore somewhat premature. The *Outlook* was one of the few calling atttention to this: "He who is accused of violating the laws of the land should be tried by the tribunals of the land. He who is accused of violating the standards of the church should be tried by the tribunals of the church. Certainly he should not be tried before the missionary body of another church which has not even the jurisdiction to try a member of the communion to which that missionary body belongs."

The dénouement of the episode was unexpected. Rockefeller had been thoroughly lambasted for weeks, and the secretary of the board had been instructed to return the money but replied that it had been already spent. Then the truth came out. The gift had not been received with "joyous surprise" but had been urgently solicited and was the result of negotiations that had lasted over two years. The Congregationalists had long been envious of the gifts that Baptist missions had been receiving from Rockefeller. Because Rockefeller's wife had been a Congregationalist before her marriage, an approach was made to her sister, Miss Lucy Spelman, who was a member of the Rockefeller household. Though she had brought up the matter at family breakfast, Rockefeller had declined to go beyond his own denomination. There followed more entreaties from the Congregationalists and finally a direct appeal to Frederick Gates, who advised Rockefeller on his charitable contributions.

Rockefeller was understandably stunned when the issue was raised as to whether a gift should be accepted that he had been begged to give; in addition, he was shocked to see the gift made an occasion for nationwide denigration of his character. Gates was taken aback when ministers who had previously solicited Rockefeller for money joined in the witch-hunt. One of these was an eminent Presbyterian divine who had written Rockefeller, endorsed Rockefeller's checks personally, and had visited Rockefeller's office in quest of money.

After the "tainted money" incident, no one expressed compunctions about accepting money from John D. Rockefeller, from whom, as someone put it, "oil blessings flow."

In November 1905 a play written by Charles Klein, and entitled *The Lion and the Mouse,* opened on Broadway. The main character, played by the noted actor Richard Bennett, is John B. Ryder, the richest man in the world, worth "a thousand million dollars." This was universally understood to be Rockefeller. Ryder is surrounded by senators and governors ready to do his bidding. One lackey says to another: "Socialism is growing in the country. Do you know, Senator, that last week a man dared to address Mr. Ryder as he was getting out of his carriage? Another dared to take his snapshot with a Kodak. In Russia he might have been shot. We must protect him against the rabble, the American people."

Ryder, who holds Congress in the hollow of his hand, is arranging to have a judge impeached and removed on a fake charge because he dared to enjoin Ryder's railroad from seizing millions of acres of public land. Ryder proclaims, "If that man goes back on the bench, every paltry Justice of Peace, every petty official, will think that he has a special mission to tear down the structures that hard work and capital have erected." The daughter of the judge, in love with Ryder's son, attacks this soulless man: "He is the greatest criminal the world ever produced. He loves money because he loves power better than mankind or womankind."

Although the play reads today like the weariest twaddle, the public must have delighted in seeing the favorite American villain represented on the stage, since the play ran for two years and smashed all existing stage records. It was later successfully novelized.

These are only two examples of the hatred poured on Rockefeller in the first decade of the century. Senator Robert M. La Follette branded him as "the greatest criminal of the age," and newspapers from one end of the country to the other, led by those owned by Joseph Pulitzer and William Randolph Hearst, pilloried him with that indictment. In cartoons he was conventionally represented as an octopus; and one cartoonist improved on the others by making him hydra-headed, and wrote as his caption, "But Where Is the Heart?"

The paradox is that the object of all this hatred was not a wicked man. On the contrary he had "heart." He was a pillar of the church, and extraordinarily generous to philanthropic causes, although he and his family lived simply. He was a good employer, paying higher wages than the average; and in 1903, two decades ahead of American industry, he installed a pension system.

In an age when the public was milked and bilked with adulterated merchandise of all kinds, there were few complaints in this country about the quality of Standard Oil products. Rockefeller had no "Public be damned" attitude.

These virtues of Rockefeller were ignored or given short shrift. Rockefeller's well-known piety, which happened to be deep and genuine, actually boomeranged on his reputation. It was regarded by the public as the last refuge of a scoundrel, a Tartuffe-like hypocrisy. "The pretense of piety" was a favorite phrase in the Pulitzer papers. Rascals had better be godless. Rockefeller's philanthropies were attributed to the need for what Mark Twain called "fire insurance—insurance against the fire of the hereafter." They were also considered a bribe campaign to buy public goodwill. Actually, such aspersions did Rockefeller grave injustice. From the time he was sixteen and began working, Rockefeller contributed part of his income to charity; and his contributions had reached substantial figures long before he became a public villain.

In 1911 the Supreme Court of the United States ordered the Standard Oil "trust" dissolved; that is, the single-company monopoly was broken up into many different companies. The decision was not based on legal principles but was a response to the overwhelming adverse public opinion against Rockefeller.

From that point Rockefeller withdrew from any connection with Standard Oil except stockholding, and from that point the miraculous transformation in the Rockefeller reputation began. In 1912 the New York *Evening Journal,* belonging to William Randolph Hearst, for years his unrelenting foe, said: "Rockefeller uses his money for all the people. He considers himself the responsible custodian of the millions he has dipped up from the golden stream of opportunity. And humanity will be better off because of his work when he shall have been dead ten thousand years." Later Hearst suggested that Rockefeller should receive a Nobel prize because of the contributions of the Rockefeller Institute to the cure of diseases.

During the First World War the Rockefeller name evoked cheers as he gave and gave again, not only by subscriptions to Liberty Bonds but also in gifts of millions to the Red Cross and Belgian Relief. It was in the twenties that America took the octopus to its heart, when the man exchanged a crown of thorns for a halo. His birthdays and annual pilgrimages to Florida became hallowed moments. John Singer Sargent, who painted a portrait of Rockefeller, an etherealized Rockefeller, said that he felt himself in the presence of St. Francis of Assisi. The odium attached to Rockefeller was becoming so dim that the New York *Evening Post* commented editorially on one of his birthdays, "Possibly a hundred years from now some historical scholar under the Rockefeller Foundation will be set to studying the United States from 1875 to 1910 and will find to his amazement that the name, Rockefeller, had in his lifetime been held to execration by millions."

In 1928 the Rockefellers launched a successful proxy campaign to oust Colonel Robert Stewart as chairman of Standard Oil of Indiana because he was "tainted" in the Teapot Dome scandals. The press rang with hosannas. I recall that as a boy, reading the papers of the time, including the columns of Arthur Brisbane, Hearst's sidekick who was Rockefeller's greatest booster, I was convinced that Rockefeller was enshrined in the Pantheon of American heroes, and would have been shocked to learn that he was for long considered infamous. I am sure that millions of my generation had the same impression.

John D. Rockefeller died in 1937. For twenty years there had been no dissonant note in the loud chorus of praise.

Sinner or saint? The literature concerning Rockefeller has swung to the same extremes as public opinion.

The reputation of Rockefeller and Standard Oil was demolished by two books. The first, a savage polemic by Henry Demarest Lloyd, *Wealth Against Commonwealth,* was published in 1894. The second, the masterpiece of the muckraking age, published ten years later, was *The History of the Standard Oil Company* by Ida Minerva Tarbell, one of the most widely discussed and influential books in our history.

In painting Rockefeller in the trappings of Satan, Lloyd did not have a single good word to say about Rockefeller. He "did not even invent the rebate." In her attack on the ruthless monopoly, Miss Tarbell made one concession. Rockefeller always kept his word, preferring not to sully piracy with dishonesty.

Stung by the Tarbell book, Rockefeller deserted his policy of silence and wrote his *Random Reminiscences of Men and Events,* a general defense containing some rationalizations and a good deal of soft soap. After the dissolution of Standard Oil he decided on a definitive biography, and while in his late seventies spoke at length to the selected historian, a sportswriter by the name of William O. Inglis.

In 1929, when the apotheosis of Rockefeller was in full bloom, John Winkler's *John D: A Portrait in Oils* appeared, an impressionistic account of the man and his career. Mirroring the popular mood, it was a hymn of affection. In one aside he shrugged off the early life of Standard Oil as "crooked." In 1932, at the bottom of the depression, John Flynn's *God's Gold* was published. Though the stock of business leaders at the time was quite low, Flynn was generous in his treatment of Rockefeller. His great fortune was "the most honestly acquired . . . the least tainted of all the great fortunes of his day."

At the request of the Rockefeller family, Professor Allan Nevins of Columbia University undertook a detailed study of the man and his times. He was supplied with the Rockefeller papers and the notes of Inglis. The result in 1940 was *John D. Rockefeller: The Heroic Age of American Enterprise.* The verdict of Norman Cousins in reviewing it is one with which this writer agrees. Referring to the American capacity to forgive and forget, Cousins said, "If it had appeared a quarter of a century ago it might have been called 'inspired whitewashing' at worst or 'warmly sympathetic' at best."

In the years since, the facts about the life of Rockefeller have been disappearing into limbo. Thus in a book about the Rockefeller family, the author, referring to the past, says, "The libels are not repeated here."

It is a disservice to blunt or gild the truth about the history of Rockefeller and the early oil industry. In terms of morality Rockefeller was one of the best of the industry builders; nevertheless he was typical of the age. What had to be done, he did. The period of our Industrial Revolution was a period of unbridled lust for fortune and of incredible corruption. That is part of our heritage, and we cannot blink it; the change since then is the measure of our progress.

The assessment must be a mixed one, of bad and good. One of Rockefeller's favorite pieces of doggerel contained the lines "There is so much bad in the best of us; there is so much good in the worst of us." The good coming out of Rockefeller's career cannot be gainsaid. An industry of immense service to the public was built that possibly could not have been built in any other way. The fortune has been poured out in a philanthropic spirit for countless charitable, religious, health, educational, and artistic purposes. This writer believes that the lives of the Rockefellers have served the public good. The reader will be able to judge for himself.

BOOK ONE

THE EMERGENCE OF ROCKEFELLER

I have ways of making money you know nothing of.
—JOHN D. ROCKEFELLER IN 1872

CHAPTER 1   *"Oil—There's Your Fortune"*

THE ROCKEFELLER FORTUNE was due in large part to luck—Rockefeller would have been the first to admit it. His famous statement "God gave me my money" implied as much, since Rockefeller realized that he had been a favored child of fortune. The first of the fortuitous circumstances was the most important. In 1859, when Rockefeller was twenty years old and on the threshold of his business career, the first oil well was drilled not far from Cleveland, where he lived and worked. The place was Titusville, a village in the northwestern corner of Pennsylvania, forty miles south of Erie, which in turn is one hundred miles east of Cleveland along Lake Erie.

In the early days of the Republic, home illumination came from candles. Candles, however, were not considered inexpensive; and most people, as from time immemorial, went to bed when darkness fell, and rose with the dawn. Thus the advent of cheap oil automatically provided more hours of waking life.

Oil lamps came into use in the beginning of the eighteenth century when the sperm whale fell prey to the harpoon. By the time of the Revolution a large whaling fleet was in business, operating from ports like Nantucket and New Bedford, and fortunes were made, one of which was to be the Hetty Green fortune. Not only could whale oil be used for lamps, but spermaceti could be used for candles, and soon sperm candles were supplanting tallow candles. In *Moby Dick*, Captain Starbuck exults that he is doing God's work by bringing light into the home. But the supply of whale oil was always thin, and became thinner; its price was far too high for an unsatisfactory illuminant—as much as three dollars a gallon. Camphene from turpentine came into use about 1830, a better light but highly dangerous. Oil was then called "burning oil," and users of camphene found this to be literally correct, since it was risky even to carry a lighted lamp.

Camphene was therefore less popular than lard-oil lamps. By the time of the Jackson Administration, a lamp was a status symbol denoting wealth, since all oils were costly.

A great advance was made in 1846 when Dr. Abraham Gesner, in Canada, found a way of distilling an oil from coal. He called it "kerosene," from the Greek *keros,* meaning "wax," and the *ene* suggested by "camphene." In 1850 the Scotsman James Young patented a method for extracting crude oil from bituminous coal, and the business of extracting oil from shale began. (It became so efficient over the years that Standard Oil was never to get a firm grip on the Scottish market because of competition with shale oil.) Samuel Downer, of South Boston, became the most energetic manufacturer of what was called coal oil or carbon oil, producing 650,000 gallons of refined oil a year. This was only one of fifty existing manufacturing plants turning out coal oil. The process required two distillations, first from the coal and then from the oil to produce kerosene, but the price undercut all other types of oils. Professor Nevins points out that as a commission merchant in 1859, Rockefeller probably handled coal oil and that in Cleveland in that year a wholesaler advertised in the Cleveland *Leader:* "It is not explosive; it will not gum or smoke when burned in proper lamps; it is 50% cheaper than lard or sperm oil; and it is 20% cheaper than gas." (Artificial gas made from coal was available in some areas.) This advertisement overrated the coal-oil illuminant. It was cheaper at $1.00 a gallon than other oils, but was still a luxury item. It was dangerous, and the lamp did become quickly clogged and crusted. None the less Downer cleared $100,000 in 1859.

When petroleum first became available in quantities in 1860, the stage was set, for the public was acquainted with illuminating oils, distributive channels were set up, distilling was familiar, and lamps were in widespread use. The transition to petroleum was so smooth that while the price of the new illuminant remained high, most users in the country were not aware that their oil came from a new source. Kerosene made from petroleum, in fact, continued to be known as coal oil.

In the new machine age lubricants were indispensable. Various animal and vegetable oils were used for that purpose. However, both James Young and a chemist in the employ of Downer, Joshua Merrill, were able to distill lubricating oils from coal and shale, and a big demand sprang up from textile mills and rail-roads.

Throughout the two decades before the Civil War attention was turning to the bluish-green, viscous, malodorous substance called petroleum, oozing from the ground in various places along the Appalachian range. Mankind had been acquainted with it in a vague way for centuries. According to legend, pitch made from it was used to build Noah's Ark and the Tower of Babel. It was used in the "everlasting fires" of Mideast cults, and the American Indians used it for their sacred fires. The only oil burned for illumination in Roman times was olive oil, which gave a weak, smoky light. The first knowledge of the distillation of petroleum came from the Arabic culture about the eighth century of the Christian Era, and it spread in later centuries.

Oil was detected at an early date in America. The earliest mention was in 1636 in G. Sagard's *Histoire du Canada et Voyages du Missionaires Récollets,* in which a letter of 1627 describes the visit of a Franciscan missionary to the oil springs of what is now Cuba, New York. In 1700 the Earl of Bellemont, colonial governor of New York, sent the Royal Engineer of the Colonies to "view a well or spring which is eight miles beyond the Senek's furthest Castle which they have told me blazes up in a flame when a lighted coale or firebrand is put into it; you will do well to taste the said water and give me your opinion thereof." In 1755 a map of Pennsylvania published in London had "Petroleum" printed over the northwestern part. In 1776 General George Washington bought a tract of land in Virginia in what was later the Kanawha Valley of West Virginia, close to what is now Charleston. Washington noted in his journal, "This tract was taken by Gen. Lewis and myself on account of the bituminous spring which it contains of so inflammable a nature as to burn as freely as spirits and is nearly as difficult to extinguish." In 1783 General Benjamin Lincoln told in a letter of the troops stopping at a spring in western Pennsylvania: "They collected the oil and bathed their joints in it. This gave them great relief and freed them of rheumatic complaints. The troops drank freely of the waters and they operated as a gentle purge." The troops had stopped at what soon appeared on maps as Oyl Creek, not far from the first well.

For years the oil was considered a dreadful nuisance. It so

fouled streams that cattle could not drink, and when carried onto pastures in floods it ruined the grazing land. Those who complained the most were the borers for saltwater used in the manufacture of salt. The presence of petroleum on the ground was supposed to be a sign that there was salt underneath, but when the borers hit saltwater and it spurted up mixed with petroleum they were exasperated. At first they abandoned such wells in disgust. Then it occurred to them that the oil might be separated, since it floated on streams; indeed, if the water was dumped into cisterns or culverts the oil came to the surface and could be skimmed off. In fact, so much was thrown into one stream along the Kanawha that it was called Greasy Run.

Here and there people were finding use for the oil. In 1847 Samuel Kier, of Pittsburgh, in partnership with his father and brother, bored wells at Tarentum, close to Pittsburgh. At four hundred feet the well brought up water mixed with petroleum. It seemed that the well was ruined. But Kier knew that the oil had qualities that made it burn and that it might be a lubricant. He sent some to a Philadelphia chemist, who gave the first expert opinion—advice to distill it and sell it as an illuminant. Kier established a refinery with a five-barrel still, and in 1858 he was selling it in New York as "carbon oil that will burn in the ordinary coal-oil lamp."

Gradually, man was moving to the final discovery. Another step—though it does not appear as such—was that Kier decided to bottle petroleum and sell it as a medicine. Indians were known to use it as a medicine. Kier's wife was suffering from consumption, and her doctor prescribed American oil, which Kier examined and found to be identical with his petroleum. Seneca Oil or American Oil could be used as a liniment; but when three teaspoonfuls of it were taken three times a day, it supposedly could do wonders for cholera morbus, liver complaints, bronchitis, and consumption. Kier bottled his petroleum and sold it through drugstores all over the country as "Kier's Petroleum or Rock Oil," an unexcelled remedy, "Celebrated for its Curative Powers." He sold a good deal of it because petroleum was so malodorous that everyone was sure that it was a powerful medicine.

To advertise his medicine Kier distributed handbills. They were in the form of bank notes that bore on the top the picture of

an artesian well. Beneath it, in bold letters, was BANK OF ALLE-
GHENY RIVER; and below that, on this ingenious advertisement
(from which Madison Avenue could learn today), where one
would expect dollars were the words FOUR HUNDRED FEET—and
then—"below the earth's surface is pumped up with the salt
water, floats on top, when a quantity accumulates is drawn off
into barrels, is bottled in its natural state without any preparation
or admixture." Thus Kier made a virtue of the fact that he did
nothing to the petroleum in its raw state but bottle it and sell it.

In 1854 a graduate of Dartmouth, George H. Bissell, who had
spent ten frustrating years in various pursuits and had finally
settled on the law, returned on a visit to his alma mater. While he
was there, a professor of chemistry showed him a bottle of petroleum and told him that it might be better than coal oil as an
illuminant. "Where did it come from?" Bissell asked. It had been
discovered floating on the surface of springs in a place called Oil
Creek in Pennsylvania and had been sent by an alumnus, Francis
Brewer, whose father was part owner of the land. Bissell was
deeply interested, and with his law partner, Jonathan Eveleth, he
bought 105 acres at Titusville for $5,000.

Because the law partners were out of funds after the purchase,
they organized the first oil company, the Pennsylvania Rock Oil
Company, organized at first under New York laws but later reorganized as a Connecticut corporation because in Connecticut
stockholders were not liable for debts of a corporation. The moving spirit in the organization became James M. Townsend, president of the City Savings Bank of New Haven, who, however, did
not want his name to appear in connection with so chimerical
an adventure.

Several barrels of oil were shipped to Professor Benjamin Silliman of Yale, whose father, by coincidence, had made a scientific
report on the oil springs at Cuba, New York, in 1833. By frac-
tional distillation Professor Silliman showed that at least 50 percent could be converted into illuminating oil that could be
burned in a camphene lamp and that in addition naphtha and
paraffin could be recovered, leaving only a 10 percent residue. As
to the lubricating oils, he was vague. About the illuminant he was
enthusiastic: "I cannot refrain from expressing my satisfaction at
the results of these photometric experiments since they have

given the oil of your company a much higher value as an illuminant than I had dared to hope." In conclusion he stated his belief
that the company had a "raw material from which by simple and
not expensive process they may manufacture very valuable products." This historic report was held up until the company could
raise $528 to pay the professor for his trouble. The report was
printed and distributed as an encouragement to would-be investors. Professor Silliman himself was so impressed that he bought
shares in the oil company. But the company was no more successful than before in raising money. Francis Brewer's father, who as
a member of Brewer & Watson had sold the company its Titusville land, wrote to his son who had invested some money,
"Beware—you are in the hands of sharpsters."

The company knew that the oil could be a bonanza. As an
illuminant it would be cheaper, last longer, be safer, and give a
better light than coal oil. The problem was to procure it in quantities. Aside from recovering oil from the salt wells, the only
methods were to dig ditches or pits, to skim oil from the surface
of streams or "tar springs," or to spread blankets over streams and
then wring out the blankets. By the wringing method a man
could obtain ten gallons a day if he worked hard. The market was
there, and waiting. A Colonel A. C. Ferris, of New York, sold
crude oil to refiners, obtaining it from every source he could, but
the total business, of which Ferris had the greatest part,
amounted to only 1,180 barrels in 1858. Though the price was
$30.00 a barrel, which at 42 gallons to the barrel was over $0.70 a
gallon wholesale, Ferris still could not meet the demand.

The Pennsylvania Rock Oil Company was almost at a standstill
—and then came the breakthrough. The story is that while Bissell
was walking along Broadway in the summer of 1856, he took
refuge from the heat under the awning of a drugstore. While he
was inspecting the window, his eyes alighted on a Kier medicine
handbill with its picture of an artesian well. Eureka! Why not
drill for oil directly, just as Kier and others drilled for saltwater?
He spoke to Townsend about it, who mulled over it but did not
agree with Bissell until the fall of 1857. Then, according to Townsend's account, the stockholders cast scorn on the idea. Oil coming out of the ground, pumping oil out of the earth as one might
pump water? What a crazy idea!

But Townsend had made up his mind; he decided to send to Titusville a fellow boarder at the Tontine Hotel in New Haven where he lived, a man who had invested $200 in the company. A tragic figure in the story of oil, Edwin L. Drake was to be infinitely more important for mankind than that other explorer, the illustrious Drake of Elizabethan times. Drake, thirty-eight, was something of a drifter. His last job had been that of conductor on the New York and New Haven Railroad, work he had had to give up because of his ill health soon after the death of his wife. Townsend sent Drake on a mission of inspection to Titusville, choosing him for no better reason, apparently, than that he was available and had a railroad pass.

Drake made the trip in December 1857, presumably to perfect title to the land, which was leased to the company because a "foreign" corporation could not own land in Pennsylvania. He stopped off at Syracuse to see the salt wells and then went by stage from Erie to Titusville, in Crawford County. It was a God-forsaken village of 125 inhabitants. Though there were farms all about, it was wild ravine country that held good deer-hunting in the winter. There were a few lumber mills in the environs. Mail reached the town once a week, and there was not a bank in the whole of Venango County, the site of the first wells. Drake was greeted there as "Colonel" Drake, a title he was to bear for the rest of his days. To impress the denizens of that rural retreat, Townsend had addressed his mail to "Colonel Drake." The "colonel" had a legal conference, inspected the oil springs, went to Tarentum to see the salt wells there, and returned home with as much enthusiasm as his innately phlegmatic personality could muster. Now the Seneca Oil Company was organized, supplanting the previous company, of which Drake became *pro forma* president.

In May 1858 Drake came to Titusville to stay. He was accompanied by his new wife and his son. For a while he seems to have puttered around, digging ditches and pits. Perhaps he had some doubts about drilling for oil. It was not until the late summer that he set about to find a driller. One agreed to come but did not show up. It appeared that he thought Drake was unbalanced, and the driller had said "yes" only to get rid of him. Another driller vanished after he got a better offer from a salt borer. There was one delay after another in assembling tools. Drake was a methodical plodder, not a dynamo of energy. When cold weather set in, all he had to show was a thirty-foot derrick and an engine house.

The inhabitants of the area, who were at first amused by the project, soon dismissed it with indifference. "Drake is fooling away his time and money," they would say. The derrick was called "Drake's yoke." Francis Brewer had become a skeptic; distributing free cigars, he said they cost him nothing—he had sold his stock for a song. Why was the idea considered fantastic? Oil experts are skeptical about the Bissell version that he got the drilling idea from Kier's circular. Certainly Professor Silliman, Kier, and others must have considered the possibility as logical. What deterred them was probably doubt as to whether there were formations of oil at all. The residents of the oil areas were unanimously convinced that there were no such formations and that the oil was from underground coal fields, and oozed to the surface by a kind of capillary action. Even if there were such formations, might they not be thousands of feet below the surface?

In May 1859 Drake began anew. He had gone to Kier's well at Tarentum and hired as driller "Uncle Billy" Smith, a Vulcan of a man who had a good deal of experience in drilling. In addition, he was a blacksmith, and could make drilling tools. Smith brought along his fifteen-year-old son, Sam, and built his home near the proposed well. Drilling began. When the well was 18 feet deep, the soil caved in. A cast-iron pipe six inches square was then driven down, through which the drilling tool was lowered, a technique to be adopted widely. At 36 feet bedrock was reached, and with the aid of a six-horsepower engine the drill began boring through the rock. On Saturday August 27, the drill seemed to hit a crevice, and operations were suspended for the weekend. The depth was 69½ feet, and Drake expected that he would have to drill at least 200 feet deeper.

The next day, Smith and his son gazed into the well where the son saw a dark liquid a foot beneath the surface of the shaft. "*Oil! Oil!*" Sam cried. Running to a neighboring sawmill, he cried, "We've struck oil!" The cry reverberated through the countryside. "The Yankee has struck oil! The Yankee has struck oil!" Within twenty-four hours, hundreds were milling around the well. Drake, who was away, did not appear upon the scene until Monday morning. Pointing to the well, Uncle Billy said to him, "Oil. There's your fortune." He could not have been more wrong. Drake was unmoved, showing the same equanimity in the face of good fortune as he did in bad. He supervised the pumping of the oil into tubs and barrels—the problem of storing oil already had loomed—and went off to wire the good news to Bissell in New York. Bissell celebrated by quietly buying up shares of Seneca Oil, telling no one but his partner, Eveleth of the strike. He then set off for Titusville to buy or lease as much of the properties on Oil Creek as he could; thus, he became wealthy. Meanwhile the Seneca Oil Company had become disillusioned with the project. After supplying Drake with $5,000, Townsend had finally sent him money to conclude his affairs and come home. Fortunately, because of the slowness of the mails, the letter arrived after oil was struck.

The Drake well was pumping twenty-five barrels a day, and a price of $20 a barrel could be anticipated. Jonathan Watson, who was Brewer's partner in the sawmill, rode around the area making leases on the day after the strike. Neighbors of Drake made preparations for well-drilling and since they could not wait for machinery they used human power, "kicking it down" by using a hickory pole set over a fulcrum, at the end of which was a platform on which men could jump up and down, activating the drill. In that way the second and third wells came in in early 1860. These were the Barnsdall and Watson wells, more prolific than the Drake well. The stream of oil was becoming a stream of dollars. Though cataclysmic events were occurring in the outside world, for John Brown had made his futile raid on Harpers Ferry in October 1859, all eyes in the oil regions were fastened on black gold, while the Union fell apart.

The news was somehow slow to reach the outside world. The first mention anywhere seems to have been in the New York *Tribune* on September 12, where a letter from "Medicus" in Titusville said, "The excitement of the discovery of this vast source of oil was fully equal to what I saw in California when a large lump of gold was accidentally turned out." The first mention in a paper in the oil regions was in the Crawford *Journal* at

Meadville, which carried an item the next day, but buried on an inside page. Rockefeller did not see anything until November 18, when the Cleveland *Leader* carried an item about the "oil springs of northern Pennsylvania" and "a rush to the oleaginous locations."

Oil did not have the same sound as *gold*, but within a few months of the Drake strike a wave of new faces was to be seen in the Oil Creek area. Unlike the Gold Rush of 1849, a continent did not have to be traversed; this strike was close to eastern centers of population, and only twenty miles from the nearest railroad. Workmen in the salt-drilling industry came early, leaving that industry prostrate. Those who had been frustrated in the California gold rush came to try their luck with oil. Farm boys from one hundred miles around flocked in, lured by tales of fancy pay for teamstering oil. Speculators and investors came looking for a quick "killing." The "grapevine" was working; a letter from "Uncle Bill" Smith was typical: "For God's sake, Mr. Peterson, come up here, there's oceans of oil." Flotsam and jetsam drifted in—adventurers, gamblers, the loafers and curious, camp followers, prostitutes known as dance-hall girls. Oil City, Titusville, Franklin, Meadville, and Tidioute were filling up. By mid-1860 an observers said of Titusville: "It is now the rendezvous of strangers eager for speculation. Never was a hive of bees in time of swarming more astir or making a greater buzz."

Where was the oil hidden underground? Offering their services were "diviners" who used a forked stick of witch hazel that vibrated in the proximity of oil, spiritualists who had established contacts in the underworld where the oil lay, and those heavenly endowed mortals the "smellers," who by applying their nose to the ground could sense oil within three hundred feet. Although the exploits of the "smellers," have gone unrecorded in the annals of Petrolia, the great Pithole field of 1865 was found with a witch-hazel stick.

At first, leases were cheap. Farms were leased for $200 down and a royalty of one-quarter down to an eighth of the value of oil obtained, if any. A story was current that the Pennsylvania Dutch farmers were so greedy and ignorant that when they were offered an eighth, they refused, demanding a tenth. But prices began to soar, and soon the farmers received fabulous amounts. Samuel C.

T. Dodd, who much later was general counsel for Standard Oil
and who won fame for devising the trust instrument, practiced
law in his youth in the oil regions. In his memoirs he told how
farmers who never saw $100 in their lives, and who often did not
know where breakfast would come from the next day, were now
suddenly enriched beyond the dreams of avarice. He recalled
how a farmer who was being paid in bank notes sat in Dodd's
office looking at the bills in his hat, and sobbing. Another farmer,
distrusting banks, kept his money in his chimney. There was a
heavy rain, and the bills got soaked. When he spread them out in
a field to dry, a strong wind came along and blew them all over
creation. But the most famous case was that of John Benninghoff,
who kept $210,000 in his house and hired armed guards as watch-
men. Professional gunmen from Philadelphia overcame the
guards and stole the money. Benninghoff offered a $50,000 re-
ward and hired detectives, who undoubtedly split the swag with
the ringleader, who escaped, though three others were convicted.
Benninghoff lost everything.

Those who joined the Oil Rush had no cause to be disappointed. The Oildorado exceeded El Dorado. All the rushes that
occurred in the United States, before and since, gold and silver
together, were small change compared to the riches that piled up
in western Pennsylvania from oil after 1860. Thus the Egbert
brothers, M. C. and A. C., from a thirty-nine-acre farm leased in
1859 shared a profit between $8 and $10 million by the mid-
sixties.

In Franklin, eighteen miles from Drake's well, James Evans
struck oil while boring for salt. Church bells pealed and court
was adjourned to celebrate. Evans' daughter joyously told everyone, "Dad's struck ile." The phrase caught on, and was heard all
over the world. An American traveler was in the bar of a hotel in
a small Australian town a year later. A sheepman came in and
clanked some coins on the bar. The barmaid giggled, and said,
"Dad's struck ile."

United States Senator Johnson N. Camden, who had been a
Standard Oil executive and who began in the oil regions, writing
in 1883 recalled the scene as "Pandemonium." Everybody was
feverishly trying to suck the oil out of the earth under the "law of
capture" before his neighbor did. Leases were broken up into

subleases, and wells were sunk on quarter-acres. It is estimated that twenty times as many wells were drilled as should have been. Four-fifths of the wells were dry holes, and since the cost of a well was $8,000 the losses were heavy.

In 1861 came the spectacular development of the "flowing" wells, gushers geysering above the derricks, driven by subterranean gas. The Empire Well flowed at 2,500 barrels daily; the Davis and Wheelock well at 1,500 barrels daily; and the Maple Shade Well at 1,000 barrels daily. Production of oil, which was only 650,000 barrels in 1860, rose to 3,056,000 barrels in 1862.

And what of Drake the explorer who first brought to the surface this miraculous source of energy that transformed civilization? Did he share in the cornucopia? Though advised to lease land, he did not try to do so until prices were out of his reach. He served as a justice of the peace, making $3,000 a year. He left the Regions in 1863 and went to Wall Street, where he soon lost his fortune of $15,000. He then moved to Long Island, where he was stricken with neuralgia that almost crippled him. In 1869 Zebulun Martin, a hotel owner of Titusville, encountered him on the streets of New York with his twelve-year-old son for whom he was looking for work. Drake was wearing the same coat he had worn in 1860. Martin gave him all the money he could spare, $20, and on his return to Titusville, raised $4,833 for Drake's benefit. The Pennsylvania state legislature voted him a pension of $1,500 in 1873. From then until his death in 1880, Drake lived on, almost in penury, and in agony from the neuralgia that completely incapacitated him.

Of Drake it was said that his epitaph should have read, "He shook the bough so that others might gather the fruit." The actual inscription on the Drake monument at Titusville is lugubrious enough: "His last days, oppressed by ills, to want no stranger, he died in comparative obscurity."

We have discussed the gold and silver lining for the few before taking up the subject of the clouds overhanging the many. Actually, there were grim problems for the oil producers. One was the demon of Fire, a problem endemic to the whole industry but particularly dangerous to crude producers, since crude oil was combustible at a lower temperature than refined. In October 1859 "Uncle Billy" Smith almost lost his life in a fire that burned up the derrick and his home. On April 17, 1861, a never-to-be-forgotten fire claimed nineteen lives. The news echoed around Titusville that a gusher, a "flowing well," had been struck near Rouseville. Henry Rouse, after whom the town was named, joined in the rush to the new well. The gusher rose sixty feet high; suddenly there seemed to be a flash of lightning followed by a roar like that of artillery. The gas from the well had been ignited by a cigar or lamp on the ground. Rouse, who minutes before had boasted that he was $50,000 richer, was caught in the flaming oil as it reached the ground, and, like others, he became a human torch. Though only parts of his body remained intact when he reached safety, he calmly dictated his will between sips of water from a teaspoon, leaving his money to public purposes, and then died.

The oil producers soon discovered that when the oil came to the surface, their troubles had not been solved; indeed, they had just begun. Where was the oil to be stored pending sale? How was it to be transported to market? What kind of price would it bring?

As soon as the Drake well started to flow, a search had begun for barrels. Any kind of barrels were sought as more wells flowed —casks that had held turpentine, molasses, whiskey, beer, cider, vinegar. Brewer & Watson, who operated a sawmill, converted it to the manufacture of barrels, but it was inadequate. Cellars and barns were ransacked, and barrels were brought from afar. Because it soon appeared that the acids in the crude dissolved the glues and shellacs of the barrels, improvements had to be made in their manufacture.

How was the oil to be stored? An early method was to construct a reservoir built of wood or lined with cement. Then wooden tanks were built to hold as much as 1,000 barrels. They were used until the end of the decade, when they were supplanted by the iron tank. Leakage, evaporation, and fire in the wooden tanks destroyed much of the oil.

How was the oil to be transported to the railroads? The closest were at Corry, eighteen miles away, and Erie, forty miles away. Barrels weighing 360 pounds were loaded on wagons and hauled there by crews of boy teamsters. The roads were little more than ribbons of mud, and a teamster who could swim was said to have an advantage over others. Detours were made on farms. Guerrilla warfare broke out between the teamster boys and the farmers, and many farmers found themselves at the end of the terrible "blacksnake" whips the boys were so ready to wield.

The oil regions were under the tyranny of these boys. Samuel Van Syckel, who built the first pipeline, recalled at a later day: "Sometimes a line of teams a mile long would be stuck in the mud. Often the teamsters would dump their load, worth $5 a barrel, and abandon it. Mules would get so discouraged that they would lie down and die in the roadway before they could be helped. The teamsters knew their power. They charged accordingly. They charged for looking at the oil to see how many barrels their teams could draw. They charged extra for every mudhole they struck, and if the wagon wheels went to the hubs they doubled their bills. The teamsters were making more money than the well owners and didn't care whether they hauled oil or not."

Another method to get oil to refining centers was to load the barrels on barges from Oil Creek to Oil City and thence transport it on the Allegheny River to Pittsburgh. Oil Creek was frozen in winter and usually too shallow in warm weather. Lumbermill owners had dams which they opened to float logs downstream—artificial freshets. The lumbermen now agreed to open the dams once or twice a week to oilmen at the price of a few cents per barrel.

"Pond freshet!" went up the cry, and thousands gathered along the banks for three hours of fun as hundreds of bargemen sought to catch the crest of the flood. Collisions and wrecks were the order of the day, and more often· than not only half the barrels that began the trip reached Oil City. The barrels were stacked on the docks at Oil City, where usually a quarter of them were stolen, then put on boats to be carried to Pittsburgh. Captain J. J. Vandergrift, who became an important Standard Oil executive, made his fortune on the river. He brought barrels up from Pittsburgh by the thousands, and hauled back oil. He conceived the idea of hauling a string of barges by means of his steamer, *Red Fox,* and later built the predecessor of the tanker, a barge hauling thousands of barrels in tin-lined compartments.

By 1863 the peak of fortune had passed for the bargemen and the teamsters, who with their ready cash made the nights red with riot and were the darlings of the dance-hall girls. Railroads were now stretching their tentacles into the oil regions. A line had been constructed from Corry to Titusville, and one was being built from Meadville to Franklin. Teamsters would now have only the traffic from the wells to the railroads.

It was evident at that early date that storage and transportation were bottlenecks that threatened the prosperity of the producers. It is estimated that only a fraction of the oil produced got to market between 1860 and 1865—perhaps ten million barrels went to waste. Those who controlled storage and transport would sit atop the producers, and that is what Rockefeller in the end managed to do.

The oil was bought by the refiners or their agents who went from well to well making bargains. At the beginning, refiners of oil from coal were undaunted, and had a banner year in 1860. But when petroleum fell below $12 a barrel, they realized that they could no longer be competitive and switched to refining petroleum. Some moved to the oil regions. Samuel Downer built a great works at Corry. At Plumer some Germans, the Ludovici brothers, constructed the Humboldt refinery at a cost of half a million, the best equipped in the world, with foundations of cut stone and with luxurious furniture and statuary. It was the talk of the nation.

Many others became refiners. As Rockefeller says in his *Reminiscences:* "The cleansing of crude petroleum was a simple and easy process and at first the profits were very large. Naturally all sorts of people went into it: the butcher, the baker, and the candlestick maker. . . ." For $200, if you were mechanically inclined, you could build a still that would refine five barrels a day. A fair-sized refinery could be built for $8,000. The process involved breaking petroleum into its components or fractions by boiling and condensing its vapors, the different components differing in their volatility. The crude in stills or retorts was heated up to 700 degrees Fahrenheit. The vapors then were passed through a cast-iron gooseneck into a copper worm immersed in water where they were condensed. Gasoline, being most volatile, was condensed first. There was little known use for it, and for years it was known as the "offal of the oil industry." Then came naphtha, benzine, runs of kerosene, lubricating oils, and paraffin, and finally there were left tars and residues. Stills were scattered all over. Samuel Van Syckel recalled that he first became interested in oil while living in Jersey City. On the flats around the city were dozens of small stills. Noxious fumes floated into the city. "Almost every day there was an explosion somewhere from the gases." Finally, the city's Common Council ordered a stop to the refining, and Van Syckel came to Titusville. At first the refining process was so inefficient that there was only a 55 percent yield of kerosene from crude, but this could easily be increased to 65 percent by mixing in some naphtha or gasoline. The user of such adulterated kerosene stood a good chance of being burned by an explosion.

Within the first three years of the life of the new industry, it learned of the curse of overproduction and ruinous prices. Oil started out at $20 a barrel, but by the spring of 1860 it was only $12. It continued to slide, and by the end of 1861 was only $0.10! A barrel weighing 70 pounds was twenty or thirty times more valuable than the petroleum within it weighing 300 pounds. Production, discouraged by such low prices, fell in 1863 and 1864.

This is a summary of the situation in the oil fields at the beginning of 1863 when John D. Rockefeller, a successful commission merchant of Cleveland, branched out into the oil business. As a resident of Cleveland he had beheld with wonderment the quick growth of a new industry, a new economy, and a new land. A classical scholar who had been enraptured by the beauty of Greece saluted it in print in those early days in an apostrophe worthy of Byron. The poet was Samuel C. T. Dodd, later to be Rockefeller's counsel:

> The Land of Grease, The Land of Grease,
>   Where burning oil is loved and sung;
> Where flourish arts of sale and lease
>   Where Rouseville rose and Tarville sprung;
> Eternal Summer gilds them not
>   But oil wells render dear each spot.

CHAPTER 2 *The Youth—*
"Pleased Although Sad"

WALKING along the streets of Cleveland, the boy of twenty-
three was the glass of fashion. He wore a high silk hat, a
frock coat, and striped trousers. Tall and handsome, he walked
with a slight stoop, his head jutting a little forward. His face
was unadorned, but in three years he would sprout fashionable
side-whiskers that would meet under his chin in a thin line.
Three years later they would meet over his upper lip in a luxuri-
ous moustache. His expression was the same as it was to be
throughout his working days, serious, intent, and thoughtful. He
was known respectfully and greeted respectfully as "Mr. Rockefeller."

What manner of man was this John D. Rockefeller who by the
time he was forty would bestride the world of oil like a Colossus,
and write an imperishable page in our nation's industrial history?

John Davison Rockefeller (whom we shall refer to in this narrative simply as "Rockefeller," distinguishing him from other
Rockefellers) was born in the small village of Richford, (appro-
priately enough) in Tioga County, New York, on July 8, 1839,
during the Administration of Martin Van Buren. It was a small
settlement not far from Binghamton, on the southern tier of the
state. He was the second child and oldest male offspring of William Avery Rockefeller and Eliza Davison Rockefeller. He had
been preceded by Lucy and was soon followed by his brother
William, who was destined to join John in Standard Oil and
acquire scores of millions. In 1843, when John was four, the family moved to the busier village of Moravia, forty miles away to
the northwest, and there were born to the couple Mary Ann and
twins, Franklin and Frances, the latter dying in infancy. Franklin,
known as Frank, would feud with his older brother throughout
his life and would die his bitter enemy.

The name Rockefeller, originally Rockenfeller, is German,
Johann Peter Rockefeller, from Sagendorf in the Rhineland, set-

19

tling in Somerville, New Jersey, in 1723. A genealogist hired by
William Rockefeller told the Rockefeller Family Association in
1907, to its delight, that the original name belonged to French
noblemen by the name of Roquefeuille (meaning "rock-leaf") in
southern France—a family that had coins bearing their name.
Because they were Huguenots, they had fled to Germany to escape religious persecutions. Perhaps this lineage is true, but more
than one ingenious and industrious genealogist has catered to the
family pride of the rich. At any rate, Rockefeller was much less
than one-quarter French nobleman. In this country the Rockefellers intermarried with spouses of British stock. Lucy Avery,
Rockefeller's paternal grandmother, was of good English blood.
The original Christopher Avery came to this country in 1630 with
the Puritans. This line has provided distinguished names in our
history, and a genealogist has claimed that the Avery line's de-
scent can be traced to King Egbert, the first King of England,
and Duncan, King of Scotland, who was murdered by Macbeth.
Eliza Davison, Rockefeller's mother, was of pure Scots blood on
both sides. Thus Rockefeller, like the other great industrial kings
of the nineteenth century, was predominantly of British par-
entage.

The union between Rockefeller's mother and father was a
strange one, and proof of the saying that opposites attract. The
daughter of a strict farmer in Niles Township, John Davison,
Eliza was equally strict, and devout, being a member of the choir
in the local Dutch Reformed church. Her choice for a husband,
William Rockefeller, apparently didn't give a fig for religion.
Neither repressed nor austere like Eliza, he was outgoing, lively,
and worldly. He liked to pretend that he was deaf and dumb, and
there is a story that he met Eliza when he went to the door of her
home and posed as a deaf-mute. Entranced by his good looks, she
said, "If he weren't deaf and dumb, I'd marry him," and was held
to her word. Though it may not be true, it's a pleasant yarn. The
Rockefellers loved the tavern. Godfrey, William's father, was
called by Ida Tarbell a well-known "tippler," and it is conceded
that he was a hard drinker. William's brother, Jacob, seems to
have been a souse. Apparently a storekeeper made a wager with
him that he could not stay sober, and when the storekeeper lost
he made an entry, "Allowed Jacob Rockefeller for not drinking

five dollars." The entry is extant today. William Rockefeller, however, was a teetotaler. As Miss Tarbell put it, he had "all the vices save one."

In his old age Rockefeller bore an uncanny facial resemblance to his mother at the same age, and the resemblance was one of spirit, too. She was taciturn and reserved, with a great deal of inner strength and serenity, traits she passed on to John but not to her other sons, William and Frank, who had the jollity and gregariousness of the father. She instilled her devout Baptist faith into her eldest son, but was less successful with the others. From his earliest days, Rockefeller recalled, he went to Sunday school, and the Sabbath was a day for pursuits more staid than levity and light reading. She was a firm disciplinarian and laid on the rod without hesitancy, but with some humor, saying that she applied it "out of love," which, Rockefeller recalled, did not make it less painful. In telling of a whipping because of some unfortunate doings in the village school, he recalled yelling to his mother that he was innocent. She replied, "Never mind. It will do for the next time."

It was because of his mother that Rockefeller became a "model boy" and a "model young man." Another influence contributed to his surprisingly early maturity. Because his mother undoubtedly suffered great loneliness, since her husband was away much of the time, she turned to her son as a confidant and for moral support. Observers of the family noted that at an early age John assumed the role of a parent to the younger children.

However, the father also played a major role in shaping John. William Avery Rockefeller may be the skeleton in the family closet, but it is clear that John adored him. In his *Reminiscences,* though he pays no tribute to his mother, he does to his father, saying: "To my father I owe a great debt in that he himself trained me to practical ways. He was engaged in different enterprises; he used to tell me about these things, explaining their significance and he taught me the principles and methods of business."

Except for a brief spell in the lumber business, his father was an itinerant quack doctor, practicing mostly on the American midwestern frontier. The practice of quack medicine was not a grave disparagement of his character, nor does it connote fraud.

More than half the practicing doctors had no formal training, and those that had, killed more often than they cured. One has only to recall that when George Washington became ill with a severe cold and a throat obstruction in 1799, three eminent doctors bled and purged him to death. In 1840 medicine was not much more advanced. In that day superstitious folk preferred esoteric nostrums and panaceas to formal doctoring. By establishing the Rockefeller Institute for Medical Research, John D. Rockefeller certainly atoned for all the empty pretensions of his father to cure diseases.

The father would leave home for a long period of time, telling no one but his wife of his destination. Setting up credit for her at the local store so that she would not want, he would then travel to a frontier town in Iowa or Illinois where, likely as not, he would visit the local editor and hire a boy to distribute hand bills: "Dr. William A. Rockefeller here for one day only. All cases of cancer cured unless they are too far gone and then they can be greatly benefited." If a patient wanted a full cancer treatment he would have to pay $25. Most bought some harmless liquid for a dollar. The good "doctor" also lent money at 12 percent, and sometimes was able to foreclose on a good property. He visited Indian settlements, and once told a friend that he pretended to be deaf and dumb because the Indians believed that those who had lost a sense possessed occult powers to heal.

He would return home in a handsome new rig with fine horses, and flashing a roll of bills, and the home rang with joy. The family gathered around the melodeon, and William played the violin, holding it at his waist. He would spend time with his children, riding, rowing, and swimming with them. He would also talk to them of the great world over the horizon and how to get green bills like those that were rolled in his pocket. When John was eight his father took him to the great city of Syracuse, where he saw the iron monsters moving on tracks and belching forth steam, and observed the hustle and bustle of the metropolis of twenty thousand souls. From that day stemmed his desire to belong to the city rather than to the country.

In his home village the father was the character who in times past has been called a sport or a slick or a card. He dazzled everyone with his clothes, his stories about his adventures in far-off lands, his ability to take charge of every situation. When the village of Moravia decided to build a new schoolhouse, he became the leader. Selecting a plot of land, he found the exact center by counting the revolutions of the wheel of his wagon on each side and dividing by half. He could excel everybody, whether at swimming, wrestling, or shooting. Ida Tarbell found an old man at Parma, close to Cleveland where the family lived in 1854, who recalled him: "How he would shoot! Bang-e-tee. You'd thought there was a whole army around."

During the stay in Moravia, the father apparently settled down in response to the wishes of his wife and went into the lumbering business, hauling logs up Owasco Lake to Auburn. He also put a little money into a log road, losing on his investment when a railroad was built on the route. Life was pleasant and there were many friends, since William was an attractive person, jolly, kind, and generous. But then—calamity and disgrace. First there were rumors that a horse-stealing "underground railroad" ring was operating; then three associates of the father were indicted and convicted. Rumors persisted that William was the man really responsible and that he had somehow shifted the blame to innocent or less guilty parties. Then, on July 23, 1849, the Court of Oyer and Terminer, sitting at Auburn, indicted William Avery Rockefeller for raping Anne Vanderbeak, a hired girl, in his home, in April of 1848. He was never arrested, and undoubtedly fled the county. At any rate, in 1850 the family was in a new home back in Tioga County, in the bustling township of Owego.

The background and resolution of this indictment are puzzling. When the assailant is known, an indictment for rape fifteen months after the event is most unusual. It suggests an ulterior motivation, which would not necessarily reflect on the truth of the charge. The indictment never came to trial. In later years Rockefeller denied that his father was ever a fugitive and that he would have known about it; but since he was only ten at the time, that is open to debate. If his father was a fugitive, the arm of the law must have been very short if he felt safe thirty-five miles away in an adjoining county. Probably the change of residence was made because of the scandal, and the girl was persuaded to forget about it. The indictment caused an irreparable breach with his father-in-law, John Davison, who lost no time in suing on notes that William had made to him for $1,200. In addition, he changed his will so that his daughter, who had married against his advice, would have only the income for life on the share of property he had previously left to her outright. He also left the allegedly ravished girl $50 in his will.

From the time the family moved to Owego, William Rockefeller resumed the practice of medicine, with occasional visits home. Possibly Eliza was just as glad to see her husband away. The signs point to a growing estrangement.

For many years it was believed that Rockefeller rose from poverty. When John Winkler, in 1929, revealed that his parents were fairly well off, it made news. Yet the misimpression was continued in John Flynn's book three years later. Rockefeller himself liked to see his life as a Horatio Alger epic. In 1907 he said to William Hoster, a reporter "What advantages had I that any other poor boy did not possess? Did any one have less to start with than I?" The answer is that many, many had less. Rockefeller's boyhood was not one of grinding poverty but one of relative comfort. One has only to examine the photographs of the spacious homes in Moravia and Owego to realize that the Rockefellers were not poor. Rockefeller's sister, Mrs. Mary Ann Rudd, derided the idea in later years, saying that although the family was not rich, "we had plenty to eat and wear and every kind of comfort." There was hired help in the house at all times.

William's father, Godfrey, was a well-to-do farmer, and Eliza's father was prosperous. When William was twenty-six he bought a farm for $480. (By checking Historical Statistics of the United States, prepared by the Bureau of the Census, I have found that the price level approximately doubled between 1840 and 1913, and has since trebled, so a multiple of six should be kept in mind.) When the family moved to Moravia, his father bought a 92-acre farm for $3,100, on which he soon paid off the mortgage. William always had a roll of bills with him, and Rockefeller recalled that his father never had less than $1,000 on his person. In those days, he said, to have $4,000 was to be accounted rich. Additional signs of the relative affluence of the family will appear in this survey of Rockefeller's early years.

Rockefeller had a happy youth—rowing, fishing, ball-playing, going nutting, skating, and coasting in the winter, and other healthy pursuits. There is no indication that he was ever under pressure to make money, and except for some reference to digging potatoes for a neighbor there is no indication that he had any job prior to the first one after high school, though the school year then was eight months and less. His parents paid him small sums for chores such as pulling weeds and milking cows, which he could do as well as anyone. In his *Reminiscences* he speaks of keeping some turkeys, which he fed on curds of milk supplied by his mother and which he sold at a profit. The coins in his china bowl piled up, the biggest accretions undoubtedly coming from gifts from his father.

The countryside in the Finger Lake area was a wonderful one for a growing boy. At Moravia was Owasco Lake, and at Owego there was the Susquehanna. There were magnificent forests dotting the landscape. Throughout his life Rockefeller was to preserve his love of trees, water, and landscapes until it became a passion with him in his old age. At his Pocantico estate he tried to re-create the images in childhood that he carried with him in his life:

> These beauteous forms,
> Through a long absence, have not been to me
> As is a landscape to a blind man's eye:
> But oft, in lonely rooms, and 'mid the din
> Of towns and cities, I have owed to them
> In hours of weariness, sensations sweet . . .*

One must tread warily among the recollections of Rockefeller's boyhood. By the time biographers got around to digging up the facts, most of his contemporaries were dead and the living had rusty or suggestive memories. A legitimate grievance against Ida Tarbell is that she failed to do much of the oral interviewing a modern reporter would have done. Her firsthand observations of men and events are limited. The next reporter, William Inglis, did not come on the scene until almost two decades later. Rockefeller's recollections themselves are not the most reliable. The risk is that what is taken for fact may be apocryphal.

Thus Flynn and Nevins tell the same story. When Rockefeller was twelve years old, at his mother's suggestion he lent a farmer

---

* Wordsworth, "Lines Composed . . . Above Tintern Abbey."

$50 from his china bowl at 7½ percent interest. The next year he did some potato digging for a nearby farmer at 37½ cents a day. At that time he collected $3.75 interest, and it occurred to him that money could work wonders. He would have had to sweat ten days to earn the money he had accumulated painlessly through interest.

This tale I cannot credit. It bespeaks a precociousness that is too rarely met. A boy of twelve has no legal capacity to make a contract, and no adult would deal with a child. Moreover, if he had made money this way at twelve he would have been a Rothschild by fifteen, but there is no further mention of lending adventures. Winkler's account seems to me the correct one. After working for the farmer, Rockefeller said it "occurred to me" that money lent at interest would have obviated the toil.

A favorite occupation of biographers is to dredge up in a man's youth the auguries of later greatness. The truth seems to be that in Rockefeller's case there were almost no adumbrations of greatness. He seems to have been completely undistinguished. In school he was not bright. In later years he said, "I was not an easy student and had to labor diligently to prepare my lessons." Books and ideas were to play no part in the life of Rockefeller, who till the end of his days had no inclination for the company of intellectuals or for intellectual pursuits. Yet one of the paradoxes of the man was that he always had an admiration for learning and was to give millions to universities. When he was in high school in Cleveland, he wrote a short essay on education that has been preserved. It contains this piquant paragraph on the value of learning, "Had Isaac Newton been an unlearned man on seeing the apple fall, would he not rather have eaten it than inquired why it fell?"

Ida Tarbell found people who remembered Rockefeller as a boy. They made such comments about him as: "He never mixed much with the rest of us." "He seemed always to be thinking." "He was different from his brothers and the rest of us." While in Owego the boys seemed to have been so backward in their studies that their mother sent them to study at the La Monte home where Susan La Monte, the oldest child, was particularly bright. This was the (later) Mrs. Susan Life who founded the Rye Female Seminary to which Rockefeller sent his oldest daughter, Bessie. In later years she recalled Rockefeller clearly: "He was just an ordinary well-behaved boy plodding along with his lessons. There was nothing about him to make anybody pay especial attention to him or speculate about his future." She said further, "He used to walk slowly along, and often seemed to be thinking as he went." David Dennis recalled that "most of the time he seemed to be going along quietly thinking things over."

Yet "the child is father to the man." There were qualities that could have commanded notice. His self-command and prudence prompted his sister Lucy to say, "When it's raining porridge, you'll find John's dish right side up." He thought long and hard over every move. Once, while playing checkers with him, David Dennis chided him for a long delay. John replied: "I'll move as soon as I've figured it out. You don't think I'm playing to get beat?" Susan La Monte's brother Cyrenus recalled of him, "Persistence. He had all the persistence there was." And then, of course, his family noted his remarkable thriftiness.

While in Owego, John and brother Will attended Owego Academy, where tuition was charged and which was attended by boys from wealthy homes. Payment of tuition also argues against indigence. In connection with his study there, another tale appears in both Flynn and Nevins that I think is a tall tale. In his old age Rockefeller showed a picture of the class to a descendant who asked why Rockefeller and his brother William were not in it. The old man replied: "William and I had to remain out of it. We did not have good enough suits." No doubt Rockefeller said this, since he liked to build the illusion about himself. But can this be credited? Who would have so humiliated the boys? And remember that both biographies also contained the stories about Rockefeller's loan of $50 as a boy. If that was so, how was it he could not afford $5 for a suit? Rockefeller's father was well dressed, and would not have allowed his sons to go about in rags. As Mrs. Life recalled: "He was the best-dressed man for miles around. You never saw him without his silk hat." The probable explanation for the absence of the two boys is that they moved in 1853 to Strongsville, fifteen miles from Cleveland, and this photograph was taken after their departure. Since it contained so many beloved faces, they wished to have it.

The family wanted the boys to have a high-school education.

For the standards of the times, this was sumptuous. The father paid to have the boys board in Cleveland and attend the only public high school at what is now in the heart of the city at Euclid and Erie. Rockefeller there met two young people whom he would know well for the rest of their lives. He became a close friend of a forceful and spirited boy, Mark Hanna, who at sixteen had engaged himself to marry. Hanna was to become political boss of the Republican party of the state of Ohio and was to make McKinley President of the United States. Another person he met was the daughter of a prosperous man, Laura Celestia Spelman. "Cettie" Spelman was to become Rockefeller's wife. The impressions of Rockefeller as a young man coincide remarkably with those of him as a boy. Lucy Spelman, Laura's sister, two years older, recalled him as "a studious boy, grave, reserved, never noisy or given to boisterous play." Another student, Darwin Jones, said of him, "reserved and studious, though always pleasant."

Rockefeller once made a declamation, then customary in high schools, which began, "I'm pleased although I'm sad." The girls burst into laughter because of the accurate self-description, and dubbed him "Old Pleased Although I'm Sad." There were like characterizations of him. Because of his demeanor and well-known churchgoing, he was called "Deacon." Soon after he left school, someone referred to him as, "Oh, that stick."

School

Apparently Rockefeller did not complete high school, though biographers say he graduated. He says. "I had nearly completed the course," which would mean, since he finished the June term, that he had a year to go. He says, "The plan had been to send me to college." College then was only for the élite, and if there had not been the wherewithal there would have been no such "plan." Colleges then were professional schools for the law, medicine, and the ministry, and since Rockefeller had no ambitions in those careers, there was little sense in his going to college. His father wanted him to plunge immediately into the business world, and paid $40 for a three-month course at Folsom's Commercial College, where he could study double-entry bookkeeping and could pick up some knowledge of banking and commercial law. Thus in September 1855, at the age of sixteen, Rockefeller was ready to make his fortune. His education was as good as that of any of

Educ

the great fortune-builders of the century except J. P. Morgan, who attended Göttingen University in Germany for two years. It is interesting that Morgan, like Rockefeller, showed little of the get-up-and-go drive that is supposed to presage the acquisition of riches. His personality in youth was described as leaden, morose, and withdrawn.

The best education for business that Rockefeller acquired was from his father, and it was a good one. During his picaresque existence William Rockefeller had to live by his wits on the frontier, where he had to contend with others who were sharp-witted too. In the business transactions in which the "doctor" engaged he had to be a shrewd bargainer, appreciating the value of a nickel gained. Rockefeller recalled: "He used to dicker with me and buy things from me. He taught me how to buy and sell." From early years he sent John on responsible errands, such as buying cordwood for the family. Sharpness, sharpness, was his constant exhortation. He boasted: "I cheat my boys every time I get a chance. I want to make them sharp. I trade with the boys and skin them and just beat them every time I can."

While Rockefeller seemed to be his mother's son in personality, the habits of thinking of his father sprang out in his business life—William's acquisitiveness, his cunning, his self-assurance, and his boldness. And make no mistake about it—this young Rockefeller, though secretive and dour, was bold and daring. He was to be much more so than his associates and his rivals. He had in his veins the boldness of the Spanish conquistador in quest of gold, like Hernando Cortez who burned his ships behind him so that his small band could only march forward toward the gold of Montezuma.

September 26 was a day always marked by Rockefeller, because it was on that day in 1855, after weeks of pounding the pavement, that he landed his first job, with the firm of Hewitt and Tuttle on Merwin Street, as an assistant bookkeeper. The firm were commission merchants and produce shippers. No pay was mentioned, but in January he was paid $50 for three months' work and was then put on a salary of $300 a year.

Looking back years afterward, Rockefeller saw that the experience he gained in this firm was extremely valuable for his future career. Because his work was done in the main office of the firm, he was almost always present when the partners discussed their affairs. Besides its regular commission business, the firm owned private residences, warehouses, and office buildings, and it was Rockefeller's job to make up and deliver the bills, collect the rents, and adjust claims. He had to learn to get along with all types of clients and customers, and maintain satisfactory relations with his employer. It was an education in what he later said was the most important quality for business success—the art of getting along with people.

As a boy of seventeen he was given responsible work to do. For example, a shipment of marble would come from Vermont, having arrived by rail, canal, and steamer. The shipment had been damaged. He was given the task of allotting the damage cost among the three carriers. Though Rockefeller had to work out solutions to problems like these, "I thought the task no hardship and so far as I can remember I never had any disagreement with any of these transportation interests."

As the partners reposed more confidence in him, they gave him accounts to be audited. He was in a neighbor's office when a plumber presented a long bill, and the businessman, with a quick glance, said, "Pay it," to his clerk. When the same plumber presented his bill to Hewitt and Tuttle, Rockefeller, checking it item by item, found discrepancies, and saved money for his firm. Slovenly methods of doing business were not for him, he decided. Careful auditing of all bills, big and small, became a cardinal tenet of the Standard Oil Company.

There is no substantial evidence that the boy in his school days dreamed of making big money. But at this time in his early work life, his desire to make money germinated. In 1905 Rockefeller told a group that one day Hewitt received a bank note from a downstate bank for $4,000. (Such odd bills existed in those days, when the Federal Government printed a three-dollar bill.) After showing it to Rockefeller, he locked it up in the safe. "Many times during the day did I open that safe to gaze longingly at the note."

In Rockefeller's *Reminiscences* the sole mention of the ambition to make money occurs in connection with an activity that would seem to be at the opposite pole—his church activity. Because church was to be the other arm of Rockefeller's life, let us look at it. In Owego he and brother Will had become regular churchgoers. When the family moved to the environs of Cleveland, the boys joined the Erie Street Baptist Church. At the age of fifteen, John was baptized there. They were taken under the wing of Deacon William Sked, and became pillars of the church. The effort to maintain the church was a cooperative one, with everyone joining for small tasks. John soon became clerk of the church, recording all expenditures. As soon as he became twenty-one, he was made one of the five trustees of the church, and became teacher of its largest Sunday-school class.

We are beginning to see the signs of an unusual young man. The recognition accorded him by his church in appointing him to these posts while a mere boy attests to his maturity and competence.

The church had a mortgage of $2,000 on it, and the mortgagee (though a deacon) insisted on payment, slow return of the interest having made him uneasy. One Sunday morning the minister announced from the pulpit that $2,000 would have to be raised or the building would be lost. At the end of the service Rockefeller stationed himself at the door and, buttonholing each member, got him to promise something for the church. The campaign lasted for months; and though it was a great undertaking to raise such a big sum in small pledges and collections, Rockefeller managed it. "My first ambition to earn more money was aroused by this and similar undertakings."

Rockefeller plunged wholeheartedly into church activity because it was the sole extracurricular activity that was available. He did not drink; he did not engage in any sports; and he did not attend the theater. Though he was given piano lessons in high school, he had no interest in music. He did not play cards or dance. He did not read, nor did he spend his time with girls, chaste or otherwise. From his *Reminiscences* it appears that he spent time talking to the landlady with whom he boarded, defending the rate of 10 percent for interest on investments that he located for his father in Cleveland. Thus the church was a Godsend for him, as an emotional outlet for a healthy youth, and a lifelong habit attachment had been formed.

The Baptist Church was Fundamentalist, and believed in original sin, hell-fire, salvation through faith, and literal interpretation of the Bible. Men and women sat separated as in the Hebrew synagogue. Actually Rockefeller, like the average Baptist, was not strong on theology. The Baptist was interested in applying the teachings of God to the problems of real life. And the church itself was life—people, mostly of lower station, enjoyed the Sunday services, the midweek services, the revival meetings, picnics, Gospel singing, men's society, and the like.

After Rockefeller got his first job in 1855, he began a record of his expenditures in a notebook he marked "Ledger A." This he kept, and it was a precious possession, the basis of many talks. He would say, "You could not get that book from me for all the modern ledgers of New York nor for all that they would bring." The ledger does show Rockefeller the youth to be remarkable. The first entry is a gift of ten cents to the "Missionary Cause." It was made in November, before he received any pay. Though Rockefeller had money saved, and did not feel pinched, it is still extraordinary that the giving habit began before the getting. In the next four months he gave almost 10 percent of what he earned. The young man felt a responsibility to the poor of New York. He gave $0.12 to the Five Points Mission there. He gave $0.25 to "a poor man in the church" and $0.50 to "a poor woman in the church." By the time he was twenty-one he had expanded his gifts beyond denominational lines, giving to a Methodist Church, a Negro church, and to "Catholic orphans." Thus the genesis of the great philanthropies lies in these gifts of nickels and dimes to a cross section of people and causes.

An expenditure that Rockefeller later professed perplexed him in Ledger A was $2.50 for a pair of gloves. A pair of mittens for a quarter would have sufficed to keep his hands warm. But it makes sense. In those days much more than today men dressed to fit their part, and the youth who saw himself on the rise would lavish money on expensive gloves. The boy was working hard to make his way. There is a notation in his ledger in which he makes a resolution for the benefit of his nonworking self. "I have this day covenated with myself not to be seen in No. 45 (Merwin Street) after 10 P.M. within thirty days." Under it there is another notation by Rockefeller. "Don't make any more such covenants." This is so cryptic that any explanation would be mere guesswork.

Rockefeller worked for the firm until March 1859, a few

months before Drake struck oil. The time of employment was three and a half years. He asked for a raise of $800 a year, but the best that Hewitt would do for him was $700. The difference of $100 set Rockefeller to looking around for another opportunity.

Maurice Clark, an Englishman, had come to America to escape prosecution for assaulting his employer. He had moved around before coming to Cleveland, and, like Rockefeller, had attended Folsom's Business College. By dint of hard industry as an employee in a commission house, he had saved $2,000. He proposed to Rockefeller, who at almost twenty was ten years his junior but whose capacity he obviously respected at that tender age, that they go into partnership in a wholesale commission business in produce, grain, meats, hay, salt, lime, and other goods in which they could act as intermediaries for a profit.

Rockefeller asked his father for a loan of $1,000. Because his father had promised to give each of his sons $1,000 when each reached his majority, he agreed to advance the $1,000 now, but John would have to pay 10 percent interest for the fifteen months until he was twenty-one. Where did the remaining $1,000 come from? Rockefeller's total salary while he was with Hewitt was about $1,250. Out of this he had to pay board and clothe himself. A year after young Rockefeller began working, in 1856, William Rockefeller moved the family from Parma, a village seven miles from Cleveland, into the city itself, into a house at 35 Cedar Street, made of brick, having no less than twelve rooms and an indoor bathroom. William was prosperous. A photograph of the boys in 1858 shows them resplendently dressed, with gold watch chains. But the father continued to "skin" his son. Since John was making his own way, he would have to pay board while at home.

Some of the $1,000 Rockefeller needed could have been savings from earnings while at Hewitt and Tuttle, but a good deal must have been savings over the years from his china bowl, which consisted mostly of gifts from his father. So while thrift was the aged Rockefeller's constant theme in homiletics to the young, and though he gave away dimes to teach thrift, his start in business was due far less to thrift than to having a daddy with money.

Cleveland was growing by leaps and bounds. It was a new city, having been founded by General Moses Cleaveland, agent of the Connecticut Land Company in the Administration of George Washington. The area became known to many as New Connecticut. In 1830 it had a population of only 1,500 but the opening of the 300-mile Ohio Canal linking it to the Ohio River had given the city a great impetus. When Rockefeller began attending school there in 1853, it had 23,000; in 1860 the population leaped to 44,000 and in 1865 to 61,000. British and German immigrants poured in. Five railroads constructed in the 1850 decade connected the city with the interior. It was close to the western terminus of the Erie Canal, and a fleet of steamers was in being for shipments on the Great Lakes. Farm produce from the interior was shipped from here to eastern points. The city was a hub for the transshipment of raw materials, iron ore from Michigan to the mills of Ohio and Pennsylvania, and coal from these states to the West.

Geographically, too, the city on Lake Erie was well located as the terminus of the "underground railroad" for slaves, for shipment to Canada and freedom. The city, a hotbed of abolitionism, seethed with excitement as it fought the hated Fugitive Slave law. In 1859 a score of residents of Oberlin and Wellington were in jail on a charge of wresting a Negro from a slave catcher and spiriting him across the Lake. The whole university town of Oberlin had joined in the exploit, and now the ringleaders, in the role of martyrs, refused bail. Mass meetings were held in front of the jail in which the accused joined from behind barred windows as business in the city virtually stopped. Rockefeller himself was profoundly moved. In a high-school essay, preserved today, he had protested against the shamefulness of human beings held in bondage. In 1859 his records show that he gave money to a Negro in Cincinnati to buy his slave wife, and in 1860 there is a notation of a similar purchase.

Lincoln's election was greeted with joy here, and there were loud cheers for the President-elect when he spoke to a large crowd at the Weddell House on his way to Washington in February 1861. A little earlier there had been an ugly riot in the city when a slave girl captured on Prospect Street had been put in a jail for safekeeping. When a mob besieged the jail, the girl was none the less conveyed back to slavery. Secession now dissolved all counsels of confusion into a contest of arms. Though the response in Cleveland was great, neither Rockefeller nor his brother Will was among the volunteers. Frank, although only sixteen, enlisted, lying about his age, and was wounded at Chancellorsville and Cedar Mountain.

Though the careers of many men, as depicted on a graph, are full of peaks and valleys, Rockefeller's career went steadily, almost vertically, up. Never, in any one year, did he fall back. The new firm of Clark and Rockefeller was a success from the day it was launched, March 18, 1859, when the Cleveland *Leader* announced, "As experienced, responsible and prompt businessmen we recommend their house to the favorable consideration of our readers." Operating at 32 River Street the firm netted $4,400 in its first year; Rockefeller's share was almost three times what he had been earning with Hewitt.

The firm sold goods, mostly farm products, on consignment, generally collecting commissions from both seller and buyer. Clark was the "outside" man, Rockefeller the "inside" man. But, as if to refute the notion that he could not pull his weight in "man to man" deals, Rockefeller in his *Reminiscences* tells of traveling in Ohio and Indiana, asking for business but disclaiming any desire to break connections that the customer might have. "To our great surprise business came in so fast that we hardly knew how to take care of it."

Rockefeller, indeed, was very persuasive. He was direct and intent. Someone commented to his sister, Mary Ann, "How's that brother of yours who can walk right up on a man's shirt bosom and sit down?" Rockefeller in his negotiations with people was developing his credo that life is not a jungle with human beings trampling on one another but a meeting ground where human beings could forge a marriage of interest for the benefit of both. The theory was not always to work out in practice. But he early showed the power to win people to his point of view. In later life he attributed success to his ability to inspire confidence in others.

The later qualities of the builder of the oil empire were visible in the fledgling. Clark later said: "He was methodical to an extreme, careful as to details and exacting to a fraction. If there was a cent due us he wanted it. If there was a cent due a customer he

wanted him to have it." His hunger for more capital was incessant. He had learned that money can work, as we have seen, and
he had also learned that borrowed money could also work for you
if the return on it exceeded the cost of borrowing. Money was
needed for advances on consignment and transportation costs
that were out of pocket. Like Oliver Twist, he wanted "more."
Clark said later, "He was the greatest borrower you ever saw."
One source of money was his prosperous father, who was always
looking for his 10 percent. Doing business with his father was less
than satisfactory because his father would show up at the most
inopportune times to ask for his money. It seemed as if he liked to
play games with his son. "The truth is that I was not particularly
pleased with his application of tests to discover if my financial
ability was equal to such shocks."

Rockefeller therefore turned to banking channels. His first loan
came from Truman P. Handy, president of the Commercial Bank,
organized in 1845. He had known Rockefeller as a schoolboy and
had been impressed with his church activities. The youth gave
him the details of his business, and asked for $2,000. Handy
replied: "All right. You can have it. Just give me your warehouse
receipts. They are good enough for me." Rockefeller said:
". . . my elation can hardly be imagined. I held up my head—
think of it, a bank had trusted me for $2,000. I felt that I was now
a man of importance in the community." Possibly out of gratitude,
Rockefeller later made Handy rich. He told him to buy Standard Oil stock. When Handy said he lacked the money, Rockefeller lent it to him, putting stock away for him to be cashed at will.

Launched as a bank borrower, Rockefeller now borrowed to
the hilt, to the consternation of Clark. The boldness of his partner
became a cause of an increasing breach between the two partners. Another cause of friction was that Rockefeller was straight-
laced and punctilious to a fault in doing business, while Clark
was free and easy. Once a good customer asked to draw in advance on a shipment before the bill of lading was in hand. Clark
agreed, but when his partner returned to the office he was
shocked. He called on the customer and explained that good
business practice enjoined such advances. The customer stormed
about, and Rockefeller told Clark that, though he feared the firm
had lost a customer, he would do it all over again. But the man

continued to trade with the firm, and never mentioned the incident again.

A year after the firm was born, it took in a new partner and became Clark, Gardner and Company. Commodore George Gardner, who became mayor of Cleveland, supplied recollections of Rockefeller. With friends, Gardner had bought a secondhand yacht, and on a Saturday afternoon he asked Rockefeller if he wanted to go for a sail. Hunched over his books, Rockefeller upbraided Gardner: "You are barely getting a start in life and yet you own an interest in a yacht. You are injuring your credit and mine at the banks. Everybody will be looking at you as a spendthrift and soon our business will be wrecked." Rockefeller once sent a huge shipment of grain to Buffalo and, since the weather was fine, decided to save the $150 insurance. But when a storm blew up over the Lake, he sent Gardner to place insurance on the cargo. Gardner returned with the receipt at the same time that a telegram arrived saying that the cargo had reached port safely. Rockefeller went home sick.

In March 1861 the firm's profits were $17,000, with Rockefeller's share almost $6,000. This was the month of Lincoln's inauguration and the coming of war. The Civil War saw business boom for Cleveland and for the firm. As traffic down the Mississippi and the Ohio ground to a halt, the importance of the two great cities of the Midwest, St. Louis and Cincinnati, faded while that of Chicago and Cleveland rose. The raw materials of the Midwest were now indispensable for the industrial East, and the great traffic was now between East and West on the trunk railways and the Great Lakes. For Rockefeller's firm the war was a boon. The government needed food—pork, breadstuffs, and other supplies. The firm was receiving shipments of salt from Saginaw, Michigan, where Rockefeller's future partner, Henry Flagler, was trying to make his fortune in salt. The army needed salt badly, and very likely the partners could not work hard enough to meet the demand. We do not know what the profits were for 1861 and 1862 but they must have been great.

In fact, business was so profitable that by the end of 1862 Rockefeller had a problem finding suitable places to invest his surplus. He wanted to use his own money in the business and collect 10 percent interest, but Clark vetoed that. (Gardner had left the firm in 1862.) Then an opportunity developed. An impecunious young Englishman named Samuel Andrews was listed in the Cleveland directory as a "candlemaker." Though he did make candles to earn a few dollars, he was actually engaged in working in a refinery in Cleveland, making oil from cannel coal and shale. He had also refined oil from petroleum, possibly the first in Cleveland to do so. He talked to his fellow Englishman, Maurice Clark, about the great profits to be made in the refining of petroleum. An expert technician, he said he could raise the yield of kerosene by making the best use of sulfuric acid in the process. Andrews interested Clark first, and then Rockefeller, who knew Andrews as a communicant of the Erie Street Baptist Church.

For the twenty-three-year-old Rockefeller the fabulous profits were too good to be passed up. At that time oil refining was as marginally speculative as a business could be without being disreputable. Rockefeller initially put $4,000 into the new firm of Andrews, Clark and Company of which he was a partner. He went into it, he said later, "thinking this was a little side-issue," and did not publicly attach his name to the venture.

CHAPTER 3   *Early Days in Oil*

At the time Rockefeller entered oil, it was a get-rich-quick business. If a man did not double his capital in a year he was disappointed, and that applied to both producing and refining. As if at a Barmecidel feast, everyone was frantically trying to cash in, impelled by the dread that the oil might disappear like a mirage. In the oil regions nobody bothered much about the cost of drilling or storage or loss by fire, accidents, leakage, or theft. In Cleveland, waste oil, gasoline, and naphtha were poured out at night into the Cuyahoga River, and passing tugboats would have fun tossing hot coals on the oil and lighting it up.

By the end of 1866 there were fifty refineries in Cleveland. "The city was flavored and saturated with oil," says the historian William Gansor. Rose. "The river and lake were smeared with it. Oil wagons rumbled through the streets and tanks blocked the railroads. Oil fires kept the city firemen eternally vigilant and filled the valley with painful apprehension . . ." A Cleveland refiner, Manuel Halle, said that at the end of the decade "Many men were failing as the market jumped up and down. In those days if you saw a big black cloud of smoke in the sky it meant that somebody's oil refinery was burning; that so much oil was being destroyed and therefore the price of refined oil might jump from fifteen or sixteen cents a gallon to eighteen or nineteen." Rockefeller recalled, "When the fire-bell rang we would all rush to the refinery and help put it out, and while the blaze was still burning I would have my pencil out making plans for rebuilding."

Early in the morning, at six-thirty, Andrews and the Clarks (two other brothers had joined the firm, James and Richard) met with Rockefeller while he was having his breakfast. Mrs. Mary Ann Rudd, Rockefeller's younger sister, recalled in later years that while everybody else was talking of the war "they were talking oil all the time. It was all foreign to me and I got sick of it and wished morning after morning that they would talk of something else; but they didn't seem to care for anything else."

Rockefeller had quickly lost interest in his commission business, although he was still engaged in it. His thoughts were all on oil. Very early he inaugurated his basic principle, which he called "attention to little details," or penny-pinching. The most expeditious route to economy was to "pay a profit to nobody," that is, unless it could not be helped. The result was that someone else's profit became yours. Instead of buying oil from jobbers, James Clark went to the Regions to buy oil, thus eliminating the jobber's profit. Instead of being dependent on independent contractors for drayage, Rockefeller built his own force of wagons, hiring them out to competitors when business was slack. The firm made its own sulfuric acid for refining.

Inevitably, a trend toward vertical integration was developing. The cost of barrels was a very heavy item, ranging up to $2.50 apiece. By installing his own cooperage plant and buying forest land for the staves, the cost was cut to a little over $1.50. The firm dried lumber in kilns before transportation to cut weight and thus save on transport costs. Samuel Andrews was a master of refining techniques, and he saw to it that very little oil was wasted. Even the sulfuric acid was recovered, and the yield of kerosene was high. The firm manufactured benzene, and during the Civil War, with the supply of turpentine from the South cut off, it was used in paints and varnishes. Paraffin was sold; it was used for candles and also for chewing gum, for which there was a great demand from ladies' sewing circles. Vaseline, then called petrolatum, was finding a demand. Residuum for lubricating oils was sold to other refiners. Until Joshua Merrill, in 1868, discovered how to deodorize lubricating oil, the demand was restricted—after that, it became an important product. Refineries were learning how to produce dyes from oil. Practically every component could be used; but the only use for gasoline was to heat stills.

Rockefeller pitched in with all the jobs to be done around the refinery. Like the others, his clothes were saturated with the malodorous oil. While visiting a nearby boarding house for lunch, at the request of the other patrons he was removed to the kitchen, where he was fed "second leavings." He said later: "I stayed out of doors day and night those days. I ran up and down the tops of freight cars when necessary."

Though assailing Rockefeller on moral counts, Ida Tarbell had to concede that his success stemmed in part from his ability to eliminate waste and cut costs. Yet even here her estimate of him is a snide one. She pictures him as a Uriah Heep: "Low voiced, soft-footed, humble, knowing every point in every man's business he never tired until he got his wares at the lowest possible figure." Rockefeller was by all accounts "smooth." She interviewed a man who told her: "The only time I ever saw John Rockefeller enthusiastic was when a report came in from the Creek that his buyer had secured a cargo of oil at a figure much below the market price. He bounded from his chair with a shout of joy, danced up and down, hugged me, threw up his hat, acted so like a madman that I have never forgotten it." This is not the only recollection of Rockefeller's joy over a good bargain. In later years he explicitly denied these bourgeois manifestations of joy over money. But Rockefeller was very young at the time and he was becoming very rich. One must suppose that he had the same. human emotions any of us would feel. Later he became more blasé about money, or better disciplined—probably both.

When Rockefeller returned home at night, his thoughts were still on oil. He would wake his brother Will in the middle of the night to tell him of a new idea. He had a habit then of talking about his problems to himself. If too exultant when he first went into business he would say to himself: "Now a little success. Soon you will be thrown down, soon you will be overthrown. Look out, or you will lose your head. Go steady." Now that he was launched, he would say to himself: "You've got a fair fortune. You have a good property now but suppose the oil gives out, suppose the oil gives out."

There was the rub. Suppose this was really a Barmecide feast? He was building for the future, not knowing how much oil there was underground or where. But beginning in 1864, strikes at Cherry Run and then at Pithole convinced Rockefeller that oil was here to stay. The demand had soared during the war, despite the facts that one-third of the population, in the South, was cut off and that the wartime tax of $1.00 a barrel on crude oil and $0.10 a gallon on refined made the price steep. In November 1861 the first shipload of oil, 3,000 barrels, had crossed the ocean to Britain. Because of the well-known flammability of oil, a crew had been secured only by getting seamen drunk and shanghaiing them. Now there was no difficulty in getting crews, and the export demand was tremendous. This was important, since the population of the United States, then 31 million, was a small fraction of that of Europe.

On January 21, 1865, the Boston *Commercial Bulletin* said:

The changes of a year or so are so great as to make one think that we are realizing in these modern days the labors of the genie of Aladdin's lamp and to ask perhaps if that celebrated genie's name was not Petroleum—the lamp slave—after all. It is folly now to denominate petroleum as a humbug or to view the oil discovery as a bubble that will soon explode or pass into history as one of the things that were. There are flourishing towns that have been built up wholly by oil discoveries, railroads solely built to convey petroleum and so blocked up with it they cannot furnish enough rolling stock to accommodate the trade. There are barrels, millions of them, oozing with petroleum. There are banks, newspapers, hotels, insurance companies all resting on the products of these wells. Through all the seasons of navigation the Allegheny has been crowded with vessels of every description laden with petroleum. Pittsburgh which used to be the iron city thinks now of little else but petroleum.

The New York *World* said in 1866, "The development of petroleum as an article of merchandise for export is one of the wonders of the Nineteenth century." In 1866 Great Britain alone took 6,250,000 gallons, and France 4,250,000 gallons. By 1872 exports had risen to 152,000,000 gallons, and they went to every corner of the world. A little country like Syria took a million gallons and Egypt a half-million. No wonder the phrase was current in the Regions, "The world is weeping for oil." A British capitalist and railroad builder who visited the United States in 1865, Sir Samuel Morton Peto, wrote in *The Resources and Prospects of America,* "It is difficult to find a parallel to such a blessing bestowed upon a nation in the hour of her direst necessity."

On September 8, 1864, Rockefeller was married to Laura Celestia Spelman. After a honeymoon in Canada and eastern cities, the couple settled in the house next to his father's house at 29 Cheshire Street. In honor of the event Rockefeller gave a dinner for his twenty-six employees that day, at which he was not present. When taking leave the day before, he said to Andrews: "Sam, keep them all at work. Keep them all busy, but don't ask anybody to do anything for nothing."

The personality of "Cettie" Spelman was an important influence in the life of Rockefeller and on the personality of the future Rockefellers. She was the daughter of Harvey Spelman, a prosperous Cleveland businessman, a former member of the state legislature, and an operator of the "underground railroad." Her mother was an ardent temperance advocate, having prayed in the saloons of Brooklyn in her youth. After graduating from high school, "Cettie" had attended one of the best finishing schools, Oread at Worcester, and then had become a teacher. A determined young lady, an essay of hers in high school was entitled "I Can Paddle My Own Canoe." She was an abolitionist as ardent as

her parents, and the Rockefeller interest in the Negro in future
years stems largely from her. While Rockefeller mixed his religion
with a good dose of pragmatism, she took her religion straight,
being practically armor-plated in religion. She not only disap-
proved of dancing, cards, and the theater as sinful, but also did
not write letters on Sunday. She believed literally in the saving of
souls. Though her family had been Congregationalist, she
switched to her husband's church and became a hard church
worker. Notebooks of a Sunday-school class she taught survive—
beside the names of most pupils is a C, indicating he was a true
Christian. Beside the name of one is the doleful notation, "Died
July 2, the first to go and not a Christian." She was far better read
and more cultured than her husband, and passed on these wider
tastes to her children.

In 1868, Rockefeller bought a home on one of the finest avenues to be found in any city, Euclid Avenue. This was then at the
outskirts, 424, later numbered 997, at the corner of Case Avenue.
There were large grounds, which pleased him immensely; and an
adjoining house was put on rollers and moved away. In the back
he built a stone stable and coach house that might have been
taken for a residence except for its stable doors. Here he had his
trotting horses, Midnight, Flash, Jesse, Baron, and Trifle. In winter and summer he liked to race other Clevelanders on Euclid
Avenue. This early home refutes the canard that Rockefeller was
mean and stingy in his personal life.

The entire circumference of his life was his business, his family,
and his church. He had no friends other than those of business
and church. He belonged to no clubs or organizations. He did not
know of society, and cared less. He never missed a church date
nor did his wife. When she was pregnant with her firstborn,
Bessie, Rockefeller took notes on the sermons and read them to
her.

A pamphlet, "Cleveland Past and Present," published in 1869
has these observations concerning the thirty-year-old Rockefeller:
"Although quite a young man he occupies a place in our business
circle second to few: Close application to one type of business, an
avoidance of all positions of honorary character that cost time . . .
keeps everything pertaining to his business in so methodical a
manner that he knows every night how he stands in the world."

A leading member of the family at this time dimmed out of

Rockefeller's life. His father had appeared in the Cleveland directory of 1857 as a "physician." He was to appear in and out of the directory for the next twenty years as "herbal doctor" or "alleopathic doctor," but he was rarely seen in Cleveland from 1860 on. He seems to have been greeted affectionately by John D. on his visits. John D. Rockefeller, Jr., recalled him in his childhood: "He gave me a .22 calibre rifle and the two of us used to shoot at marks and targets. Grandfather was a great story-teller. All the family loved him. He was a very entertaining man, coming and going when he felt like it. He lived a detached kind of life and I didn't know much about it."

At increasingly longer intervals he would reappear. George D. Rogers, Rockefeller's private secretary, told of a visit by William to New York when he was past eighty, his huge bulk having grown enormously fat and powerful-looking, but still his ebullient self. Associates of his father sometimes asked John D. for his address but were put off. On one trip John assembled his old cronies, and to them the father said merely that he lived "'way out yonder."

In March 1889, Rockefeller's mother died at the age of seventy-six. At her burial were all her children but not her husband. Though he was alive, and very much so, her tombstone bore the inscription "Mrs. Eliza Rockefeller, Widow of William Rockefeller." No doubt that was done at her request. Later there was a sensational revelation. In July 1905, Ida Tarbell published a photograph of William Rockefeller and stated that his whereabouts was a mystery. She urged that all about Rockefeller's "origins" should be publicized. "A man who possesses the influence that Rockefeller does cannot be allowed to live in the dark. It is the duty of the public to know who he is. . . ." The New York *World* offered a reward for information concerning William. In retrospect it is hard to see any justification for this outrageous invasion of Rockefeller's privacy. It reflects the vindictive hatred of Rockefeller that existed, or more probably the morbid fascination he had for the public. The whereabouts of a father who had dropped out of sight when Rockefeller was an adult seems remote from his "origins."

On February 2, 1908, the New York *World* published a two-column lead story solving the mystery. Unless it was a brazen fabrication, William Rockefeller had lived in bigamy since 1855 with a girl of twenty, whom he had married when he was forty-five, until his death at the age of ninety-six in 1906. He had assumed the name of Dr. William Levingston. (He had either been born in Livingston, New York, or his parents had lived there soon before his birth.) The photograph of Dr. Levingston and of William Rockefeller show the same man or identical twins. The alleged proofs are numerous in the article—deeds of land Dr. Levingston made were in the name of William Rockefeller; his photograph bore the same birth date as William Rockefeller's; and his widow said: "If you want to know the facts go to John D. Rockefeller. Let him tell if he will." A doctor who traveled with him on his trips in which he purported to cure cancer and kidney trouble knew him as Rockefeller. The article claimed that John D. Rockefeller knew the truth about his father and that his father had cashed Standard Oil drafts made out to Dr. Levingston. Rockefeller did not deny the story, though his brother Frank did.

The published version is part of the record. It proves nothing at all about Rockefeller's character except that one student of Rockefeller, William H. Allen, may have had a deep insight when he attributed Rockefeller's abnormal secretiveness in part to a habit of concealment of his father's derelictions that arose in his youth.

Returning now to the main thread of our narrative—while his father was leaving his life, a new generation was joining it. There arrived Bessie, Edith, and Alta. Rockefeller was "pleased although sad," since he wanted an heir. On January 29, 1874, John D. Rockefeller, Jr., was born, and the father rushed to his office to break the news with tears of joy and was embraced by his associates.

The men who embraced Rockefeller were new associates, Henry M. Flagler and Oliver H. Payne. Maurice Clark had parted ways with Rockefeller years earlier. Clark, like so many of Rockefeller's future associates, was, unlike himself, a lively, worldly fellow, attractive and fond of company. He was a good business-man who subsequently became rich. But there were irritations in his relationship with Rockefeller. He would jibe at his junior member of the firm, "What would you have done without me?" Rockefeller did not relish this downgrading of his contribution.

Then, too, Maurice's brother, James Clark, was hard to stomach. He had been with Hussey and McBride, a rival refiner, and he liked to boast of the tricks he had played on Hussey behind his back. Rockefeller, taking no chances that the same tricks would be played on him, made him account for every barrel of oil he bought and made him furnish exact expense accounts. James Clark retaliated with open sneers at the "Sunday-school superintendent."

The biggest bone of contention was Rockefeller's incessant borrowing, which terrified Maurice Clark. Rockefeller says, "I had worn out the knees of my pants these days begging for credit." He went to bed wondering how he was going to repay a large sum he had borrowed and awoke wondering where he was going to borrow more. This policy brought him into collision with Clark. One day Clark, exasperated, said to him: "We have been asking for too many loans in order to extend this oil business. Why, altogether we have borrowed $100,000." Rockefeller replied, "We should borrow whenever we can safely extend the business by doing so." Clark answered, "If that's the way you want to do business we'd better dissolve and let you run your own affairs to suit yourself."

Though it was probably bad temper and bluff on Clark's part, Rockefeller lost not a moment in putting a notice of dissolution in the paper. He felt that the timid Clark was a drag on him. He had scouted Andrews and knew that he would stay with him. The auction of the oil business was set. The price zoomed up in the bidding between Clark and Rockefeller until the latter bid $72,500 and the former said: "I'll go no higher, John. The business is yours." The loser took the commission business *in toto* as a consolation prize. Rockefeller said, "This was really my start in the oil trade," and he regarded it as the beginning of his success. In the Cleveland *Leader* of February 15, 1865, was a notice that the former business of Andrews, Clark and Company would be operated from then on as Rockefeller and Andrews.

Now Rockefeller had a free hand, and had to account to no one. John Andrews, Sam's brother, took over the purchasing in the Regions that had been done by James Clark. John brought his brother William into the business, organizing William Rockefeller and Company to build a second refinery. Like the first one, the

Excelsior Works, the second, the Standard Works, was at the head of Kingbury Run, beside the tracks of the Atlantic and Great Western, which ran a spur from the main line to the works. By the end of 1866, another company, Rockefeller and Company, was incorporated in New York to handle export sales. It had an office at 181 Pearl Street. At that time the firm used export agents and regular channels of trade. It was not for some years that Rockefeller undertook to eliminate middlemen.

The addition of William Rockefeller was no act of nepotism. Will, a shrewd man but jolly and likable, was a tremendous asset, all students of Standard Oil agree, including Miss Tarbell. He had made a success in business on his own, becoming a partner in a commission house. He was like his father, and much different in temperament and outlook from his older brother. For one thing, he believed wholly in living and not in giving.

The $72,500 that Rockefeller had paid Clark for the business had not only cleaned out all his cash but had undoubtedly strained all his credit facilities. Rockefeller, too, was not a loner, and was looking for a partner with acumen matching his to carry the load. All he hoped for and more came with Henry M. Flagler, whose alliance with Rockefeller was one of the luckiest events of his career.

Flagler was nine years older than Rockefeller, having been born near Canandaigua, New York, in 1830. He was the son of a Presbyterian minister. It is remarkable that the three men closest to Rockefeller in his business career were sons of ministers: Henry Flagler, John D. Archbold, and Frederick T. Gates. His counsel, Samuel Calvin Tait Dodd, though not born to a minister, was weaned on the Bible, the study of which became a passion with him.

Flagler left home at the age of fourteen because his presence was a financial burden on the family. He walked nine miles to Medina, where he got his first transportation. He worked his way on a canalboat, and landed in Republic, Ohio, almost penniless; there he joined his half-brother, Dan Harkness, the son of his mother by a previous marriage, her third. They worked together in a store owned by Dan's uncle, Lamon Harkness. It was so cold in the back room where the boys slept, he recalled, that he used to sleep under the counter swathed in wrapping paper. Dan married one of the daughters of Lamon, Isabella, and Henry Flagler married the other, Mary Harkness. Showing great acuteness as a businessman, Flagler was made a member of Lamon's firm, Harkness and Company. By 1862 Flagler had $50,000. The salt-mining business was going great guns in Saginaw, Michigan, the business of boring for saltwater having collapsed because all the workers flocked to the oil wells. For a time Flagler made money; but in 1865 prices collapsed at the end of the war, and Flagler had lost his $50,000 and was $50,000 in debt. Dan Harkness lent him $50,000, and now Flagler was back east in Cleveland, looking for another fortune.

One of Flagler's relatives by marriage had had a stroke of luck. Dan Harkness had a half-brother, Stephen V. Harkness, by the previous marriage of his father. Thus Henry Flagler had a half-brother, Dan Harkness, who had a half-brother, Stephen Harkness, but Flagler and Stephen Harkness were unrelated by blood, while his wife, Mary Harkness, was a first cousin of Stephen. (This network was due to the fact that in those days the widowed did not remain long unspoused.) Stephen, who was twelve years older than Flagler, was in the grain commission business in Monroeville, Ohio, and also operated a distillery. Stephen happened to be a good friend of Senator John Sherman, who was a member of the Senate Finance Committee, and gave him a tip. The first comprehensive Internal Revenue Act of 1862, a Civil War measure, would impose a tax of $2 on every gallon of distilled spirits. (This was a very heavy tax, so heavy in fact, that the term "bootlegging" originated from the habit of hiding untaxed liquor in the high boots worn then).

Stephen decided to make a killing. He bought all the liquor in sight. He borrowed from every bank that would lend him a dime. He sold grain for farmers and staved off payment while he bought liquor with the proceeds. At the time he sent a wire to Rockefeller, then in the commission business: "Why the hell don't you remit for the last car of corn I shipped? Unless I get it soon I will bust." Thus by hook and crook he cornered a good supply of liquor that he sold for a fat profit when the tax was imposed and the price went up. He made $300,000. Moving to Cleveland, he made some more hundreds of thousands in real estate and was perhaps the richest man in the city.

Rockefeller had known Flagler in the days before his salt venture when they had done business together. Now they renewed their friendship. They had office space together in the Sexton Building. Flagler first had tried to market a process for making the perfect horseshoe, but this had failed. Then he had resumed the grain commission business, became a buyer for Maurice Clark in the commission business he inherited from Rockefeller, built up a business of his own, and then bought out Clark. Being the heir of Rockefeller's old business, he had a link with him.

Rockefeller took an immediate liking to Flagler. He proposed to Flagler that he join him in the oil business and that he tap Harkness for capital. Harkness was quite willing to be convinced, and so a new era began. A notice was published in Cleveland newspapers of an agreement dated February 28, 1867, for a limited partnership, under the name of Rockefeller, Andrews & Flagler, the limited partner (limited in liability) being Harkness, with a published investment in the notice of $70,000. It is believed that the investment was over $100,000, the rest being a loan to Flagler.

The new company solved the problem of capital. No longer would Rockefeller have to go about begging for loans. Since the oil business was considered speculative, such loans were often for short terms and at high rates of interest. Harkness's name behind the firm as silent partner was such a solid guarantee that if credit was needed, there would be little difficulty in getting it. Harkness himself was always ready with help. In 1872 Standard had a fire in New York and lost $700,000 in property; the insurance company delayed payment. When Rockefeller called on Harkness, he said, "John, I'll give you all I've got." Rockefeller recalled, "That was the kind of man Harkness was." And what a wonderful investment it was for Harkness, bringing in hundreds of millions! When the trust was dissolved in 1911, the Harkness family interest was second only to that of Rockefeller.

In Flagler, Rockefeller gained a mental and spiritual kin. They lived with each other all day, sharing the same office, walking to and fro from work, spending many evenings with each other. They were much alike, although the handsome, glossy-haired, distinguished-looking Flagler seemed more the man of the world or *bon vivant*. He was actually extremely religious, having been a

Sunday-school superintendent at Saginaw. He was a devoted family man; his wife, Mary, was almost an invalid, and he made it a cardinal rule to spend at least five nights a week at home. Dalliance with women was for a later day. Like Rockefeller, he was not given to uttering unnecessary words. Rockefeller once recalled that Flagler had said spontaneously, "John, isn't a friendship founded on business a lot better than a business founded on friendship?" Their thinking was so close that Rockefeller might have addressed him the same way that Richard III addressed Buckingham in the heyday of their friendship: "My other self, my counsel's consistory, my oracle, my prophet."

Flagler was bold and he had vision. The man who later spent $50 million in building the East Coast of Florida into our greatest resort area and who conceived the railroad from Jacksonville to Key West, surviving to see it completed, could also make grandiose plans for the oil industry and the leadership of his company in it. Rockefeller says that he was eye to eye with him on the importance of building for permanency: ". . . he insisted that when a refinery was to be put up, it should be different from the flimsy shacks which it was then the custom to build. Everyone was so afraid that the oil would disappear and that the money expended in buildings would be a loss that the meanest and cheapest buildings were erected for use as refineries." Flagler had one quality in better supply than Rockefeller, and the latter prized it: the ability to deal with people. Flagler therefore undertook more of the negotiation of contracts. Rockefeller said of this quality, "The ability to deal with people is as purchasable a commodity as sugar or coffee, and I pay more for that ability than for any other under the sun."

Let us imagine the sort of problems that Rockefeller and Flagler discussed in their daily conversations. There was certainly little to complain about for the present. The firm was the largest in Cleveland. A credit statement of a Cleveland Bank supplied at that time to a New York bank says that Rockefeller's firm had a capital of $1 million, of which $360,000 was invested in the refinery and real estate and $600,000 in the business. It also had big storage facilities for oil. This was decidedly an asset, since the price of crude and refined varied so much that the art of making

The Drake Well at Titusville, Pennsylvania, pumped 25 barrels of oil a day, selling for £7 2s 6d a barrel

John D. Rockefeller was eighteen when this photograph was taken in 1857

Rockefeller at the age of forty one . . . 'I have ways of making money you know nothing of'

money in oil was largely a strategy of when to buy and when to sell. Oil storage, therefore, was vital.

But problems were looming. Production of oil had almost doubled from 1863 to 1870, from 2,631,000 barrels to 4,659,000 barrels, while refinery capacity had grown faster. However, consumer demand had not kept pace. The margin between crude prices and refined was dropping. When Rockefeller went into the oil business at the start of 1863, crude sold for $2.00 a barrel, which at 42 gallons per barrel meant less than $0.05 cents a gallon. The refined price was $0.40. This was quite a margin, even though five gallons of crude were needed to make three gallons of refined. In addition, the cost of barrels and transportation was high, and the cost of refining was $0.05 cents a gallon.

Later, the margin began to shrink. In the beginning of 1869, crude at $7.00 a barrel was $0.16 a gallon, but refined sold for only $0.34. The margin from 1864 to 1869 had shrunk from $0.38½ to $0.18. Though the cost of barrels had been cut, transport costs were lower, and refining costs had fallen from $0.05 to $0.03 a gallon, the profit per barrel had dropped drastically. The operations of the free market might yet wreck all the refiners if the margin kept going down.

They also talked about the future of Cleveland as a refining center. Could it compete with the other refining cities, Pittsburgh, New York, and Philadelphia? Could it compete with the refineries built in the oil regions themselves? By 1865 there were thirty located there. What could be more logical than to locate refineries close to oil, the raw material? But the theory did not work out well. Machinery and chemicals had to be transported into the Regions at a high cost; and labor, real estate, and raw materials cost 40 percent more than in Cleveland and Pittsburgh.

Pittsburgh was less than 60 miles from Oil City, and by 1865 had 80 refineries. It was only 355 miles from Philadelphia, an export outlet, a considerably shorter distance than Philadelphia was from Oil City. It had plenty of coal and labor, and was connected to the southern market by rail and river.

Cleveland seemed to be least favorably placed. Oil had to be shipped 148 miles northwest to Cleveland and then 609 miles to New York. The combined trip was 750 miles. A refiner in the Regions had a trip of 500 miles to reach New York. A refiner in

New York or Philadelphia was much closer to the oil regions. (Of course, he had to buy five barrels of crude for every three barrels of refined produced from the crude, and pay freight on the five barrels on the long trip to the Eastern Seaboard; the Cleveland refining center required that the five barrels of crude be carried only for the short trip to Cleveland.)

Cleveland had a geographical problem in competition. Its fate depended on railroad rates. Situated on the Great Lakes, it excelled all other points in access to the West. To compete in the East and in foreign markets it had to have more liberal treatment if it was to survive. As the Cleveland Board of Trade said in 1866, "Cleveland possesses the natural advantages for becoming the greatest refining center in the United States, a position she will speedily take if our railroad and lake transportation men will adopt a liberal policy as to freights and establish a low and uniform rate to the seaboard which will enable us at all times to compete with Pittsburgh."

Cleveland was in an excellent bargaining position. First of all, since it was on the Lake, close to the Erie Canal, it could use the canal to ship oil as long as it was ice-free. Then it had another ace to play. There was not one railroad from Cleveland to the Regions, but two: the Atlantic and Great Western, which was for a long time leased by the Erie Railroad and later allied to it, and the Lake Shore Railroad, which was a part of the New York Central. From Cleveland to New York there were two roads, the Erie and the New York Central. Thus Cleveland could always play one road against the other to get lower rates. But Pittsburgh was at the mercy of one road, the Pennsylvania.

Rockefeller and Flagler talked of this problem, and in that connection undoubtedly discussed the oil regions. Many times Rockefeller must have said, "What a crazy breed of men those oil producers are!" Indeed, the spectacle in the Regions was enough to disconcert any sober businessman like Rockefeller.

The Oildorado reached its most feverish pitch as the Civil War came to its end. Soldiers swarmed into the oil regions, and employers took pride in the number of heroes they could hire. These new arrivals came at the same time as rich new strikes were made. The revels now took on their gaudiest hue. J. T. Trowbridge, writing in the *Atlantic Monthly* in 1869, said, "Almost everybody you meet has been suddenly enriched or suddenly ruined (perhaps both within a short space of time) or knows plenty of people who have."

The rags-to-riches-to-rags romance was epitomized in the well-publicized career of "Coal Oil Johnny." Mixed with legend, the story lived on for years, and many came to believe that "Coal Oil Johnny" could only be John D. Rockefeller. Heaven forbid!

John W. Steele was the nineteen-year-old adopted son of Widow McClintock, owner of one of the biggest wells, who was burned to death in 1864. Johnny had a brief conference with a lawyer who advised him as to his affairs, "Let things be," and charged him $500. That was his first experience in getting plucked. He began an orgy of spending that amazed the country. Blazing with diamonds, he leased the Continental Hotel in Philadelphia for a day for $8,000 because they had refused to fire a clerk who had offended him. Johnny held open house, everything free to all comers. He hired a minstrel show and put them on a fully equipped private train he had bought, paying all salaries out of his pocket for weeks, including reimbursement to the treasurer for house receipts they were not collecting. When the Chicago Opera House said it would not "rent to a nigger show," he offered to buy it for $200,000. He lighted cigars with $100 bills, tipped bootblacks with gifts of the same denomination, and gave gifts of expensive diamonds to anyone who struck his fancy.

After spending half a million, he went broke when his well went dry. He ended as a baggage clerk. Although many jeered at the exploits of "Coal Oil Johnny," he had fun losing his fortune; others just saw theirs go down the drain.

Fortune hunters poured into the area. On a trip to Oil Creek, Andrew Carnegie was amused to see a sign by a derrick, "To hell or China." He and his partners bought a farm and set up a company to drill for oil on it. The farm rose in value to $5,000,-000, and the wealth helped to establish the great Carnegie fortune.

In the fall of 1864, another fortune hunter was living with three other men in a room in the United States Hotel in Franklin. Samuel C. T. Dodd, who got to know him well, said in his memoirs that "he was exceptionally good-looking." From a theatrical family, he regaled Dodd with anecdotes. "I became very fond of him," Dodd wrote. Dodd noted that he was uninterested in the presidential contest then going on between Lincoln and General McClellan, and was uninterested in the war. The youth played billiards every day with Alf Smiley, a roommate, and was a free spender. "I have plenty of money and I enjoy your company so please let me pay for you." Smiley later recalled that the fortune hunter was uninterested in politics and the war then in progress. He had paid $5,000 for a partnership in the Fuller farm, which was a dud. He was in and out of the Regions, going to Canada at the same time Rockefeller went on his honeymoon. In February he was at Pithole, paying $1,000 for a thirtieth interest on a lease owned by the Boston Company. He then left the Regions for good, and returned to Washington. John Wilkes Booth was on his way to play his last and most famous role in Ford's Theatre on April 14.

The short life of the city of Pithole was so bizarre that a few years later there was wonderment as to whether it had been a reality or a dream. Oil was found in early 1865 on the farm of Thomas Holmden, six miles from Plumer. Reputedly it was found by the vibrations of a witch-hazel stick. It was a small clearing in the woods, with many pitholes in the earth nearby. In May there was a surge to the area, and in a month the city of Pithole existed. It was said to have 15,000 inhabitants, and the daily volume of mail received was third in the state, next to that of Philadelphia and Pittsburgh. It was a city of "shreds and patches." Buildings, all of wood, were constructed in five days, and sometimes immediately collapsed. Newcomers had to sleep one hundred to a barn, paying a dollar each, and considered any shelter at all a luxury. But in less than a year it had banks, newspapers, and a score of fine hotels. Murphy's Theater had 1,100 seats and had chandeliers from Tiffany's. An actress who was playing Lady Macbeth one night pleased a patron so much that he tossed a $500 bill to the lady, who interrupted her sleep-walking soliloquy to grab it. A drink of water cost a dime, a pail a dollar. The standard way to get your mail was to pay a dollar to a boy on line for his place. Every day at noon forty soiled doves from the leading sporting house staged a procession on horse-back, demurely seated side-saddle, thus giving the residents a chance to appraise the horseflesh. There was a lot of good clean horseplay, too. An "R.C.T." club was organized: "Rum, cards, and tobacco." A minister on being told it meant "Religious Counsels Treasured" preached sermons there.

Mud was everywhere. "Crocus" (Charles G. Leonard), who wrote the *History of Pithole* in 1867, said that the single plank that served for a sidewalk was "so far beneath the surface that more than ordinary length of limb is required to reach it." A correspondent sent back to his paper a drawing of a pair of boots upended in mud with a sign sticking out, "Who will take care of Mother now?" An ingenious young inventor of Pithole decided that he would use the menace of mud to fight the menace of fire, and invented a machine to throw mud on fires. In the first demonstration he got caught in the machinery, fell into the hopper, was catapulted into the fire, and burned to death. So say the chronicles.

On every streetcorner hawkers were peddling choice oil stocks or oil leases. It was said that there was not $100,000 within twenty miles of Oil Creek before the Drake well, but a lease on a small plot of land in Pithole could go for $100,000. Many were defrauded. A favorite trick was to run oil by subterranean pipes into dry wells. One person got caught when he made the mistake of pumping out kerosene from a well.

The magic city of Pithole so suddenly conjured from the earth was as suddenly swallowed up. In February 1866 there were complaints of oil in water wells and water in oil wells. Gushers began to fade, owing, it is said, to a failure of subterranean gas caused by too much drilling. Then fires broke out, followed by a flood. The people decided to evacuate. A curse was on the town. A good part of the population had fled before it was acknowledged that there was no more oil. The pool was a rectangle only two miles long and a mile wide. By 1870 there were only a handful left in the ghost city that had disappeared from the map.

This saga of Pithole is typical of the riot and recklessness of the Regions, where hundreds of thousands of worthless oil securities were sold, where Dr. A. C. Egbert, who had kept $1,800,000 in cash in his house, wound up broke in Cleveland, a harmless crank asking Rockefeller for a loan of a million; where even the train running along the Allegheny from Pittsburgh speeded so recklessly that the route was dubbed "The Valley of the Shadow of Death," and where, as J. N. Camden recalled, "The simple statement of a man's connection with oil was a severe blow to his credit."

This bacchanal is not recounted only to amuse the reader. Its significance is vital. It explains how the conflict between the oil producers and Rockefeller was grounded in a difference in basic outlook and psychology. The parsimonious Rockefeller was appalled at the profligacy of the Regions; the Regions derided Rockefeller as "the man with the notebook" who counted each penny. Reconciliation was not possible.

But, unlike the ephemeral city of Pithole, progress was being made in the Regions. Investment is indicated by the fact that the paid-in capital of oil companies in 1870 was estimated at $350,-000,000. The appetite for oil stocks was such that when a company in Philadelphia opened its subscription books, a line of buyers three blocks long formed. Corry, which in 1859 had been only farmland and a stopping point for deerhunters, by 1865 had a population of 10,000, twenty banks, and an oil exchange that exerted more influence on the country than anything done at Philadelphia. Oil City, which had been a farm village named Cornplanter, after an Indian chief, was battling Corry for supremacy. By 1870 Titusville had a population of 10,000.

The most revolutionary development for oil producers (next to the linkage of the Regions by rail) was the introduction of pipelines. Early pipelines were built in 1863, relying mostly on gravity, such as the line from the Tarr farm to the Humboldt refinery. Samuel Van Syckel came to the Regions as a producer and would have made money at Pithole if the teamsters had not devoured his profits. He determined to build a pipeline from the wells to the railroad. He was ridiculed even by his friends: "Do you expect to put a girdle around the earth? Can you make water run uphill?" He was so mocked that he was forced to eat in the kitchen of the Morey Hotel in Pithole, going in by the back way. But he built the line. With three relay pumps, oil flowed through two two-inch lines side by side for four miles. Then, as he related, the teamsters would "drive astraddle of it, dig down to it, putting logging chains around it and pull it out of the ground. I sent to New York for some carbines, hired 25 men to patrol the line and put a stop to it." Like Drake, this pioneer got nothing out of it. He lost the line because of debt, later got into ruinous litigation with Standard Oil, and died forgotten and penniless.

Henry Harley built the next pipeline. He was a colorful character, typifying the devil-may-care attitude of the period. An associate of Jim Fisk and Jay Gould, the Erie buccaneers, he landed in jail, where his wife, a cultured woman, took up her abode with him. Samuel Dodd, in his memoirs, describes how he found him in New York so destitute that he was begging for a dollar, yet would not travel a block except by cab and was resplendent in paste diamonds. Harley built a line that met even fiercer resistance from the teamsters, who not only tore up the line but also burned the storage tanks and the wells using the pipe. The governor called out troops to beat them into submission. It was Custer's Last Stand for the teamsters.

The system of sale of oil now became simplified. When the storage tanks at a well became full, the stopcocks were opened, and oil was run off to the stations of the pipeline. The amount run off was measured on a gauge, and the wellowner was given credit by certificates, usually for a thousand barrels. These certificates were negotiable and were an article of commerce on the oil exchange. A Farmers' Train ran the length of Oil Creek, making stops at all the wells enroute, and became an informal exchange where oil certificates could be sold to jobbers or refiners. If the oil was not sold immediately, a storage charge was made by the pipeline company.

The rails carried oil in barrels, and continued to do so for a long time. But wooden tanks, two to a car, invented by Amos Densmore, came into use, and then were supplanted by upright iron tanks. By 1869 the horizontal boiler came along, with a cupola or dome that allowed for gas expansion and thus reduced the toll of explosions and fires.

Derricks were twice as high, and wells at 600 feet were twice as deep as in Drake's day. Many of the wells became clogged with paraffin. A valuable new device was tried in January 1865, a "torpedo," a flask filled with gunpowder patented by Colonel E. A. Roberts. At 365 feet, the first experiment "operated like a stomach pump." By 1869 nitroglycerine was substituted, and many a "torpedo man" met his Maker sooner than he planned.

In *Wealth Against Commonwealth*, speaking proudly of the advance in the Regions, Henry Demarest Lloyd says: "But shadows of sunset began to creep over the field in its morning time and the strange spectacle came of widespread ruin in an industry prospering by leaps and bounds. . . . As early as 1865 strange perturbations were felt, showing that some undiscovered body was pulling the others out of their regular orbits." And the consequence? "Everything withers—even charity."

What was this miscreant heavenly body? (Lloyd had undoubtedly been reading of the discovery of the planet Neptune.) It was Standard Oil, of course, five years before it was born.

Ida Tarbell wrote in the same vein. The Regions were on their way to solving their problems. "There was nothing too good for them. But suddenly at the very heyday of this confidence a big hand reached out from nobody knew where to steal their conquest and throttle their future."

Whose hand? Mr. Rockefeller's, of course.

This is nonsense. The Regions had a chronic economic problem that was a millstone around its neck—overproduction. In consequence, the price of crude oil skidded up and down, but mostly within a range below the subsistence level for the small producer. From $20.00 it fell to 0.10 a barrel in December 1861 and shot up to $14.00 in July 1864, then down to $4.00 in August 1865 and $1.35 in December 1866. It rose to $5.75 in July 1868, $7.00 the following January, but fell to $2.70 in August 1870.

Most producers felt no prosperity at all. Producers were discussing combining to make better terms with refiners as early as 1866. The Oil City *Register* said, "Producers at Titusville and other places are clamoring for a Convention of interested persons to take some action looking for better prices for oil." In 1867 an oilman, John Ponton, warned that the only salvation for the producers was to combine and build their own pipeline. Because Rockefeller was able to combine refiners, and producers were unable to combine among themselves, he earned their undying hatred.

CHAPTER 4 *Rebate*

IN 1899, Lewis Emery, Jr., a lifelong competitor of Rockefeller, testifying before the United States Industrial Commission, said, "The milk in the cocoanut of the success of Standard Oil Company is transportation." Transportation, indeed, is the key. The advantage in rail rates that Rockefeller obtained in the early days of oil was a competitive advantage that was a prime secret of his success and of the garroting of his rivals. They were called "rebates," and Rockefeller admitted that he received them up to 1880. Thereafter he got privileges in one form or another from the railroads, even if they did not technically warrant the label of rebate. By 1880, Standard Oil through its pipelines had itself become a transporter of oil, which enabled it to put even more pressure on the railroads for rate concessions.

"Rebate": the most controversial word in Rockefeller's career. It comes from the French *rebattre*, meaning "to beat down again." Applied to a business transaction, it came to mean a refund or a remission of payment. Originally it was a secret repayment of a railroad rate to one party rather than a special rate to a group. This beneficence in rates for certain parties came into being in other industries as well. In 1899, the Interstate Commerce Commission reported to Congress that "No one thing does so much to force out the small operator and to build up those trusts and monopolies against which law and public opinion alike beat in vain as discrimination in freight rates."

Why were the railroads so accommodating as to give Rockefeller rebates? Let us first see how Rockefeller explained it. In his *Reminiscences* he says:

> It [Standard] offered freights in large quantity, carloads and train loads. It furnished loading facilities and discharging facilities at great cost. It provided regular traffic so that a railroad could conduct its transportation to the best advantage and use its equipment to the full extent of its hauling capacity without waiting for the refiner's convenience. It exempted railroads

from liability for fire and carried its own insurance. It provided, at its own expense, terminal facilities which permitted economies in handling. For these services it obtained special allowances on freight.

In 1917, Rockefeller said to William Inglis: "Who can buy beef the cheapest—the housewife for her family, the steward for a club or hotel, or the commissary for an army? Who is entitled to better rebates from a railroad, those who give it for transportation 5,000 barrels a day, or those who give 500 barrels—or 50 barrels?"

This explanation of rebates as quantity discounts has been adopted by others than Rockefeller, such as John Flynn. Yet it is far from being an adequate explanation. A quantity discount, as we know it, is a shading in price or a moderate reduction. A reduction in price of 50 percent hardly answers the description. That is indeed a horse of a different color. Then this begs the question as to how in the first place the Rockefeller firm grew to the strength that it was able to offer oil in greater quantities for shipment than its competitors. How did Caesar acquire the meat on which he fed to make him so great before he became Caesar? Then, again, it should be noted that competitors of Rockefeller testified that they offered loading and terminal facilities and other services equal to those offered by Rockefeller, but were rebuffed by the rails when they sought rates as low as those given to Standard Oil.

To comprehend how Rockefeller was successful in getting rebates, we must envision the situation a hundred years ago. Railroads were still very new. In 1830 there were only 23 miles of rail; in 1840, 2,818 miles; and in 1860, 30,000 miles. The railroad was a revolutionary development of unparalleled significance. Prior to the railroad, most goods had been carried on inland waterways, canals, or coastal traffic. On the poor roads there had been only the unwieldy Conestoga wagons. Now transport was swift and sure. For a town to be "off the railroad" was an unmitigated disaster; to be "on the railroad" was a boon. Cities and towns floated bond issues to raise money to "persuade" the road to connect with them. In 1853 the per capita railroad debt of Wheeling was $55 and of Baltimore $43. When the rails reached the town, there were processions of notables, fireworks, and banquets. Thus when the Atlantic and Great Western reached Cleveland from the Regions in November 1863, Rockefeller must have read and heard of the banquets tendered to Sir Samuel Morton Peto, the British capitalist responsible for the financing of the road—nine varieties of fish, six of game, nine of other meats, fourteen kinds of pastries.

This power was heady wine for railroad managers, who looked on themselves as among the masters of America, and brooked no opposition or criticism. It was the most prestigious occupation, as evidenced by the influx of Civil War leaders, including General George B. McClellan, who joined the Atlantic and Great Western as president; Assistant Secretary of War Thomas Scott, who became vice president of the Pennsylvania Railroad; and Assistant Secretary of War Peter Watson, who became general freight agent for the Lake Shore Railroad. The arrogance of the rail chiefs was akin to that in Britain, where Arthur Hadley wrote, "A complainant is a marked man and the [railroad] commission cannot protect him against the vengeance of the railroad."

Railroad men were venal in a venal age. Colonel Joseph Potts related that when he congratulated Tom Scott on his appointment as Assistant Secretary of War, Scott joyfully replied, "This job is worth $100,000 to me," and he was not thinking of the salaries he would receive after the war. Andrew Carnegie received a salary of $125 a month as a division superintendent of a railroad, and at the end of six years with about the same salary, he wrote in his memoirs, "My investments now began to require so much of my attention that I resolved to leave the service of the railway company."

Ida Tarbell charged that railroad chiefs were "bribed" to give rebates to Standard Oil, and in 1876, in testimony before Congress, Rockefeller's brother, Frank, then at odds with him, said that rebates were "divided up between the Standard Oil Company and the railroad officials." There were indignant denials, and no supporting proof was offered for the allegation. However, it is a matter of record that prominent rail officials like William H. Vanderbilt became stockholders of Standard Oil under unexplained circumstances and for an unstated consideration (if any), thereby acquiring a stake in the success of Standard Oil.

Rail rates were not uniform. The rates were set pragmatically, the object being to maximize the return to the railroad. There was then no legal restraint as to the obligations of a common carrier. Ida Tarbell, among numerous inconsistencies, stated that "the railways were bound as public carriers to give equal rates" but that the theory then was "not so definitely crystallized into law." The latter statement is the correct one. There was nothing firm in the common law or then on the statute books to prohibit rebates, and implications that Rockefeller connived to breach the law are on unsound footing.

There was a published rate, but all agreed that it was the starting point for haggling. Logan MacPherson, in his book *Railroad Freight Rates in Relation to the Industry and Commerce of the United States,* says, "Indeed, transportation was regarded by both railroads and shippers as a matter of bargain and sale, the shrewdest shippers securing the lowest rates and the cleverest freight solicitor the largest traffic." An infant industry that showed prospects of growth could get a lower rate, that being often the inducement for locating along the line. The most frequent occasion for the special rate was to meet competition from another railroad. That resulted often in a lower "through" rate than a "local" rate from a much closer point, or more for the short haul than for the long haul. Thus at one time it was cheaper to ship from Pittsburgh west to Cincinnati and from there east to Philadelphia than to ship directly from Pittsburgh to Philadelphia, because the rate from Pittsburgh was a "local" rate, and the rate from Cincinnati was "through." As A. J. Cassatt, vice-president of the Pennsylvania Railroad, put it: "Through rates are governed by competition. That forces below paying-rates sometimes. If we put local rates down to the same charge per ton mile, the road could not live." The local rate was set as high "as the traffic would bear."

Even Henry Demarest Lloyd admitted that his *bête noire,* Rockefeller, did not invent the rebate. Professor Nevins cites abundant evidence of special rates and discrimination in investigations conducted in 1867 by the state senates in Ohio and Pennsylvania. Thus a Harrisburg freight agent admitted that "all the prominent parties have special rates" in the shipment of iron and steel. There was also testimony on the secrecy of such rates. An ironmaster said: "We must have a special rate given us by the general agent in Philadelphia. We cannot live by the sheet rates. Those rates seem to be arbitrary [sic]."

In 1890, J. M. Bonham wrote in *Railway Secrecy and Trusts* this plausible rationalization for Rockefeller's acceptance of rebates: "They [Standard] found a system of secret rebates and discriminations in flourishing existence. Should they become participants of them or become the victims of them? . . . They naturally chose the second alternative." It is to be noted that no one was so Pecksniffian that he passed up a rebate opportunity, which confirms Rockefeller's joke about the Scotsman who was asked what he thought of rebates. He replied, "Laddie, I'm against them—unless I'm in on 'em."

Even while defending rebates as quantity discounts, Rockefeller mentions that it was competitive pressure from different methods of transport that made the rails amenable to giving rebates. Cleveland with two different railroad systems—from the oil regions and to the East and the availability of shipment by the Lake and then the Erie Canal—was in a prime position to "bully" the roads. But rather than start a general rate war, the rails preferred to confine the rate favoritism to one company and take its chances with the others.

The most apt explanation from the standpoint of the railroad's own self-interest was the testimony of a railroad man named Wicker before the Cullom Committee of the United States Congress in 1886:

> I am speaking now as a railroad man. Here is quite a grain point in Iowa where there are five or six grain elevators. As a railroad man, I would try and hold all those dealers on a level keel, awarding them all the same traffic rate. But suppose there was a road four miles across the country and those dealers should begin to drop in on me and tell me that road was reaching within a mile or two of our station and drawing to itself all the grain. You might say that it will be the just and right thing to give all the five or six dealers a special rate to meet this competition. But as a railroad man I can accomplish the purpose better by picking out one good, smart live man and give him a concession, let him go there and scoop the

business. I would get the tonnage and that is what I want. But if I go to the five it is known in a very short time. I can illustrate that by a story told by Mr. Vanderbilt. A broker came and said, "Mr. Vanderbilt, I would like to take in my friend John Smith." Vanderbilt replied, "Here are you and myself in the deal now. We take in John Smith. That makes 111. I guess I won't do it."

Rockefeller was that one "good, smart, live" man chosen. In their purblindedness, the rails did not foresee that the process would be cumulative. As Rockefeller grew stronger by rebates, he demanded bigger rebates. As rail expert William Z. Ripley commented, "Sinbad is soon overwhelmed by the Old Man of the Sea." Simon Sterne, counsel of the Hepburn Committee investigation of 1879, spoke in the same vein of the supreme folly of the railroads in falling prey to Rockefeller.

"Foolish, shortsighted people not to have foreseen that such a monopoly when erected would eventually dictate terms to the railways and become a modern Frankenstein, a monster that would plague its inventors."

On January 10, 1870, the Rockefeller firm, hitherto a limited partnership, was reorganized as a corporation, the Standard Oil Company of Ohio. The capitalization was $1,000,000, consisting of 10,000 shares of $100 each. Rockefeller took 2,667 shares worth nominally over $250,000. That was not his entire wealth. About that time, he wrote to his wife, "You know we are independently rich outside investments in oil." Stephen Harkness had 1,334 shares, and Henry Flagler, Samuel Andrews, and William Rockefeller 1,333 shares each. Rockefeller was president of the new company, William Rockefeller vice-president, and Flagler secretary. The firm was undercapitalized, which was to be a characteristic of the company in the future. Heavy investments were made by O. B. Jennings, a brother-in-law of William Rockefeller, and Benjamin Brewster, vice-president of the Omaha Railroad, who became stockholders. The corporate form was assumed, not for the purpose of selling stock to the public, but for greater convenience in doing business and to facilitate future entrance of capital.

This company, progenitor of the great trust, adopted the name "Standard" from the Standard Works, one of its two refineries. It was a useful name because it connoted "standard oil," that is, oil of a good quality and up to a standard, an important consideration when consumers were worried about oil of poor quality that might explode. In 1868, refiners held a national convention on the subject of eliminating cheap "benzoin," which was dangerous, and generally improving the quality of oil.

The company soon acquired the Long Island Oil Company in Brooklyn. It owned, besides refineries, a fleet of tank cars, warehouses, lake transshipping facilities, timberlands, and paint and barrelmaking plants. It was among the largest refineries in the world. It had a capacity of 1,500 barrels a day. The capacity of all refineries in Cleveland, 25 in number, was 12,000 barrels, far beyond that of Pittsburgh. At this time the total number of refineries in the nation was 250, and Standard's share was between 3 percent and 4 percent. Of the capacity actually in operation, since there was a surplus of refined, it was a greater percentage.

Rebates had already played a major part in promoting the success of the Rockefeller firm. Since the essence of the rebate was secrecy, the time of the first rebates and their amounts have been surrounded by confusion and contradiction. Relatively recent proof has come to light shedding light on the early rebates. These are contained in documents that were the property of Roger Sherman, an attorney of Titusville who was prominent in the fight of the oil producers against Standard Oil and who later joined Standard's legal staff. In June 1946 these contracts, drafted by Sherman, were published in the *Mississippi Valley Historical Review* with a commentary by Professor Chester McArthur Destler.

The contracts show that Rockefeller was the recipient of rate favors from the Erie ring of Jay Gould, Jim Fisk, and Henry Harley. By contract of June 5, 1868, three Cleveland refiners, Rockefeller, Andrews, and Flagler; Clark, Payne and Company; and Westlake, Hutchens and Company acquired a quarter interest in the Allegheny Transportation Company, the pipeline belonging to Henry Harley and members of the Erie ring. Clark, Payne and Company by 1872 joined the Standard Oil Company, and it has been suggested that the Westlake firm in 1868 was little more than a dummy company through which rebates were channeled to the other two firms.

The Allegheny Transportation Company was to receive from

the Atlantic and Great Western Railroad, which was leased by
the Erie, $5.00 "per car for each and every carload of bulk oil
loaded for Cleveland at points between Oil City and Titusville
inclusive passing over the Atlantic and Great Western Railroad. . . ." The pipeline also would receive $12.00 per car for oil
shipped East via the Atlantic and Great Western and the Erie
Railroad with which it was linked.

The three refiners, by virtue of their quarter interest in Allegheny, would receive a quarter of these payments. In addition,
on oil shipped to Cleveland that belonged to them they would
receive three-quarters of the $5.00 payment. On August 27, 1868,
the $12.00 payment (referred to as a "drawback" in the docu-
ments) was raised to $15.00.

By another contract of March 19, 1870, the Standard Oil Com-
pany received another rebate of $0.05 per barrel on oil shipped to
Cleveland conditioned on its exclusive use of the Atlantic and
Great Western for shipments to Cleveland.

An interesting feature to be kept in mind for future reference
was that Rockefeller through his ownership of the interest in
Allegheny transportation shared in rebates paid *on oil shipped by
others*. These rebates were probably not the total that the Rockefeller firm collected, but, as Professor Destler comments, "They
furnish the first adequate explanation of the swift, unprecedented
expansion of Rockefeller, Andrews and Flagler from a concern of
modest proportions into the largest producer of refined oil and its
byproducts in the United States. No explanation based upon the
utilization of the processes and economies employed by other
successful refiners nor the Horatio Alger tales of thrift, industry
and business efficiency can account for the phenomenal development." This statement cannot be seriously challenged, since even
defenders and admirers of Standard Oil have conceded that the
early success of the company was due more to rail rebates than to
superiority in management.

Our next evidence is an affidavit filed in a court case in 1880 by
General J. H. Devereux, who became vice-president of the Lake
Shore Railroad in 1868. This road reached from Cleveland to
Franklin in the Regions by 1868 and by 1870 was extended to the
center of the producing district at Oil City. Devereux swore that
when he took over he found no record that his predecessor,

Amasa Stone, had granted rebates, despite many rumors to the contrary that had been bruited about. Devereux swore that in 1870 Henry Flagler came to him and made a proposition. (Flagler said later he was in charge of all transportation matters for Standard; and Rockefeller said that he was the "contract" man because of his exactness and ingenuity.) Flagler told Devereux that Standard was shipping oil east by canal for as low as $0.90 a barrel. The existing rail price was $0.40 from the Regions and $2.00 to New York, a sum of $2.40. If Devereux would cut the rate to $1.65, $0.35 from the Regions and $1.30 to New York, Devereux could have a guarantee of 60 carloads a day of refined from Standard to be shipped east by the Lake Shore and New York Central.

Devereux said he made a mental calculation that this steady business would mean that solid oil trains could be run instead of mixing oil cars with other cars, that it would reduce the round trip to 10 days from 30 days, and that the capital investment would be cut to $300,000 from $900,000. He said Yes.

The figures given by General Devereux are perplexing, since Standard Oil, with a capacity of 1,500 barrels a day in 1870, could not have furnished 60 carloads a day for shipment east. Three years later, in 1873, General Devereux became president of the Atlantic and Great Western, and in that capacity negotiated rebates with Standard Oil. It is reasonable to believe that Devereux confused the figures as to Standard Oil's capacity in 1870 with the greatly enlarged size of the firm after it had exterminated most of its rivals in Cleveland in 1872. It is also reasonable to believe that Devereux omitted to mention the prime bargaining weapon that Flagler threw on the table; namely, the rebates already being received from the Erie Railroad and the Atlantic and Great Western. The critics of Rockefeller and Standard Oil have maintained that rebates were extorted (whether by threats or cajolery) because of competition, not on the basis of savings to the road. Even under the figures cited by Devereux, it is doubtful whether the savings on the investment in rolling stock, labor, and handling charges would have justified a reduction to $1.65.

The problems in the oil industry were at a crisis stage in the latter part of 1871. It was evident that a blowoff was inevitable.

The refining industry was in the doldrums or depression, although Standard Oil was making money as it always had. The general picture of crisis presented Rockefeller with a rare opportunity. From later events it is evident that there must have been deep cogitation between Rockefeller and Flagler. The problems, complex as they were, can best be illuminated in the form of an imaginary conversation between the two strategists in the fall of 1871:

FLAGLER: Refining has turned into a sour business. The bonanza days are over. Crude is selling for $5.00 a barrel or $0.12 a gallon, and refined for $0.24. That's a margin of only $0.12, and we need five barrels of crude to make three of refined. In the last two years the margin has been cut by 33 percent. We can survive and make money on that margin because of our rebates, our new distilling equipment, and our other economies, but our profit rate is on the downgrade. For the other refiners it's all misery. They can't break even on that margin. Some are suspending operations.

ROCKEFELLER: The refining industry is blown up beyond all reality. There is a refining capacity of 45,000 barrels a day, but that's three times in excess of what's needed. There are too many in the business, too many fly-by-night operators. Today, by price-cutting, they lead themselves to a slow grave and in the meanwhile impoverish the others. Many must go.

FLAGLER: The price of refined must rise. That can happen only with fewer refiners or by combination among refiners, or both. I agree with you that competition in refining is idiotic, senseless, and self-destructive.

ROCKEFELLER: Pittsburgh refiners are aching like those in Cleveland. Here the Pittsburgh *Gazette* says, "There must be a decline in crude, although the producers continue obstinate and refuse to make concessions." Of course they refuse. Crude is up about a dollar above the average of last year; but still, at today's price, lots of small producers can't make a go of it. Speculative rings are trying all the time to jack up the price. Two years ago they formed the Petroleum Producers' Association and tried to raise crude prices by getting an agreement to stop drilling. It didn't work out. Jobbers are always trying to combine. Recently a producer-representative told me that a producer association would like to arrange things so that refiners like Standard Oil work for producers on a commission basis. We would lose our independence. That's what we can expect if we are put under their heel, so we'd better combine first if we want to maintain our interests.

FLAGLER: The refiners in the Regions are as insolent as the producers. Two years ago the papers in Titusville and Oil City were saying that Cleveland as a refining center would be wiped out "as with a sponge," and they are saying the same thing today.

ROCKEFELLER: That's because the Pennsylvania Railroad is cutting rates from Regions again. Did you notice that the Cleveland *Leader* said today, "Fortunately the Erie managers have a keen eye on Mr. Scott [of the Pennsylvania] and one may rely on them to so adapt their oil rates to the market that Cleveland refining interests will not suffer." And the New York Central also isn't going to take the risk that we Cleveland refiners will perish. They are going to hold on to our oil traffic and not let the Pennsylvania take it away.

FLAGLER: Actually, John, these rails by engaging in this rate warfare are cutting their own throats. Each year they make a convention on rates, and then one rail breaks it and all hell busts loose. It ends up so that no one of the three rails, the Pennsylvania, the Erie, and the New York Central, makes any money or any money to speak of out of the oil traffic. They would be much better off if they could arrange to get a stable, regular cut of the oil traffic by making a deal with the refiners.

ROCKEFELLER: Henry, I think that our minds are moving along the same lines. There is a way of arranging a marriage of interest between the rails and the refiners so that both parties may profit. There are too many refiners. Some union is imperative to reduce output. The rails can help us and we can help them.

FLAGLER: Yes, if the rails would grant rebates only to certain refiners, only those refiners will be able to live in today's market when the profit margin is so low. Then those refiners who survive will be in a healthy state and they will reward the rails by allotting them each a fair share of the oil traffic. The result will be a healthy refining industry and healthy and wealthy railroad lines to carry the oil. The only ones who will suffer will be the inefficient refiners who don't deserve to live anyway.

ROCKEFELLER: And another object can be accomplished at the same time. Foreign governments are becoming a nuisance. They want to import crude and do their own refining. France has just put an import tax on refined. The rails as a further favor to us will agree to carry only refined oil to the seaboard, except for the crude needed by the refiners in New York or Philadelphia who will survive under this new arrangement. So no crude will be exported, and we will continue to get for ourselves that rich export trade in refined.

There is a good deal of argument as to what Rockefeller planned at this stage. The writer believes that this conversation must have represented approximately Rockefeller's thinking at the time. It is certain that the blueprint that emerged did not spring into being fullblown, but was the product of much deliberation, over a period of months. It was the celebrated South Improvement Plan, the most cold-blooded, Draconic scheme for extinguishing competition that was ever put forth under a free society. It was built on the foundation of the rebate, but it had other ingenious devices.

CHAPTER 5   *The Oil War of 1872*

IN LATE NOVEMBER OF 1871 Rockefeller wrote to his wife after talking with Peter Watson, general freight agent for the Lake Shore, which, as we have said, was part of the New York Central alliance. "There is a new view of the question just introduced and I don't know how it may turn out though I am hopeful —indeed the project grows on me." This is probably the first allusion to the South Improvement Plan, famous and malodorous in the history of oil.

All the executives then and later who were connected with Standard Oil disowned it, claiming that it was an idea that was a brainchild of the railroads. Their statements were made after the plan had been thoroughly discredited. Many years later, Rockefeller said to Inglis: "It was not our idea. We had an idea of our own." Flagler said in 1888, "We did not believe in it but the view of other gentlemen was pressed on us to the extent that we acquiesced in it." Orville T. Waring, a Pittsburgh refiner who was in the plan, said, "We went into the plan on the suggestion of Thomas A. Scott [vice-president] of the Pennsylvania Railroad. It was he who originated the plan."

Scott, it is known, had become dubious about the prospects for building up his subsidiary line, the Philadelphia and Erie, as a crude carrier from the Regions, since he was running into the red. He was jaded by the rate wars. But who begat the final plan is overrated as to its significance, for it is known that Rockefeller, refiners, and the rails were putting their heads together to map a stabilization for the oil industry and for rail traffic. One or the other of the parties might have come forward with what was to be the final blueprint.

The plan was bold, brazen, and simple. The rails would greatly increase their rates on oil, crude and refined. However, they would give rebates to a few refiners, in effect picking the "good, smart, live" ones. Among the refiners the expectation was that only those inside the ring could live; all others would have to go under. If it would work—and secrecy, of course, was of the essence—there would be a combine in no time. In return for the favor, each of the rails would get a stable share of oil traffic.

The first step was to get a charter for the new combination. This was no easy matter, since the common law prevented corporations from holding stocks of other companies, especially those outside the state. But here was a piece of luck. The Pennsylvania legislature had just created a number of special corporations. One was the Pennsylvania Company, which was in the future to be the backbone of the Pennsylvania Railroad, and another the Reading Company, which was to serve the same use for the Reading Railroad. Another was a company called the South Improvement Company, which was chartered to do anything under the sun but for which no use had yet been found. Like the others it was called a "Tom Scott company," passed by a legislature under Scott's domination. Promoters of the oil scheme bought the charter of the South Improvement Company on January 2, 1872. Did the vagueness of the name appeal to them? They rejected a proposal to change the name to the American Cooperative Refining Company.

Later, the stock was distributed. The complete list of stockholders was as follows:

William Frew, Philadelphia	10 shares
W. P. Logan, Philadelphia	10 shares
John F. Logan, Philadelphia	10 shares
Charles Lockhart, Pittsburgh	10 shares
Richard S. Waring, Pittsburgh	10 shares
W. G. Warden, Philadelphia	475 shares
O. T. Waring, Pittsburgh	475 shares
P. H. Watson, Ashtabula, Ohio	100 shares
H. M. Flagler, Cleveland	180 shares
O. H. Payne, Cleveland	180 shares
William Rockefeller, Cleveland	180 shares
J. A. Bostwick, New York	180 shares
John D. Rockefeller, Cleveland	180 shares
TOTAL	2,000 shares

O. H. Payne had just sold his firm, Clark, Payne and Company, to Standard Oil and had become an executive of the company. Peter Watson, representing the Lake Shore Railroad at Cleveland, would, of course, have Rockefeller's interest at heart. Jabez Bostwick, head of the jobbing firm of Bostwick and Company in New York, would soon join his firm to Standard Oil. Therefore, of the 2,000 shares, *Rockefeller interests held 1,000, or half.* The other half belonged to refining firms that were nominated by the Pennsylvania Railroad, which did not serve Cleveland. They were Lockhart, Waring, and Warden of Pittsburgh; Warden, Frew and Company of Philadelphia; and Atlantic Refining Company of Philadelphia.

Contracts were then signed by the company with the railroads, Commodore Vanderbilt for the New York Central, Jay Gould for the Erie, General George B. McClellan for the Atlantic and Great Western, H. F. Clark for the Lake Shore, and Tom Scott for the Pennsylvania. There was some discussion of allowing producers into the combination, and a penciled draft was prepared that set a fair price for crude, provided production were curtailed. However, this draft was put aside and fell into limbo. It seems that it was never seriously pushed.

When the details of the contract came to light, it was seen that for sheer impudence it could not be matched. The general level of freight rates for oil was boosted, and rates were sometimes doubled. But members of the South Improvement Company were to get substantial rebates. For instance, the rate to Cleveland from the Regions was to be $0.80 barrel, and to New York from Cleveland for refined $2.00, or a total of $2.80. That was for the outsiders. Rockefeller, as the sole Cleveland member, would get a rebate to Cleveland from the Regions of $0.40, and to New York from Cleveland of $0.50; his rate therefore, would be only $1.90. Other members of the combination in Philadelphia and Pittsburgh would get similar rebates.

This amazing scheme went further, piling Ossa upon Pelion. Section 4 of Article Two said the rails would pay "On all transported for other parties drawbacks of like amounts as the rebates from the gross rates, the same to be deducted and retained by the party of the first part . . ." Thus on every barrel shipped by his competitor from the Regions to Cleveland, Rockefeller would collect not only $0.40 as a rebate on his oil, but another $0.40 as a drawback on the competitor's oil. For every barrel shipped to New York by him and a competitor, he would collect $0.50 as a rebate and $0.50 as a drawback. His total rate would be cut to $1.00 a barrel as against a minimum $2.80 for a rival competitor in Cleveland.

The plan was a windfall for the Pittsburgh and Philadelphia refiners who would be included, but the greatest windfall went to Rockefeller, who got lower rates though Cleveland was more distant from the seaboard. And what did the railroads get out of it? The oil traffic would be "evened" by the refiners, the Pennsylvania to get 45 percent and the Erie and Central each 27½ percent. No longer would they have to engage in cutthroat competition on rates.

To make this fully effective as a machine to destroy competition, the members were to get copies of waybills showing the consignor, consignee, and destination and freight charges. No better system of espionage on competitors could have been set up. To make things even more complete, the railroads pledged "to maintain the business of the members against loss or injury by competition . . . and to that end shall lower or raise the gross rates of transportation . . . for such times and to such extent as may be necessary to overcome competition." Could the rails promise to do more?

We are still in the dark today about exact details of the genesis of the plan, the ultimate purposes, and the sponsorship. How many refiners were to be admitted? The railroads later asserted in their defense that they thought that the majority of refiners were represented, but they could hardly have been unaware that only 10 percent of the refining capacity was represented by the original stockholders. We know from the statements of John D. Archbold and Henry Rogers, stating that they refused membership, that some other refiners were asked to join. Selected ones undoubtedly were invited. William Warden, of Warden, Frew and Company, when grilled in a congressional hearing said, "It never entered my head that the refiners would not all be brought in." But note this further testimony:

Q. In case you could take all the refineries in, the railroads proposed to give you a rebate upon their freight charges?

A. No sir, it was not put in that form; we were to put the refineries all in, upon the same terms; it was the understanding with the railroad companies that we were to have a rebate; there was no rebate given in consideration of our putting the companies all in but we told them we would do it.

Q. But if you did form a company composed of the proprietors of all these refineries, you were to have a rebate on your freight charges?

A. No, we were to have the rebate anyhow but were to give all the refineries the privilege of coming in.

Q. You were to have the rebate whether they came in or not?
A. Yes, sir.

If refiner members were to get rebates whether others joined or not, why would they share them with additional refiners?

It is not credible that Rockefeller contemplated that the South Improvement Plan would admit all or many refiners. Since refinery capacity was almost triple oil demand, would he integrate Standard refineries in a plan for output curtailment or quotas so that his refineries would be restricted, like other unsuccessful refiners, to a third of capacity? It must be borne in mind that he was making money even in bleak 1871. As a clincher we shall see in the next chapter that Cleveland refiners who succumbed to Rockefeller in 1872 did not dream of being admitted to the South Improvement Ring.

It has been claimed by Rockefeller and Flagler that they had their own "plan" and decided only to give the South Improvement scheme a whirl. This theory has been put forward by Professor Nevins, who, like others, has branded Rockefeller's association with South Improvement as a black mark. But if it was only a whirl, what a whirl it was! Of the stockholdings in South Improvement, Standard Oil had the lion's share, a half, and far in excess of any other refiner. From this evidence it would appear to be a Rockefeller scheme. As the correspondence shows, Rockefeller worked his heart out for the plan. His letters to his wife, which we will advert to later, when the plan came under attack, show that. In 1899, before the United States Industrial Commission, his lieutenant John Archbold branded the plan as "an outrage on the business as a whole that was not included." Rockefeller's attitude was quite different. When he decided in 1906, after the Tarbell book was published, to have his own history of Standard Oil written, he assigned to the Reverend Leonard Woolsey Bacon as his first task to write a defense of the South Improvement Plan. In later years he said, "I shall never cease to regret that at that time we never called in the reporters." Rockefeller said to Inglis: "I had our plan clearly in mind. It was right. I knew it as a matter of conscience. It was right between me and my God. If I had to do it again tomorrow I would do it the same way." This must have meant the South Improvement Plan. The reference to "our plan" introduces some element of ambiguity in defense of his conduct; but even if he had another plan in mind the success of South Improvement, for which he fought hard, would have shelved it. Details of any other plan Rockefeller might have had would undoubtedly have envisaged the same objectives as South Improvement.

The new rail rates were not scheduled to go into effect until some time after March 1, but rumors began to sweep the oil belt before that time. Commodore Vanderbilt was right that a secret known by 3 meant 111 who were in on it. There were leaks even though all who had been approached had to sign a pledge of secrecy (another indication that membership was to be restricted, since if it were to be open to all there would have been no need for silence).

On February 21 the Cleveland *Plain Dealer* said that "a gigantic little game has been going on in oil circles in Cleveland" to the effect that Rockefeller and Andrews were proposing with another refiner to monopolize the oil business in league with the railroads. The *Petroleum Centre Record* the next day spoke of "a rumored scheme of gigantic combination among certain railroads and refiners to control the purchase and shipment of crude and refined oil from the region." On February 26 the news came out prematurely.

The general freight agent of the Lake Shore at Titusville had a son who was mortally ill. Quitting his office, the agent abruptly left the new freight schedules on his desk. On February 26, without instructions, a subordinate put them into effect. Suddenly the Regions found their freight rates doubled. New York and Philadelphia refiners buying crude gasped with dismay. When the news about the South Improvement Plan came to light close on the heels of the new rates, the Regions let out a shriek of anguish followed by a roar of rage. The Pennsylvania Railroad had sold them down the river. No refiner in the Regions was in the plan, and none could compete under the new rates. The producers were not injured overtly, since refiners outside the Regions paid the freight rates, but a combination of refiners would be able to grind down the price of crude. The oil producers had always felt, too, that their safety was closely linked with the independence of the refiners of the Regions.

At the outset it appeared that the chances that the Regions would be able to overturn the new compact were very dim. The railroads were so powerful that few had the courage to take them on in combat. There were no laws on the statute books to fall back on. The corrupt Pennsylvania legislature was named the "Tom Scott legislature." But the unlikely did happen—this was the first case in which a monopoly was to be overcome by the force of enraged public opinion. It was the first time the railroads were forced to their knees, and the little-known device of the boycott was instrumental in foiling the holdup. (The term itself was unknown, since the experience of Captain Boycott occurred in Ireland in 1880.)

Virtually all business stopped in the Regions. Pumping of wells, drilling of new wells halted while the population turned out into the streets. A mass meeting was held in Parshall's Opera House in Titusville where 3,000 denounced the combination, the railroads, and the state legislature for "putting chains on the people." Banners read: "Down with the Conspirators," "Don't Give Up the Ship," "No Compromise." Telegrams were read at the meeting. One from General McClellan read that "Neither the Atlantic and Great Western or any of its officers are interested in the South Improvement"; but amid loud laughter a wire from Jay Gould was then read exposing the falsehood: "I only signed it after it was signed by all the other parties." Yet a victory had been scored; General McClellan characteristically had had another case of what Lincoln had called his "Slows."

On March 1, at Love's Opera House at Oil City, a second mass meeting was held. Emotions were whipped to a high pitch when a speaker said that the new company was well named. "In the South they enslave blacks. And this is an improvement on the South since it is intended to enslave whites." A young refiner, who at twenty-four looked even more boyish, told how some refiners had heard of the plan and had gone to the railroads to remonstrate. He said that afterward he had been invited to join but had refused because it was an "iniquity."

Let us pause to look at this youth—John Archbold, who was destined to be second in power only to Rockefeller in Standard Oil. He was the son of a circuit preacher and had so little schooling that it is said that he had to invent his own system of arithmetic. At sixteen he went to work for W. H. Abbott, who was an associate of Henry Harley in the pipeline business, and also a refiner. By the age of twenty-one Archbold was a partner in the refining company of Porter, Moreland and Company. He was a rousing extrovert, convivial, and a tippler, fond of all-night poker but ready the next day to captain the local baseball nine. Rockefeller said that he first encountered his name during this period when he went to Titusville and saw it registered with "$4 a barrel" beside his signature. It is not certain exactly what Archbold had in mind, whether he thought that crude should sell for that price, whether he had some oil for sale at that price, or, what was most likely, was trying to impress the hotel owner's daughter with whom he was in love. At this time he was pitted against Rockefeller, and so was another refiner who would become in time a Standard titan, Captain J. J. Vandergrift.

At this second meeting, resolutions were offered by Lewis Emery, Jr., and adopted. A new combine of producers was formed, the Petroleum Producers' Union. The meeting resolved to drill no new wells, and abandon Sunday work. Most important, a boycott was voted—no oil was to be sold to refiners who were members of the South Improvement Plan. Emery got the ball rolling on a further means of strengthening the price of crude oil—a production cut of one-third.

The Oil City *Derrick*, under the editorship of C. E. Bishop, was taking the lead in whipping up indignation in the Regions. On its masthead Bishop printed the names of the eight South Improvement members on the blacklist. Rockefeller's name was seventh on the list. Under it, Bishop printed, "Behold the Anaconda in All Its Deformity." Bishop at this time coined the terms "anaconda" and "octopus" in relation to monopoly, and they were to survive as stock epithets.

The editorials of the *Derrick* were choice, and for the first time in his career Rockefeller got roasted by name. He was called the "Mephistopheles of Cleveland." The Cleveland *Leader* praised the refineries of that city, and the *Derrick* retorted, "Rockefeller subsidized the Cleveland press, requesting it to say nothing inimical to him." In another issue it said, "Mr. Rockefeller is said to be a pillar of the Baptist Church but he would make a better pillar of salt although we would not give much for the article." Commenting on South Improvement, it said, "Those who get into it will need improvement and the best place will be south." To an editorial in the Cleveland *Leader*, "It Will Blow Over," the Derrick said, "That is what Boss Tweed said until the storm blew him over."

A third mass meeting was held at Franklin, and there final

plans were made for shutting off oil from the miscreant refineries. Among the demonstrators were members of the new Oil Men's League, a secret society modeled on the Ku Klux Klan, with passwords and fiery symbols. A petition ninety-three feet long was prepared for submission to the legislature, and a march was prepared on Harrisburg. A delegation was sent to Washington to ask for an investigation by Congress.

It was apparent that the campaign against South Improvement was gaining momentum. The indignation in the Regions was described a year later to the Pennsylvania Constitutional Convention by Samuel C. T. Dodd: "Had the companies not cancelled the contract . . . I venture to say that there would not have been one mile of track left in the County of Venango—the people had come to that pitch of desperation." A million dollars had been raised to finance the Creek refiners. Representatives of New York refiners came to the Regions to pledge their support, among them one who attracted all eyes by his personal magnetism, Henry H. Rogers, of Charles Pratt & Company, another opponent of Rockefeller who would become in time a power in Standard Oil. Rockefeller, who was never petty, would hold no grudges against anyone after this fracas was over.

New York newspapers joined in the attack. Thus the New York *Tribune* said, "Under the thin guise of assisting in the development of oil refining in Cleveland and Pittsburgh this combination has laid its hand on the throat of the oil traffic with a demand to stand and deliver." The Oil City *Derrick* tried to enlist support outside the Regions by pointing out that the consumer would pay the bill. The price of refined would be raised at least four cents a gallon. In testimony before Congress, Peter Watson made a weak defense. Although the price of refined might go up, the combination would for the future stabilize the price. When fluctuations take place, "The retailers are very quick to note a rise in prices but very slow to notice a fall, so that the average price of a retail purchaser is very much above the average wholesale price." But with stabilization the retailers would not be able to make these advances in price. That was for the future—for the present the price would rise.

To Rockefeller this commotion seemed incredible, and he was disposed to attribute it to a few soreheads. But when his oil stopped coming to Cleveland and his production dropped, that was a different matter. The boycott was effective. A producer who sold to Rockefeller faced the threat of being dropped from the Oil Exchange. A small producer, Franklin Tarbell, father of Ida Tarbell, refused an offer by Standard Oil of a year's output sale at premium prices.

During all the turbulence, Rockefeller's backing for the plan did not falter. His letters to his wife from New York show that. On March 15 he wrote, "We will do right and not be nervous or troubled by what the papers say." On March 17, "It may take weeks or months yet to succeed but the Union of American refiners is worth much labor and patient effort." On March 21, "I am still persevering and hopeful," and on March 23, "I haven't any idea of giving up ship . . . it is no business of the public to change our private contracts." That would be the key to Rockefeller's attitude for all the years to come in his struggle with public opinion. "It is no business of the public to change our private contracts."

However, the railroads were losing heart. Commodore Cornelius Vanderbilt said, "I told Billy [his son, William] to stay clear of that scheme," and Billy said, "They were too sharp for me." Tom Scott backtracked. In an interview with the producers and independent refiners on March 18, he said that he had entered the pact only because he believed that he was dealing with the whole industry but now that he had learned differently (the height of malarkey) he was prepared to deal with this group (even though he knew that it represented only the smaller refiners). When the committee met with the Erie and the Atlantic and Great Western they were asked if they didn't want a scheme concocted for them like the South Improvement Plan! The rails were so used to special concessions and deals by this time that they did not understand a plea simply to deal openly and evenly. It is interesting that most of the indignation in the Regions was directed against the evil refiners and far less against the rails. The explanation is that no one was under any illusion about railroads —they were thieving magpies—but the refiners were supposed to be actuated by human sentiments.

The Pennsylvania legislature seemed on the point of passing a free pipeline bill, giving a pipeline to carry oil the right to eminent domain such as a railroad obtains, and Scott was anxious to capitulate without any further ado. On March 25, the railroad men met in the Grand Opera House on Eighth Avenue and Twenty-third Street in New York. The New York *Times* in its account mentioned Rockefeller for the first time in a metropolitan paper, saying that there was a crowd milling before the conference room. "Among them were Messrs. Rockafellow [*sic*] and Watson of the South Improvement Company who were evidently chagrined at being denied admission." Watson got in but was shouted down by the producers, who said, "We want nothing to do with you," and so he left. The *Times* said that "Rockafellow disappeared looking rather blue."

The railroads now agreed to scuttle the South Improvement Plan and make a new contract with producers. Under the new rates, even though Cleveland was over two hundred miles farther west from New York, it would have to pay only the same rate as from the Regions; but of course crude would have to be carried from the Regions to Cleveland, while oil was at the doorsteps of the Regions refineries. It was a great victory for the Regions and East Coast refineries. All rates were to be public and on "a basis of perfect equality to all shippers, producers and refiners and no rebates, drawbacks or other arrangements of any character shall be made or allowed."

The railroads acted in time. A few days later the charter of the South Improvement Company was repealed and a free pipeline bill was passed. Because Allegheny County was excepted, where the Pittsburgh refineries and the Pennsylvania Railroad terminus were located, Scott did not worry about it.

Rockefeller, considered the prime mover of the plan, from that time was a marked man in the Regions. The boycott continued for a few weeks after the capitulation. When Fisher Brothers, a firm of oil brokers in the Regions, announced that they had made a contract for 20,000 barrels with Standard, it was kicked out of the Producers Union, censured by the Oil Exchange, canceled out of contracts, and showered with words of abuse, such as "betrayal" and "infamy." Another producer, had it not been for an armed guard, would have seen his shipment of 5,000 barrels, bound for Standard in Cleveland, burned by a mob. But the boycott was hampered by the fact that Rockefeller owned valuable rolling stock, such as tank cars, and the producers needed his business. Therefore when Rockefeller sent a telegram on April 8 saying that his company had canceled all its prior contracts with the rails and with the South Improvement Company, the boycott was lifted. Reflecting the malignant rumors circulating about him, he inserted in the wire a categorical denial that he or any Standard member "threatened to depress oil."

What were the long-range implications of the South Improvement Plan, aside from the cloud on Rockefeller's name? The two different views can be pegged to two quips. In later years Rockefeller said the mudslinging about the plan reminded him of the darky who complained to the judge that his wife was asking a dollar a day from him. The judge asked, "What is she doing with all that money? And the darky replied: "I dunno, Jedge. I ain't give her none yet." If nothing happened under a plan that failed, why all the fuss? asked Rockefeller.

The other point of view was expressed by Henry Demarest Lloyd. He said that Mark Twain, in describing the labors of the missionaries in the Sandwich Islands, said that they were so successful that the vices of the natives no longer exist in name—only in reality. The South Improvement Plan no longer continued in name—only in reality, said Lloyd.

The truth seems to lie between the two points of view. The South Improvement Plan died—but over the years the arrangements Rockefeller made with the rails were suspiciously akin to the main features of South Improvement.

Although the South Improvement Plan was scuttled, it had immediate consequences of a profound nature in Cleveland, as we shall now see.

Right, John's mother, Eliza Davison
Rockefeller; *below*, his father William
Avery; *bottom right*, Ida Tarbell, a
leading anti-Rockefeller campaigner

Left, Henry Flagler . . . his ability to deal with people was highly valued by Rockefeller; *below*, the seventy-nine-acre Forest Hill estate in Cleveland which John Rockefeller bought in 1873

CHAPTER 6 *Massacre in Cleveland*

AFTER THE SMOKE OF BATTLE over the South Improvement Plan had cleared away, the oil industry awoke to find that Rockefeller had not lost after all. He had staged a sensational coup. Using the South Improvement Plan as a sharp ax, he had whacked off the heads of almost all the competitors he had had in Cleveland. Of 26 refineries in Cleveland, he had taken over 21. The barrel capacity of Standard in one stroke leaped from 1,500 a day to almost 11,000, or a quarter of the capacity in the country. Rockefeller alone had a greater capacity than all the refineries of New York or of the Regions. At the age of thirty-two, he was the dominant figure in the oil industry—indeed, a dominant figure in American industry, although he was to remain unknown to the public for many years.

The coup had been managed quickly and silently. It was not until February 21, 1872, that the Cleveland *Plain Dealer* said, "A gigantic 'little game' has been going on in oil circles in Cleveland to the effect that a single firm has bought up or got control of all the refineries of the city and proposes to monopolize the business." In mid-March the Titusville *Herald* printed a list of the refineries that had been absorbed by Standard Oil. A month later, after the demise of the plan, the New York *Bulletin* said, "The trade here regards the Standard Oil Company as taking the place of the South Improvement Company and as being ready at any moment to make the same attempt to control the trade as its progenitor did." This, of course, was exaggerating the effect of the new monopoly, which was confined to Cleveland.

The strategy Rockefeller employed put him in the class of Napoleon as a field general, an honor accorded him by so captious a critic as Miss Tarbell. It was said of Rockefeller in the oil regions that he could wait and wait. "To Rockefeller a day is as a year and a year is as a day. He never gives up." But when the time was ripe, he could strike like a cobra. His forte was planning. As John Archbold once said, all the leaders of Standard tried to see ahead, but Rockefeller could see around corners.

Let us examine the great leap forward. As soon as the rails agreed to the South Improvement Plan, Rockefeller saw that this was the tide "which, if taken at the flood, leads on to fortune." He launched a battle on two fronts, first to put over the South Improvement Plan nationwide, which at least in the first instance would put the country's refineries in a few hands, and, second, immediately to take over the refineries of Cleveland. His weapon was the advantages he would get under the plan. His freight advantage by rebate and drawback over his Cleveland competitors was at the minimum $1.80, including Regions to Cleveland and then refined from Cleveland to New York. This competitive advantage amounted to over $0.04 a gallon at a time when refined had fallen to $0.22 a gallon. Under these circumstances no refiner in Cleveland was in a position to compete with him any longer.

Rockefeller's first step was to arrange a meeting with Colonel Oliver H. Payne, the head of his biggest competitor in Cleveland, Clark, Payne and Company. (Payne's other partners in the business were Maurice and James Clark, Rockefeller's erstwhile partners.) Rockefeller proposed to Payne that he sell out his company to Standard and that he (but not the Clarks) should join the active management of Standard. The terms of this proposal are significant—Payne would join Rockefeller as an ally; he would not join after being intimidated or subdued. The inducement to Payne was that his firm would be able in this way to enjoy with Rockefeller the immense benefits of the South Improvement Plan. Payne replied: "Your idea strikes me favorably. I shall consult with my partners and let you know their view as soon as possible." The answer was "Yes," and terms of purchase were then negotiated.

Colonel Oliver H. Payne was an aristocrat. The only college graduate to become a member of the early ruling hierarchy of Standard, he was a graduate of Andover and Yale. Flagler found his hauteur painful, describing him as "kin to God." His father, Congressman Henry B. Payne, was a nationally known Democrat, whose election to the United States Senate in 1884, allegedly obtained by Standard Oil money when his son was Standard treasurer, was to be a *cause célèbre*. The addition of Clark, Payne and Company in 1872 fortified Standard as a refining power, and the addition of Oliver Payne gave the company more prestige.

The next step was to recapitalize Standard Oil, which was done on January 1, 1872. The stock was increased from 10,000 shares to 25,000 shares and the capitalization from $1,000,000 to $2,500,-000. Because Rockefeller had 5,821 shares, his interest was worth nominally a half-million. Of the new shares, 4,000, with a nominal value of $400,000, were distributed to Clark, Payne and Company as the purchase price. Immediately 700 shares were given to buy Jabez A. Bostwick and Company, the New York oil jobber who had valuable terminal property there, and 200 shares to buy out a small refiner, J. Stanley, of Cleveland.

Joining the company as a stockholder was Peter H. Watson, general freight agent of the Lake Shore Railroad, who was given (?) 500 shares with a nominal value of $50,000. Continuing in the company with increased shares were three bank heads, Amasa Stone, Jr., Stillman Witt, and T. P. Handy. Thus the three principal banks of Cleveland were in Rockefeller's corner, the Second National, Commercial National, and Merchants' National.

Rockefeller was now ready to go to work on his mop-up operation. He called in the refiners of Cleveland one by one to his second-floor offices in the Cushing Block and told each the score. What he said was this—The competitor had the option to sell out to him or perish. No one could compete with him under the South Improvement Plan. The refining business was wallowing in a sea of red ink, and would get worse. He was offering the only path to safety. All the powerful were in league with him. Oliver Payne had joined him. Peter Watson had joined him, showing how the railroads stood. Because all the leading banks were with him, credit in Cleveland to carry or to bail out a refinery in money trouble would be impossible. Why not give up gracefully? Rockefeller would set appraisers to evaluate their works and would pay in cash or, if the competitor was willing, would pay in Standard Oil stock. (Under the recapitalization Rockefeller had been awarded 1,200 shares as agent of the company for purchase of refining properties.)

Panic spread among the refiners as they learned what was up. There is a story that one refiner meeting another on the street said that he was not afraid, to which the other replied, "You may not be afraid to lose your head but your body will suffer." W. H. Doane, a Cleveland refiner, told a congressional committee a few months later, "They [refiners] were forced to sell; the railroads had put up the rates and it scared them; they became frightened and disposed of their property."

In 1879, before the Hepburn Committee of the New York State Assembly, witnesses told of their frantic but hopeless efforts to extricate themselves from the enveloping net. Isaac Hewitt, who was a partner in Alexander, Scofield and Company, was the commission merchant who first hired Rockefeller as a bookkeeper. He went to see William Vanderbilt in New York but was rebuffed. Then he went to see Peter Watson, who said, "You'd better sell —you'd better get clear—better sell out—no help for it." He then went to see his former employee, who now rode the waves. Rockefeller offered him fifty cents on the dollar of the book value of the works. Hewitt testified: "I would not have sold out if I could have got a fair show with the railways. My business instead of being a business to buy and sell became degraded into running after the railways and getting an equal chance with others. That was the business of the oil trade."

When the settlement came around, Rockefeller urged Hewitt to take stock in Standard Oil instead of cash. Urging the wisdom of the course, he said, "I have ways of making money you know nothing of." There are more things in heaven and earth, Horatio . . .

Robert Hanna (uncle of Mark Hanna), of the refining firm of Hanna, Baslington and Company, was most reluctant to sell. He had been making 30 percent on his investment yearly. He said that Rockefeller told him that his career in oil was over. "You can't compete with Standard. We have all the large refineries now. If you refuse to sell it will end in your being crushed." He went to see General Devereux of the Lake Shore, who said that the rates given to Standard could be given to them only if they could furnish the same quantities with the same regularity. He had to sell out on Rockefeller's terms. Frank Rockefeller, then with Alexander, Scofield and Company, said his brother told him, "If you don't sell your property it will be valueless because we have got the advantages with railroads."

This stone wall of indifference by the rails proved that the South Improvement Plan was not an open-end organization for entry. Rockefeller's competitors in Cleveland would gladly have joined if they had been able, but the privileges under the plan were reserved for Rockefeller.

In later years Rockefeller waxed very emotional in his defense against the charge that he had ruthlessly slaughtered his competitors. His defense happens to be a good one—its defect is that the defense was made good only by later history. In early 1872 one would have had to be clairvoyant enough to read the future and to foresee that Standard Oil stock would be a gold mine.

First, Rockefeller makes the good point that the refining business was in bad shape and that the "paralysis of fear" that was attributed by refiners to the South Improvement Plan was a "paralysis" engendered by the depression in refining. Rockefeller's assumption that most of the refiners were lucky to get out with some capital is to some extent borne out by future events. The next year saw the Panic of 1873, and many refiners who had been paid off in cash would have gone into bankruptcy. Again, Rockefeller seems to be correct that most of the refineries he bought were obsolete, "old junk, fit for the scrap heap." He scrapped most of them, retaining only a small percentage of the capacity bought.

His principal contention was that he offered the refiner whom he had crushed an option: cash or stock in Standard Oil. If Rockefeller's advice had been followed, the refiner would have accepted stock, would have become Rockefeller's partner, and would have become fabulously rich.

Mr. Dooley, the turn-of-the-century satirist, once said, "There's wan thing fr'm what I can see, an' that is that Jawn D. hasn't an idea that he iver did wrong to anywan." Indeed, according to Rockefeller, he not only did no one wrong but actually showered manna from heaven, if only the ignorant could have seen it. To Inglis, Rockefeller said: "The Standard was an angel of mercy, reaching down from the sky and saying 'Get into the ark. Put in your old junk. We'll take all the risks.'" Again he said to Inglis: "The procedure was without precedent. We find here the strongest and most prosperous concern in the business which had made money in each year of its existence, turning to its less fortunate competitors, who, it well knew, had been losing money and becoming discouraged and saying to them, practically 'We will stand on for the risks and hazards of the refining business. You need not contribute, come with us and we will do you good. We will undertake to save you from the wrecks of this refining business.'"

And thus Rockefeller can conclude that the disgruntlement came only from those who did not accept his generosity. The criticism "came from those who having been offered the choice to take cash or stock had not faith enough to take the stock."

This is as sudsy a tub of Rockefeller soft soap as one will be able to find. At the time Rockefeller had no Good Samaritan impulses. For proof, note this in his *Reminiscences:* "We very much preferred to have them take the stock because a dollar in those days looked as large as a cart-wheel." Standard merely wanted to save cash.

Then, too, how many were in a position to take stock? Dispossessed refiners needed capital to eat with and to launch another business. In his *Reminiscences* Rockefeller tells how Flagler met a German baker who was in refining but was a misfit in it. Flagler said to Rockefeller: "I'd feel better if we invited him to join us. I've got him on my conscience." This may be a fairy tale, but at any rate the story goes on that the baker was glad to have his plant appraised and get half in stock and half in cash. Rockefeller does not explain whether Flagler's pocketbook was in any way linked to his conscience, how the baker was able to start in another business with his attenuated capital, and how he would have been able to "join us" if he had chosen to take all in cash.

We know of only one firm that took stock. Frank Arter had a refinery that cost $12,000 and for which Rockefeller gave only $3,000. Arter took it in Standard Oil stock and had a hard time surviving. Meeting him on the street, Rockefeller asked, "Are you still holding your stock?" Arter said yes, though it was pledged as collateral for a loan. Rockefeller replied, "Good. Sell everything you have, even the shirt on your back, but hold on to that stock." Of course he was right. In a few years Arter was wealthy and a member of the Standard's Board of Directors.

At the time, though, no one could have foreseen the fantastic rise of Standard Oil and of its fabulous stock. Sober and skilled minds thought little of the stock. Robert Hanna told his partners: "Don't touch the stock. It has no future. The organization will fall of its own weight." James Clark, of Clark, Payne & Company, who got some of the 4000 shares allotted to the firm, cussed Rockefeller over and over again. "That Standard Company can't succeed. They'll bust sure." He sold the stock for $110,000. It was worth a million in a few years, and he cussed Rockefeller even harder.

Let us examine the Rockefeller defense further. He says in his *Reminiscences:* "It has been said that I forced the men who became my partners in the oil business to join me. I would not have been so short-sighted . . . would it have been possible to make of such men life-companions?" To Inglis he said, "How could our company succeed if its members had been forced to join in it and were working under the lash?"

This is as disingenuous a statement as can be found. It conveys the impression that all the heads of firms that were crushed and taken over by Rockefeller joined Standard Oil as partners. This is not true. Oliver Payne alone joined as a partner in Cleveland. His firm, Clark, Payne and Company, was paid off mostly in stock and to the tune of $400,000. But note the contrast with the other firms that were taken over. The Payne firm was paid most generously for its goodwill—the others were paid off skimpily, and only for the "use-value" of the firms. Alexander, Scofield and Company were paid $65,000 for a refinery on which they had expended as much as $120,000, and its capacity was only slightly less than that of Clark, Payne and Company. Hanna, Baslington and Company was paid only $45,000 for a plant that they said cost them $76,000. Hanna said that they were netting 30 percent on the investment; so the selling price was only twice the annual earnings, while the usual multiple is ten or more. But, to be sure, if those firms had had the foresight to take Standard stock instead of cash, they would have thereby made their fortunes.

If the policy of 1872 had been the continuing policy of Rockefeller, because of the option he extended to receive payment in stock, he might build a case for himself as a benefactor. Some writers, like Mark Sullivan in *Our Times,* mistakenly accept the 1872 policy as the enduring policy. But that was a unique situation in which Rockefeller chose not to leave the attrition of competitors to the processes of time. From that point on, his policy was harsher. Where there were facilities or executives he wanted (and he was as much interested in brainpower as in physical facilities), he would pay generously in stock (or cash if the owner preferred), giving a high valuation to the goodwill and giving responsible jobs to the executives of those firms. In short, the Oliver Payne treatment. Thus Rockefeller's enemy, Lewis Emery, Jr., complained in 1898 to the United States Industrial Commission, "All or nearly all of them [purchases] were made at prices grossly in excess of the reasonable value of the business sold, the chief consideration being the accumulation of power which the monopoly was acquiring."

As for other firms in which Rockefeller was interested, from a negative viewpoint—that is, removing them from the scene—the policy differed, depending on the situation and on whether the Standard Oil executive in charge of executions was interested in building his record on his celerity in dispatching the victims or the cheapness of the buying price. The general policy was to pay as little as possible. Only occasionally would the refiner who had been bought out get some Standard Oil stock or be able to keep stock in his refinery. Only in occasional "blackmail" cases was a refiner able to hold up Standard Oil and collect for "goodwill." In most cases the payment would be for "use-value" and sometimes only for junk value. Sometimes Standard would negotiate immediately for terms of sale; sometimes it would try to run the competitor to the ground before making an offer; and sometimes it would just let the refinery wither and die. Sometimes there would be room for a job for the refiner who had been bought out. At any rate the 1872 offer to all refiners to accept Standard Oil stock in payment made the policy generous compared to that applied in succeeding years.

The gravamen of the charges brought against Rockefeller in later years was his harshness to competitors. Compared to the malefactions of others who gathered fortunes in the nineteenth century, it is a light charge. In the departments of knavery and rascality, John D. Rockefeller does not rate with the leading "robber barons."

Gustavus Myers, in his monumental study *The History of the*

Great American Fortunes, says of the period, "All the confluent facts of the time show conclusively that every stratum of commercial society was permeated with fraud, and this fraud was accepted generally as a routine fixture of the process of gathering property and profits."

Let us review a few in this gallery of august personages who later commanded public awe and respect on account of their wealth.

Stephen Girard made a fortune in the shipping trade in the Revolution by trading with the British after taking an oath of allegiance to the Americans. He was always on the sharp lookout for a quick dollar. During a revolt against the planters in Santo Domingo, the planters put their valuables on his ship and went to shore for more. When they failed to return, Girard sailed away with his valuable cargo.

John Jacob Astor amassed a fortune through his American Fur Company, getting the Indians drunk and then swindling them. No angle was overlooked in this trade. Even the liquor the Indians bought and the goods Astor exchanged were overpriced.

Cornelius Vanderbilt made his start in Hudson River shipping by bribing city officials to give him exclusive docking facilities. As a transatlantic shipper he got a rich payoff out of the annual pork-barrel shipping subsidies voted by Congress, most of his money being extorted from other shippers under threats of competing against them in carrying the mails.

Becoming a railroad promoter, Vanderbilt engaged in a contest for rail control in New York State with Jay Gould, a promoter of rascality *sans pareil.* They debauched the legislature with bribes, one state senator accepting $75,000 from Vanderbilt and then turning around to accept $100,000 from Gould. Railroad stocks were shamelessly watered; it was estimated by a rail expert, Charles Francis Adams, that there were $50,000 water in every mile of track between New York City and Buffalo. Gould's direct loot from the Erie Railroad, exclusive of profits from stock manipulation, has been put at $12,000,000.

Russell Sage began as a member of a firm that was seeking to swindle the creditors of a property and wound up by swindling his partners. As a city official of Troy, New York, he betrayed

Troy into selling a railroad that he had sold to the New York Central at a great profit.

Collis P. Huntington, Leland Stanford, Charles Crocker, and Mark Hopkins who built the Central Pacific and the Southern Pacific were a quartet of confidence men. They used their slender capital to bribe the California legislature and Congress to grant them franchises and land grants. They amassed their fortunes by setting up a construction company to build the roads for a fantastic sum. Since they owned the construction company, they thereby lined their own pockets. Thomas Cochran, in *The Age of Enterprise,* says that while the notorious Union Pacific paid out $400,000 in graft between 1866 and 1872, the Central Pacific between 1875 and 1878 handed out $500,000 annually.

J. Pierpont Morgan began his amazing career by financing a deal during the early Civil War to sell to General Frémont in the West 5,000 rifles that had been condemned in the East because they were defective, shooting off the thumbs of the soldiers firing them. The rifles cost $3 and he sold them for $22. During the war he sold the dollar short by buying options in gold. He had no qualms of conscience, though many felt it unpatriotic to make money out of Union reverses. The Union League Club of New York passed a resolution that such speculators should be publicly hanged.

As a big steel magnate, Andrew Carnegie sold much armor plate to the government for the building of our navy. In 1893, former employees in the Homestead plant brought information to the navy that the armor plate was defective and that certain plates selected for ballistic tests were treated secretly at night to hoodwink the inspectors. The Carnegie firm was fined $141,000 by President Cleveland.

The catalogue could be prolonged. But to put matters in their proper perspective, we must note that the circumambient ethics and morality in business practices of those days, or the lack of it, are not comparable with those of the present day. Men fought bare-fisted for business conquest, without benefit of Marquis of Queensberry rules, as they did in the prize ring. No quarter was given and none was expected; no one was expected to be his brother's keeper. "What do I care about the law," said Commodore Vanderbilt. "Ain't I got the power?" But until the close of the century there were few laws to circumscribe business conduct —in the federal area only the Interstate Commerce Act, a feeble instrument, and the Sherman Antitrust Act, a dead letter. Restraints imposed by business ethics were few. The prevailing mores were expressed by Artemus Ward, "Them that has, gits," and by David Harum, "Do unto others as they would do unto you—and do it fust."

BOOK TWO

THE ROAD TO
THE TRUST

The coal-oil business belongs to us.
—JOHN D. ROCKEFELLER IN 1876

CHAPTER 7 *Swallowing Up the Refineries*

IN THE FEW YEARS that followed the South Improvement Plan, between 1872 and 1879, the share of refining capacity held by Standard Oil soared from 25 percent to 95 percent, or into a nationwide monopoly position. The impression created by Henry Demarest Lloyd and Ida Tarbell is that this monopoly was obtained by Rockefeller by predatory, piratical methods. "The Assyrian came down like a wolf on the fold." According to their accounts, the refineries competing with Rockefeller were crushed with brute force and perfidy, and most important, by the perfidious rebate, by which, as Lloyd put it, "rivals are blown out of the highways, busy mills and refineries turn to dust, hearts break, and strong men go mad or commit suicide. . . ."

If this is not a misrepresentation, as Rockefeller and his defenders declared, it is at least an oversimplification. The Lloyd-Tarbell theory certainly does not apply to leading refiners throughout the country who voluntarily threw in their lot with Standard in 1875 as working partners, much as Oliver Payne did in 1872. There are other elements in a picture that have a bearing on the question as to how much villainy was perpetrated by Mr. Rockefeller.

First, by 1875 there was a technological revolution within the industry that made it far less possible for the small refiner with limited capital to survive. A process of "destructive distillation" was introduced for "cracking" kerosene and thus increasing the yield of kerosene from crude to well over 75 percent. This was carried on in stills holding as much as 3,000 barrels. In 1865 it was considered that the minimum size of a refinery for efficiency was 240 barrels a day, but in 1870 the figure was a minimum of 900 barrels a day. In 1860 an efficient refinery could be built for $10,000, but in 1870 the figure was between $60,000 and $80,000. The Octave Refinery built in Titusville by John Archbold in 1869 cost $88,900, and the Harkness Refinery built in Philadelphia in 1870 cost $120,000.

This leap in capital requirements automatically put a great deal of pressure on existing or would-be small refiners. In assessing the role of small business in America, one must give heavy emphasis to the increasing technology and the ever-increasing need for capital that have conspired to keep small businesses small or have erased them altogether.

A second factor that must be considered is that the years 1872–1875 were very poor years for refiners, many of whom would have disappeared anyway. At the time of the "massacre" in Cleveland, the price of refined was $0.22 per gallon, a price at which refiners could not operate profitably. But in December 1873, the year of the Panic, the price had fallen to $0.13. In November 1874, the refined price had dipped to $0.11. Bankruptcies among refiners were common. Standard was able to increase its profits not only by rebates but also by economies in refining and by more extensive utilization of by-products. Its cost of refining per gallon, which was 2½ cents in 1870, declined further. Its astounding success in cutting costs is demonstrated by the fact that in 1885 refining costs per gallon for Standard Oil had fallen to .452 of a cent.

A third factor is that the superiority of Standard was won as much by brainpower, astuteness, and foresightedness as by ruthlessness. "I wanted able men with me," Rockefeller said. And he succeeded in surrounding himself with able men.

In the hearings of the Hepburn Committee in 1879, William Vanderbilt was on the stand:

Q. Can you attribute, or do you attribute, in your own mind the fact of there being one refiner instead of fifty now to any other cause except the larger capital of the Standard Oil Company?

A. There are a great many causes; it is not from their capital alone that they have built up this business; there is no question about it but that these men—and if you come into contact with them, I guess you will come to the same conclusion I have long ago—I think they are smarter fellows than I am, a good deal; they are very enterprising and smart men; I never came into contact with any class of men as smart and able as they are in business, and I think a great deal is to be attributed to that.

Q. Would that alone monopolize a business of that sort?

A. It would go a long way toward building it up.

A fourth factor was adverted to by William Vanderbilt in his testimony. He said, "I think these gentlemen from their shrewdness have been able to take advantage of the competition that existed between the railroads for their business, as it grew, and that they have availed themselves of that there is not a question of doubt."

In their greed for the rich Standard oil traffic, in their desire to ingratiate themselves with Rockefeller, the three rail systems, the Erie, the New York Central with the Lake Shore, and the Pennsylvania made themselves willing victims. Rockefeller had hardly to exert himself or engage in deep machinations to get rebates and favors. Unable to reach agreement among themselves, the rails turned to Rockefeller as master to keep peace among them by dividing up the oil traffic.

Subservient to the big shipper, the rails gave scant consideration to the small shipper. Although the railroad had claimed the right of eminent domain and the right to cross state highways as public carriers when the rails were built, they none the less repudiated any obligations to serve the public as common carriers. Government was very tardy in imposing restraints. In 1869 Massachusetts established the first railroad commission, but it had only investigative and publicity powers. Attempts by oil producers and refiners in Pennsylvania to force the legislature to issue rules for the rails brought this verdict in 1879 from the Oil Producers' Council: "It has been simply a history of failure and disgrace. If it has taught us anything it is that our present lawmakers are as a body ignorant, corrupt and unprincipled." Henry Demarest Lloyd commented that Rockefeller "had done everything to the Pennsylvania legislature except refine it."

The situation in Washington was equally unpromising for rail control where the rails had well-paid lobbies. One critic said, "The House of Representatives was like an auction room where more valuable considerations were disposed of under the Speaker's hammer than in any other place on earth." In 1876, after much agitation, a resolution was introduced in the House for a special committe to investigate the railroads. There was an objection from a member, Henry Payne, father of the Standard executive. His objection is worth a chuckle in these days of big government—such a special committee would require the hiring of an extra clerk. The objection was heeded, and so the House Committee on Commerce undertook the inquiry. As adviser to the chairman the committee had J. N. Camden, head of a refinery belonging to Standard Oil. The investigation ended soon after it had begun.

Though a final factor to be considered is the most important one, it is not recognized at all in the books of Lloyd or Miss Tarbell. The oil combination created by Rockefeller was not a unique phenomenon, as those authors pictured it; it was typical in the Industrial Revolution that occurred in this country between 1850 and 1900. By 1890 there were one hundred combinations in whiskey, sugar, tobacco, cattle feed, beef, wire nails, and bicycles among others. The oil industry responded to the economic imperatives of large nationwide industries with great aggregations of capital to achieve standardization and economies of scale. Cutthroat competition between small units in oil was destined in the end to go, and if Rockefeller had not been the agent, another one would have emerged. As Professor George Stocking says of the events of 1872 in *The Oil Industry and the Competitive System:* "An economic situation had arisen wherein competition threatened loss and centralized control meant economies and increased profit. Such a situation waits only the appearance of shrewd business acumen and judgment until monopoly will develop."

Before the transformation of the American scene by the railroad, small industries thrived autonomously in each community of any size. Before the Civil War, as John Flynn points out, Cleveland, a small city of 25,000, had 21 flour mills, 27 clothing factories, 17 boot and shoe plants, 13 furniture factories, 17 machine factories, and 50 lumber mills. These "factories," of course, were all small shops. But rail ties made these small shops impracticable when compared with the ability of larger ones to offer quality and cheapness in goods. While tears have been shed for the small number of refiners put out of business by Standard Oil, no one has attempted to count the mortality in untold thousands of these small shops.

By 1893 more than 150,000 miles of rail had been laid, compared with 30,000 at the time of the Civil War. The binding of the nation together with swift transport was accompanied by new inventions. The Bessemer process put the local steel furnace out of existence; the roller process for grain inaugurated by Pillsbury put an end to countless local flour mills; refrigerator cars underpriced local slaughterers; the McCormick reaper supplanted local shops or the blacksmith who made agricultural tools; new sewing machines made ready-made clothing available more cheaply from distant clothing factories. The average farm-implement factory increased from 5 workers and a capital investment of $2,674 in 1850 to 79 workers and an investment of $400,000 in 1910; the average steel mill from 53 workers and an investment of $46,000 in 1850 to 426 and an investment of $2,280,000 in 1910.

The oil industry is only a part of the general pattern. Large refineries built with large capital and operating with lower cost made the small local refiner obsolete.

The railroads agreed in the peace pact of March 25, 1872, settling the South Improvement Plan conflict, that "no rebates, drawbacks or other arrangements of any character" would be allowed. No sooner was the ink dry on this solemn contract than the rails agreed to give rebates to Rockefeller. Such cynicism as to one's published word would be hard to match.

And yet such a result could have been anticipated. As oilman W. T. Scheide testified before the Hepburn Committee in 1879, it was "an impossible agreement." He added, "The immediate effect of it would have been to have utterly destroyed fifty-five per cent of the refining interest of the country, that is, Cleveland and Pittsburgh." That is an extreme statement; but certainly Cleveland, more distant from the Eastern seaboard than other refining centers, needed a special rate.

Testifying before the Ohio State legislature in 1879, Henry Flagler read a contract of Standard Oil with the Lake Shore–New York Central for rates to the seaboard "From the first of April to the middle of November 1872, about seven months, $1.25." This was $0.25 less than the rate stated in the March 25 agreement, so a rebate went into force less than a week after that agreement.

We have seen that on April 8, seven days after the effective date of this agreement, Rockefeller wired to the oil producers that he had no contract with any rail. Either Rockefeller later got a contract that was made retroactive or he lied. The latter would be quite consistent with Rockefeller's view that the rebates he obtained were private contracts between himself and the rails and that they were no business of anyone else.

There is additional corroboration as to the length of the no-rebate agreement. George R. Blanchard testified in 1879 that he became general freight agent of the Erie Railroad in October 1872 and that he was astonished to find that rebates were being paid. "I asked why that contract [of March 25] was not being observed and was then convinced in reply that the agreement of March 25 lasted less than two weeks and that at an early date the Empire Line was receiving a large drawback or commission from the Pennsylvania Railroad."

Under Colonel Joseph Potts, the Empire Transportation System to which he referred was becoming a formidable factor in the oil picture. It was in essence a fast-freight service. With no less than ten railroads stretching between New York and Omaha, and sometimes requiring innumerable connections, Empire took care of all freight service for shippers. As an ally of the Pennsylvania Railroad, it routed its shipments east over the Philadelphia and Erie Railroad, a Pennsylvania Railroad subsidiary. It owned hundreds of miles of pipelines in the Regions and transported oil in its own green cars to the eastern seaboard. Getting rebates on its shipments from the Pennsylvania Railroad, it was a staunch friend to refiners in the Regions and in New York and Philadelphia but no friend to Rockefeller, who had to do better on rebates than the clients of the Empire.

Because Rockefeller heard that the Pennsylvania had cut the rate from the Regions to New York to only $1.05, Flagler went to see William Vanderbilt in December 1872. He demanded a rate of $1.05 from Cleveland, which was of course a much greater distance to New York than that from the Regions. Vanderbilt reluctantly assented, but one month later restored the rate to

$1.25, which caused Standard Oil to cut back its shipments over the Central, and induced it to ship east by canal.

In March 1874 Standard scored a triumph in bargaining that gives ample testimony to its bargaining power. Erie was dissatisfied with its share of the oil traffic, carrying only a sixth as much as the Pennsylvania. It entered into negotiations with Standard, which was now at odds with the Central. The reply of Standard to the overtures was that it had its own terminal and cooperage works (which it had acquired with Bostwick and Company) at Hunter's Point on Long Island opposite midtown New York. Central usually delivered its oil to these works in tank cars; there it was barreled or cased for shipment, most of it going abroad. Why should it pay Erie for the use of Erie's oil terminal at Weehawken, New Jersey, on the Hudson River? The Erie then made a novel proposal. It would turn over its oil terminal to Standard Oil, which could use it free of charge. In return, Standard would give Erie half of its oil traffic and agree to equal treatment for all oil shippers at the Erie terminal, Standard to get a fair profit for the services rendered to others.

An astonishing concession! The Erie, a public carrier, would turn over part of its railroad property to one shipper. Rockefeller gleefully assented. Of course, by running the terminal he would have a complete espionage and information service as to the shipments of his competitors. However, by 1879 only Standard was using the Erie Terminal. As Simon Sterne, counsel to the Hepburn Committee, said: "They [Standard] have the exclusive shipment of oil and therefore nobody could ship oil and there was no oil handled for anyone else. But if the Erie should send some for someone else, why, the sloop could not get to the dock and the machinery of the dock would not and could not work by any possibility so as to get the oil out of that dock and into a ship, except at the end of a lawsuit."

During the summer months of 1874, the rails again tried to find some permanent solution to the seemingly endless internecine warfare among them on rates. They came up with another rate pattern amending the one of March 25, 1872, obviously hoping that the new one would abate the pressure for rebates. Released on September 9 in a private circular by James H. Rutter, freight agent for the New York Central, it was known as the Rutter

Circular. It was a stab in the vitals for the Regions. The rate on refined from the Regions to New York was raised from $1.50 to $2.00. The rate from Cleveland to New York was also raised from $1.50 to $2.00. But a radical change was introduced for the benefit of Cleveland and Pittsburgh. Crude oil would be carried from the Regions free to the refineries there—14 barrels of crude for every 10 barrels of refined later transported to the East. In other words, Cleveland would pay the same rate as the Regions to New York, although, including the shipment of crude to Cleveland, 300 more miles of transportation were required.

The authorship of this clause has been attributed to Rockefeller. Undoubtedly it was Standard's idea, though this time Rockefeller stayed in the background. In return for the indirect rebate he would "even" the oil traffic between the three roads.

The Rutter Circular had the effrontery to state, "You will observe that under this system the rate is even and fair to all parties, preventing one locality taking advantage of its neighbor by reason of some alleged or real facility that it may possess." Geographical advantage, one of the prime factors for location of businesses since the day commerce began, was to be erased as an "alleged facility."

The Regions greeted the Rutter Circular with dismay. Not only did the new principle of "equalization" strike hard at the Regions; there was an additional blow. The rate on crude to New York was raised only from $1.35 to $1.50, while the rate on refined went up $0.50. This was a gift to refiners along the seaboard. But it was against the principle of equalization that the loudest protests were raised. If that was a desirable principle, why shouldn't the Regions be able to buy sulfuric acid, paint and glue for the prices at which they were sold in New York, where they were much cheaper? Why shouldn't the Regions pay the low prices prevailing for barrels in Cleveland?

The 1872 agreement had provided that no changes in rates were to be made unless on ninety days' notice. But when the producers addressed a courteous protest to the Pennsylvania calling notice to this clause, they received, after a three-week wait, a brusque reply that the new rates ensured equality and that the interests of all parties would be promoted.

There was still a large refining interest in the Regions, consisting of twenty-five refineries, and there was a move to revive the insurrectionary spirit that earlier had toppled the South Improvement Plan, but it was to prove abortive. The Oil City *Derrick* cried: "The enemies of the producers have made another bold stroke. Arouse at once! Gather your forces immediately! Titusville producers have sounded the first cry of organization; let our other towns follow her example." Two years, however, had significantly changed the configurations of power. Producers were more disunited than ever, since there was a host of new ones who, operating with small capital, could not afford to stop the drill. Furthermore, any threat to institute a boycott of Standard Oil was futile, since Standard was now in the pipeline business and had huge storage tanks full of oil.

The Regions were fed up with the Pennsylvania Railroad, and so was Pittsburgh. Under the principle of equalization, the rate from Pittsburgh to Philadelphia was only $0.15 less than from Cleveland to New York, but the distance from the Regions to Pittsburgh was only 60 miles and then to Philadelphia another 350 miles. The total mileage in the Cleveland circuit was twice as much, yet the rates were almost the same. There was widespread backing of a project advanced by Dr. David Hostetter, the manufacturer of the famous medicine Hostetter's Bitters, to build a pipeline to Pittsburgh. From there the crude could be carried over the Baltimore and Ohio's Connellsville branch to Baltimore refineries, or it could be refined in Pittsburgh. Another plan was to carry oil by barge to Pittsburgh, and there, after refining, carry it again by barge to Huntington, West Virginia, and from there by the Richmond and Chesapeake Railroad to Richmond for export.

These plans came to grief. Because the pipelines in league with the Pennsylvania refused to pipe oil to the barges, transport by water had to be abandoned. The Columbia Conduit Company, the Hostetter project, met stiff resistance from the Pennsylvania, since the pipeline had to cross the railroad at several points. At one point, nearing Pittsburgh, Hostetter laid his pipes on the bed of a stream where the rail crossed by a culvert. Hostetter claimed that he had bought the bed of the stream, but a force of Pennsylvania workers tore up the pipe and guarded the crossing with guns. Court litigation dragged on into 1875, and in disgust Hostetter in May 1875 leased the line to three young men destined to acquire fame later in Tidewater Oil history: Byron D. Benson, Robert E. Hopkins, and David McKelvy. They hit on the ingenious idea of carrying the oil across the blockaded run by wagon and then repiping it to Pittsburgh. Some oil reached Pittsburgh that way by the summer of 1875. This method was laborious, and every now and then the Pennsylvania would block the route completely with a long line of cars. The Pennsylvania legislature closed the last door for the Columbia Conduit Company when it refused to pass a free-pipeline bill.

The Regions believed that they would be able to live with "equalization" because it would put an end to further rebates for Rockefeller. They were mistaken. In 1875, Rockefeller got another rebate of 10 percent from all the roads. Colonel Joseph Potts said that some Cassandras bewailed that the "favorite" would soon swallow all, but Rockefeller soothed their alarm. As Colonel Potts put it:

> Their [Standard's] little rebate was enough for them. Everybody else should prosper. They needed no more refineries; they already had more than they could employ. It was the railroads they chiefly cared for and next in their affection stood the 100 rival refineries. Such beneficent longings as still remained spread out in steady waves toward the poor producers. This unselfish language soothed all alarm into quiet slumbering. It resembles the gentle fanning of the vampire's wings, and it had the same end in view—the undisturbed abstraction of the victim's blood.

According to Ida Tarbell, her favorite vampire, John D. Rockefeller, had a "mind which stopped by a wall burrows under or creeps around" but never gives up. Stymied when the South Improvement Plan collapsed, he undertook other methods. In May 1872, to the amazement of the people of the Regions, Rockefeller was in Titusville, shaking hands, winning friends and influencing people in behalf of what was called the "Pittsburgh Plan," a plan for an open combination all refiners could join. A central board would allot quotas or shut down some refineries altogether, but all would share dividends equally. This plan was rejected by the Region refiners, sentiment turning against it when the word spread that those who joined would get rebates from the rails. What disconcerted the Regions most during the debate was that leading refiners who had led the fight against the South Improvement Plan now sided with Rockefeller. They included John D. Archbold and J. J. Vandergrift. This was a mild shock to some; to more discerning observers it showed which way the wind was blowing.

In August 1872 another combination was formed, the National Refiners' Association, with Rockefeller as president and Vandergrift as vice-president. This association lasted until June of the following year, when it had to be dissolved because of widespread noncompliance with quotas. The Regions hailed with delight the death of the "Junior Anaconda." Producers always looked with hostility on a combination of refiners who might grind down the price of crude.

Between 1872 and 1875 Rockefeller concentrated on building up Standard Oil. In 1873 he bought the Devoe Manufacturing Company, which not only refined oil in its Long Island, New York plant but also cased it for export. In the same year he took a step that was to have the most important consequences for the future. He went into the pipeline business, commissioning Daniel O'Day, a rough-and-tough oilman working for Jabez Bostwick, to build short lines in Clarion County and later in Bradford County. He then bought a third interest in the Vandergrift-Forman pipelines, which together with the lines built by O'Day became known as the United Pipe Lines, four hundred miles of pipe that were a formidable competitor to the lines operated by the Empire Transportation Company.

Other significant steps were taken in 1874. The Imperial Refining Company, biggest in the Regions, owned by Vandergrift, became part of the Standard empire. Then Rockefeller entered another new field. He bought a 50 percent interest in Chess, Carley and Company of Louisville, which not only had a refinery there but was the leading jobber of oil in the southeastern United States.

In 1875 Rockefeller decided that the time was ripe for the final fruition of "Our Plan." The refineries of the country would be unified under the banner of Standard Oil. There were at the time, aside from Standard, 15 refineries in New York, 12 in Philadelphia,

22 in Pittsburgh, and 27 Creek refiners and a scattering elsewhere.

In the summer of 1874, W. G. Warden, of Philadelphia, and
Charles Lockhart, of Pittsburgh, met Rockefeller and Flagler at
Saratoga, New York. After enjoying the races, they had a conference in which Rockefeller urged Warden and Lockhart to throw
in their lot with Standard, to sell their companies to Standard and
take seats on the active management of the rising oil colossus. He
pointed out to them the rich rebates from the rails, which he
could share with them, and also the economies he had achieved
in manufacturing. They took a trip to Cleveland and inspected
his books—indeed, Rockefeller could sell profitably at a price
below their own actual cost of manufacture. They consented.
Thus Warden, Frew and Company came into the fold, bringing
along the large Atlantic Refining plant and Lockhart, Frew and
Company, which had seven plants in Pittsburgh. Three months
later Charles Pratt and Company of New York agreed to join, and
the remarkable Henry H. Rogers of the Pratt firm now lent his
unique talents to Rockefeller.

Standard Oil was recapitalized in March 1875 from $2,500,000
to $3,500,000 to provide for stock to pay for the new acquisitions.
The shares were now valued at $265 each in the marketplace,
instead of the par value of $100. Together with cash put up by
the new companies, Standard gave $1,000,000 in stock at par
value for properties worth $3,000,000, indicating that the stock
was considered to be worth at least $300 a share. Rockefeller had
been picking up new stock. "I was a regular dumping ground for
stock," he said later. Because he now had 4,549 shares, his holdings of stock alone were worth over $1,200,000 by the most con-
servative valuation in 1875. It is interesting that one of the
stockholders appearing in 1875 is William H. Vanderbilt. The
terms on which he became a stockholder of Standard Oil are
unexplained.

The new firms joining Standard as new partners were to be the
nuclei for absorbing refineries in Philadelphia, Pittsburgh, and
New York. The agent for corraling refineries in the Regions was
John D. Archbold, who formed the Acme Refining Company out
of his firm of Porter, Moreland and Company and another refiner,
and became part of Standard Oil. This firm was to have great

success in eliminating Standard competitors. By 1878 Archbold
testified that all but two refineries in the Regions had "retired
from the business gloriously."

How were refiners driven into the corral? Critics of Rockefeller
say that it was by the most remorseless and brutal economic
pressure. Standard companies enjoyed big rebates that their
competitors did not have and thus they could be readily under-
sold. Not only did the markets of these refineries disappear but a
new complaint was voiced with increasing frequency—they could
not get tank cars for oil shipment because the cars were being
monopolized by Standard Oil.

A. H. Tack, a partner in Citizens' Refining Company of Pittsburgh, testified before a congressional committee in 1888 that
from 1872 he found it hard to compete. Although he seemed to be
doing everything the best way, he still had no margin of profit.
He realized, as all did, that it was the baneful influence of Standard Oil that was responsible. He went to Rockefeller to see if
there were any terms on which he could survive.

As Rockefeller swallowed another oyster he shed another tear.
"There is no hope for any of us," he said, "The weakest must go
first."

> "I weep for you," the Walrus said:
> "I deeply sympathize."
> With sobs and tears he sorted out
> Those of the largest size,
> Holding his pocket-handkerchief
> Before his streaming eyes.

Morehouse and Freeman was a refinery in Cleveland engaged
in the manufacture of lubricants. They had a deal with Rockefeller by which they were supplied daily with 85 barrels of residuum, which Standard, concentrating on kerosene production, discarded. Then in 1874, Morehouse said, he was suddenly cut down
to 12 barrels. Morehouse testified before the Hepburn Committee: "I saw readily what that meant, that meant squeeze you out,
buy your works. They have got the works and are running them.
I am without anything. They paid about $15,000 for what cost
me $41,000." He said, "My refinery was built with the express

understanding from John D. Rockefeller that I should have all the stock I wanted to run the works with."

But now Rockefeller told him: "The coal-oil business belongs to us. We have sufficient money laid aside to wipe out any concern that starts in this business."

William H. Harkness testified that his refinery made money until 1874, when he found he could not sell during several months of the year except at a loss; but when he could sell profitably he could not get tank cars, and thus became dependent on Warden, Frew and Company of Standard Oil for oil supplies. "I was dissatisfied and wanted to do an independent business or give it up." At the Centennial Exposition of 1876, in Philadelphia, while standing before the Corliss Engine, he decided that there was a new powerful engine at work in the world of oil, and determined to sell out.

W. T. Scheide, of the large oil jobber Neyhart and Grandin, decided to give up the struggle in 1875. He saw that refiners were buying oil from him only because they wanted to use him, an independent source of supply, as a bargaining weapon to force more money for their refineries out of Standard Oil. His final decision to quit came when the general freight agent of the Erie indiscreetly told him, in order to persuade him not to quit, that he had thus far resisted all offers of money from Standard Oil to get Erie to shift the Neyhart cars to them. The effect was the opposite of the intended one of reassurance, since it convinced Scheide that it was only a matter of time before Standard would see to it that he would have no cars. As a matter of principle, he would not sell the company to Standard Oil; instead he sold it to Charles Pratt and Company, not learning until later that the purchaser was a Standard Oil unit. With Neyhart and Grandin gone, refiners who bought oil from them had to come hat in hand to Standard.

Thus the acquisitions went on. If a competitor resisted, then the thing to do according to a phrase used often by Archbold and Flagler and by Rockefeller himself was to make him "sweat" or "feel sick" and then resume the parley.

We have some succulent details of the superb Trojan Horse job done by J. N. Camden in behalf of Standard in taking over refineries in the territory served by the Baltimore and Ohio Railroad, principally in Parkersburg, West Virginia, and Baltimore. His refinery in Parkersburg was almost bankrupt when it was taken over by Standard as the Camden Consolidated Oil Company in May 1875. Of this affiliation the world was ignorant, since under West Virginia law the recording of a bill of sale was not required. Camden posed successfully as an enemy of Standard, and for years got away with it.

Camden became the darling of Robert Garrett, the head of the B.&O., who was engaged in a war with Standard. Camden wrote to Oliver Payne: "Mr. Garrett is coming to see us tomorrow. I suppose he will encourage us to keep up our oil business and fight the 'combination.'" Garrett was giving special rates on the Connellsville branch reaching Pittsburgh, and he was either carrying crude to Baltimore to be refined from the Columbia Conduit Company or carrying refined to that port for export. Baltimore was making sensational progress at the expense of other ports, its exports of 37,330 barrels in the first three weeks of 1875 being ten times as much as in 1874.

Camden spiked Garrett's hopes for building up independent refineries on the route of his railroad. On the strength of his masquerade, Garrett gave Camden, the supposedly indomitable foe of Standard Oil, an enormous rebate. While the open rate on refined to Baltimore was $1.75, Camden paid only $0.66½. On lubricating oils he paid only half the open rate of $1.12½. When the impostor had established his base of operations in Baltimore, he exulted to Payne that he could undersell the leading refiners there. When the leading refiner there, West and Company, balked at selling out to Standard, Camden advised that he would give the firm another dose of competition, writing to Flagler, "Let it end there until they become very sick."

To put refiners in Pittsburgh through the wringer and thus soften them up so that they would be willing to sell out to Lockhart, Frew and Company of Standard Oil, Camden worked out a deal with the distributor in Cincinnati who supplied them with staves for barrels, to sell his entire surplus to Standard. Thus, as he explained to Payne, there was in Pittsburgh "little capital in the cooperage business and no supplies on hand." The result of a shortage would be "ruinous prices" for barrels for all independent refiners. When the deal was completed, Camden gloated, "We are fully masters of the situation."

He dealt summarily with the small refiners in Parkersburg. "We will either get them or starve them," he wrote to Rockefeller. "I will protect your flank this Fall in the most practicable way it can be done." The next month he wrote that it would be better to crush the small refiners than to buy them out. "The object of the whole crew of broken-down oil men is to pension themselves upon us, and to take them all in would clean us out like grasshoppers." So Camden devised a plan for buying out the entire crude supply from West Virginia wells in order to "starve them out."

With this fearless Captain Kidd in command, it is no wonder that the Camden company netted 200 percent on its capital in 1876.

This type of bold deception in setting up a phony or phantom competitor to Standard Oil was to be repeated many times afterward. Apparently, Rockefeller considered it a legitimate tool of competition. The secrecy surrounding the Standard operations was to be a hallmark of the company under Rockefeller. Not only was the B.&O. duped about Camden, but the Erie and Pennsylvania railroads did not know for some time after the 1875 absorptions which were Standard companies and which were not. Cipher communication carried on by Camden also became a general practice. In Camden's letters "morose" stood for Standard, "doubters" for refiners, "Mitre" for Garrett, and "droplet" for Baltimore. The lexicon had broadened since the early exuberant days of the company when Rockefeller and Flagler had one code word between them, "Amelia," for "The goose hangs high."

CHAPTER 8 *The Scofield Case*

DURING THIS PERIOD of amalgamation, Rockefeller ran into conflict with owners of three refineries. The disputes were publicized by his detractors, and did harm to Rockefeller's reputation —in two instances grievous harm because the owners of the refineries happened to be widows, objects of tender sympathy during the Victorian period. Yet in examining the facts, it appears that the equities are not all on one side and that sometimes the pot was calling the kettle black.

In 1872, William Scofield, of Alexander, Scofield and Company, having been bought out by Rockefeller, agreed not to reenter refining. The same pledge was made by John Teagle, of Squire and Teagle. None the less in 1875 a new refinery appeared in Cleveland—Scofield, Schurmer, and Teagle, built at a cost of $65,000. Rockefeller, who always regarded a contract as sacrosanct, was indignant. To Inglis, in later years, he said that the new firm had left the ship when it was foundering (not too precise history); but "when we had saved it, they came aboard the ship again and looted it. They were a lot of pirates."

In its first year the company cleared $41,000. In 1876 Rockefeller made an agreement with them, the contract being labeled "Agreement for an Adventure." Although the Scofield refinery could refine as much as 200,000 barrels a year, it agreed to restrict itself to 85,000 barrels. Standard Oil would supply $10,000 additional capital, would purchase and transport the crude and sell and transport the refined. The first profits up to $35,000 would go to Scofield, the next $35,000 in profits would go to Standard, and thereafter the profits would be equally divided. This arrangement was to be so hush-hush that correspondence between the two parties was to be carried on through Post Office Box 125 in Cleveland, belonging to an imaginary G. A. Mason. The partners swore later that Rockefeller enjoined them not to tell even their wives about the contract and not to buy fast horses or fine rigs lest their

new wealth be betrayed. While an authority like Professor Nevins
has scoffed at this statement, it must be borne in mind that
Rockefeller's desire for secrecy was becoming a fetish and that in
this case there might have been good reason for secrecy.

Henry Demarest Lloyd made much of this contract in his book,
using it as an example of the *peine forte et dure* suffered by
refiners oppressed by Rockefeller. This firm, he said, had been
deprived of its God-given right to refine. A firm, alien to it, invested only $10,000 and no more, and yet pocketed $315,345.58 in
four years "with no work." Lloyd forbore to mention that it was
also a "mint" to the Scofield firm, which pocketed the same sum
in four years compared to its profit of $41,000 in 1875 prior to the
agreement. Moreover, it was not true that Standard Oil contributed no work. It had done all the work in building up the rebate
system and all the other emoluments flowing from the monopoly
it had created. That enabled the profit per barrel for the Scofield
firm to soar from $0.34 to $2.05.

As so often happens, appetite mounted with the greater profits,
and the Scofield firm refused to adhere to the 85,000-barrel limit,
although entreated by Rockefeller, who pointed out that without
output limitation the price of refined would dive and that output
restriction was the heart of the "adventure." Finally Rockefeller
went to court for an injunction, asking for specific performance of
the contract. Scofield broke with his two partners and wrote to
Rockefeller, "I think you will soon discover [the stand of his
partners] is only blackmail."

The affidavits filed by both parties in the suit abounded with
the usual distortions to be characteristic of claims by Standard
and its enemies in the years to come. The Scofield firm claimed
that the contract was against the public interest and should be
outlawed as a restraint of trade under the common law. It
claimed that the demand for oil could not be satisfied if all refineries were operated at full capacity. But Standard was keeping a
good deal of its own capacity idle, and Rockefeller in his answer-
ing affidavit swore that refining capacity was twice as great as
demand. Other statements that he made at best skirt the truth,
such as that Standard had no monopoly. He swore that "the
Standard Oil Company owns and operates its refineries in Cleveland, Ohio and its refinery at Bayonne, New Jersey; that it has no

other refineries nor any interest in any other refineries. . . ." This
was in 1880, the year of the first trust, and only a Philadelphia
lawyer could have found technicalities to support that statement.

Rockefeller, moreover, supplied a fanciful explanation for the
extermination of his competitors in Cleveland in 1872. At that
time, he said, "it was deemed advisable by many of the persons
engaged in refining, for the sake of economy to concentrate the
business and associate their joint capital therein." What happened? "That at this time the Standard Oil Company, by reason
of its facilities and its large cash capital was agreed upon as the
one best adapted to concentrate the business." Rockefeller presumably accepted the responsibility as a sad duty, or out of
mercy.

The court ruled against Rockefeller, and the decision gave
credence to the idea that Rockefeller was actively seeking to limit
output in order to raise the price of oil for the American home.
The Scofield firm continued to be a thorn in his side, as we shall
see later.

As a part of the defense, an affidavit was included from a Mrs.
Fred A. Backus, the former owner of a refinery turning out lubricating oils. She was the widow of a man who had established one
of the first refineries in Cleveland in 1860. Fred Backus had denounced Rockefeller openly at the time of the South Improvement Plan. He had survived the "massacre," since he specialized
in lubricating oils, which Standard did not manufacture at the
time. They had a contract for reciprocity, Backus handing over
kerosene to Standard and receiving in return lubricating oils,
which he mixed with animal and vegetable oils to make the final
product.

Backus died in 1874, leaving a wife and three children. He had
been a good churchman (whose piety Rockefeller undoubtedly
approved), having been president of the local Y.M.C.A. Mrs.
Backus continued to run the business, and made an annual income of $25,000.

In November 1878, she negotiated with Standard Oil for the
sale of her refinery, for which a purchase price of $79,000 was
paid, of which she received seven-tenths, having sold previously
three-tenths of her stock of the company. At this time Standard

was picking up almost all the refineries in the country and was engaged in making lubricating oils—we have seen that in 1874 it took over the lubricating business of Morehouse and Freeman. Mrs. Backus had seen the handwriting on the wall: her profits were declining, and she, like other refiners, had been unable to get tank cars for oil shipments.

Since the time of sale, her brother-in-law later stated in a letter to Rockefeller, "she thinks that you literally robbed her of millions and feeds her children on that diet three times a day more or less, principally more, until it has become a mania with her." In the Scofield case she filed an affidavit for the defense, saying that Rockefeller had swindled her. Lloyd and Tarbell gave circulation to her story, and since the image of the cowed, defenseless widow with three children nestling in her skirts had a powerful sentimental appeal, the story hurt Rockefeller perhaps more than any other charge in his life. In his *Reminiscences* Rockefeller devotes more space to the Backus charge than to any other subject.

Mrs. Backus claimed that when she was approached about selling the business she insisted that she would deal only with Rockefeller, who visited her. Of her interview with him, she said: "I told Mr. Rockefeller that I realized the fact that the Backus Oil Company was entirely in the power of Standard Oil Company and that all I could do would be to appeal to his honour as a gentleman and to his sympathy to do with me the best he could; and I begged of him to consider his wife in my position—that I had been left with this business and with my fatherless children and with a large indebtedness that Mr. Backus had contracted for the first time in his life. He said he was aware of what I had done and that his wife could never have accomplished so much. . . . He promised with tears in his eyes that he would stand by me in this transaction and that I should not be wronged."

She claimed that she was wronged. She did not see Rockefeller again—and this seems to have been part of her complaint about being wronged, since she had expected him to "stand by her" in the flesh. She asked for $200,000 but had to accept the last offer, which was $79,000—$60,000 for the works, goodwill, and successorship, and $19,000 for the oil on hand. The Backus Company was to continue under its own name (the outside world was not to know of the change in ownership). She claimed that in their interview Rockefeller had consented to her retaining stock in the Backus Company since he said that he wanted only majority control, but in the end his representatives gave a cold shoulder to her request for stockownership, saying that no outsiders were wanted.

When the papers were brought to her she said (according to her): "It is like signing my death warrant. I believe it will prove my death warrant." She then wrote a scorching letter to Rockefeller:

> Were it not for the knowledge that there is a God in heaven and that you will be compelled to give an account for all the deeds done here, and there in the presence of my husband will have to confess whether you have wronged me and his fatherless children—were it not for this knowledge, I could not endure it for a moment, the fact that a man possessed of millions that you are, will permit to be taken from a widow a business that had been the hard life-work and pride of herself and her husband, one that was paying the handsome profit of nearly twenty-five thousand dollars per annum and give me in return what a paltry sum that will net me less than three thousand dollars; and it is done in a manner that says, Take this or we will crush you out. . . . I cannot tell you the sorrow it has caused me to have one tell me within the last few days that it was enough to drive honest men away from the Church of God when professing Christians do as you have done by me.

This must have shaken Rockefeller. He immediately replied that he was not anxious to have the refinery, that Mrs. Backus two years earlier had been willing to sell out for considerably less and with some of the payments deferred, while now she would receive all in cash; that the present cost to reproduce the refinery was one-third of the $60,000 paid by him; that he would cancel the sale if she preferred, or since she complained that she had been denied the privilege of holding stock, he would permit her to hold up to 300 shares, or three-tenths of the company.

Affidavits in Rockefeller's behalf were printed in the Oil City *Derrick*, at that date a Standard Oil mouthpiece, after Miss Tarbell had aired Mrs. Backus's case in *McClure's* in 1902. They included statements by Mrs. Backus's brother-in-law, H. M. Backus; Charles Marr, who represented her in the sale; and Mr. Malony, her plant superintendent. They must be accepted with a *caveat* since they relate events occurring almost a quarter of a century before, and Mrs. Backus was now dead. Mr. Backus's letter is particularly fishy. He admits he wrote the letter after talking with the superintendent of the Buckeye Pipe Line Company, a Standard Oil company. He gushes "respect and admiration" for Rockefeller, and says, referring to his own hard luck, "I have had my ups and downs but I have tried to take my medicine and look pleasant instead of sitting down under the juniper tree and blaming my losses on John D. Rockefeller."

Surveying all the evidence, what do we find?

Mrs. Backus was given the opportunity by Rockefeller to hold stock in the Backus Company. Why did she not do so? It would appear that she really was eager to liquidate her entire interest in the company. This would be consistent with the statement of Marr that during the negotiations she "frequently urged affiant to bring the same to a conclusion as she was anxious to dispose of said business." In his letter, Rockefeller said that in their conversation he understood that if she sold the business she would want to be through with it completely. According to Lloyd, she told the court that she did not accept the offer to keep Backus Company stock because she had already disposed of the proceeds; but if so, she must have invested her money with the speed of lightning, since all the events occurred in the space of a few days.

It appears that she actually received more than seven-tenths of $79,000. She admitted that the sale price did not include cash on hand and accounts receivable. Marr swore that the total amount she realized was $133,000—not far from the real asking price of $150,000 (not $200,000 as she said). This figure of $133,000 can be discounted as an *ex parte* statement, since it seems excessive.

Malony said he was, of course, as plant superintendent familiar with the works, and he knew they could be replaced for only $25,000. H. M. Backus said the same. Miss Tarbell admits, "It is probably true as Mr. Rockefeller states that he could have reproduced Mrs. Backus' works for $25,000."

If this was so, then under the prevailing circumstances it does not appear Mrs. Backus was wronged, comparing her settlement with sums received by other casualties. Rockefeller seems to have leaned over backward, giving her a large sum for goodwill, which he usually did not recognize, restricting the amount he paid in such cases to use-value. It is quite likely that Marr was telling the truth when he said that when the offer was made "she [Mrs. Backus] expressed herself as entirely satisfied therewith." Her subsequent exasperation and emotional explosion were directed to the entire monopoly situation that had forced her to the wall and reduced her bargaining power to the nuisance value of her plant. And in truth, if she had been able to survive, her annual profit of $25,000 from the refinery when properly capitalized would have warranted a sale price of a quarter-million for her, at the very least.

When Mrs. Backus died, she left $350,000, so she was not pauperized by Mr. Rockefeller. In his *Reminiscences,* Rockefeller has the last word. If she had kept stock in the company it would eventually have been exchanged for Standard stock, and she or her estate would have had millions.

In 1877 Mrs. Sylvia Hunt, a widow of Baltimore, leased her refinery in Baltimore to the Camden Consolidated Oil Company, the Standard subsidiary. She was a woman with a good deal of spunk, having rebuilt her refinery within a few months after it burned down. Colonel Joseph Potts, who was not enamoured of Rockefeller after Potts' Empire Transportation Company had been destroyed by Standard (as we shall read in the next chapter), wrote of her: "It could fairly have been expected that something of chivalrous feeling would be inspired by the sight of this indomitable spirit who had wrought so noble a work against such odds. They [Standard] crushed her business and spirit as remorselessly as they would have killed a dog." Ida Tarbell gave currency to this statement.

This seems to be an outright libel. In December 1877, Camden wrote of his first meeting with the widow, who impressed him tremendously; "Mrs. Hunt drove up to our office to see me this evening with an elegant turn-out Driver in Livery and she in diamonds." Because she wanted a deal to bring her plant into the Standard ranks and manage it herself, a lease was worked out at $5,000 a year.

Rockefeller apparently enjoined Camden to be considerate to her, since the latter wrote, "Knowing your disposition to avoid having any trouble with her I have conceded everything she has asked and have been most kind and yielding to her." But by May 1878 Camden wrote to Rockefeller, "I really believe that Mrs. Hunt is not in her right mind."

She harassed Camden constantly with requests for accommodations and changes in the arrangement, to which Camden acceded—but these led only to fresh requests. First, Camden hired her sales agent in Baltimore and then her son. Then he raised the lease rent to $7,500; then she wanted an agreement from Standard Oil to buy the plant at the end of five years; then she wanted the value fixed immediately; and then she wanted to be released from any further personal service.

In despair Camden wrote, "I do not see anything more that can be done." To cap it all, the lady, while being paid by Standard, enticed Standard employees into her employ and set up a new competing oil refinery that she tried to sell to Standard.

CHAPTER 9   *The Struggle with the Empire Transportation Co.*

COLONEL JOSEPH D. POTTS, head of the Empire Transportation Company, saw the emergent situation in the beginning of 1877 with cold clarity. As he testified in 1888 before a United States congressional committee: "We reached the conclusion that there were three great divisions in the petroleum business— the production, the carriage of it and the preparation of it for market. If any one party controlled absolutely any one of these divisions, they practically would have a very fair show of controlling the others."

And that was what was happening. Standard Oil, asserting its control over all refining, was stretching its tentacles into the pipeline business, and had made the three trunk railroads abject suitors for the oil traffic. "Each kind of commodity," wrote the English economist J. A. Hobson, "as it passes through the many processes from the earth to the consumer may be looked upon as a stream whose channel is broader at some point and narrow at others." Astride the narrow bottleneck of refining, Rockefeller was now nearing control of the whole stream.

Colonel Potts, who decided at this late hour that a blow must be struck for freedom, was a worthy antagonist for Rockefeller, and, fittingly, a good deal like him. "A shrewd, oily man, as smooth as oil," Rockefeller summed him up years later, but those were the very words often replied to Rockefeller himself by his antagonists. Like Rockefeller, Potts was a religious man who lived simply and worked hard. Like Rockefeller, he was also a man known for his ability to plan far ahead. The Empire Transportation had been built, like Standard Oil, on rebates. Since Empire was to all intents a subsidiary of the Pennsylvania Railroad, it had taken the initiative in getting rebates from that road for its customers and thus had played a role in upsetting previous no-rebate pacts among the roads.

Empire, as we have noted, was basically a fast-freight expediter from the east to the Midwest frontier, but its main revenues were from the soliciting of oil business. Empire owned 5,000 tank cars, about 1,500 in its famous "Green Line," and furnishing these cars gave it a constant excuse for rebates that it passed on to its customers. It was rich in property, having a fleet of Great Lake steamers, one of the best oil terminals at Communipaw in New Jersey, piers of its own there, warehouses, tank storage, grain elevators, and, most important of all, over 500 miles of pipelines in the oil regions.

Potts foresaw an even greater future for Empire; on the other hand he foresaw also that the growth of Standard Oil could wipe it out. If Standard took over all the nation's refineries, Empire could lose a vital part of its business. Its main traffic by volume was crude oil carried east over the Philadelphia and Erie, an artery that belonged to the Pennsylvania Railroad, and this involved the Pennsylvania in Empire's future. The Pennsylvania also had cause to be concerned that Standard might at some time shut down its Pittsburgh refineries or might ship the refined east

over the Baltimore and Ohio, cutting out the Pennsylvania altogether.

In January 1877, Potts worked out a deal with Tom Scott,
having persuaded Scott, now the Pennsylvania Railroad president, that he must go along with Empire in self-protection. Empire pledged itself that it would build up its own refineries,
whether through purchase or control, and the Pennsylvania
would support Empire with special low rates, to be repaid out of
Empire's profits in refining, if any. In other words the railroad
would subsidize the establishment of a refining alliance that
would challenge Standard Oil. Prospects that Empire would be
able to block Standard in this way seemed very promising indeed. Oil producers would side against Rockefeller; a large number of independent refiners were ready to fight for their existence;
and not only was Empire rich, but the Pennsylvania Railroad,
with profits of $25,000,000 a year, was the greatest corporation in
the country. The other rails, the Erie and Central, might split
apart, and thus Rockefeller would be left with no support.

Soon Rockefeller learned what was afoot. Empire took over the
large Sone & Fleming refinery on Long Island and began building
another refinery in Philadelphia. Rockefeller went to see Scott
and A. J. Cassatt, third vice-president of the Pennsylvania. What
did this mean? The Empire was entering a foreign activity,
Rockefeller protested (overlooking the fact that he himself now
had both feet in the pipeline business). According to Potts's account, on the theory that the best defense was a bold offense,
Rockefeller took the occasion to ask for more rebates. Getting no
satisfaction, he threw down the gauntlet. This, gentlemen, is war.

Standard Oil was well heeled for battle. In the previous fall,
vessels to carry oil for the winter season to foreign ports gathered
in New York harbor. The price of refined was only $0.14 a gallon
in June and $0.16 in July. But crude supply was down; and
Standard, in the driver's seat because of the shortage, demanded
$0.26 a gallon. Foreigners refused to buy. The price went up to
$0.19 in August, and by September foreign buyers were helpless.
Their resistance collapsed, and refined went to $0.26, where it
stayed for the next three months. Because of the lush profits from
the "holdup," during the heat of the Empire struggle Standard
was able to declare a dividend of $80 on every $100 par value of

capital stock. Even after that melon to stockholders, the treasury of Standard bulged with cash reserves.

The first step in the military offensive that Rockefeller took was to close down his Pittsburgh refineries, immediately depriving the Pennsylvania of two-thirds of its oil traffic. Then Rockefeller called on the Erie and Central railroads to cut their rates. We observe now how the parallel to clauses in the South Improvement Plan appear. That plan required the rails to lower or raise the rates of transportation to such extent as might be necessary to overcome competition on behalf of Standard Oil and other members; and this obligation was apparently recognized and carried out by the rails, now under Rockefeller's thumb, as it would be carried out later in the battle with the Tidewater. Certainly Standard Oil had no financial need for such rate cuts; the Erie and Central apparently cut their rates under Rockefeller's orders, and at the expense of their treasury, only to hurt the Pennsylvania. Thus far they carried gratitude, "the expectation of later favors to come."

Why did they jump at Standard's command? Jewett, president of the Erie Line, could explain only feebly to the Hepburn Committee, "We were opposed to permitting the Empire Line, a creature of the Pennsylvania Railroad, to be building refineries, to become the owners of pipelines leading into the oil fields and leading to the coast, without a contest." Not much illumination for a course of hara-kiri. Before a congressional committee in 1888, Flagler could only say that when the situation was called to the attention of the other roads they said "that it was unfair to them that the Pennsylvania did not divest itself of the manufacturing business."

Soon Empire and Pennsylvania found themselves knee-deep in hot water—or more accurately, red ink. The rate cuts became so steep that, according to Cassatt's later testimony, one large oil buyer, Henry G. Ohlen, got a contract from the Pennsylvania for the transport of his oil at $0.08 a barrel below the out-of-pocket cost to the road. Wherever a refinery allied to Empire tried to sell its refined, it found itself undercut by Standard. Wherever Empire went into the market to buy crude for its refineries, Standard bid up the price. Sentiment in the old fields was all with Potts, and he was cheered wherever he appeared; but where dollars and cents were concerned, producers and refineries chased the best deal. They had a golden opportunity to deal a blow here to the octopus Rockefeller, the single buyer, but their greed was too great. As Potts said later, "They found the opportunity for immediate profit too tempting to resist by playing one belligerent against another." Producers sold to Standard when they could get a higher price, and refiners squeezed the lowest freight rate from the Pennsylvania.

The rate war spread to all commodities and to passenger traffic as well, so that a passenger could travel from New York to Chicago for $15. The Pennsylvania lost $1,000,000 in three months; Philadelphia received only a third as much oil as it did before the war with Standard.

The Rockefeller luck held again, conclusively. In July a bloody labor war erupted. Workers struck on the Baltimore and Ohio, and rioting began that quickly spread to the Pennsylvania, which had cut railroad wages by 20 percent and then announced a doubling of the length of freight trains, which would result in loss of jobs. In Pittsburgh the worst violence occurred when a pitched battle was fought between workers and the state militia, in which twenty-five lost their lives. The Pennsylvania suffered a grievous property loss. As one report read: "Where lately stood magnificent buildings teeming with life and business are seen nought but charred timbers and heaps of ashes. Of the hundreds of railroad cars remain but wheels and axles which are broken and twisted in all possible shapes."

The Pennsylvania Railroad for the first time in its history passed its dividend, and the stock fell to 27, almost half of par value. The financial situation of the Pennsylvania was weaker than outsiders were aware. The stock, like that of all railroad issues, was highly watered, and lush dividends had left the cupboard bare.

For the Pennsylvania, humbled in this war, there was nothing to do but to go to Canossa. Scott and other executives went to Cleveland in August, and Rockefeller and his staff repaid the courtesy with a trip to Philadelphia the next month for the peace conclave. Rockefeller demanded that Empire abandon its refineries, which Standard Oil would absorb along with the pipelines of Empire. Standard took the lion's share of Empire's tank cars.

Because Potts, though crushed by the adversity, refused to surrender Pennsylvania exercised its legal option to take over Empire's property. The Pennsylvania Railroad's small stockholders were in truth delighted to see Empire disappear, having felt all along that Empire skimmed the cream off the freight business and that Pennsylvania officials lined their pockets by holding its stock. The purchase price was $3,400,000, which Rockefeller raised by collecting cash from all the banks that were in his camp, buggying from one to another in Cleveland. The mammoth sum paid over by a company that had been capitalized for a million dollars only seven years earlier was the sensation of the business world. In 1879 William Vanderbilt testified, "I was surprised at the amount of ready cash they were able to provide."

The capitulation by the Pennsylvania marked a new era for Standard Oil. After subduing the most powerful railroad in the country it held the whiphand over all the rails. By acquiring the tank cars of the Empire, in addition to virtually all the tank cars on the Central and Erie, it made it difficult for any large opposing refinery interest to arise. And now, by taking over the pipelines of Empire, Standard was not only the major refiner of oil, but overnight became the major transporter of oil, threatening producers within its grip. As soon as the agreement with the Pennsylvania was announced, newspapers in the oil country referred to Rockefeller as "Lord of the Regions."

The white flag of surrender was hoisted on many battlements. Dr. Hostetter came to see Rockefeller with his Columbia Conduit Company to sell, and a bargain was agreed upon. The line, like the Empire's lines, was incorporated into United Pipe Lines belonging to Standard Oil. The Baltimore and Ohio for the first time decided to enter the railroad pool with the three others, Pennsylvania, Erie, and Central, and an agreement was made. The sale of the Columbia Conduit Company convinced the B.&O. that thereafter it would have to do business with Rockefeller if it wanted any oil business at all. The Standard agreed to give 47 percent of the oil traffic to the Pennsylvania, 21 percent each to the Erie and Central, and 11 percent to the B.&O.

The shaken refineries were now dropping easily into Standard's lap. In late 1877 and early 1878, John Archbold completed twenty-

seven purchases and leases. J. N. Camden reported from his territory, "We have cleaned up every seed in which a refining interest
could spring in Baltimore." In April 1878, Flagler estimated that
the total investment in refining in the nation was $36,000,000; of
this, Standard owned or controlled $33,000,000.

Independent refiners who persisted in competition with Standard were told who was boss without any attempt to disguise the
truth. Here are two cases that later came to light:

William Harkness, who had sold out in 1876 to Warden, Frew
and Company in Philadelphia, tried to reenter the business in
1877. He wanted to build a refinery of 10,000 barrels a day, and
went to see the Pennsylvania. "I was almost on my knees begging
to be allowed to do that." He asked if he could get a rate on
crude as cheap as that given to Standard Oil, and said he would
agree to stay in refining for ten years. The answer ·vas No. A. J.
Cassatt said to him, "That is not practicable, and you know the
reason why." No one could misunderstand the Delphic utterance.

Rufus Bush, of the firm of Denslow and Bush, said that because
their contract with the Empire expired in May 1878, they got an
interview with the Pennsylvania in March concerning renewal.
Bush said that members of his firm asked if they could get the
same rate as Standard, and again the answer was No. The answer
was still No to a query as to what the situation would be if they
shipped the same amount as Standard. "He [Cassatt] intimated
that each road had a certain percentage of the oil business and
they [Standard] could divide that up and give each road its
proportion and keep harmony, which we could not." Cassatt suggested that they go to Standard and "fix it up," which they understood to mean euphemistically that they should sell out.

In June they had another interview, and this time their complaint was about tank cars. Because the firm was never allotted
enough by the road, Bush suggested that the firm would like to
put some on which they would supply. Tom Scott became irate
and said that if there were not enough cars, the Pennsylvania
would build more. Scott added, "Well, you have cost us in fighting for you now a million dollars and we don't propose to go into
another fight." Scott made another proposal to the firm as well as
to the firm of Ayres, Lombard and Company, which was present.
According to the account of Josiah Lombard, ". . . he [Scott] said

there would be no peace and profit in the business until we made some arrangement with the Standard Oil Company."

And what of the rates paid by Standard? For its trouble in performing the service of "evener," Standard was to get a "commission" of 10 percent on its own oil shipments and on the freight "under its control." The latter phrase would cover cases such as the contract with Scofield, Schurmer and Teagle, and Lord knows what other kinds of arrangements. The service performed by Standard was explained by Flagler before a congressional committee in 1888:

> It was incumbent upon us during the succeeding month to ship over the road or roads which had received less than its percentages an amount during that following month sufficient to bring up the deficit of the previous month. Undertaking to do that meant, as I well knew at the time, a responsibility imposed upon us, and an obligation to run refineries at certain localities which perhaps at the time it was unprofitable for us to run. It meant a steady continuance of a large volume of business at periods of time when it might not be profitable to run them. . . . I say it was no light task and realizing that I said to these gentlemen "we will undertake to do this business for you, to secure to each one of you the percentage we may have agreed upon, upon condition that we are paid for that service a sum which shall be equal to 10% of the rate you receive for doing the business."

Since Standard laid out its production plans far in advance, whatever juggling of quotas would be necessary month by month to ensure each rail its fixed percentage would not seem to have been an onerous task. As if to buttress a weak argument, Flagler threw in the fact that Standard assumed all risk of fire and provided terminals on the seaboard free of charge. Even if a 10 percent rebate were not to be deemed excessive, there can be no rationalization in savings to the road for the rebate that was actually given, according to the report in trade circles. There was a good deal of testimony that while the published rate from Cleveland to New York in 1878-1879 was $1.44½, *the actual rate to Standard Oil was only $0.80.*

But this was not all. The iniquitous "drawback" that had appeared in the South Improvement Plan now cropped up again. On February 15, 1878, Daniel O'Day, manager of the American Transfer Company, one of the Standard's pipelines, wrote a note to A. J. Cassatt, vice-president of the Pennsylvania Railroad. He informed him: "I here repeat to you what I once stated to you and which I asked you to receive and treat as strictly confidential, that we have been for many months receiving from the New York Central and Erie railroads certain sums of money, in no instance less than twenty cents per barrel on every barrel of crude carried by each of these roads."

O'Day asked the same amount of twenty cents per barrel, dating from February 1, on every barrel the Pennsylvania hauled, whether for Standard or for a competitor. Cassatt investigated, and finding that, since the preceding October, Central had been paying the rebate and drawback of thirty-five cents and Erie thirty cents, he ordered his comptroller to pay twenty cents per barrel for the next three months. It is estimated that the amount the American Transfer Company thus extracted in 1878 amounted to $3,093,000—almost enough for the Standard to have paid a dividend of 100 percent on the par value of its capital stock. There is no explanation for this payment on crude shipped by parties other than Standard but coercion—the rails had no course except to consent if they wanted to keep the goodwill of Standard.

Observe the fine delicacy with which the money is lifted out of the Pennsylvania's pocket. This is not a request for a conference and negotiation from one company potentate to another. It comes from the manager of a small Standard Oil branch capitalized at $100,000. O'Day reminds Cassatt that Standard now has a pipeline running to Pittsburgh, that B.&O.'s share of the traffic has been cut to 11 percent, that the Chesapeake and Ohio is getting none, and that the other rails are making the payment. Then, as casual as coffee talk, like light *causerie* in the afternoon, "I am constrained to say to you that in justice to the interest I represent we should receive from your company at least twenty cents on each barrel of crude oil you represent." That letter was all that was needed.

When examined about this payment to Standard, Cassatt said, "We pay as a commission to them to aid in securing us our share of the trade." The Pennsylvania comptroller said, "We pay it for procuring oil to go over the lines in which the Pennsylvania Railroad Company is interested as against the New York lines and the New York Central." But an independent shipper, H. G. Ohlen, had shipped 30,000 barrels in February and March 1878 on which the drawback was paid, and no one could demonstrate that Standard Oil had anything in the world to do with that shipment.

As another instance of the iron hand in the iron glove, here is the text of a note with a dictatorial ring sent by Flagler to William Vanderbilt and the other rail presidents on April 23, 1878:

DEAR SIR:

I am anxious to meet the representatives of the Trunk Lines at the earliest moment possible, in respect to oil rates from the first of May.

May I ask you to use your influence in bringing about such a meeting not later than Friday of this week if possible.

Yrs truly,

H. M. FLAGLER
Secretary

It is fair to surmise that no other customers of the railroads dared to address rail presidents so peremptorily.

CHAPTER 10   *The Struggle with Petroleum Producers*

CLOSE ON THE HEELS of his conquest of the Empire, Rockefeller was compelled to engage in a battle royal with the oil producers of the Regions. In the course of a dramatic contest he was indicted for criminal conspiracy and had to face a swarm of suits and investigations. From this time on, Rockefeller was destined to be in the public pillory.

The Regions had always dreaded the specter of the single buyer. In the Empire struggle all their sympathies were with

Empire, though they did nothing to help, extracting the last drop in prices and rebates. Though they had contributed nothing that might lead to any other result, the sudden capitulation shocked them, and they were thrown into a panic by the realization that there was now virtually only one buyer of oil and also only one gatherer of oil. There was a general confluence of thought that this was the last time to act or be smothered, and events soon convinced them that Rockefeller meant to smother them. Before studying the events of 1878, it is instructive to revert in time to the first combination formed by oil producers in 1872 after they had humbled Rockefeller in the South Improvement Plan fracas. The events of 1878 form a sequel to what occurred then.

It was not long after the demise of the South Improvement Plan that Rockefeller and Flagler were in the Regions urging the adoption of a plan for stabilization that would embrace all refiners and would shore up the price of crude oil. Rockefeller's soiled reputation did not help the cause for the Pittsburgh Plan. Thus the *Petroleum Centre Record* expressed the hope that the Regions "would not allow themselves to be soft-soaped by the honeyed words of monopolists and conspirators." On May 15, in a meeting at Titusville, John Archbold and J. J. Vandergrift, Region refiners, spoke for the plan but it was rejected. Region refiners in the majority feared that the plan would be dominated by Pittsburgh and Cleveland refiners.

However, Rockefeller when blocked only turned direction, and in September he had a new combination of refiners in being, the National Refiners' Association, with a pledge to reduce refinery output by half and to observe minimum prices. With four-fifths of the refiners as members, the single buyer was now a real possibility. Another circumstance frightened the producers into action. There had been an onrush of production in Clarion County, increasing in a year from 12,000 barrels a day to 16,000 barrels, and the price of crude was falling like a shot, dropping in August to $3.37 compared to $4.42 a year earlier. Could there be any more compelling relationship between supply and demand? And what if a single buyer should control demand? The price could slump to $3. Many wells were five-barrel-a-day affairs. Since it cost $8 a day to operate such a well, there would be only a few dollars left for royalty and paying off the $6,000 average cost of the well.

There was a spontaneous call among producers for action. Captain William Hasson, elected president of the Petroleum Producers' Association, was one of the few oilmen who was not a carpetbagger. His farm on the site of Oil City had been bought from the Indian chief Cornplanter in 1796 and had been sold for $750,000 when it was found to contain oil. His plan was to stop the drill and stop leases to drill, for six months, enforced by a pledge to be signed by producers, "This we agree to and bind ourselves to each other under a forfeiture of $2,000 for each well commenced," the pledge not extending to any well where the rig had been commenced. Hasson's agents toured the Regions, exhorting and searching out lawbreakers. The chief pocket of resistance was among the native Clarion County farmers, who thought the pledge a scheme to rob them.

Stopping the drill could affect output only for the future. Some drastic step was necessary for the present. When the price of crude dropped below $3 to $2.75 the association decided to close all wells for thirty days. The sight of a highly individualistic industry employing ten thousand men stopping in unison was, according to the Oil City *Derrick* "a spectacle that takes one's breath away." The producers organized to burn well rigs and destroy the engines of recalcitrants. At Rouseville a mob of three hundred closed thirty wells by force. (Rockefeller was stigmatized as a lawbreaker, but when violence was used in the Regions it was pardonable because the cause was holy.) Miss Tarbell, with apparent approbation, said: "Men who appeared in church on Sunday in silk hats carrying gold-headed canes—there were such in the Oil region in 1872—now stole out at night to remote localities to hunt down rumors of drilling wells. If they found them true, their dignity did not prevent their cutting the tools loose or carrying off a band wheel."

The success was a limited one in terms of reduction of output. At some time the pumps had to start again, and the embargo was lifted at the end of October. Now production shot up to the unheard-of figure of 22,000 barrels a day. A voluntary output-curb would not work.

The next step was the organization of a pool to control distribution rather than output. The Petroleum Producers' Agency was organized with a capital of a million dollars to be subscribed by the producing community. It would purchase oil at $5 a barrel and would pay the producer part in cash, part in tank certificates. If the oil could be sold for $5, well and good; if not, it would be held in storage until it could be sold at that price. In effect refiners and jobbers (who often accumulated stocks and gambled with them) would be confronted with a united front by the producers.

The formation of the pool among producers alarmed Rockefeller and other refiners. It appeared that it could work. The solid public opinion behind the pool was evidenced by the fact that after a few weeks a million dollars of capital was subscribed. The producers might have the refiners over the barrel with their demand for $5 a barrel for oil. Consumers might have to pay through the nose, and the New York *Herald* said in alarm, "The consumers are likely to take a hand in the matter and use their efforts to frustrate the design and intent of the shutdown by refusing to pay higher prices."

Now Rockefeller appeared on the scene with the pipe of peace. He did not want to fight the producers, he said, but to join with them in supporting the price of crude. He immediately put in an order for 6,000 barrels of oil at $4.75. For the future, said Rockefeller, "We are willing to go further and buy only of the producers' agent, hence the order we have given you. . . . We do this to convince producers of our sincerity and to assist in establishing the market."

Why did Rockefeller make this and the purchases to follow? The oil producers could see only an antithesis of interest between producers and refiners, and later ascribed Rockefeller's actions to base Machiavellian motives, slimy tactics to subvert the producers' pool and wreck it. On the other hand, Rockefeller may in all sincerity have seen the way for a marriage of interest between producers and refiners. It was hard to stabilize the price of refined when the price of crude behaved like a Mexican jumping bean. Another reason—he did not want the producing element forever locking horns with him, and he was no doubt disconcerted when a mass meeting of producers passed a resolution asking that pressure be put on foreign governments to put a tariff on refined, no doubt the only time that Americans have ever asked that a foreign tariff be put on American goods. Another reason—dropping prices for crude always disrupted the market for refined, since wholesalers and foreign buyers would stop buying, waiting for lower prices. And, in the long run, low prices for crude would destroy the incentive for exploration for oil on which the industry depended. Thus Rockefeller's intentions may have been completely honest and aboveboard.

"Timeo Danaos et dona ferentes"—liberal translation: mind your eye when the Cleveland refiners get generous—proclaimed the Oil City *Derrick,* which had a weakness for Latin phrases. There were many who regarded Rockefeller's offers of support as a Circean song that ultimately would dash the producers on the rocks. The agency should dictate, not negotiate. Any long-term alliance with Rockefeller could lead to disaster, since the agency might be caught off guard at the most unfavorable moment.

But the bargaining power of the agency was weak. By the end of November a price of $4 a barrel was already a farce. Wildcat wells had come in big, opening up new territory. A million barrels was already in storage, and the surplus was rising all the time. It was futile to ask for another embargo, since it was too expensive to keep machinery idle. So the Regions were ready for a compact with the devil.

The devil was very reasonable. If the agency would deal only with the National Refiners' Association, the refiners would agree to deal only with the producers' agency. The price would be $4.00 a barrel, geared to the then refined price of $0.26 a gallon—for every cent rise in refined, $0.25 was to be added to the crude price until it reached $5.00 a barrel. Over Captain Hasson's protest, the producers agreed to the so-called Treaty of Titusville.

The auguries were bad from the start. No sooner was the agreement signed than the price of crude dived. Rockefeller gave an order for 200,000 barrels at the emergency price of $3.25, which the producers were glad to get.

Another clause in the agreement was that the refiners would agree to accept no rebates. Rockefeller, who was receiving substantial rebates at the time, agreed to this with a straight face. His agents were saying privately that he could give a good price to producers because he was getting rebates from the rails.

The end came rapidly. On January 14, 1873, suddenly and without warning, Rockefeller canceled the contract for the oil not yet delivered. The price of $3.25 he said was ridiculous when crude was being sold at $2.50 and as low as $2.25. The producers had not kept their oral agreement that they would stabilize the price by holding the well output in check. Culver, the negotiator with Rockefeller, said, according to the Titusville *Herald* on January 16: "I believe they are the most honorable set of business men I ever met, . . . I further believe that if the producers showed any indication of being able to control themselves, these men would be willing to take the balance of the oil even if the open price was down to $1 a barrel."

To many in the Regions, despite Culver's statement, the incident proved that he who sups with the devil should use a long spoon. To others it proved that the producers had failed the test. No new combination attempt would be inaugurated for many years. Ida Tarbell said, "Nature outraged that her generosity should be so manipulated as to benefit a few had opened her veins to flood the earth with oil." Rockefeller, commenting on this passage, said, "Nature would not have opened her veins if the producers had not compelled her to do so."

For his part, the experience of 1872 convinced Rockefeller that the oil producers were unruly and undisciplined. His later comments were that the Regions were a "mining camp" and the producers "men like spoiled children." The profligacy of the oil producers was a never-ending source of astonishment not only to Rockefeller but even to their partisans. Miss Tarbell said, "Nobody looked with favor on economy and everybody despised small things." No one sent a letter when he could send a telegram; no one bothered to repair tools; they were simply replaced. The trouble was, said the Oil City *Derrick* in a burst of frankness, "Their business was born in a balloon going up and spent all its early years in the sky."

Producers saw the need for combination, and there was an apparent community of interest, but there were subsurface rifts making for centrifugal tendencies. The small wellowner with five barrels a day depended on the price of oil for survival, but to the wildcat operator who hit a big well, price meant less than what quantity he could market. In the spring of 1874 a combination move got nowhere, since small producers said they would go broke if the drill and the pumps were stopped, while the rich producers, with thousands of barrels of oil in storage, would profit by a price rise on that oil. They decided, "We can all go to hell together," and by November 1874 oil was selling at the heartbreak price of $0.62 a barrel, which destroyed small producers by the score. The disunity within the ranks of producers was pointed up by the Titusville *Herald* in April 1874 when it said, "Were not those who were resoluting most loudly indoors to 'hold on' and 'pull together' secretly giving their brokers orders to sell?" As a matter of fact, no sooner was the agreement of December 15, 1872, signed with Rockefeller, fixing a price of $3.25 a barrel, than a member of the executive committee sabotaged it by selling a large amount at a figure slashed far below $3.25.

With the absorption of Empire by Standard, the tocsin was sounded for action in the Regions. On October 21, 1877, the first meeting of the Petroleum Parliament was held in Titusville. They met secretly for three days and again in December for four days. While they talked up the familiar ideas about restricting the drill, the emphasis was on building their own pipeline to the sea and, thus wriggling out from the deadly embrace of Standard. At the coast, crude could either be refined by independent refiners or shipped overseas. One proposal, backed by Lewis Emery, Jr., was for a pipeline to Buffalo, where oil could be transferred to oil barges for the trip to New York on the Erie Canal. The other proposal, backed by Benson, McKelvy, and Hopkins, who had formerly operated the Columbia Conduit Company under lease from Dr. Hostetter, was to build a 235-mile line from the Allegheny River to Baltimore. To get a right of way for the latter line, the oil producers backed legislation by the Pennsylvania legislature to give the pipeline the right of eminent domain. In April 1878 the Pennsylvania House passed the bill but the Senate turned it down. It was no doubt influenced by Standard propaganda that this was a plot of European refiners to starve out United States refiners. The fact that the terminus was in Baltimore and not in Philadelphia hurt the bill, since there was a strong protest from Pennsylvania interests that it would cost the state 250,000 jobs. An amendment to make Philadelphia the terminus was made too late.

The defiant moves by the producers to turn their backs on

Standard Oil and the rails it controlled did not serve to endear them to Rockefeller when a crisis arose. The policy he adopted in 1878 may have been unnecessarily harsh as a result.

It was a new outpouring of oil, the new Bradford field in McKean County, that caused the crisis. In 1872 an output of 22,000 barrels a day had been enough to wreck the combination plan, but now output soared to 42,000 barrels a day. The new field was so rich that wells could be laid out "like rows of corn and every well could be a success."

As to the first step taken by Standard Oil to cope with the new flood there is no dispute. The United Pipe Lines, the Standard subsidiary, built pipelines in a thousand directions to tap the new wells. Storage tanks were hurriedly built for the new supply. As Ida Tarbell wrote, it was "one of the greatest construction feats the country has ever seen. . . . It was a wonderful illustration of the surpassing intelligence, energy and courage with which the Standard Oil attacks its problems." But as to what ensued, there is a considerable difference of opinion.

As a common carrier, United Pipe Lines acknowledged that it was under an obligation to take all oil offered for storage or pipage. When the tanks at a well were full, the wellowner would request that it be run into the pipeline. He would then receive a certificate for his credit balance that was negotiable and could be sold to someone else, who would then order the pipeline to transfer the oil to him.

Standard Oil warned in December 1877 that the phenomenal outpouring of oil was taxing its pipelines, and pleaded that the drilling be stopped. But the supply continued to mount, and in early January the blow struck. The pipelines under Standard control announced they would take no more than one-quarter of the oil to be run off from the wells for storage—the rest would have to be sold immediately under what was called the "immediate shipment" policy. In other words, producers would have to take whatever price they could get. There was only one large buyer of oil, Standard Oil again, wearing the garb of J. A. Bostwick and Company, and Bostwick would buy only at a discount from the current price of from $0.02 to $0.25 a barrel. Producers saw in this a shameless squeeze play, what in later years would be termed "chiseling." To pile humiliation upon humiliation, producers had to stand for hours in front of United Pipe Lines offices and would have to return in five days to be told whether their offer for sale of oil was accepted. Later, in place of oral negotiation, a policy of sealed bids was inaugurated so that oil producers were put in the position of bidding against one another, in the most effective method of "bearing" the market. Since Standard held the whiphand, the Regions had to endure this galling procedure or starve. As one producer was heard to say, "Working for a principle is all right but it don't feed the babies."

The "immediate shipment" policy was rescinded in April but was renewed again in July. Indignation swept the oil fields. The Standard was using the storage shortage as an excuse for getting oil cheaper. Was not crude cheap enough? Between February and September 1878 the price per barrel slumped from $1.87 to $0.78. Why must further discounts be squeezed from producers? But the producers were helpless. It was impossible for many to stop the wells for fear of damage by saltwater; unable to store, they had no choice but to pump oil onto the ground, which many did.

The situation became further aggravated during the summer months. Many wellowners had storage tanks which they had leased to United and for which they paid no storage charge on their own oil stored there. Now, on the grounds that the pipelines were full, United refused to run the oil from the wells into their own tankage, although the oil stored there had been sold. Excitement was raised to a fever pitch in June 1878 when the rails said that there was a shortage of tank cars. Independent shippers found it impossible to ship oil and therefore impossible to buy. B. E. Campbell, president of the Producers' Association, told rail officials that "the idea of a scarcity of cars on shipments of less than 30,000 barrels a day was such an absurd bare-faced pretence that he could not expect men of ordinary intelligence to accept it." Two days later, Campbell testified that the express train on which he was riding was delayed for over half an hour in passing through hundreds of empty oil cars. He thought that these cars were bound to pick up "immediate shipment" oil. Independent shippers told of their inability to get cars. H. G. Ohlen got an order for one hundred cars from the Erie Railroad but Daniel O'Day of United Pipe Lines refused to load them.

When Ohlen protested that he had an order from the railroad, O'Day answered, "That makes no difference. I cannot load cars except on an order from Pratt [Charles Pratt of Standard]."

There was genuine danger that rioting would grow out of the increasing resentment and frustration. As Ida Tarbell wrote: "Crowds gathered about the offices of the Standard threatening and jeering. Mysterious things, cross-bones and death-heads were found plentifully sprinkled on the buildings owned by Standard. More than once the slumber of the oil towns was disturbed by marching bodies of men. It was certain that a species of Ku Klux had hold of the Bradford regions and that a very little spark was needed to touch off the United Pipe Lines."

In retrospect it appears that there were equities to be weighed on both sides to the controversy. In its role as the owner of the pipelines and the monopoly buyer, Standard Oil had a stranglehold on the Regions and it seems that it squeezed harder than necessary. On the other hand, Ida Tarbell admits that the lack of tankage was an undoubted fact in the Bradford area—of the 4,000,000-barrel tankage in the Regions there was only 200,000 there in December 1877. Rockefeller built tankage there frantically but at great expense. He himself admitted to Inglis that the discount on "immediate shipment" oil was used to pay off the heavy investment he made in construction of pipes and tanks there. Rockefeller seems to have justified himself self-righteously by likening the discount to a penalty that the producers had to pay for their improvidence in producing the glut. In view of the high profits that Standard was continuing to make in a year when many producers went broke, this profit could have been foregone. Then, too, the producers could not understand why the "immediate shipment" policy was imposed in the lower Regions where there was no glut and tankage was adequate. On the other hand it is hard to muster sympathy for producers who made no move to help themselves. A meeting of producers in June 1878 pushed through this resolution: "Resolved the shortest way to $2.00 oil is through $.25 oil. Resolved, that we favor pushing the drill as rapidly and diligently as possible until the goal of $.25 oil is reached." This was idiocy.

Rockefeller can be indicted, too, for blocking the wheels of progress by using his power to prevent pipelines to distant points from being built which would have alleviated the hardships of the Regions. The Standard Oil influence was instrumental in defeating the free-pipeline bill in the Pennsylvania legislature. Then, too, he used his hold on the rails to block Lewis Emery's pipeline to Buffalo. Thus in March 1878 Rockefeller wrote to Daniel O'Day: "There are two ways to prevent the pipe going over the right-of-way of the Buffalo & Jamestown Road, the one in giving them some refined business and the other in bidding higher prices for such right-of-way than the other parties but I leave this to you. Don't let them get a pipeline to Buffalo." To President Jewett of the Erie he wrote, "It occurred to me you might desire to exert an influence with the Jamestown and Buffalo Road against the carrying out of this agreement." Emery did manage to reach Buffalo by pipeline in August, but again the roads responded to Rockefeller's edict that they protect him against competition, and they cut the rate from the Bradford fields to New York so drastically that in the winter, when the Erie Canal was closed, Emery became discouraged and sold out.

It was only hope of intervention by the courts and by the State of Pennsylvania that averted violence on the oil fields. The producers asked that the state institute proceedings to obtain a writ of quo warranto compelling United Pipe Lines to do its duty as a common carrier. When Governor John Hartranft listened in person to the grievances of the producers, he gasped in astonishment at the power of Standard Oil, "How has all this been produced?"

Because the proceedings on the writ got bogged down in delays, the governor directed the secretary of internal affairs to hear the charges. The verdict of William McCandless on October 14 was: "The charges of the oil producers have not been substantiated in any way that demands action." The Regions went wild with rage. "Buck" McCandless was hanged in effigy in Bradford, Parker's Landing, and Tarpot. In Bradford there was a check hanging from the pocket of the effigy signed by John D. Rockefeller for $20,000 and endorsed by the Pennsylvania Railroad.

Progress was made in other directions as the mills of the law ground ahead slowly. Bills in equity were filed by the Attorney general asking for an injunction against the railroads to compel them to fulfill their duties as common carriers, and cease discriminations. The star witness was A. J. Cassatt, vice-president of the

Pennsylvania, who gave full testimony on the Empire struggle and the drawbacks paid to Standard after it was over. The Ohio legislature began an investigation that, though short-lived, heard much testimony from Flagler about rebates. The Hepburn Committee hearings took place in 1879, an investigation conducted by a committee of the New York State Assembly. Although testimony from oil producers and refiners who had been injured by Standard was abundant, and there was some from railroad men like William Vanderbilt, there was little that could be gleaned from Standard Oil representatives when they took the stand. In its report the committee branded Standard as "a mysterious organization whose business and transactions are of such a character that its members decline giving a history or description of it lest this testimony be used to convict them of crime."

Thus John D. Archbold denied that he had anything to do with the administration of Standard Oil or knew of its transportation policies. Later he admitted that he was a stockholder as well as a director of Standard Oil. The committee counsel, Simon Sterne, asked, "Well, Mr. Archbold what function do you play in the Standard Oil now as director?" Archbold replied, "I am a clamorer for dividends." Sterne persisted, "What dividends do they pay?" To that Archbold replied flippantly, "I never have difficulty in carrying mine off." As for railroad rates, Archbold's memory failed him as to rates paid six months before. In his *Reminiscences* Rockefeller dwells with delight on this exchange, reflecting Rockefeller's feelings about prying legislative inquiries.

Because the confidence of the producers rose with the response they were getting from governmental agencies, with misgivings from many producers, they pressed ahead on another front. A grand jury in Clarion County indicted Rockefeller and eight other Standard officers for criminal conspiracy on various counts, such as conspiracy to obtain a monopoly and extort unreasonable commissions and rebates. While some Standard officials were arrested and gave bail, Rockefeller, his brother William, and Flagler defied the process and fought extradition. Their claim was that extradition was possible only if they were in Pennsylvania at the time the crime was committed and had fled into another state.

The strategy of Standard Oil was to get the suits for injunctive relief postponed indefinitely on the ground that any testimony given in that suit could be used against the defendants in the criminal suit. As producers had feared, the criminal indictment would stymie indefinitely the stronger civil suits. The plan, too, was that in either criminal or civil suits the Standard officers would thumb their noses at the court and say they knew nothing. Thus Flagler wrote to Rockefeller about testimony that Vandergrift might have to give: "We can, of course, emphatically deny any connection between United Pipe Lines and the Standard Oil Company. As to discrimination in rates made by the United Pipe Lines he knows there never have been any. If it is a question of railroad freights and discriminations in them, my judgment is he knows nothing or of knowing will not be compelled to answer." These are instructions for committing perjury.

Standard officials had been in conference with the new governor, Henry Hoyt, and there had been pressure from Tom Scott and other railroad men. (Scott and Cassatt had escaped indictment because, according to the Producers' Union, "they professed the greatest desire to get rid of Standard domination and were loudly asserting that they had been victimized and compelled at times to carry oil freights at less than cost.") It was therefore no surprise that after many excuses for delay, Governor Hoyt declined to take action on obtaining the extradition of Rockefeller and his associates from New York. In January 1881, in a message to the legislature, he explained why he had not acted: ". . . requests were presented in the interests of the petitioners [Producers' Union] to the Governor not to issue the requisition followed again by requests that they go out. Finding that the highest process of the Commonwealth was being used simply as leverage for and against the parties to these negotiations . . . and they were being regarded as a mere make-weight in the stages of private diplomacy," he had declined to act.

A very strange justification indeed for a governor of a state to disregard the indictment presented in a court of his own state, even if the facts were true. However, the producers emphatically denied the charge that they had ever wavered about their desire to bring Rockefeller to justice.

Now general discouragement spread among the producers, a feeling that Rockefeller was invincible—he had bribed the Pennsylvania legislature to defeat the free-pipeline bill; he had bribed

"Buck" McCandless; and now he had bribed Governor Hoyt. With his fine sense of timing, Rockefeller now came forward holding the dove of peace. He made an offer to buy a large quantity of crude at a price far above the prevailing $1.00 a barrel. But the producers remembered how Rockefeller had left them high and dry with a contract of that kind in 1872, and, looking for the cloven foot, they refused to negotiate. Then came a thaw. President Campbell of the Producers' Union was ready to listen to Rockefeller's offers "as a first rate gauge to test how badly they are scared." When the price of crude dropped to $0.70 a barrel in 1879, and the conspiracy suit was delayed and delayed, a peace party came openly to the fore.

In January 1880 a peace conference was held in the Fifth Avenue Hotel in New York. The terms that were agreed upon were that Standard Oil would not object to the entire abrogation of rebates, drawbacks, and secret rates, and the Pennsylvania said that all rates were to be open on demand. None the less rebates were not explicitly abandoned—the rails were only "at liberty" to give equally favorable rates to others who shipped "like quantities." There were real concessions—United Pipe Lines would take and store all oil up to 65,000 barrels a day, and there would be no discount on "immediate shipment" oil. There would be no discrimination in distribution of tank cars.

There was keen disappointment among the producers that discriminations in freight rates, which were considered the backbone of Standard's power, could still continue. In the meeting of the Grand Council of the Union that ratified the pact, Campbell sat throughout with tears streaming down his face. But the council was now attended by only forty members as compared to two hundred in November 1878. Producers interested in quick results had lost interest. Most important, there was no money to continue the litigation. As a part of the peace, Rockefeller had paid the union $40,000 for legal expenses. One whom Miss Tarbell called "a very frank and intelligent producer" branded the oil producers a "damned cowardly, disorganized mob." In a letter to President Campbell, he further said:

All this high-flown talk is buncombe of the worst kind. The producers are willing to meet in a mass meeting held out of doors where it costs nothing for rent of a hall and pass any kind of a resolution that is offered. It costs nothing to do this, but when asked to contribute a dollar to the prosecution of these plunderers, robbers and fugitives from justice, they either positively refuse . . . say that the Council is doing nothing, that the suits are interminable, that there is no justice to be obtained in the courts of Pennsylvania, etc., etc. or else plead poverty and say they have contributed all they are able to.

This aspersion and others regarding the producers were printed by Ida Tarbell, and she implicitly recognized the truth of them. Emotionally rather than rationally she was bound to their cause. Her girlhood was spent in the Regions at the time when the events related in this chapter took place, and at that time hatred for Standard Oil reached a high pitch of intensity. People in the Regions spat after Standard Oil representatives, and mothers used the image of Rockefeller to keep children in line much as British mothers used Napoleon at the beginning of the century: "Rockefeller will get you if you don't behave." It was this venom, which she imbibed in her youth, that molded the bias of her classic attack on Standard Oil during her mature years.

CHAPTER 11   *The Struggle with the Tidewater Pipe Co.*

I T WAS THE BOAST of Standard Oil in later years that its monopoly had not only brought about economies possible only with large-scale production but that monopoly had also enabled the company to introduce the latest innovations and technological improvements, thus bringing about cheapness and wider uses for oil. There was certainly substance to this boast. Yet, as to one of the most revolutionary developments, the pipeline for transporting oil long distances, Rockefeller stood in the doorway as long as he could. The reason was due to circumstances of the moment.

The long-distance pipeline was undertaken just a year after he had subdued the rails, when he enjoyed without challenge all kinds of preferential arrangements. If pipelines now supplanted the rails for carrying oil, and were operated by others, his laboriously built-up advantages might be erased.

His resistance was therefore stiff. The trio of Byron Benson, Robert Hopkins, and David McKelvy had abandoned the plan to reach Baltimore from the oil fields on the ground that it was too long a span for the still-untried long-distance pipeline, and a shorter route was settled upon, from Corryville to Williamsport, Pennsylvania, where a connection would be made with the Reading Railroad, which would carry the oil to the seaboard. The Tidewater Pipe Company was organized, with a capital of $625,000, of which Franklin Gowen, president of the Reading Railroad, persuaded his line to buy $250,000; the right of way that Lewis Emery, Jr., had bought for the abandoned Equitable route to Buffalo was purchased; the Reading, eager for oil traffic of which it had practically none, gave an order to the Reading Iron Works for two hundred tank cars.

Propaganda appeared in farmers' newspapers, undoubtedly stemming from Standard Oil, that a farmer who leased his land for the pipeline would find that oil leakage had ruined his fields and buildings. Stories were spread that the chief engineer, General Herman Haupt, was a visionary who once built a bridge that collapsed and had made other bad blunders. Standard tried to buy up a continuous band of land across the state from north to south to block off Tidewater. The play did not succeed, since General Haupt did some broken-field running that would have done credit to an all-American. Feinting to one direction by making surveys, he would be buying quietly in the opposite one, and Standard agents were thrown off balance by sudden flanking movements. At one time the blockade seemed complete, but by exhaustive search of titles it was found that there was a sixteen-foot-wide strip on the bed of a stream between two farms; the strip was purchased from the state, and the pipeline traversed the strip. Rockefeller tried to prevent tank cars from being built for his opponent to carry oil by rail from Williamsport. On March 7, 1879, Vandergrift, replying to his telegram, wrote, "I will see them [Riter and Conley] at as early a date as possible and try to keep them from building tanks for Tidewater."

During the early months of 1879, the pipeline was being extended farther—6-inch pipe, in sections of 18 feet. Rockefeller remained skeptical of its practicability. On May 13 he wrote to Camden, "Rather doubt they will pump oil by the 25th inst. as has been published . . . am not a little skeptical about their doing it. They are quite likely to have some disappointments yet, before consummating all their plans in that direction." His lieutenants had been more realistic than he of the inevitability of the new development. A year before, William Warden had written him after a conference with Tom Scott, "I think the Col. quite agrees with me that it would have been far better for the S. O. Co. to have built the Line than to have others do it." And months before, around Christmas of 1877, William Frew had written him that whether or not Tidewater obtained its capital, "it is quite probable a seaboard pipeline will be built before a great while."

On May 28 a great crowd assembled at Corryville. The pump, a new type of 80 horsepower, started, and the oil chugged audibly through the pipe, pushing it, at a rate of 250 barrels an hour, to a point 28 miles away and 700 feet higher. The oil traveled as fast as a man could walk. At Olmsted a second pumping station lifted the oil 1,800 feet higher. From the peak elevation it descended the rest of the way to Williamsport by gravity, reaching there seven days later. It was a success. A new era in the oil industry had come to pass. One more step had to be taken to make the pipe feasible. During the summer the heat so expanded the pipe laid aboveground that it curled up, uprooting trees and telegraph poles. The next step was to bury the line beneath the earth, where pipelines have remained since.

Like the superb field general he was, Rockefeller would deploy not one but several columns against the enemy. The first and most massive assault was for the rails to respond as usual to Rockefeller's demand that they cut rates to protect him against competition, as they did when he was under assault by Empire. It was estimated by General Haupt that the cost of piping to Williamsport and then by Reading Railroad to the East was $0.30 a barrel compared to $0.80 charged to Standard by rail and the charge of at least $1.35 to its competitors. The rails cut their rates bone-deep to $0.20 and then to $0.15 a barrel, and Standard reduced the charge of its pipelines for pipage down to $0.05.

Flagler, testifying in 1888, claimed that he was against the rails committing hara-kiri, telling them at Saratoga in June 1879: "We can make a satisfactory arrangement with the Tidewater and avoid this contest. It is not necessary for you to throw away any money." He said President Jewett of Erie replied, "But look at our investment." Flagler said that Standard went along with the slashing of rates, "like fools." That was Flagler's version.

Standard Oil profited by the lower rates, while, as in the Empire struggle, the rails suffered grievously. (It should be borne in mind that the reductions applied only to crude. Refined was not yet carried through the pipeline.) The rate slashes proved futile. Tidewater was a small company with a small capitalization, and its losses could be replenished by those who were convinced that Tidewater was riding the wave of the future. For Standard Oil it was like a giant exhausting itself by trying to swat a fly.

A second line of attack was for Standard to build its own trunk pipelines. Under the management of Daniel O'Day, pipelines were built from the Regions to refineries in Cleveland, Pittsburgh, and Philadelphia, accompanied by a good deal of reassurance to the rails that Standard was not abandoning them as carriers. It also built a pipeline to Bayonne, New Jersey, intending to link it with its refineries at Communipaw and Constable Hook, but ran into difficulty there. The Central Railroad of New Jersey, determined not to lose this traffic, had the mayor of Bayonne in its pocket. He vetoed the franchise to Standard voted by the Common Council. In September 1880 a mayor was in office who was in Standard's pocket. The Jersey Central was prepared to go to court to get an injunction if permission were granted. On September 22 a night session was held of Bayonne's mayor and council, and Standard was voted a right of way. Word was flashed to the Standard yards; the gates swung open, and a work crew of 300 got into action, an army that had been carefully instructed. Under the light of lamps, while the city slept, the line was laid, streets were repaired, and when the morning came the oil was flowing. It was too late for the Jersey Central to do anything about it.

A third assault by Rockefeller was to stop up the demand at the other end of the pipeline by buying up all independent refiners who might be in the market for the crude carried by Tidewater. The offensive to wipe out the independents was pursued more

Right, John Archbold, whose published letters damaged the reputation of the Standard Oil Company; *bottom right,* Frederick Gates played a leading rôle in Rockefeller's life; *below,* Henry Demarest Lloyd, the author of *Wealth Against Commonwealth,* a bitter attack on the Standard Oil Monopoly

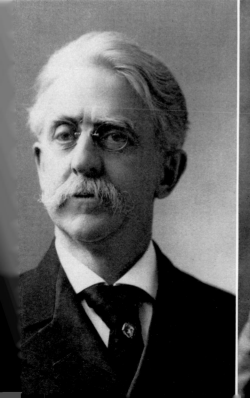

Rockefeller in 1904, shortly after a nervous disease

aggressively than ever after April 1879. Tidewater, in self-defense, built its own refinery at Chester, Pennsylvania. An independent, the new Solar Works at Williamsport, used 1,000 barrels a day of crude. The ingenious J. N. Camden sent an agent to buy 250 barrels a day of refined from Solar. Dealers left stranded switched to Camden's refineries, and when they were securely bound by contract, Camden's agent stopped his purchases and left Solar in the lurch. Solar sold out to Standard in 1880.

There were innumerable ways in which the giant Standard could torment its weak, younger rival. Rockefeller wanted tank cars withheld from Tidewater. Thus he prodded Payne in December 1880, "We do not want cars left around loose." Tidewater, of course, relied on the rails to transport its refined to dealers, and the rails made life difficult. To carry refined to Washington, the Pennsylvania Railroad charged Tidewater a rate that was higher than it charged Standard for carrying oil from Pittsburgh to Washington, though the latter distance was three times as great. The Pennsylvania quoted a rate from Chester to Lock Haven, but wrote that "we cannot make a rate on the empty cars returning," which prompted President Gowen of the Reading to remark, "They must be taken by wheelbarrow, or by canal or by balloon." Another tack of Standard was to preempt as much crude as possible by outbidding Tidewater at the wells close to the beginning of the pipeline. Rockefeller wrote to Archbold, "I think it is the cheapest way for us to compete with Tidewater." Rockefeller characteristically assumed a loftiness of motive, as displayed in a letter to Payne relating to his struggle with Tidewater: "We are not able to see the end yet but will persevere and keep going with a view of securing the rights of free American citizens, etc., etc."

The nimble Tidewater none the less continued to grow, and soon began to extend its pipeline from Williamsport to the East. However, the volume of oil it was handling was no more than 3,000 barrels a day as against the 6,000-barrel capacity of the line, and it was feeling the pressure. On March 10, 1880, Daniel O'Day revealed to Rockefeller that by accident he had encountered President Benson of Tidewater, who said to him, "I want to let the bars down for any overtures your company may want to make looking to an adjustment of the question." Also making clear that he was against any cutthroat competition, Benson said, "The

Tidewater stands ready at any time to reach an agreement on advancing rates." He thus pledged by implication that the new pipeline would not be used as a club to beat Standard over the head. From this time on, the parties got closer together in secret negotiations.

There were then extensive efforts by Standard to undermine the company by internal subversion. The Tidewater Company sold a $2,000,000 issue of bonds to the First National Bank of New York, headed by George F. Baker, and immediately the bank was besieged by warnings that the company was insolvent. That information may not have been far from the truth, since Miss Tarbell, while implying that this was all a black Rockefeller tactic, says the company survived by "borrowing money, speculating in oil, exchanging credit, chasing checks from bank to bank, 'hustling' in short, as few men ever did to keep a business alive." Franklin Gowen went to Europe to market the securities; no sooner had he arrived than warnings were cabled all over that he had to sell the securities abroad because everyone in the United States knew the company was on the rocks. The stocks and bonds were ultimately disposed of, but the terms were so harsh that the financing weakened the company more than it helped it.

A character now enters the picture whom it is worth while examining, since he typifies the process by which so many of Standard Oil's enemies became its friends and pawns. It shows, too, how the lure of lucre was instrumental in bringing them into camp.

E. G. Patterson had been among the most fanatical enemies of Rockefeller. He had been a leader in the revolt against the South Improvement Plan, and in 1877 he was again a leader of the oil producers. He was effective in getting the State of Pennsylvania to act against Standard Oil, and was a prominent witness before the Hepburn Committee.

In February 1878 a new auditor-general of Pennsylvania, William P. Schell, wrote to Standard Oil in Ohio, asking for a statement of its capital stock so that Standard might be taxed as a business doing business in the State of Pennsylvania. This sent tremors of fear through Flagler, who after many evasions finally replied that the company only bought oil but did not do business in the state. Thereupon the auditor, on the basis of what informa-

tion he could scrape together, levied a tax amounting to
$3,145,000 for the past ten years, and the state brought suit to
collect.

Patterson now stepped into the case as an expert on Standard
Oil, giving his help to the attorney general prosecuting the suit.
Standard shelved its policy of silence, and William Rockefeller
offered to disclose all the facts the state wanted to know, and the
case could come to trial with an agreement on the facts. Over
Patterson's objections this voluntary disclosure was made, the attorney general cut down the amount requested to $796,650, and
the court levied the tax on so much of the capital stock as represented by property in Pennsylvania, awarding only $22,600. Pat-
terson pleaded with the attorney general to ask for a new trial
and elicit the real facts under examination instead of accepting
Standard's facts, but was turned down.

After the case had come up for trial, Patterson sent word to
Standard, through an intermediary, that he would not be bound
by the agreement as to the facts and that "I propose to attack."
John Archbold then asked the intermediary why Patterson was so
antagonistic, and "whether it would not be possible for us, if he
was needing business, to find some position in which he could
legitimately find a living." After the court decision Patterson was
downcast, particularly since his compensation was to be geared to
the amount recovered. Archbold then paid Patterson off. He gave
him $7,500, in cash, with another $7,500 to follow. This, and a
salary of $5,000 for services for a year, would be contingent on
good behavior.

The Pennsylvania legislature investigated this payment. Archbold testified that the payment had nothing to do with suppress-
ing evidence relating to the tax suits, but merely to have "him
desist from further malicious attacks upon our company." Archbold explained how simple it all was: "He came to my room at
the Continental; I told him that so bright and smart a man as he
ought to be in a better business than attacking corporations
merely because they were successful. Patterson said if we would
reimburse him for money he had expended in the litigations and
for his trouble he would feel it right to cease his attacks."

And now the pitiful Patterson, in tow to Standard, holding fifty
shares of Tidewater worth $5,000, came into court saying that

Tidewater was insolvent and asking that a receiver be appointed. But a judge refused to grant the petition, branding the petition as a "nefarious plot."

Next move. There was a minority group headed by H. L. Taylor and John Satterfield. It appears that Taylor's Union Oil Company had been sold to Standard in 1882 and that he was a heavy stockholder in Standard. It had been published that the regular stockholders' meeting of Tidewater in January 1883 would be postponed to February. On the formal date, when management planned to adjourn the meeting quickly, Taylor and Satterfield appeared. Holding the majority of stock present, they voted themselves into office, throwing out the proxies of the management group. McKelvy barricaded himself in his office to prevent Satterfield from taking over as the new president. The newly elected group went to court, but the same Judge Pierson Church, who had decided against Patterson, now termed the election of the insurgents "farcical, fraudulent and void."

Tidewater lost a good deal of public sympathy when credence was put in an affidavit by Archbold that Tidewater officers, far from waging uncompromising war, had been proposing for some time an entente based on a division of business and fixing of rates. The truth is that Tidewater management had been playing ball with Standard. It had obtained a loan from Standard in the summer of 1881 in return for a block of voting stock. Tidewater stockholders had not an iota of knowledge of this amazing transaction. The camel had its head and forelegs already under the tent.

In October 1883 a final settlement was made. It was a boon to the badly exhausted Tidewater and a victory for Standard that subjugated its rival to a minor role—Tidewater's pipelines would carry only 11.5 percent of the crude to the East, while Standard would take the rest. If other pipelines had been laid close on the heels of the Tidewater, the Standard empire might have crumbled; but Rockefeller had rushed into the breach, building trunk pipelines of his own, absorbing all the stray oil-field pipelines into the gigantic National Transit Company of April 1881, a $30,000,000 company. The United Pipe Lines and American Transfer system belonging to Standard were absorbed into this company.

Thus Tidewater became a satellite, no longer a foe. The pipeline rates were to be uniform with the rail rates. It would cost $0.40 to carry a barrel to Philadelphia and $0.45 to New York. Pipage rates for pipelines in the oil fields were $0.20 a barrel no matter the distance.

The rails were guaranteed 26 percent of the traffic whether they carried the oil or not. Thus the rails that started out by giving rebates to Rockefeller would now receive rebates from him. For the traffic in the 26 percent share they did not actually carry, the pipelines would pay them $0.08 a barrel.

Since the cost of piping oil through his own pipes to the East Coast was only $0.06, it was immaterial to Rockefeller if competitors paid $0.40 to ship by rail or by Tidewater. The Standard refineries paid $0.16 to the National Transit Company, which was, of course, only a bookkeeping charge.

Thus, with the advent of the pipeline, the monopoly continued to enjoy an advantage in transportation charges, and enjoyed even greater ascendancy over the rails.

CHAPTER 12 *The Trust Triumphant*

THE WORD "TRUST" in English means confidence or belief. It is derived from the word "true," and "troth" is another derivative. In the Danish and Swedish *tröst* means comfort or consolation. In the English common law a trust describes the relationship that exists when property is confided to one for the benefit of another, such as a guardian holding property for a minor until he comes of age. These are meanings of "trust." Yet in the 1880's, by a peculiar evolution, the word came to mean an industrial combination, such as the oil trust or the whiskey trust, and Congress passed what were named Antitrust laws. Let us see how this came about.

The organization of the various units in the far-flung empire of

Standard Oil presented a problem that continually perplexed Rockefeller and his associates. The laws of the time did not contemplate interstate empires or indeed any empires at all. A corporation in Ohio, as in other states, could not hold stock of another company, except by special enactment of the legislature (occasionally passed for the benefit of railroads). Standard Oil was engaged in buying refineries in different states and building national pipelines. An overriding priority problem in the late seventies was to find some legal way to expand the business and to maintain unitary central control.

The first legal device adopted was to have the business taken over engage in business for the account of Standard Oil. This was done in the case of Bostwick and Company. The next step adopted, in the case of the Long Island Oil Company, was to transfer its securities to one person as trustee, in this case to Henry Flagler. Devoe Manufacturing Company and the Vandergrift and Forman Pipelines by this device came under Standard domination. However, this piecemeal solution was unsatisfactory. How effective could the control of the trustee over the manager of the plant be? Could different individual trustees be effectively coordinated? If Rockefeller died, could the trustee be readily dislodged from control of the property?

Out of this legal fiction, came the all-embracing trust. The authorship of the trust instrument is credited to Samuel C. T. Dodd, the lawyer in the Regions whom we have encountered before. He had represented Vandergrift interests for some time until he learned to his astonishment that Vandergrift was an appanage of Standard Oil—a reflection of the unusual secrecy surrounding the operations of Standard Oil. He had been losing his voice, and, fearing for his courtroom practice, was amenable to an offer from Rockefeller to join him as legal counsel, one of the first prominent lawyers in America to enter the service of one client exclusively. Accepting the offer, Dodd remarked, "Well, as the ministers say as they get a call to a higher salary, it seems to be the Lord's will." But the earnest Dodd was concerned about preserving his independence of mind in order to give the most disinterested counsel, and therefore refused a salary higher than $25,000 a year and an offer of stock that would have made him rich.

In April 1879 the first trust agreement was executed. The former individual trustees for companies that had been taken over, the thirty-seven existing stockholders, and the Standard Oil Company of Ohio conveyed all the stock of the subsidiaries to three "dummy" trustees, Myron Keith, George Chester, and George Vilas, who were to manage the stock for the benefit of the stockholders. The legal theory was that the subsidiaries no longer belonged to Standard Oil of Ohio but to the trustees. On the basis of this thin legal fiction, Rockefeller swore in the Scofield case that besides its refineries in Cleveland and Bayonne, Standard Oil "has no other refineries nor any interest in any other refinery."

In 1879 Henry H. Rogers testified before the Hepburn Committee. It was the existence of the trust agreement, with its loose reins, that enabled him to give this amusing if vague description of the relations between different members of the Standard kingdom:

Q. You said that substantially 95 percent of the refineries were in the Standard arrangement.

A. I said 90 to 95 percent I thought were in harmony.

Q. When you speak of their being in harmony with the Standard, what do you mean by that?

A. I mean just what harmony implies.

Q. Do you mean that they have an arrangement with the Standard?

A. If I am in harmony with my wife, I presume I am at peace with her and am working with her.

Q. You are married to her and have a contract with her?

A. Yes, sir.

Q. Is that what you mean?

A. Well, some people live in harmony without being married.

Q. Without having a contract?

A. Yes, I have heard so.

Q. Now, which do you mean? Do you mean the people who are in the Standard arrangement and are in harmony with it, are married to the Standard or in a state of freedom—celibacy.

A. Not necessarily, as long as they are happy.

Q. Is it the harmony that arises from a marriage contract?

A. Not necessarily so long as they are happy.

Q. When you speak of their harmony is it a relation of contract?

A. I mean by harmony that if you and I agree to go to Wall Street and buy a hundred shares of Erie at 33 and we agree to sell it at 40, that is harmony.

Henry Huttleston Rogers, testifying here, was one of the most colorful characters in the Standard Oil hierarchy. In the latter years of the trust, by virtue of his talents he would rank next to Archbold, third in command in the company, and become a leader in the world of finance. After an impoverished boyhood in Fairhaven, Massachusetts, he entered refining as a technician, inventing an improved still that was widely adopted; and he found methods for separating naphtha fractions from kerosene. He entered Standard Oil together with Charles Pratt and Company in 1876. He was magnetic and commanding in personality, polished, histrionic, and a great raconteur. Generous to a fault, he pensioned off old oilmen out of his own funds, built a monument to "Colonel" Drake in Titusville, and paid for Helen Keller's education. He was a great admirer of Mark Twain, and when the author was in financial straits he befriended Twain, let him go into bankruptcy but attended creditors' meetings with him, and by unremitting counsel nursed his financial condition back to solvency. But when it came to business, Rogers was quite another person, "Hell-Hound Rogers." As Thomas Lawson, the author of *Frenzied Finance*, said in that book: "He is considerate, kindly, generous, helpful and everything a man should be to his friends. But when he goes aboard his private brig and hoists the Jolly Roger, God help you. He is a relentless, ravenous creature, as pitiless as a shark."

The 1879 trust agreement was unsatisfactory. The trustees managed the stock but could not manage the companies. There was a need for welding together the units, including Standard Oil of Ohio, which was not in the trust. When Pennsylvania sought to put a tax on the entire capital stock of a corporation doing business in the state, it was a shocker; and there was the possibility that other states might follow suit. It was imperative that steps be taken to divorce Standard Oil of Ohio from its holdings in other states. After much consideration of the alternatives, particularly a single corporation holding company to be chartered by the New York State legislature, it was recommended by Dodd that the trust instrument be further expanded. In January 1882 the definitive trust instrument was signed, a unique step forward in industrial history.

The three trustees, the now forty-two stockholders, and Standard Oil of Ohio conveyed all the stock to nine trustees, who included Rockefeller and other powers, such as William Rockefeller, Payne, Flagler, and Archbold. The new combination had no name, no charter; it was simply a common-law trust. Each stockholder received in place of each share twenty trust certificates representing slices of the total holdings. The nine trustees were to "exercise general supervision of the several Standard Oil companies and as far as practicable over the other companies and partnerships any portion of whose stock is held in trust." The capitalization of the trust was a modest one, $70,000,000. On the basis of earnings averaging over $10,000,000 a year, it could have been much higher, and in its undercapitalization was to be almost unique among trusts. Rockefeller, with almost a fourth of the shares, had a total wealth in the company of $18,000,000. Within eight years, by 1890, the earnings would be $19,131,000 and the dividends $11,200,000, of which Rockefeller would receive a fourth.

There certainly was no cleavage here between ownership and control such as would characterize the American corporation in the years to come. Rockefeller's exertions on behalf of stockholders besides himself was recognized by the grant of a salary—$12,000 in 1875, which rose to $30,000 by 1900, a bagatelle.

The general outline of the trust agreement became known and was the model of the whiskey trust and the sugar trust, which soon followed. It was not until 1888, when the New York State Senate examined Rockefeller, that the full text was published. The verdict of Ida Tarbell is this:

Thirty-nine corporations, each of them having legal existence, obliged by the laws of the state creating it to limit its operations to certain lines and to make certain reports, had turned over their affairs to an organization having no legal existence, independent of all authority, able to do anything it wanted anywhere; and to this point (viz. 1904) working in absolute darkness. . . . You could argue its existence from its effects but you could never prove it. You could no more grasp it than you could an eel.

The trust as set up in 1882 included 14 companies wholly owned, the largest of which was Standard Oil of Ohio at $3,500,000; next were Charles Pratt and Company and Atlantic Refining at $500,000 and $400,000 respectively. There was 26 companies partly owned, the largest of which was National Transit Company, 85.4 percent owned, with a capitalization of $30,000,000. This mammoth capitalization is consistent with the fact that by 1885 refining took second place to transportation as the source of income for the trust, 36 percent as against 53 percent.

Policies for the vast aggregation of companies were formulated by committees—Rockefeller was probably the first to use the committee system extensively in the corporation. At the apex was the Executive Committee headed by Rockefeller and on which the grand nabobs sat, meeting every day. Below were committees like Transportation and Export Trade; Manufacturing, Case and Can; Lubricating, and so forth. The committees were effective in furnishing unity, cross-fertilization of ideas, and harmonization of conflicting ideas.

Though the various units operated autonomously, they of course did not compete in selling. The old brands that had won popular favor continued to be sold: Devoe's High Screw and Pratt's Astral, Brilliant, Peerless, and Royal Daylight. The units competed with one another as far as efficiency was concerned, one refinery trying to turn out a product cheaper than another. Sometimes the performance of companies was compiled without names, and sometimes the name of the most efficient unit was published and representatives of other plants would visit it for study.

The competition between units might be won by extreme scrimping, and the Cyclopean eye of the Executive Committee inspected every corner for savings. Ida Tarbell wrote that when she visited the largest of the can factories, the Devoe on the East

River in New York, "At the entrance of the place a man was sweeping up carefully the dirt on the floor, and wheeling it away—not to be dumped in the river, however. The dirt was to be sifted for tin filings and solder dust."

The search for economies was carried to seemingly absurd lengths. Rockefeller one day was watching refined oil being packed for export. When the can was full enough, solder was dropped to fasten and seal the lid. Rockefeller asked, "How many drops of solder do you use on each can?" The answer was "Forty." Rockefeller said: "Have you tried thirty-eight? Would you mind having some sealed with thirty-eight and let me know?" It turned out that a good many cans leaked with two drops less of solder. However, none of them leaked with thirty-nine drops. From that time on, there was a saving of one drop of solder per can.

A story widely circulated to illustrate Rockefeller's watchful supervision over trifles happens to be apocryphal, made up by a wag in the oil regions in a spirit of ridicule. None the less it could have happened. Bungs for barrels were as expendable as household pins, but Rockefeller addressed a letter to a refiner about his monthly report: "Last month you reported on hand 1,119 bungs. Ten thousand were sent you at the beginning of this month. You have used 9,527 this month. You report 1,012 on hand. What has happened to the other 580?"

There is another story, this time a true one, and it illustrates the Rockefeller maxim that the company should "pay a profit to no one" unless it could not be helped. In 1882 Rockefeller and his associate Orville Waring were riding in a train on the outskirts of Cleveland when Waring called attention to a large, handsome house on a high hill. Rockefeller said: "Whew! That's an expensive house. It belongs to George Hopper who builds barrels for us. I wonder if Hopper isn't making too much money out of us." Rockefeller analyzed the contracts, and decided that it would be cheaper for Hopper's company to become part of Standard Oil, which was what happened.

The barrel, "the holy blue barrel," as the Standard barrel was irreverently called, was an object of Rockefeller's constant attentions. By 1885 the barrel cost only $1.25, a radical reduction from early cost. He drove to supply all his own supplies and components. Shooks for cases had been purchased, but by 1884 the Oswego Manufacturing Company turned them out for Rockefeller in his own plant. At Bayonne, Rockefeller had his own glue works. Five-gallon tin cans were made at the Devoe Works to carry oil to tropical and Oriental countries, transport by barrels being impractical for hot or distant lands. Machines devised by Herman Miller, known in Standard-land as "the father of the tin can," could turn out 8,000 cans in a day with three men in 1880 and 24,000 in 1893. In Elizabeth and Bergenport, New Jersey, Standard could turn out its own acid, and by the early days of the trust the company was making its own tank cars in Buffalo and its own pumps in Oil City.

In 1911 Charles Woodbury, an old-time employee of Standard, wrote: "Chicane still taints the ways of the Standard, but its main foundation and business structure are of better material. Tricks may build a small business—never a large one." Nowhere was enterprise better displayed than in the wide variety and uses of its products. Before the United States Industrial Commission in 1899, Theodore Westgate, of Pure Oil Company, the first Standard competitor, said: "I believe that the Standard Oil Company is employing the very best brains engaged in the manufacture of oil. They have certainly brought forward a great many inventions in the refining of crude oil. I certainly believe that. A man cannot help but see that they are improving every day."

The multiplication of products was astounding. There were, in the early years of the twentieth century, 174 different kinds of refined distillates used for illuminating oils; there were 29 grades of naphthas; there were 833 kinds of lubricating oils—axle grease, gear grease, cup grease, spindle lubricants, cylinder oils, valve lubricants, oils for looms, dynamo engines, and so forth. Different grades of gasoline, naphtha, and benzine were made for use in vapor and sponge lamps on streets and in homes, for removal of fat from wool, for purifying paraffin wax, for extracting oil from seed, for manufacturing varnishes, lacquers, oilcloth, and patent leather, for thinning paint and for cleansing. Vaseline, made by Chesebrough, was in every household. Galena-Signal lubricating oils were used on 95 percent of the railroad mileage of the country, sold with a guarantee that the cost would be equal to or below that of any other oil. In 1911 the Bayonne plant made eight types of macadam binder and twenty-one kinds of asphalt. Paraffin, used for candles, matches, and chewing gum, had become indispensable for insulation of wires in electrical installations and telephone wiring because it was an unexcelled nonconductor. Even the residue of distillation had uses. Acid sludge, formerly dumped at sea, went to fertilizer manufacturers for raw material.

Standard launched an intensive campaign to sell American housewives on the merits of the gasoline stove, the first extensive use for gasoline. The early models were dangerous—in 1871 an expert said, "A keg of gunpowder in a building is not as dangerous as one of these stoves"; but refinements were made, and in the 1880's Standard was plastering the country with advertisements for the stoves: "less than a half a cent an hour" and "guaranteed not to smoke, smell or gum the burner." A great market was developed for such stoves in the Midwest areas that lacked a wood supply. When Rockefeller decided to launch a campaign in New England to sell the stoves, he found that the demand for gasoline for internal-combustion engines was preempting the supply of gasoline.

It is almost a trite observation that fortune smiled on Standard Oil in bringing the automobile with its vast demand for gasoline and lubricants almost step by step to fill the gap as the kerosene lamp gave way to the electric bulb. There were only 800 registered autos in 1898. In 1904 there was an automobile race from New York to Paris by way of the Bering Straits, and Standard got big publicity when it set up supply stations for the autos. By 1911 there were 618,000 autos, and in that year, for the first time, sales of gasoline and naphtha exceeded sales of kerosene.

Rockefeller frankly admitted that he did not anticipate the gargantuan development of the automobile industry, but he was not the only poor prophet. The *Literary Digest* in 1900 said, "The ordinary 'horseless' carriage is at present a luxury for the wealthy, and although its price will probably fall in the future, it will never, of course, come into common use as the bicycle."

There was another market on the distant horizon. In 1903, at Kitty Hawk, Standard Oil salesmen brought wooden barrels of gasoline and cans of lubricants for use of the Wright brothers and their new flying-machine.

An equally providential stroke of fortune "to fill the gap" was the successful exploitation of the new Lima field in northwestern Ohio and eastern Indiana. From the beginning of his oil career Rockefeller had been haunted by the specter of the exhaustion of the Pennsylvania fields; and by 1885, as the Bradford field was failing, it became evident that the twilight of the Pennsylvania fields was on hand. There was skepticism about the possibility of new oil deposits in the United States of any magnitude. John Archbold, who sold some of his Standard Oil stock at this time, said to someone who suggested oil in Oklahoma, "Are you crazy, man? I'll drink every gallon of oil produced west of the Mississippi."

Luckily, just at this time the new Lima field was tapped. By 1886 over a million barrels were produced, and in 1890 more than 15 million barrels. Initially this crude presented serious problems. The oil had a sulfur content averaging .65 percent which imparted to it a skunk-like odor, a minor matter beside other difficulties. The yield of deodorized kerosene and naphtha combined was only 57 percent compared to 75 percent plus from Pennsylvania crude; the cost of refining per barrel was ten cents higher, and there was still enough sulfur left to cause smoking and encrustation of wicks.

Rockefeller showed his foresight and courage. He decided to buy large quantities of the Lima crude and store it until some method had been found of clearing it of the sulfur. The price of the Lima crude was fantastically low, dipping to $0.15 a barrel (gushers made profits possible even at that level for producers). Up to this point Rockefeller had stayed clear of production. Archbold had firmly opposed it, saying that it "would make new food for demagogues, politicians, papers and howlers of all descriptions" bellowing the charge that Standard was crushing small producers. Rockefeller overruled him and decided to forge ahead in buying oil properties. By 1891 Standard had invested $8,000,000 in Ohio oil properties and owned 70 percent of the oil tankage in the state.

In this course Rockefeller encountered resistance from Pratt and others who felt that this investment in Lima crude was too hazardous and that there might never be a return. Rockefeller told Inglis in later years that he had carried the day with the

Executive Committee only when he said, "Very well, gentlemen. At my own personal risk I will put up the money to care for this product; two million—three million if necessary."

To find a way to refine the oil, Standard Oil selected another Flying Dutchman, the famous Herman Frasch, a German immigrant, an energetic and even explosive character, who was a genius in industrial chemistry. He had had success in refining Ontario, Canada, crude, which had a high sulfur content. When he joined Standard in 1886 he applied this process to Lima crude—the process consisting of a chemical union of the sulfur with metallic oxide that would form a precipitate that could then be removed.

For two years Frasch had no success, as one experiment after another failed. In the meantime there was nothing to do with the crude but to push its use as industrial fuel. A pipeline was built to Chicago to facilitate its use by the western trade. Though thousands of barrels were given away as samples, it did not catch on. In Russia, railroads and factories were using oil as fuel, but in the United States coal was too cheap.

By 1888, working in the new Solar Refinery in Lima, Frasch reported success. The cost of the "Herman Experiment" had been $200,000, and just before success even the daring Henry Rogers had joined Pratt in believing the venture unwise.

The patents gained by Frasch were to be the foundation of Standard Oil profits for the next seventeen years. Bradstreet's stated that it was "one of the greatest bonanzas ever struck." The price of Lima oil on the strength of the discovery rose from $0.15 to $1.00 a barrel. The oil was refined at the new Whiting Refinery built seventeen miles from Chicago, just across the Indiana boundary. The original plan was to build it close to the terminus of the pipeline in Chicago, but the fumes of the sulfur-laden crude forced a move to the more distant site in a woody country trampled over mostly by duck hunters. There Standard Oil of Indiana built the largest refinery in the world. The town of Whiting sprang up, and it soon had ancillary works: a can factory, cooperage works and acid works. It was so gigantic that even Archbold found it "almost impossible to comprehend." The Whiting Refinery superseded the Cleveland refineries, and the city of Cleveland, which had taken so great a pride in Rockefeller and its refining industry, found itself without both by the end of the century.

> It lights the dwellings, temples, and the mosques amid the ruins of ancient Babylon and Nineveh; it is the light of Bagdad, the City of the Thousand and one nights; of Orpha, birthplace of Abraham, and of Damascus, gem of the Orient. It burns in the grotto of the Nativity at Bethlehem, in the Church of the Holy Sepulchre in Jerusalem; amidst the pyramids of Egypt; on the Acropolis of Athens; on the plains of Troy . . .

Thus wrote the Oil City *Derrick* in 1874 of the "Light of the World." And in the years to come the ships carrying illuminating oil to foreign ports bore heavier cargos. In 1873, 175,000,000 gallons were exported, and in 1888, 367,000,000 gallons. By 1900 that figure had doubled. Standard Oil boasted that its oil was "carried wherever a wheel can roll or a camel's hoof be planted."

In his *Reminiscences* Rockefeller says, "One of our greatest helpers has been the State Department in Washington. Our ambassadors and ministers and consuls have aided to push our way into new markets to the utmost corners of the world." Indeed, consular reports speak of their struggles for the acceptance of Standard Oil as if it were a cause in which the United States had a primary dollars-and-cents interest. Yet there was no malign influence behind this partisanship for a private interest. Standard Oil was a valuable goodwill ambassador, much as Coca-Cola was to be many decades later, and in addition, as Rockefeller points out, it brought a million dollars a week in gold to this country.

The acceptance of our oil was so widespread and our monopoly so complete that early problems were minor. In England there was competition from oil produced from Scottish shale, an industry that had made great strides in efficiency. Their oil also produced a valuable by-product, sulfate of ammonia, helping to reduce the price of the illuminant phase of the business. In China vendors of peanut oil fought against the sale of petroleum; because many Chinese could not afford lamps, Standard Oil distributed small brass or tin lamps with diminutive wicks for next to nothing.

Such little snags pale into insignificance when compared with the problems created by the offensive for markets waged with intensity from 1880 by Russian oil. Russian oil had many natural competitive advantages. In contrast to the dispersion of our fields, the Baku field on the Caspian Sea was compressed into five square kilometers. Because most wells were gushers, the average well was producing 280 barrels a day, while our wells averaged only four to five barrels. Labor costs were half or less than ours. Because of the shortage of coal, there was a big demand for heavy fuel for transport and industry, and the kerosene became almost a by-product that could be dumped abroad.

By 1883 a railroad had been built from Baku to the port of Batum on the Black Sea, and oil could be carried by tanker through the Dardenelles to European ports. The Czar opened the doors to foreigners, and the Swedish brothers Robert and Ludwig Nobel entered the business on a large scale, operating tank cars and tank steamers. The Nobel Brothers Petroleum Company, Ltd., owned the most modern refineries, as well as integrated marketing organizations in Europe. Baron Alphonse de Rothschild became interested, and with Rothschild money, the Caspian and Black Sea Company became the largest exporter of kerosene soon after its organization in 1884. By 1885 there was fierce competition from Russian oil in Europe. Proximity to the markets in southern Europe and the Near East favored the Russians. The Far East was within a month's shipping time from Batum by way of the Suez Canal, while it was a three-and-a-half-month trip by sailing vessel from New York. (Steamers were not used for Far-Eastern shipping because of fear of ignition of the oil.)

There has been a good deal of argument as to the relative merits of American and Russian oil. Professor Nevins has contended that the American oil was of better quality. But Ralph and Muriel Hidy in their study of Standard Oil, *Pioneering in Big Business*, almost an official company tract, say, "There appears to have been little difference in the burning quality of the best kerosene from either country if used in lamps and with wicks designed for that oil. In the early 1880's when lamps and wicks were designed to burn American kerosene, that oil gave a better light and smoked less. The performance of Russian illuminating oil was considerably enhanced by the introduction of special lamps and wicks."

But Standard did not ship abroad its "best" kerosene, but kerosene of inferior quality. In this country only Water White met safety regulations; to foreign countries Standard shipped the cheaper and more dangerous yellowish Standard White. Its inferior quality led to repeated complaints. An international congress of oil dealers in Bremen in 1879 protested against the poor quality of oil, demanding better refining methods. In 1893 Germany was considering a total ban on the importation of cheap Lima crude. The strongest protest centered on the alleged danger of the American oils, the claim being made that they were responsible for explosions and deaths.

The debate on the subject was severe in Britain, where there continued to be a healthy market for Scottish shale oil and where Russian oil jumped from 0 to 30 percent of the market by 1888. The argument raged about the flash-point test. The flash point is the temperature at which oil will give off vapor that when mixed with air is explosive. In 1868 the flash point for safety was fixed at 100 degrees Fahrenheit. The cup in which the test was conducted was defective, and oil that was actually giving off explosive vapor at 73 degrees did not flash in the cup until it reached 100 degrees. Then Sir Frederick Abel invented a proper instrument. But instead of making the flash point 100 degrees it was made "73 degrees Abel," thus perpetuating an error made in the previous test with the defective cup.

The argument was made that the test of "73 degrees Abel" was a minimum safety standard so low that it was responsible for most of the 473 accidents in London in 1895, causing many deaths. It was pointed out that there were about sixty days in London in which the weather temperature went above 73 degrees; the test had legalized oil that might explode in ordinary summer heat. In Glascow, where Scottish oil was sold with a 100-degree flash point, the number of accidents was many times smaller than in London. Why should not the public be protected by setting a test of 100 degrees Abel if the government required a 100-degree test for oil in its barracks and one of 145 degrees in its lighthouses? The subject was the occasion for a full-dress debate in the House of Commons in 1899, and tempers were assuaged only by a government pledge that it would investigate. Nothing came of it. The Russian oil was safer. According to Ralph and Muriel Hidy, "most of the shipments from Baku were of Water White kerosene which met a flash test of 83° on the Abel instrument while the majority of the American kerosene was Standard White of 73° flash test."

Russian competition was the subject of many top-level conferences at the headquarters of the trust at 26 Broadway in New York. One of the methods of meeting the threat was price-cutting. In 1893 the price of export oil was as low as $0.05 2/10 a gallon. The low price at which Rockefeller had acquired Lima crude turned out to be a formidable competitive advantage in the Russo-American oil war. To cut costs, tank steamers were introduced, the first used by Standard being the *Gluckhauf* in 1887, carrying 20,000 barrels in the skin of the ship rather than in tanks. The savings were such that in seven years about three-fourths of the oil was carried in such ships. The *Narragansett*, the largest tanker in the world, carried 77,000 barrels. The next step was to eliminate the profit paid to export houses here, to importing firms abroad, and to all middlemen. The Anglo-American Oil Company, Ltd., the first of many foreign affiliates, was formed in 1888, to be followed in 1890 by the Deutsch-Amerikanische Gesellschaft. By 1895 Standard Oil had 17 manufacturing plants in Europe, innumerable warehouses and storage depots, 200 tank cars and 4,000 tank wagons serving retailers.

Despite the most energetic attempts to drive out its competitors, by 1910 Standard Oil had less than 60 percent of the foreign market. Not only did Standard Oil have to contend with Russian oil; there were also new competitors. The Shell Transport and Trading Company, under the former Lord Mayor of London, Sir Marcus Samuel, originally dealt in Russian oil but later developed the rich oil deposits of Borneo. In Sumatra, Standard Oil was unsuccessful in attempts to buy the Moera Enim Company, which was bought by the Royal Dutch Petroleum Company. Soon exports by Royal Dutch to China and India outstripped those of Standard Oil by a considerable margin.

But as to the overall volume of business done by Standard Oil, Rockefeller could have no complaint. In his *Reminiscences* he said, "None of us ever dreamed of the magnitude of what proved to be the later expansion."

CHAPTER 13 *Rockefeller—A Character Study*

"**M**AD ABOUT MONEY, though sane in everything else." That was the opinion of Rockefeller attributed to Mark Hanna, the Ohio Republican boss so closely associated with the career of William McKinley. Hanna, who had attended high school in Cleveland with Rockefeller and was his lifelong friend, had himself no mean contempt for money, which gives added flavor to the statement.

One wonders how much truth there is in Hanna's verdict as an explanation for Rockefeller's personal drive. How many times in his career could he have rested on his fortune and how many times did he drive ahead to further goals? Certainly he never pursued wealth for what wealth could bring in material satisfactions. He lived simply and unostentatiously, compared to what his vast wealth could bring. As he did not seek domination of his fellowmen, neither did he seek recognition or adulation from them. He was uninterested in fame. Though by 1879 he was one of the nation's richest men, he was so little known that when a leading trade paper, *The Oil, Paint and Drug Reporter* published an editorial in 1879 on Standard Oil it referred to him as "John A. Rockafeller." In 1884, when a Cleveland writer, Sarah Bolton, wanted to include Rockefeller's biography among those of the most notable Americans she was preparing, he declined to give her any help. He was content to let the country remain ignorant of the virtues she had promised to publicize.

To Inglis, Rockefeller gave a conventional explanation for his ambition. How erroneous it is to say that because a man accumulates wealth he is after wealth. He spoke of accomplishment. "That is it—accomplishment. That is the goal of every man who tries to do his part in the world. One builds a ship. It is of a certain size and power and model. He runs it in a certain way and makes money—but knows he will do better with the next one he builds. . . . That's the thing. Accomplishment. Playing the game."

To be sure Rockefeller wanted to point with pride to the edifice he had built, and to leave it as a legacy. Accomplishment, yes. But no student of Rockefeller can be oblivious to his pecuniary drive, his obsession with the daily balance sheet of his wealth that we know was prepared for him during all his working life. Certainly his pride in accomplishment was identified with that dollar figure. This raises the question as to whether his obsession with that figure, the symbol of his wealth, was the real power-drive behind the building of Standard Oil.

Rockefeller once described himself as "a man of figures," and his associates retained vivid recollections of the way his life orbited around figures. His secretary, George Rogers, recounted how Rockefeller delighted in testing him by giving him sums of figures to add up. Others told of his delight when he made a deal to buy Hostetter's pipeline for a million; he prolonged the conversation with Hostetter with trivia while he mentally devised a method of payment that would save him $30,000 in interest charges. Charles Woodbury, an old employee, writing in 1911, told how Rockefeller, still the bookkeeper, liked to visit the bookkeepers' den and inspect their books, having a great facility for detecting errors.

"Figures are as near to his soul as when his chief joy was a successful trade," wrote Woodbury. To substantiate that, he cites an illuminating sidelight from Rockefeller's *Reminiscences*, wherein the magnate dwells on his love of landscaping, and says that his stories of landscaping "will offset the business talks which occupy so much of my story." Yet even here, when we are led to expect a diversion, he cannot get away from his figures, and plunges immediately into a discussion as to how his Pocantico estate makes a bookkeeping profit by growing young trees for a few cents each and selling them to his Lakewood estate for $1.50 to $2.00 each.

There are stories of Rockerfeller in old age that illustrate his fixation on money. He liked to talk to all sorts of people, and on several occasions talked with an old Scandinavian sailor. In taking leave of him, Rockefeller summed him up in one sentence, "He has $75,000." The man's total experience, his philosophy and worth as an individual were reduced to a stark dollar equivalence. At this time, though buried in wealth, he was actively playing the market, and his secretary would run to the links with the latest quotes. He was concerned with the rearing of his grandchildren, but the virtue most to be inculcated is evidenced in this letter to John D., Jr.: "I know that you and Abby will be careful to educate the children in financial matters as we sought to educate you that they may understand the value of money and make the best use of it."

Yet while Rockefeller was a conservationist, who walked through the offices of Standard Oil at night turning down gas jets, he was never a miser. He never suffered from the familiar money disease that afflicted Commodore Cornelius Vanderbilt or Hetty Green, which is celebrated in literature in Ben Jonson's *Volpone* or Molière's *L'Avare*. He lived well, buying first his Forest Hill estate in Cleveland, comprising seventy-nine acres, in 1873, and then in 1884 his West Fifty-fourth Street home in New York for $600,000. He loved fine horses, and collected a small stable of them for his riding pleasure. His family traveled in a private parlor car. But there was no regal splendor, none of the gaudy, conspicuous consumption that his wealth would have warranted. While racing stables were the earliest ostentation of the rich in the eighties and nineties, he never owned a race horse. Unlike others of the *nouveau riche*, he did not have a $500,000 yacht— he had no yacht at all. His New York home did not compare with that of Henry Frick, which cost $15,000,000, or with Charles Schwab's mansion in Riverside Drive, which had seventy-five rooms, forty baths, and a refrigerator that could hold twenty tons of beef. He did not have a bedstead of carved oak and ebony inlaid with gold, at a cost of $200,000, or decorate his walls with enamel and gold at a cost of $200,000. That was left to others of Ward McAllister's magic "400," with whom Rockefeller had no traffic.

Simplicity was the keynote. When Frederick Gates first traveled with Rockefeller, he noted that while his clothes were of the finest materials and workmanship, Rockefeller was inconspicuously dressed and wore no jewelry—no rings, watch chain or guard, not even a stickpin. His method of tipping was simplicity itself—he extended a handful of change to the porter or waiter, and told him to take what he wanted. The windows of his Forest Hill home were uncurtained to admit more sunlight, and the furniture did not match. His four children shared one velocipede "to teach them to give up to another." Rockefeller once wrote to Rockefeller, Jr., about his ideal "to get down more to the Benjamin Franklin idea of living and take our bowl of porridge on a table without any table-cloth."

His expenditures in business were on the thriftiest scale, those for living on a more liberal scale, and for philanthropy on a much more lavish scale. This required a fine compartmentalization in his mind for the different phases of his living. But his habits of thinking in the business compartment were so ingrained that they invaded other compartments. When Rockefeller, Jr., was furnishing the Pocantico estate for his father, and wanted to buy a statue of Aphrodite by Praxiteles, Rockefeller wrote to his son: "The price you propose to offer for it is four times as much as the price at which we supposed we had secured it at the beginning. I am wondering if we could realize this on it." There is something poignant in this picture of Rockefeller, in the evening of his life, so accustomed to seeking a successful trade that he could not comprehend a work of art except in terms of its resale value.

A propos, it was true that Rockefeller had no appreciation of the visual arts, even as he had no appreciation of literature, poetry, music, or any other form of "culture." His idea of good music was "Darling Nelly Gray"; his taste for poetry stopped at doggerel. He shunned the company of intellectuals. He read very few books—one of the few for which he had a long attachment was the work of the humorist Artemus Ward—Rockefeller had known Ward (Charles Farrar Browne) personally before the Civil War, when Browne was a reporter on the *Plain Dealer* in Cleveland. Rockefeller attended no lectures, except in his own church, though lectures were popular in his day; he attended no concerts; he did not attend the theatre until he was past sixty years of age, and then seemed to have enjoyed the sentimental David Belasco play *The Music Master*.

"Narrow" was the word for Rockefeller. Aside from his talent and specialty, the making of money, he had no scope. (Many of us would forego scope for that specialty.) In his long lifetime there were upheavals and revolutions in every phase of life, political, economic, social, and intellectual, but they left his mind unmarked. After he retired from business, the world looked on him as a great sage, and was ready to hang on to every syllable he uttered. However, he had nothing to contribute but advice on golf.

In his deportment he was always exquisitely courteous and gracious. Ida Tarbell told of a man who was thrown in Rockefeller's company for three days who reported that Rockefeller invariably begged his pardon before addressing him. Miss Tarbell said this was a reflection of Rockefeller's humility because of his great crimes. It happened to be a lifetime habit. Associates said of him that he always liked everything "nice"—nice manners, nice clothes, nice talk, nice people. He never gave blunt orders to anyone working for him—it was always "Have you thought of such and such?" "Perhaps this would do," and so on. At legislative hearings, his benignity, even when there was a cutting edge to what he had to say, disarmed the interrogators. Thus, typically, in the 1888 New York Senate hearings, when asked for the minutes of the trust, he said: "It seems to me, Mr. Chairman, there should be left some little thing that you did not exact of us. It would leave a lasting and pleasant impression of the day's experience."

He referred to the oil producers at a legislative hearing as "the dear people," though well aware that they abominated him. Of a reporter who broke a confidence, he said, "I could cry for that young man." Of a writer who made a slanderous remark about him, he said, "He may injure my reputation, but what's worse, he is blighting his character."

In his home life he was reported to have been gay. He sang at the table, and balanced, or tried to balance, crackers and plates on his nose. His children found him a boon companion, whether in badinage or in blind-man's buff or in swimming around the lake with them, a straw hat on his head.

Outside his home and in his business life he was a different person, reserved and austere. As Charles Woodbury described it, Rockefeller's spirit permeated his offices in the Standard Oil building at 26 Broadway, the base of company operations since 1884. Everything was on his model, "exemplary, devout, reticent." Anything unconventional in dress, demeanor, or style of living was frowned upon. An executive with marital trouble was exiled.

John Archbold, a sometime tippler in the 1880's, had to take a
temperance pledge and report to Rockefeller once a month. He
caught the spirit of the institution and would walk through the
halls whistling "Onward Christian Soldiers."

At his desk, Rockefeller worked silently and intensively over
the documents before him. So minutely had he delegated tasks in
his organization that he had a Negro servant beside him to blot
the paper as he proceeded. He was known to work as long as an
hour over a three-line wire, writing and rewriting it. Since he
was sending it over his private wire, this was not for economy
but to satisfy his desire for perfection, Gates wrote, "If genius
was the art of taking pains, then Rockefeller was a genius."

He would not be deflected or hurried from the schedule of
decisions before him. His secretary, George Rogers, told of a man
who left papers with Rockefeller in connection with a deal. Returning three days later he expressed disgruntlement that there
was no decision, saying, "Mr. Rockefeller promised to look over
my papers." When told of this, Rockefeller picked up the papers,
put them under his chin, and said, "Tell the gentleman I have
looked over his papers." That was the end of the deal.

Luncheon at 26 Broadway was an important function. A true
conservationist, he would not allow lunch only for the business of
eating when business of oil could be discussed. The high nabobs
assembled in their frock coats, silk hats, and gloves, taking their
regularly assigned seats. Invitation to lunch was a sign of status.
With typical graciousness, Rockefeller gave the place at the head
of the table to Charles Pratt, his senior. Others at the table might
be Flagler, Payne, Archbold, Rogers, William Rockefeller, William Warden, Jabel Bostwick, Orville Waring, William Frew,
Charles Lockhart, J. J. Vandergrift, Benjamin Brewster, and
Samuel C. T. Dodd. A missing name is that of a founding father,
Samuel Andrews, who had departed from Standard Oil in 1874.
At that time he had expressed dissatisfaction with the company's
policy of plowing back profits into expansion rather than paying
dividends. "Sam, you don't have faith in the way this company is
operating," Rockefeller said to him. "What will you take for your
holdings?" A bargain was struck for a million dollars, which
Andrews thought extremely generous, but when the stock soared

in later years Andrews felt he had been cheated, and in 1879 gave testimony hostile to Rockefeller before the Hepburn hearings.

To all Rockefeller gave his ear but to few his voice. Frederick Gates wrote, "If he was nice and precise in his choice of words, he was nice and accurate in his choice of silences." He always dealt at arm's-length with his associates, not as a bosom friend. One of his favorite Bible-class lectures was on these lines: "Don't be a good fellow. I love my fellowman and I take great interest in him. But don't be convivial, always ready to pitch in and be one of the crowd. Be moderate. Be very moderate." No one could mistake Rockefeller for a "good fellow." His correspondence with his associates is notable for its impersonality, for the absence of the joshing that is normally found in business communications between friends. Except for such perfunctory remarks as "Take care of your health" and "Be sure to take a vacation," little concern is evinced for the human being.

Over the other members of the hierarchy Rockefeller did not preside as an autocrat but merely as *primus inter pares* who sought to win his way by reasoning. Like Napoleon, he invited debate; but, unlike Napoleon, he did not insist on winning every argument. He often gave way to his colleagues.

A sense of humor seemed to be completely lacking in his literal matter-of-fact mind. Sardonic or wry statements were his closest approaches to humor. Thus while pummeling the pygmy Tidewater, he wrote to Payne that "we are not discouraged but hope in some way there will be left for us something of value in the business we have worked so hard to build up." Again, in a letter to William Warden: "Enclosed is a letter from Lewis Meredith. I did not know there was so wise a man as that in Philadelphia." He was never known to laugh out loud. As his sister-in-law Lucy Spelman described him, he was "soberly mirthful." His grimness in business was evidenced by his secretiveness, which became almost an obsession. He kept company information from his colleagues, saying: "You'd better not know. You might be subpoenaed by a congressional committee." Employees were instructed not to discuss company affairs on the outside; if they did so, they ran the risk of dismissal.

Possibly for enlightened self-interest he was a better than average employer. Wages were higher than ordinary to attract ability.

Even the lowliest errand boy was regarded as a brick in the structure, and was dumped if he did not prove out. More than pay scales, workers prized the continuous employment Standard could give, and the settled policy of promotion from within. Years before the rest of American industry, Rockefeller instituted fringe-benefits programs. Before there were workmen's compensation laws he paid hospital expenses in accidents and half the wages due. In 1903 he instituted a pension plan, though initially it helped few—those with twenty-five years of service at sixty-five received 25 percent of average pay in the last ten years. Policy toward personnel grew noticeably warmer after Standard became embroiled with the government. An employee parody of 1907 discussed the more liberal policy "ever since they made that jab at you in St. Louis," a reference to the antitrust suit.

It was not true, as has been stated, that Standard Oil in the days of the trust had no labor troubles, but it is true that the strikes were few and localized. Rockefeller refused to countenance unionism. He maintained an espionage system among his workers. When an agent spotted an agitator, he was transferred to a new locality where he could do no harm. Rockefeller had the true spirit of paternalism—he knew best what was good for the worker. Once he explained why he did not give his employees at his Pocantico estate a holiday on Labor Day: "Instead of spending money on amusements my employees will have an opportunity of adding to their savings. Had they been given a holiday, money would have been spent foolishly." No doubt Rockefeller would have endorsed the classic remark of the industrial magnate George Baer: "The rights and interests of the laboring man will be protected and cared for—not by the labor agitators but by the Christian men to whom God in his infinite wisdom has given control of the property interests of the country. . . ."

While Rockefeller was a ruthless competitor without pretense, it is hard to substantiate a case where he swindled or fleeced anyone under false pretenses. The only instance of moral turpitude that Ida Tarbell was able to find—and she made the most of it—was his dealings with the colorful James Corrigan, who in partnership with Frank Rockefeller bought the Franklin Iron Mining Company in Wisconsin but got into financial troubles in the post-1893 depression. He put up 2,500 shares of Standard Oil stock he owned as security for loans from Rockefeller, which Rockefeller took over at $168 a share. Two years later the shares were selling for $500, and Corrigan brought suit. His charges were broadcast by Ida Tarbell. He claimed that Rockefeller had lied about the value of the shares in order to get them at a bargain price. Rockefeller, he charged, had told him that the trust was earning no money, that it had the severest competition it had ever had, and that there was no surplus left in the treasury.

Miss Tarbell's account played down the fact that three arbitrators in 1899 had decided in Rockefeller's favor and that their verdict had been upheld by the Ohio Supreme Court. After Miss Tarbell's story appeared in *McClure's*, Rockefeller's attorney, Virgil P. Kline, published parts of the arbitrators' report showing that Rockefeller had offered to give Corrigan all the information bearing on the value of the stock that was available but that Corrigan had not seen fit to avail himself of it. Far from wanting to get hold of more stock cheaply, the evidence showed that he had immediately put them on the market and in ninety days had sold half for a price slightly higher than he had paid.

The quarrel caused an irreparable breach with Frank Rockefeller, who removed the bodies of his two children from the family burial plot in Cleveland so that they would not lie close to his older brother. Frank's greatest fear during his fatal illness in 1917 was that his older brother might visit him. During the last fifteen years of his life his statements about his brother were the most vitriolic in public print.

Rockefeller had only this to say, "Poor Frank. I held him in my arms when he was a baby." What is more surprising is to find in Ralph and Muriel Hidy's study of Standard Oil records that Frank was carried on the payroll from 1899 until 1912, the year after the dissolution, at the salary of a vice-president, though he did no work. One can only conjecture as to what lies behind this.

Let us turn to another facet of Rockefeller's life—his religious worship. His mounting riches did not affect his regular attendance at the Euclid Avenue Baptist Church in Cleveland and the Fifth Avenue Baptist Church in New York. As long as he was in Cleveland (after 1884 he spent only summers at Forest Hill) he was Sunday-school superintendent. His Sunday-school classes were large (filled with aspirants for jobs), and there was a good deal of interest in what Rockefeller had to say. John M. Siddall, a writer, told how when he was a cub reporter in Cleveland he attended a class and Rockefeller noticed him taking shorthand notes. It was a stumbling talk; afterward the titan took a seat beside Siddall and asked him as a favor to "chop down" the talk and "fix it up." Weeks later, on a streetcar (he rode the trolleys in Cleveland, the Elevated in New York), Rockefeller recognized Siddall and, shaking his hand, said, "You fixed that speech up so that it was first rate. Thank you."

Perhaps because of his diffidence, we have records of few talks, but they seem to have been on a very secular note, about practical approaches to life, rather than on theological themes. The following is supposed to be an authentic excerpt from a talk in which Rockefeller likened an investment in salvation to an investment in business:

> When you come to the church and associate yourself with it, you must put something into it. When the businessmen associate themselves for the manufacture of these gas fixtures or the window glasses or many of the things we see about us, each man contributes some money for the just undertaking. In proportion to what they put in, do they receive returns or dividends. Now, it is not necessary that you put in a great amount of money into this work that you are becoming a part of, but that the whole may accomplish the most it is necessary that each contribute something. Be it money or what it may. Put something in. And according you put something in, the greater will be your dividends of salvation.

H. L. Mencken, who was irreverent to earthly success, seems to have had a genuine admiration for Rockefeller. Once he paid him this tribute:

> The most interesting thing about Rockefeller in the last analysis is his fidelity to this rustic and preposterous faith. Most Americans when they accumlate money climb the golden ramparts of the nearest Episcopal Church where the crude Yahveh of the backwoods is polished and refined and

speaks the vulgate with an English A. But the Rockefellers
cling to the primeval rain-God of the American hinterland,
and show no sign of being ashamed of him. The Hell of the
Bible is Hell enough for them.

Of the two vectors fixing his existence outside his family,
moneymaking and religion, there is an incident that shows which
was the more important influence. During the tankage crisis in
the Bradford field in 1878, the devout Bostwick was outraged that
tank cars were being loaded on Sunday. He appealed to Rockefeller, pointing out that cars were being loaded for Cleveland on
the holy day. He felt confident that Rockefeller would uphold
him—but he was overruled, and had to bow. He wrote to Rockefeller: "Although I do not agree with you and the others that
we are morally right in doing so, I will give the order."

Rockefeller was not unusual among the new kings of industry
in being a devout churchgoer. Most of them were. J. P. Morgan
was the greatest layman of the Episcopal Church, and his voice
bellowed hymns in St. George's Church; Daniel Drew spent
hours in solitary prayer; Jay Cooke observed the Sabbath sol-
emnly, and exhorted his employees to go and do likewise. The
wondrously ingenious Thorstein Veblen pondered upon the link,
and found the answer, like others, in anthropology: The "predatory" instinct was a relic of barbaric times, and the modern
money conquerors made offerings to propitiate the Lord just as
barbaric ancestors made offerings to propitiate the spirits. Be that
as it may, heathenism was uncommon among the money kings.

Rockefeller regarded himself as a good Christian—*Integer
vitae scelerisque purus.* It was the most unkindest cut of all when
the minister of his own Euclid Avenue Baptist Church said, during the "tainted money" controversy, "People charge Mr. Rockefeller with stealing the money he gave to the church, but he has
laid it on the altar and thus sanctified it." As Rockefeller saw it,
he had not stolen anything.

In truth, the prevailing attitude of religion sanctified riches. As
explained by R. H. Tawney in *Religion and the Rise of Capitalism,* the Calvinist approach, the "Puritan ethic," was that man
fulfills the Lord's plan by eschewing idleness, turning out the

world's goods, and laying up wealth for his family. In turn, riches was the sign of divine favor. When Rockefeller said, "God gave me my wealth," he said no more than did Cotton Mather: "Sirs, you cannot but acknowledge that it is the sovereign God who has bestowed upon you the riches that distinguish you," or Bishop William Lawrence, of Massachusetts, who said, "Godliness is in league with riches." And did not John Wesley say: "Gain all you can. Save all you can. Give all you can"? Rockefeller knew and repeated that saying.

There is a report of a Bible-class lecture by Rockefeller in which he told of the incident in his early business life with Maurice Clark when he refused an advance to a business client even though it seemed to mean the loss of his business. Rockefeller declared that he later learned that a banker had arranged the request to test him. From the tone of his talk, it is evident that Rockefeller identified good business practice with good religion and that in this case he had been tested by temptation and sin, and, like St. Anthony, had emerged with flying colors.

What was in God's plan was also in Nature's plan. The prevailing mold of thinking was reinforced by the transposition of the new biological theories of Charles Darwin to economic life. Economic society was in evolution; man rose to the top by survival of the fittest; and everyone's struggle for existence played a part in inevitable progress. It was all mechanistic and preordained. When Andrew Carnegie read an essay by the popularizer of this theory, Herbert Spencer, he said, "Light came as a flood and all was clear."

Rockefeller apparently did seek and find social justification for his business career in service to his fellowman. More than once he referred thoughtfully to petroleum as "the poor man's light." He wrote to an executive in 1885 about reductions in manufacturing costs: "Let the good work go on. We must ever remember we are refining oil for the poor man and he must have it cheap and good."

In 1907, when the attack on him was at its peak and there were calls for him to divorce himself from Standard Oil, Rockefeller issued this statement through the Reverend Robert S. MacArthur, of New York's Calvary Baptist Church: "I am the trustee of the property of others through the providence of God committed to my care. Therefore I find it my duty to God and to the people and to whatever money is invested in my company to continue active in its welfare."

He could not have made more clear his belief that his life and career were all in the divine purpose.

CHAPTER 14   *Adventure in Iron*

DURING THE 1890's Rockefeller, as an extracurricular activity, became deeply involved in the development of the Mesabi ore deposits of Minnesota, which in 1900 provided more than 60 percent of the ore used in the nation. The story is important for several reasons—it concerns the development of one of our great natural resources that was essential in the early life of United States Steel; it resulted in the addition of $50,000,000 to the Rockefeller fortune, seemingly by accident or perhaps as further proof of divine intervention in behalf of Rockefeller; it brought another lawsuit that besmirched his reputation; and, last, it brings for the first time into the limelight a personality who played a leading role in Rockefeller's life and left a lasting imprint on philanthropy, Frederick T. Gates.

When Gates entered Rockefeller's employ in 1891, he was a thirty-nine-year-old Baptist minister, a man of finely modeled features and wavy hair. A son of a Baptist minister who was as impecunious as the rest of the clergy, Gates came from the same central area of New York State as did Rockefeller. After graduation from the Rochester Theological Seminary, he took a small pastorate in Minneapolis. There an event occurred that lifted him from pastoral activities and into broader public-spirited avenues of service. The wealthy miller, George A. Pillsbury, told him that he was suffering from an incurable disease and that he wanted to leave money to the Owatonna Academy, a Baptist school, but

Right, Rockefeller was sixty when he took up golf in 1897; *below*, the Pocantico Hills estate, comprising 4,180 acres and 75 buildings

Above, 'The Casements' at Ormond Beach, Florida, where Rockefeller became a popular figure among his neighbours; *below*, the Music Room of the Rockefeller's home at Pocantico

feared that the Baptists had no interest in it. Gates suggested that he give $50,000 at once on condition that it be matched by contributions. The millionaire assented, and Gates, devoting all his time to raising the money, succeeded in raising in excess of the amount. His next job was as secretary to the American Baptist Education Society. In that capacity he campaigned for the establishment of the Baptist University, which would become the University of Chicago; the target of the campaign for money was the source "from whom oil blessings flow," John D. Rockefeller.

During the discussions about the university, the magnate had become impressed with the young, effervescent minister who seemed abundantly possessed of ideas and the zest to put them over. At the time Rockefeller was harried from pillar to post by importunities for money, since it was now well known that he was not only possessed of one of the largest fortunes in the nation but was also a "giving" man. It was to advise him on his philanthropies that Gates became associated with Rockefeller. He was destined to be the great almoner of the Rockfeller fortune—but interstitially he was to serve as a wizard of finance.

The Rockefeller fortune was snowballing. By 1890 it was in nine figures; his Standard Oil dividends were three millions a year; and returns from outside investments were greater. To find and manage outlets for this vast sum was a task that Rockefeller was discharging single-handed, along with running Standard Oil. It is no wonder that he had a breakdown in 1892, accompanied by a severe stomach disorder, giving him warning that he had to delegate more responsibilities to others.

On many investments, because of the inability to conduct his own firsthand investigation and the need to rely on the counsel of others, Rockefeller was badly deceived. He made investments, sight unseen, in the Pacific Northwest around what is now the city of Everett, Washington, including mines, steel mills, paper mills, a nail factory, hotel, railroad, smelting properties, and lumber fields. The Panic of 1893 collapsed the boom there with terrifying suddenness. By financial legerdemain—forcing some companies into receivership, liquidating his interest in some, nursing some companies to solvency, and finally, thanks to the skyrocketing values of the lumber fields, which were sold to the

Weyerhaeuser interests—Rockefeller was able to salvage his original investment and even add to it.

Because Rockefeller believed that Gates had a good stock of common sense, one day when Gates set out on a trip to the South it occurred to Rockefeller to ask him to look over an iron mill in which he had an interest. His report, which was unfavorable, was a model of what such a report should be, thought Rockefeller. Another assignment followed. Gates looked into the West Superior Iron and Steel Company at West Superior, Wisconsin, of which Rockefeller held $600,000 in bonds. Instead of supposedly making $1,000 a day, Gates found that the company was losing that much, that the mortgage of lands securing the bonds was fraudulent, and that in fact the steel company was a front for a land-selling scheme. This, like the Everett investments, was a path down which Rockefeller had been led, blindly following the recommendations of two fellow members of his Fifth Avenue Church, the Wall Street promoters Colgate Hoyt and Charles L. Colby. Only by virtue of Gates's timely information was Rockefeller able to prevent the investment in West Superior from being lost. Similarly, when Gates looked into the San Miguel Consolidated Mines in Colorado—Rockefeller had been led to believe that he had been privileged to invest in a Comstock lode—he found the truth shocking. The claims were utterly worthless; the promoter was using the invested funds to pay himself a munificent salary; and visitors who had previously been beguiled by his optimistic predictions were entertained royally in order to keep them away from the property and from discovering that the operation was a sham. Gates had learned the truth by visiting independent experts before he met the promoter.

These experiences convinced Rockefeller that for his self-protection he needed staff advice and administration. To head the staff he chose Gates, who now moved into 26 Broadway to be at the right-hand side of Rockefeller. Scaling the heights of Wall Street via the Rochester Theological Seminary rather than the Harvard Business School, the only previous business experience Gates had had was briefly selling harrows, a few months as a clerk in a country store, as a cashier in a country bank, and as manager of the finances of his church. Yet as manager of Rockefeller's investments he was to be a great success. Rockefeller wrote of his "rare business ability very highly developed and very honorably exercised. . . ." The admiration was reciprocated. In a statement written many years later, Gates wrote, "In all my acquaintance with him, acquaintance covering periods of trial and temptation, never have I known him to depart one hair's breadth from the best standards of business rectitude." While some would say this was inaccurate or insincere, it may be noted that Gates was divorced from knowledge of the Standard Oil operations and that at the time of Gates's association, Rockefeller could have his way in investments by sheer economic power.

Gates was largely instrumental in managing the recovery operations in the Puget Sound area, from which Rockefeller ultimately emerged with a profit. He was also in the thick of the remarkable Missabe (later known as Mesabi) investment and the litigation with the Merritts. After the testimony of Leonidas Merritt at the Stanley Committee hearings in 1911, which, as Gates, said, made it appear that he was a wolf in pastor's clothing, he published his pamphlet "The Truth About the Merritts," presenting a case for himself and Rockefeller that has been uncontradicted.

Through Colby and Hoyt, Rockefeller had been buying into iron mines, one in Cuba, two others in the rich Gogebic Range in Wisconsin, and other ore properties in Minnesota and Michigan. A new area with great potentials was being explored by the Merritt family. Leonidas Merritt, a tough, hardy man of the woods, was the leader of the clan, the others being his five brothers and three nephews. In 1890 their messianic fervor was rewarded when they struck rich deposits in the Missabe Range north and west of Lake Superior, the ore lying almost at the surface of the ground. By 1893 they had a 40 percent interest in mines with beds having as much as 50,000,000 tons of ore. They had built a 65-mile railroad to Superior that cost $660,000 but against which they issued $2,400,000 in securities, half in stocks and half in bonds. The Merritts were reckless promoters.

The Merritts decided to extend their railroad to Duluth; meeting obstruction from the stockholders of the road, they bought control for $665,000, more than the cost of the original road. This depleted their cash resources. For the extension of the road they undertook to sell $1,600,000 worth of bonds. The Merritts became close friends of a New York financier, Charles H. Wetmore, who was on close terms with Messrs. Colby and Hoyt. Through this linkup, Rockefeller bought $400,000 of the bonds. The story that Gates gives is that Rockefeller was persuaded to do so, but Anna Youngman, writing about this investment in the *Journal of Political Economy* in 1907, issued by the University of Chicago, which initially was endowed by Rockefeller, says "They [Merritts] were approached by an agent of Mr. Rockefeller who made them an offer." One wonders if Gates is correct in picturing Rockefeller as the passive object of petitions by the Merritts throughout the episode or whether he did not at least open the door of the parlor to the fly.

Then came the Panic of 1893, which spelled doom for so many. The mines were idle; the railroad trembled on the brink of receivership. There were labor riots, and men demanded pay at the end of drawn revolvers. Struggling to save themselves, the Merritts proposed two consolidation agreements with the Colby-Hoyt interests, which failed. When it appeared that the Merritt collateral might all go down the drain, Rockefeller, who was already involved to the tune of $400,000, appeared as the deliverer. A holding company, the Lake Superior Consolidated Iron Mines was formed, in which the Merritt interests were joined with mines held by Rockefeller in Cuba and in the Gogebic Range. Rockefeller for his part took $4,300,000 in bonds—he gave $2,000,000 in cash to the railroads and $150,000 to the Merritts to bail them out. Since Rockefeller took only bonds, this left the Merritts free to grab all the common stock for themselves. The maximum cash value they estimated for the properties was around $10,000,000. As Gates wrote, they "shut their eyes" and issued $26,000,000 of stock, of which they kept $10,000,000 for themselves and used most of the rest to pay creditors. The amount actually invested by the Merritts was only about $2,000,000 of borrowed money. We have noted before that they were promoters par excellence.

It was the formation of this holding company that was the subject of the lawsuit. The contract was signed and sealed on July 12, 1893. According to Gates, Lon Merritt was so overjoyed that he asked for a meeting with Rockefeller on that date; the two men met, shook hands, and exchanged pleasantries. As Merritt saw it, the crisis point was passed. "Perfect confidence is restored," he wrote.

The Panic, however, was followed by a depression, and conditions got worse. Blast furnaces were closing down, and there was no demand for iron ore. Besides, the Missabe ore was of a fine, powdery consistency, unfit for most furnaces of the day; it was either blown out over the countryside, exposing the steel company to suit, or else, if it were too closely confined, wrecked the furnace. In September 1893 the Merritts asked for a new loan of $100,000, but Gates refused, saying, "I have today on my desk urgent appeals to save old friends from ruin amounting to many hundreds of thousands of dollars."

In February 1894, after further futile appeals for loans, Rockefeller bought from the Merritts 90,000 shares of Consolidated stock for $10 a share, but granted the Merritts an option to buy back 55,000 shares at the same price within a year. Lon's brother, Lewis, and his son Hulett were carried by Rockefeller on extensions of the option for years until they bought back the stock at the option price and became millionaires, but Lon and the others did not choose to avail themselves of, or ask for, an extension of this option. (The stock was eventually worth $160 a share.) Instead they brought suit against Rockefeller, charging fraud and misrepresentation in the value of the mine properties which he contributed to the merger into Consolidated.

Gates claims that they were induced to bring suit by an unscrupulous attorney, Anak A. Harris. He says that Harris came to Rockefeller's office in July 1894 and tried to sell a block of Consolidated stock at a price far above the market, saying that he had great influence with the Merritts and could dissuade them from bringing suit.

In July 1895 the trial took place in Duluth. Lon and Alf testified that they met Rockefeller in June 1893 before the signing of the contract (Gates says that it was after the signing on July 12) and that Rockefeller spoke loquaciously (he never spoke loquaciously) about his mine properties, saying they were "gilt edged," "solvent and prosperous" and "owed little money," which the Merritts said was false. Their testimony was legally artful since, according to them, Rockefeller advised them to tell the other Merritts what he said, thus laying a foundation for suits by the

others, and also said that Gates could speak for him, thus en-
meshing alleged statements by Gates into the conspiracy.

The jury found Rockefeller guilty and awarded Alf Merritt,
who was the sole litigant in this test case, the sum of $940,000 in
damages. The Circuit Court of Appeals reversed the judgment on
the ground that the award was excessive, and ordered a new trial.
Rockefeller settled the case for $525,000 and received a retrac-
tion from all the Merritts.

The jury verdict has been attributed to the fact that in the
small mining city of Duluth, sympathy was all for the underdog
Merritts against the tycoon Rockefeller, who would not be hurt
by making a contribution to the city. (The Merritts owed money
all over Duluth.) If Rockefeller was blameless, why did he pay so
much in settlement? What he did is understandable and not unusual. He now owned almost all the common stock of Consolidated, and wanted to develop the properties. Since there were
twenty-three Merritts and a swarm of creditors, he might be
harassed indefinitely by a hornet's nest of suits.

Rockefeller was clubbed with this stick about the Merritts for
years. In 1910 the New York *World* published a long article by
Lon's daughter, Hephzibah, "What Rockefeller Did to Us."
Gates's defense is threefold:

First, all the evidence, including letters from Lon Merritt,
shows that the consolidation resulted from the entreaties of the
Merritts. Second, the meeting of Lon Merritt and Rockefeller
took place on July 12, after the contract was signed, and not in
June. In fact, Anak Harris, the Merritts' lawyer, offered to sell to
Rockefeller for $25,000 a telegram of July 12 from Lon Merritt
stating that he had met Rockefeller that day. Third, the properties Rockefeller put up were fully as valuable as he said they
were. Wetmore, who was the close friend of the Merritts, was
counsel for those companies, and knew all the facts as to their
value, of which he apprised the Merritts.

Having control of the ore fields, which he insisted was thrust
upon him rather than sought after, Rockefeller now turned with
enthusiasm to the development of their value. Rockefeller had
the richest ore potential in existence. The steel leaders had been
caught napping, and the press was filled with speculation that
Rockefeller might add the kingdom of steel to his kingdom of oil.

Rockefeller later mused: "It was a surprise to me that the great iron and steel manufacturers did not place what seemed to be an adequate value on these mines. The lands which contained a good many of our very best ore mines could have been purchased very cheaply before we became interested."

However, Rockefeller had no intention of going into the steel business. In 1896 he made an agreement with Carnegie under which the latter leased Rockefeller's mines for $0.25 cents a ton, half the usual royalty rate, and agreed to mine not less than 600,-000 tons a year. That ore and the ore from Carnegie's own mines were to pay freight over Rockefeller's Duluth railroad and his ore-carrying vessels. Carnegie did not think it wise to decline the offer. "We should lose the friendship of Mr. Rockefeller. . . . I think Mr. Rockefeller is the coming man in ore." President Leishman, of the Carnegie Company, feared that Rockefeller might enter the steel business. "I think very few people are hunting places to invest 15 millions a year." Now, by compact, Rockefeller would concentrate on transportation of ore, and Carnegie would stay out of further ore-mining properties.

To carry out his commitment it was necessary for Rockefeller to have ore-carrying ships of five thousand tons each. The railroad took the ore to Duluth; then the trains backed out onto trestles, and the ore was dumped into ships for carriage to the Lake ports. Rockefeller recounted with gusto the stratagem he used to get the best price for construction of these ships. There were twelve shipbuilding concerns, and they were asked how many ships they could build. The answer was twelve—one by each. Rockefeller wanted exactly that number built and no more, but if he had broken the news the shipbuilders would have been in the driver's seat as to price. Each was asked to submit bids for what the concern thought would be at most two ships. Each concern's representative conferred at a hotel with Rockefeller's representative, Samuel Mather, and hoped that he was the lucky one. Then each received a note from Mather that he had been chosen to build one ship. "They all rushed with a common impulse to the hotel lobby, each bent on displaying his note and commiserating with his unsuccessful rivals only to discover that each had a contract for all he could do and that each had been bidding against nobody but himself. Great was the hilarity which covered their chagrin." Rockefeller was "soberly mirth-ful," because in this way he got rock-bottom prices.

The iron and steel business had a period of prosperity between 1897 and 1900, but it was evident that lasting prosperity would be enhanced if competition were eliminated. In 1901, under the skilled hand of J. P. Morgan, the Federal Steel Company, belong-ing to Elbert Gary, and the Carnegie Steel Company were put under one roof, the United States Steel Company. Rockefeller, however, owned the richest ore mines, and in the Bessemer Steamship Company the biggest and most efficient system of water carriage. It was imperative that the new steel company obtain these before they fell into other hands.

Judge Gary suggested to Morgan that he go to see Rockefeller. Morgan replied: "I would not think of it. I don't like him." But Morgan finally did make the call on Rockefeller, which Rockefel-ler stipulated was to be a social call only, since he had retired from business. This was only maneuvering for position. When Morgan told Rockefeller that he must acquire his ore fields, the reply was: "I am sorry but I am retired. You must see my son and Frederick Gates. They are in charge of my investments."

Henry H. Rogers took John D. Rockefeller, Jr., then a stripling of twenty-six, to see Morgan. The leonine tycoon, in conference with one of his partners, paid no notice to the two when they were ushered into his office. Then he roared, "Well, what's your price?" Rockefeller, Jr., not at all unnerved, said coolly: "Mr. Morgan, I think there must be some mistake. I did not come here to sell. I understand you wish to buy." Morgan became more conciliatory.

Morgan proposed an "outside" figure of $75,000,000. The par-ties then agreed that Henry Frick should act as a negotiator between buyer and seller. Rockefeller now dropped his pose that he was retired, and in a talk with Frick at his home at Pocantico said that he objected to the imposition of an "outside" figure. That objection on principle seems to have cost Morgan $5,000,-000, since Rockefeller added that amount to the "outside" figure. Gary, who had set the "outside" figure, had to swallow the pill. After all, in a transaction of half a billion what did another five million amount to?

For the ore-carrying fleet another $8,500,000 in cash was added to the $80,000,000, which was paid half in common stock and half in preferred stock. Rockefeller became a director of the United States Steel Corporation and the largest single stockholder. The profit on the Missabe transaction from beginning to end was calculated at $50,000,000.

BOOK THREE

THE DESTRUCTION OF THE TRUST

We think no disinterested mind can survey the period in question without being inevitably driven to the conclusion that the very genius for commercial development and organization, which it would seem was manifested from the beginning, soon begat an interest and purpose to exclude others which was frequently manifested by actions and dealings wholly inconsistent with the theory that they were made with the single conception of advancing the development of business power by usual methods, but which, on the contrary, necessarily involved the intent to drive others from the field and exclude them from their right to trade and thus accomplish the mastery which was the end in view.

—CHIEF JUSTICE WHITE, SPEAKING FOR THE UNITED STATES SUPREME COURT IN *Standard Oil Company* v. *United States,* 221 U.S. REPORTS 1,76.

CHAPTER 15 *The Tribulations of George Rice*

T HE NEXT FEW CHAPTERS narrate the events that culminated
in the dissolution of the oil trust under order of the Supreme
Court of the United States in 1911. In truth, it was a cyclone of
angry public opinion that blew the trust apart, since, as the sage
Mr. Dooley commented, the Supreme Court followed the election
returns.

This angry public opinion was whipped up by two books that
we have often cited, those of Henry Demarest Lloyd and Ida
Tarbell. The dragon was slain, not by St. George with a sword,
but by two middle-aged, mild-mannered intellectuals, a man and
a woman armed with pen and ink. "Yes, sir," said Mr. Dooley of
the galvanizing effect of the written word in that muckraking age,
"the hand that rocks the fountain pen is th' hand that rules the
wurruld." It is ironic that conquest by book happened to John D.
Rockefeller, who, though an admirer and patron of higher education, was himself a most unbookish person who must have been
astounded when the pen proved mightier than the Almighty Dollar.

There were two cases occurring in the 1880's that received
extensive treatment by both authors and which consequently
brought odium upon the name of Standard Oil not only when
they occurred but also in succeeding years. The first was the so-
called "Buffalo Case," in which a Standard Oil subsidiary was accused of having attempted to blow up a competing refinery. In
spite of the notoriety of the case, we shall discuss it only briefly
here, since no one has seriously contended that Standard Oil
adopted the practice of blowing up its competitors as an article
of doing business. The second case, that of George B. Rice, we
shall consider at greater length because Rice became a symbol
of the wrongs and oppression of the individual of which the
Standard Oil monopoly was guilty.

In 1879 H. B. and C. M. Everest, father and son, sold a three-quarters interest in their Vacuum Oil Works of Rochester, New York, to Standard Oil, the Everests remaining as managers. In 1880 three employees of the company defected and established a competing refinery in Buffalo, the Buffalo Lubricating Oil Company, despite threats from the Everests that their supply of oil would be cut off. One of the partners of the new firm, the still technician, Albert Miller, was terrified by the threats; fearing that he would lose his investment, he conferred with the Everests about ways of backing out of his contractual relations with the new firm. A lawyer whom they jointly consulted for advice testified at the trial that in the course of the meeting, after he advised Miller about the contract liability, H. B. Everest said: "I think there is other ways for Miller to get out of it. Suppose he should arrange the machinery so it would bust up or smash up. What would the consequence be?" The lawyer said he advised against it.

None the less, Miller testified that he was urged by the Everests to "do something" or "give them a scare." It took months for the new firm to get started, since Miller was the only technical expert of the three partners and he was absent for long periods of time. Finally a still was ready for operations. According to the fireman's testimony, Miller ordered a heavy fire to be built and to be made heavier and heavier until, as the fireman said, it was "an inordinary fire," cherry-red in its intensity. Miller disappeared. The brickwork around the still began to crack, and then the safety valve, although packed with plaster, blew off. A mass of yellow gas escaped that might have been ignited by a spark but blew away with a favoring wind. If the safety valve had not blown off, the still would have exploded and the next stop for several workers would have been Kingdom Come.

Miller took off and joined H. B. Everest at the Union Square Hotel in New York, then went to Boston, where Everest gave Miller a fictitious name. Although Miller was simply loafing, Everest agreed to give him $1,500 a year, which was more than he had earned when he was working for Everest, who now said to him, "You won't have much to do and you can stay here in Boston and keep away from those fellows and we will still protect you." Then Miller went to California, where H. B. Everest said he had a job for him in a cannery—but he loafed there too. All in all, Miller received $4,000. One lawyer said at the trial that Miller "never earned enough to cover the end of your knife blade with salt at dinner."

Meanwhile, for three years, from 1880, Charles Matthews, head of the Buffalo Lubricating Company, had been harassed by suits for infringement of patents brought by Vacuum Oil, and his employees had been enticed away. He brought a civil suit for $100,-000 in damages against the Everests. Then Miller drifted back to Rochester from California and told Matthews the whole story. Matthews not only broadened his civil suit but went before a grand jury, with the result that not only were the Everests indicted for criminal conspiracy to blow up his plant, but John D. Archbold, Henry Rogers, and Ambrose McGregor of Standard Oil were also indicted on the ground that they were partners in the conspiracy.

In view of the prominence of Archbold and Rogers, the case drew nationwide attention when it came to trial in May 1886, in Buffalo. Rockefeller was present at the trial, and gave testimony of little value; the interest in Vacuum was held by the three officers of Standard who were indicted, and not by the company. Very much agitated by the charges, Rockefeller shook his fist at Matthews several times. The trial judge dismissed the indictments against Archbold, Rogers, and McGregor, since there was not a scintilla of evidence to connect them with the conspiracy. On the other hand, the Everests were convicted. However, for this heinous offense they were fined $250 each, which prompted a good deal of acerb press opinion, such as the comment of the Erie *Dispatch:* "It [the monopoly] can afford to blow up a rival refinery every day in the year at the price." The costs of the litigation ruined Matthews. He won a judgment in the civil suit for $85,000, but the company went into the hands of a receiver, who paid off the lawyers with most of it.

Ida Tarbell, while exonerating Standard Oil from any responsibility for the actions of the Everests, none the less managed to use the indictment as another proof of the immorality of the company: "It [the case] shows to what lengths a hostile public will go in interpreting the acts of men whom it has come to believe are lawless and relentless in pursuing their own ends. The public, particularly the oil public, has always been willing to believe the worst of the Standard Oil Company." The implication is that only the black conduct of Standard Oil previously could have brought about the mistaken belief that it was responsible for the crime in Buffalo. *Q.E.D.*

There is a legitimate charge that can be leveled against Rockefeller in connection with the Buffalo Case. Those in the organization were infused by him with the spirit that the company could do no wrong. An ex-employee, Charles Woodbury, put it this way in 1911: "The regnant principle throughout, under which all the work was done, was first, last and all the time to play the game; that the Standard Oil Company must do—must be—the oil business. 'Overzeal' was an error on the safe side, a venial offense." Rockefeller, in his *Reminiscences*, said, "It would be surprising if in an organization which included a great number of men there should not be an occasional employee here and there who acted in connection with the business in a way which might be criticized."

Woodbury's comment stands—there is no instance where Rockefeller chastised or rebuked an employee for "overzeal" in behalf of Standard Oil, no matter what the employee resorted to—which implies his condoning their acts. The Everests, far from being chastised, prospered in the trust.

The other case, besides that of the Buffalo Lubricating Works, was that of George Rice, who seemingly suffered the afflictions of Job in trying to survive as an independent refiner, and became in the eyes of many a typical victim of the vices of the trust.

I am a citizen of the United States, born in the state of Vermont, producer of petroleum for more than 30 years and a refiner of same for 29 years. But my refinery has been shut down during the past three years, owing to the powerful and all-prevailing machinations of the Standard Oil trust, in criminal collusion and conspiracy with the railroads, to destroy my business of 20 years of patient industry, toil and money in building up, wholly by and through unlawful freight discriminations. I have been driven from pillar to post, from one railway line to another, for 20 years, in the absolutely vain endeavour to get equal and just freight rates with the Standard Oil Trust, so as to be able to run my refinery at anything approaching a profit, but which I have been utterly unable to do. I have had to consequently shut down with my business absolutely ruined. This has been a very sad, bitter and ruinous experience for me to endure . . . but I am still living in hopes though I may die in despair.

This was the opening of George Rice's statement before the United States Industrial Commission in 1899. In the Pithole days, Rice had been a producer, but had then moved to Marietta, Ohio, where in 1876 he was refining as much as 500 barrels a week. Standard Oil also had a refinery in Marietta. Then, suddenly, in January 1879, freight rates were raised by all railroads simultaneously on only one commodity, oil, and all from one point, Marietta. Rail rates were left unchanged on refined from Cleveland, Wheeling, Parkersburg, and other points where Standard Oil had refineries. Standard could readily have closed its Marietta refinery and shifted production to other points, but this was not done, apparently because the increase in rates was not enforced against Standard's Marietta refinery. All the independent refiners in Marietta died as a result of the freight boost—except Rice.

Rice refused to die. He shrieked so loudly that the Ohio State legislature began an investigation of the rate boost. Nothing came of it. Rice saw that any legislative action, when it came, would help only posterity. Because freight rates made it impracticable for him to sell in the North, West, and East he turned to the South, and by analysis of freight schedules and adaptation to them built up a market that warranted a great expansion of his refinery. Now, a new trouble arose. Rice could not get crude oil. The pipeline that had brought it to the Allegheny River for shipment by water to him was torn up by the National Transit Company belonging to Standard. Rice therefore made a shift and got his crude from a field near Macksburg, Ohio, shuttling one tank car back and forth.

Then came the next blow. The Cleveland and Marietta Railroad suddenly doubled his rate from $0.17½ a barrel to $0.35, while it charged Standard only $0.10 a barrel. Moreover, Daniel O'Day, the Standard pipeline executive, notified the receiver of the road, a fussy old gentleman with the Dickensian name of Phineas Pease, that the road must remit to Standard Oil $0.25 of the $0.35 a barrel paid by Rice as a drawback. If he did not consent, Standard Oil would construct a pipeline to Marietta for its oil, and presto—no more traffic. Mr. Pease was upset—Standard's traffic on his road was seven times that of Rice. Although, as a receiver, Pease was an officer of the court and should have turned to the court for instructions, he asked for counsel from a lawyer in New York, who advised him that while he could not remit Rice's money to Standard, it would be quite legal to give Standard a discount amounting to the same amount—and so he did.

Rice was outraged by the freight discrimination and the drawback. He applied for relief to the United States Circuit Court of Appeals, asking that Pease report on all his contracts. The order was granted on the same day, and within twelve days the money paid to Standard by the railroad was refunded by it for repayment to Rice. Soon thereafter Judge Baxter, in a stinging opinion, ordered Pease removed: "The discrimination complained of in this case is so wanton and oppressive it could hardly have been accepted by an honest man having due regard for the rights of others . . . and a judge who would tolerate such a wrong or retain a receiver capable of perpetrating it, ought to be impeached and degraded from his position."

On December 11, 1885, the New York *Times* commented editorially on Judge Baxter's opinion, "No further disclosures were needed for a complete exhibition of the greed, injustice and oppression that are a part of the Standard Oil Company's stock in trade."

Five years later, in an interview with the New York *World*, Rockefeller discussed this case, but his excuses do not stand up. He said, "We repudiated the contract before it was passed on by the courts and made full recompense." The refund, however, was made twelve days after the order to produce the contract, an order that indicated clearly what the court would say. Rockefeller said, "The railroad company proposed [this] to our agent." But the fact was that the court found that Standard had "compelled" the railroad into the agreement.

Rice now got rid of the railroad entirely by building his own pipeline to the Muskingum River, over which he barged his oil to Marietta. In building his southern market he came into collision with the Standard Oil distributor, Chess, Carley and Company of Louisville. In Clarksville, Tennessee, Rice was underselling

Carley, and a dealer was ready to buy from Rice but went to see Carley first. Rice's agent reported that the dealer, Armstrong, was "scared almost out of his boots" when Carley told him that Standard Oil "had authorized him to spend $10,000 to break up any concern that bought oil from anyone else." Carley threatened that if he bought oil from Rice, he, Carley, would hunt up all Armstrong's customers who were grocers and sell them groceries at 5 percent below Armstrong's prices.

A wholesaler, Wilkinson and Company of Nashville, began buying from Rice, and received a letter from Carley: "It is with great reluctance that we undertake serious competition with any one and certainly this competition will not be confined to coal-oil or any one article and will not be limited to any one year."

Wilkinson, however, continued to buy from Rice, and on June 17, 1881, Chess, Carley addressed a letter to the Louisville and Nashville Railroad:

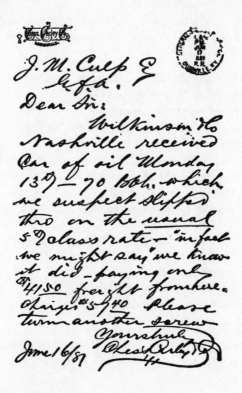

Rice testified before a congressional committee what that meant. "My rates were raised on that road over 50 percent in five days." He was asked, "Was it necessary to turn on more than one screw in that direction to put a stop to your business?" To this he replied, "One was sufficient."

This "turn another screw" letter was the subject of testimony in hearings of the United States House Committee on Manufacturers in 1888. J. M. Culp of the railroad to whom the letter was addressed, testified, "The man who wrote this must evidently have been crazy. He afterwards died in the insane asylum." But Carley said that his man, Hathaway, was sane and that the letter was routine where a competitive shipment was made, through carelessness, "below the regular rate." Amid derisive laughter Carley said, "I used to complain to Hathaway and he writes this letter to ask them to tighten the machinery of their office up there using this unfortunate expression."

The letter speaks for itself about the tight esponiage of Rice's shipments. Before the Interstate Commerce Commission a Standard agent testified in 1887:

Q. How do your agents tell the number of barrels he shipped in April, May and June?

A. See it arrive at the depot.

Q. How often do your agents go to the depot to make the examination?

A. They visit the depot once a day, not only for that purpose but to look after the shipment of our own oil.

Q. Do they keep a record of Mr. Rice's shipments?

A. They send us word whenever they find Mr. Rice has shipped a carload of oil.

Q. What do their statements show with respect to Mr. Rice's shipments besides that?

A. They show the number of barrels received at any point shipped by Mr. Rice or by anybody else.

Q. How often are these statements sent to the company?

A. Sent in monthly, I think.

Frank Carley testified that "99.9 percent of all the first-class merchants of the South are in close sympathetical cooperation with us in all our history." Letters collected by Rice showed that the attitude of many was not "sympathetical." One letter from Texas, covered by Standard's Waters-Pierce Oil Company, said, "Oil was selling at this point for $2.50 a case and as soon as your car arrived it was put down to $1.50." Indicative of the minute watch kept on Rice's shipments was another letter, "On the strength of my not having your oil today, I am told they have popped up the price 3½ cents."

During 1885, while Rice was in New Orleans, he got a wire that his rates to Memphis and New Orleans had been doubled. He rushed home and, after months of work, got the rates reduced; but in the following year, 1886 (the year before the Interstate Commerce Act was passed), his rates were raised on all his shipments, according to his testimony, from 43 percent to 162 percent, while rates charged to Standard Oil were not changed. The Interstate Commerce Commission, which in its early years had few teeth, after exhaustive testimony supported his claim as to discriminations, which, it said, were made "on no principle. Neither greater risks, greater expense, competition by water transportation, nor any other fact or circumstance brought forward in defense, can account for these differences."

From 1886 on, as Rice testified, "It takes about all my time to look after rates," not to mention time in tracing shipments delayed or sidetracked. He managed to reach some markets and get bare survival rates by interconnecting local routes, transferring his oil from one rail to the next. Thus he used seven rails to get to Birmingham, a total transport of 1,155 miles, instead of the direct route of 685 miles. To Nashville, he used five rails, shipping 805 miles instead of the direct route of 502 miles.

In order to survive, as he described it, he was kept writing, telegraphing, traveling, protesting, begging, litigating, threatening, and agitating by press, prosecutions, and investigations.

In November 1890 the general freight agent of the Little Rock and Memphis Railroad wrote to him: "We are hauling your oil. This, of course, we expect, as common carriers, to be compelled to do. It is a fact, nevertheless, that on account of handling your oil the Standard Oil Company will not route any of their freight over our lines."

Rice knew that it was cheaper to ship by tank cars as Standard shipped. For one thing, the rails charged him for the weight of the barrel, while it did not charge Standard Oil for the weight of the tanks, and also gave them free the use of the flatcars on which the tanks were carried. First he asked for tank-car rates from the Queen City and Crescent Railroad. After a correspondence of five months, in which he was shuttlecocked from one official to another, the general manager of the road finally wrote to him, "I was not aware that you had asked for rates on oil in tank cars." Rice ordered tank cars from manufacturers, and then the bankers who were to finance him backed out. Because of his feud with Standard, they feared that "You could not use these cars to advantage if the railroads should be hostile to your interests."

He did get a few tank cars, but the advantages proved illusory. Excuses for extra freight charges were piled on. For Standard a practice of "blind-billing" was followed—that is, it was presumed that tank cars belonging to them carried 20,000 pounds, even though they actually carried as much as 35,000 or 44,000 pounds. As for Rice, he had to pay for every pound he shipped. It was estimated that by "blind-billing" Standard shipped a quarter of its oil free—and that was not the only privilege Standard got on tank-car shipments.

Standard Oil had distributed to the rails a catalogue showing the number and capacity of each tank car. This was accepted by the rails implicitly, and was the basis for "blind-billing." In August 1887, Rice brought a complaint to the Interstate Commerce Commission, with proof supplied by a former Standard employee that the capacities listed were false. Suddenly the 3,000 tank cars of Standard Oil went to the shops to be repainted and renumbered. Rice's proof was worthless—the car numbers on the manifests and on the cars no longer matched. The sheerest coincidence, said Standard, of the repainting order. It admitted that the cars had been "changed as to classification slightly."

Before every tribunal and before every commission Rice won; repeatedly he was declared the victor in principle. But he, his funds, and his customers were exhausted by the long struggle, and his business succumbed. On October 11, 1898, Rockefeller testified at a hearing conducted by state authorities of Ohio on its decree dissolving the trust. Leaving the stand, Rockefeller saw

Rice, and in his usual benign fashion, extending his hand, said: "How are you, Mr. Rice? We are getting to be old men now. Don't you wish you had taken my advice years ago?"

Rice, ignoring the extended hand, exclaimed bitterly, "You ruined me."

Rockefeller tut-tutted, and moved away.

CHAPTER 16   *The Competitive Practices of Standard Oil*

W E HAVE TOLD the melancholy story of Rice—but there is another side to the story, putting Rice in another light. It appears that Rice may have belonged to a breed of refiner whom Standard Oil called "blackmailers," those who made themselves obnoxious to Standard Oil in the hope they would be bought out and got rid of for an exorbitant price. According to testimony before the Industrial Commission: Rice's wife offered to sell the Rice refinery for $24,000 in 1876; in 1882 Rice offered to give F. D. Squire, of Standard Oil of Ohio, $50,000 if he could bring about a sale to Standard for $250,000; in 1890 Rice now wanted all of $500,000 for his refinery, saying that otherwise he would institute bothersome suits. Rice admitted the $500,000 offer, saying, "Yes, I did."

Rice either grew bolder in "shaking down" Standard Oil as he became a more notorious foe or, if his refinery really did rise in value, Standard had been singularly ineffective in placing an obstacle before his progression in wealth. Rockefeller had the former view: "That was his idea—to raise a row, lose some money and make the Standard Oil lose a good deal and make a bargain. That is the whole story of George Rice."

In the "Buffalo Case" the same element appeared in the testimony. When the new company was being formed, Matthews said that Standard Oil might pay $150,000 or $200,000 to dissuade them from going in business. When Albert Miller returned from California, his initial motive was to hold up Standard Oil. "I am going to bust the Standard," he said, if he did not collect $50,000.

"Blackmailing" was a continuous occupational hazard of the monopoly. Extortion attempts were made brazenly, as this brief letter to Rockefeller from one S. W. Hall in 1883 shows: "I have leased the Seaboard Oil Works. Would it be to your interest to have it run or not run, as you might suggest?" Such machinations provoked Rockefeller's holy wrath, as in one letter to Camden: "They will be sick unto death now having failed in their wicked scheme. A good sweating will be healthy for them."

In this poisonous atmosphere of blackmail and fear of blackmail it is no wonder that competition was in terms of "dog eat dog."

This does not derogate from the fact that Rice got rough treatment from Standard Oil. The experience of Rice cannot be accepted as typical, since a slice of refining always remained in the hands of independents, and grew from 5 percent in 1879 to around 18 percent in the 1900's, rising at one time to 24 percent in 1884.

Rockefeller's inclination was to have no competition at all. At one time he authorized price cuts "to secure our *full* share of the business." At another time he wrote that where competition threatened to reduce Standard's business, "it may be a very serious question whether we had not better make an important reduction with a view of taking substantially all the business there is." But he seems to have yielded to pleas that total victory was neither feasible nor good sense. In 1884 Charles Pratt wrote to him: "*Competitors we must have, competitors we must have,* while they are out I think we are safe. And if we absorb them, be sure it will bring in another." Benjamin Brewster counseled, "If we make the fight too sharp, we face retaliatory measures."

Of the competitive methods that were relied upon, the advantage in transportation rates was a prime weapon. Rockefeller claimed that after 1880 he did not accept rebates, but what's in a name? There were plenty of ways to skin the cat. Rates could be ostensibly equal to all, yet favoring Standard Oil. One method was to keep the rates low from the cities where Standard had its refineries and high from the cities where its competitors were located. Since Standard used pipelines to transport its crude, another method was to keep rail rates high on crude. In 1880 Rockefeller wrote to Oliver Payne that he should advise the Erie and New York Central that if they kept up rail rates to Cleveland, "we will not be pressing for reduction of westbound rates." In 1880 William Warden wrote to Charles Lockhart about a competitor "making a desperate effort for a large blackmail," and asked that he approach the Pennsylvania about charging a stiff rate to that refiner. A third example was in shipments of oil to California before oil was found there. During the time when Standard was shipping heavily for storage, rail rates were lowered; afterward, rates were raised.

Actually, rates were not equal to all. Where Standard and a competitor used rail from the same points, rates continued to be discriminatory. Thus Standard Oil shipped refined by rail from Cleveland to Chicago, and so did Scofield, Schurmer and Teagle, whom we have met in a previous court case. From July to November 1881, the Scofield firm claimed, the rate charged by the Lake Shore Railroad for them was $0.70 a barrel, but for Standard only $0.35. So they brought suit in the courts of Ohio, won in the district court, and the case went to the supreme court of the state. Standard Oil claimed that it was entitled to a lower rate on the ground that it furnished a switch, terminal facilities, and loading racks, and exempted the rail from liability for fire. The Scofield firm showed that it furnished similar facilities. Then Standard claimed that it was entitled to the lower rate because it furnished much greater quantities. The Supreme Court (43 Ohio State Reports 571) struck down the lower rate to Standard in a scathing decision: "The understanding was to keep the price down for the favored customer but up for all the others and the inevitable effect of this contract was to enable the Standard Oil to establish and maintain an overshadowing monopoly, to ruin all other operators and drive them out of business." As for the claim that Standard Oil was entitled to a rebate for larger quantities, the Court said it was "a discrimination in favor of capital" and it would "add largely to the accumulated power of capital and money and drive out all enterprise not backed by overshadowing wealth."

This court decision on the legality of Standard Oil freight concessions had only one effect: the discriminations to Standard became less direct and more adroitly conceived.

Standard Oil, as we have noted, owned tank cars, and its competitors had virtually none, and this made discrimination easy. We have noted some discriminations practiced in the previous chapter. In addition to their complaint about "blind-billing," refiners who used barrels for shipments claimed that another piece of skulduggery was used. Because of the variety of refined products, each having a different weight, the railroad had to use an average figure of weight per gallon. For tank cars, barrel users claimed that it was an underestimate of weight, but for barrels it was an overestimate, thus penalizing them.

To that was added a horrendous discrimination. While there was return freightage charged on empty barrels, the roads actually paid Standard Oil three-quarters of a cent mileage allowance for hauling its tank cars *whether they were full or empty.* It was a rebate exacted under duress by Standard Oil on the threadbare excuse that by furnishing its own tank cars Standard was performing a service to the rails even when the cars were empty. It was said that during slack periods tank cars were routed home by circuitous routes to increase mileage allowances.

In 1891 Rockefeller ordered that legal title to all tank cars be vested in the Union Tank Line Company, which was set up as a separate corporation under New Jersey law. This company "rented" the cars to the different Standard refineries—a device to get around trouble for Standard under the antitrust law. The rental charge was a fiction. The revenue for Union Tank Line came from the mileage allowance paid by the roads, and it piled up, the only expense being the cost of a dozen clerks.

In 1894 the western roads rebelled and refused to pay the mileage allowance, demanding that it be drastically cut. The story is told by Albert Carr in *Mr. Rockefeller's Secret Weapon.* The leader in the revolt was Alpheus B. Stickney, president of the Chicago and Great Western line. This road got no business from Standard, possibly because Stickney was the author of a book, *The Railway Question,* in which he attacked Standard Oil for playing one road against the others. Howard Page, executive officer of UTL, bluntly addressed the revolters. If they continued to be wayward, Standard would select "the weakest road in moral stamina"; all shipments would be concentrated on it; and then the other rails would cry for restoration of the *status quo*. So it proved. And the weak sister who broke the united front was A. B. Stickney, in behalf of the Chicago and Great Western, who agreed to pay the full mileage allowance in return for a large share of the oil traffic.

This tale speaks eloquently in explaining the rise of Standard Oil by use of the "divide and conquer" principle.

The ruthlessness of Standard Oil's marketing policies have become a byword in our industrial history. The underlying spirit undoubtedly emanated from 26 Broadway, New York, but there is some extenuation in the fact that there was considerable autonomy among the different distributive units. Two of them, renowned for their ruthlessness, Chess, Carley and Company of Louisville, which had the Southeast Territory, and Waters-Pierce Company of St. Louis, which had the Southwest, were headed by forceful feudal-baron types whom Standard had difficulty in controlling. Standard believed that F. D. Carley made sham fights with independents, meanwhile lining his own pockets. Of Henry Clay Pierce, Standard executive Charles Higgins said: "He wouldn't play ball with the crowd and he liked to pull fast ones. He wouldn't do a thing straight if it could be done crooked."

The most morally offensive practice, perhaps, was the espionage network that Standard Oil set up. This unilateral industrial research seems to have been a Rockefeller hallmark, and the ophidian methods used must be charged to him. The Standard Oil agent in any territory had to file a monthly statement not only of all oil sold by him but also of all sold by anybody else. He had to list the names of all sellers, how much and what brands. One way to get such information was to go to the depot and examine the shipments. Another was to get on good terms with the railroad people who might supply the information. Waters-Pierce once complimented a Texas agent, "We are glad to know that you are on such good terms with the railroad people that Mr. Clem gains nothing by marking his shipments by numbers instead of names." Clem was a jobber of oil sold by the enemy.

Here is a sample page of a record of competing oil sold, kept regularly at the headquarters of a Standard Oil marketing division:

Bonds Reports	Date Ship'd	Date Rec'd	SHIPPER	FROM	CONSIGNEE	DESTINATION	Refined Barrels	Naptha Barrels	Lub'ing Barrels	CAR		REMARKS
										Initial	No.	
	May											
5/20	5/18	1	Penn. Mfg Co.	Oil City	L. M O Co	Georgeville		93		L M	7741	
5/22	5/15	16	Warren R. & Co	Strauthers	A. Spence Co	"		76		P.L M	432	
5/7	5/2	7	Capital Oil Co	Oil City	Hawestown Oil Co	"	64		12	E K	1684	
5/12	5/6	9	Clear Lorian R	Strauthers	X. Y 3. 62 C	"	112			L M	43	
			Empire Oil Tp.	Reno	Boston Mut Co	"	63			P L M	64378	
5/17	5/23	25	Warren L & Co	Strauthers	"	"		87		B K	63748	
6/7	6/1		Tiona Refg Co	Clarendon	"	"	75			B.K	66042	
6/14	6/30	30	Titusville Oil Wo	Titusville	Long Manty Co	"		92		B T Co	37421	
	5/22	22	Pittsburg Refg Co	Cooperts	Henry Whitebar	"		92		"	94	
6/11	27	9/1	Savoy Refg Co	Bradford	X. Y 3 Oil Co	"		122		S K	496	
4/14	5/22	26	Clamp & Co	Titusville	"	"		126		P. L M	643	

Many enemies of Rockefeller, Lewis Emery, John Teagle, and Rice's daughter, Mrs. G. C. Butts, told of bribes paid to their employees to give information to Standard. A typical case is described by the testimony of a refiner, Theodore F. Davis, before the Industrial Commission:

Q. You intimated just now that your competitors sometimes secured information with reference to your methods of doing business in ways that were ordinarily not considered normal. What were some of the methods employed?

A. On one occasion we had an office boy who became shipping clerk and attended to making shipments of oil by river and by rail. The young fellow was approached by an agent of the Standard Oil Company who offered to pay him for a report from day to day, giving the names of the persons we were shipping to, and the invoice price of the product.

The government, in its brief in its antitrust suit against Standard Oil, submitted letters from 1898 to 1900 from one Maywood Maxon, in charge of the Decatur territory for Standard Oil, to Elliot and Stanley in the Cincinnati office. In May 1898 he wrote: "I wish you would please send me check for $21.40 as promptly as you can. $4.40 is for information about the shipments of Mr. T. D. Wilson at Litchfield and $10.00 is for information up to date at St. Louis." The money obviously went to railroad employees. A dozen letters were submitted, asking for funds, but a year and a half after the first letter, in November 1899, came the final letter:

> Now, in reference to Decatur, I wish to frankly admit that I cannot make arrangements here to get this information. It might be that you could come in here and do so being a complete stranger. There has been quite a number of changes in the railroad people in the freight houses in this city, and there are a great many more on the anxious seat.

The information as to volume of competitors' shipments was compiled so that Standard could know the exact business done by each refiner and jobber. It enabled Standard to judge whether the threat in each area was serious and should be met, or was minor and could be ignored. Miss Tarbell and other opponents of Standard maintained that it was its consistent policy to "cut to kill." However, as correspondence of Standard officials demonstrates, there was a genuine reluctance to cut prices unless it was felt necessary. This was so for an obvious reason—since Standard's volume of sales was so much greater than its competitors, it lost much more by price-cutting than its small rival. Standard had to be on its guard against a refiner like George Rice who thrust rapierlike into a territory, dumped a small amount of oil, forced all sellers of Standard Oil to slash their prices, and then departed. The lot of a near-monopoly seller is not always a happy one.

Where the circumstances demanded it, there was no hesitancy to cut prices. The usual contract with the jobber or retailer who was a grocer, druggist, or hardware man guaranteed him a specific net profit, so the retailer on call of Standard could cut his price without loss to himself. Threats to cut prices could intimidate recalcitrant jobbers and retailers, and make actual price cuts unnecessary.

As an example of such a threat, Peter Shull of the Independent Oil Company of Mansfield, Ohio, produced a letter from a dealer before the Ohio investigation of 1898:

> I am sorry to say that a Standard Oil man from your city followed your oil car and oil to my place and told me that he would not let me make a dollar on that oil, and was dogging me around for two days to buy that [Standard] oil, and made

all kinds of threats and persuaded me to sell [countermand the order] and I was in a stew what I should do but I yielded. I thought I would hate to see the bottom knocked out of prices.

Before the Industrial Commission, a letter was offered from the Standard Oil office in Portland, Oregon, to a dealer in South Bend, Washington, who told of a competitor shipping "Sun Light" oil into the town:

We will state for your information that never a drop of oil has reached South Bend of better quality than what we have always shipped into that territory. They can name it "Sun Light," "Moon Light" or "Star Light"; it makes no difference. You can rest assured that if another carload of "Sun Light" oil arrives at your place, it will be sold very cheap. We do not propose to allow another carload to come into that territory unless it is put on the market at one-half its actual cost.

Peter Shull gave this crisp summary of the prospect for a dealer of independent oil: "You take $10,000 and go into the business and I will guarantee you won't be in the business ninety days. Their motto is that anybody going into the oil business in opposition to them they will make life a burden to him. That is about as near as you can get to it."

Since there was some independent oil sold, that was not always the rule. A rival refiner, T. B. Westgate, testified before the Industrial Commission that often competition was "very agreeable." He explained that it was "agreeable" if he remained content with 10 percent of the trade. If he tried to expand it to a third or a half, there would then be a price war from Standard Oil. The rule was: "Only gentlemen competitors wanted by Standard Oil."

Where Standard Oil decided to slash the price, it would slash it deeply. In Austin, Texas, the price dropped from $0.22 to $0.10, in Little Rock from $0.16 to $0.06 a gallon. In the price war of 1892, the same oil that sold at Montrose and Gunnison for $0.25 sold in Denver for $0.07. These price cuts were only a temporary boon for consumers. When the war was over, the price bounced up, not to its original level, but higher, so that the consumer could pay reparations to Standard for the damage done. Such conquest by Standard had a salutary effect in other communities.

As Charles Woodbury explained, it spread the fear that independents might disappear there, too. "Was it wise to provoke the animosity of Standard Oil for the sake of continuing the purchase of certain favorite brands?"

Dealers might not want to handle Standard Oil. From Standard records, it appears that the distaste for the monopoly was shared by many. In that case another device came into play. Dealers would get the opportunity to buy from Company XYZ, which would offer them oil at a cut-rate price. Company XYZ was a bogus company, in reality a Standard offspring. The real independent would be unable to meet the price of the fake independent, and would be driven from the territory. Then Company XYZ would raise its prices to match those of Standard.

Perhaps the most flagrant instance of playing a fake role was the fight against the Tiona Oil Company, which had bested Standard Oil at Oneonta, New York. The Albany manager of Standard, Mason, sent an agent, Charles Farrell, to Binghamton to buy Tiona Oil at the wholesale price and then sell it door to door in Oneonta as "Tiona Oil—8 cents a gallon," the same price he had paid. This started a price war that drove the price down to nothing. The demoralized retailers were incensed at Tiona, from whom they bought their oil, for starting the war, and Tiona lost its goodwill. Mason wrote to Farrell, "Our salesmen who visit Oneonta know nothing of who you are and under no circumstances whatever do we want anyone to get the slightest hint that we are in any way connected in this matter. Burn it up, don't tear this letter since someone might get hold of it."

Whether Standard's competitors employed the same methods on occasion was a subject not explored at the time. Possibly no one could adopt a holier-than-thou pose. In the antitrust case against it, Standard introduced testimony in its behalf by E. N. Wooten, who left Kentucky Standard to join a competitor in 1904. In 1908 he asked to be reemployed, his letter reading: "Since leaving the employ of the company my opinion of them [Standard officials] has materially altered and I do not regard their policies as very different in principle to those generally in vogue commercially throughout the country in small and large concerns."

CHAPTER 17   *The Trust Under Attack*

IN 1887 William Warden wrote to his chief, John D. Rockefeller:

> We have met with a success unparalleled in commercial his-
> tory, our name is known all over the world, and our public
> character is not one to be envied. We are quoted as the repre-
> sentative of all that is evil, hard-hearted, oppressive, cruel (we
> think unjustly) but men look askance at us, we are pointed out
> with contempt, and while some good men flatter us, it is only
> for our money, and we scorn them for it, and it leads to
> further hardness of heart.

It is thus evident that worrisome public hostility to Standard
Oil antedates the muckraking age. The virus of hatred had been
already at work, the foci of infection being the angry oil producers of the Regions, refiners who felt that they had been expro-
priated and independent jobbers and dealers who rebelled
against the heavy hand of the monopoly. The animus had seeped
into the minds of the public at large. A perennial problem faced
by Standard Oil was that practically everyone bought its product
and could get excited about the oil trust—few bought steel, nuts
and bolts or cattle feed, and so few got excited about the trusts in
those items, feeling too remote from their evils.

But the oil trust was not alone. By 1890 there were at least one
hundred industrial combinations and pools of substantial size.
There were trusts following the pattern of Standard Oil, not only
in major commodities like whiskey, sugar, glass, copper, lead, and
coal but even in minor items like bicycles and school supplies.
Standard Oil stock was never "watered." The company was always undercapitalized rather than overcapitalized, a somewhat
academic point since the stock was not sold by the company to
the public; in fact, it was not even listed on the New York Stock
Exchange. The most reckless, even fantastic, manipulation attended the launching of the new trusts, the stocks of which were
shamelessly "watered." The National Steel Company capitalized

at $59,000,000 and the American Steel Hoop Company capitalized at $33,000,000 had an actual investment of less than half that amount. Promoters voted themselves huge blocks of the stock for selling it to the public; manipulators William Whitney and Thomas Fortune Ryan were said to have gained control of the $10,000,000 tobacco trust with an investment of only $50,000.

The overcapitalization necessitated higher prices and higher profits to pay dividends, which was one of the primary purposes of forming the trust anyway. As for the quality of goods, *caveat emptor*. This was not the credo of Standard Oil, whose success had been built in good part on an endeavor to please the public. Any and every complaint of consumers was followed up. The prices of its products was considered reasonable until President Roosevelt set out to prove otherwise, and quality was considered the best possible, at least in this country. Nor did Standard Oil grow rich by getting favors from the government, as did other industries. The steel trust and the sugar trust thrived on the favors accorded by the protective tariff, which Henry Havemeyer, head of the sugar trust, called the "mother of trusts." Railroad fortunes were built on grants of land from the Federal Government—in the twenty-five years before 1885 the government gave away public lands amounting to 150 million acres—larger than New England and New York combined.

Rockefeller, however, was not interested in pleading his case—not until much later, when it was too late. At this time his policy was one of strict silence. While walking along Euclid Avenue in Cleveland one day, he explained why to a friend: "Look at that worm on the ground. If I step on it, I call attention to it. But if I ignore it, it disappears." There were only slight deviations from the policy. In 1881 George Rice put out an anti-Standard pamphlet, "Black Death," which contained many statements about the dangers of its oil; Henry Flagler added a section with statements in favor of Standard Oil, and distributed it. *The Oil, Paint and Drug Reporter* said, "It is very unusual for Standard Oil to squeal but in this case they have been made to fairly burst out."

The public image repelled. Rockefeller very rarely gave interviews, and presented a front of arctic indifference to the public. He had no endearing qualities, and his personality appeared so frigid that it might have been said of him, as was said of President Benjamin Harrison, that "he sweated ice water" When he had to go on public view, as in legislative inquiries, he exuded sanctimony and soft soap which the public could not swallow. Thus, to put a competitor out of business was to "save" him, and Standard Oil, which was earning 100 percent on its capital stock every year, was a philanthropic institution engaged in bringing cheap light to the world. The image of the company was even less palatable than that of the man. It appeared to be a secret Mafia-like organization operating in the openhearted American community behind a Chinese wall. The employees said nothing to outsiders, communicated with one another by secret cipher, and practiced extensive espionage of their competitors prior to cutting their throats.

In 1887 Congress took the first step in what was to be a long road to put a checkrein on hitherto unfettered business. This first departure from laissez–faire was the establishment of the Interstate Commerce Commission. It was a weak and tentative step, and gave the Standard Oil monopoly little to fear. As Commissioner Prouty said a year after the Act was passed: "If the Interstate Commerce Commission were worth buying, the railroads would try to buy it. The only reason they have not is that the body is valueless in its ability to correct railroad abuses."

The impotence of the new commission was demonstrated in the battle waged by small refiners against the order of the Pennsylvania and other northern roads in September 1888, raising freight rates on barreled oil to the eastern seaboard on the ground that freight must be paid on the weight of the barrel. Previously the barrel was carried free, but now barreled oil of the small refiners had to pay a higher charge than Standard's oil carried in tanks.

The background for this increase in rates is somewhat humorous. The railroads, justifying their rate raise on barrels, said that the commission had ruled in a case six months previously that "he [the shipper] must pay freight on barrels as well as oil." The commission in reply said that the full sentence showed that it was only deploring a prevailing practice in the South, and not making a ruling. The full sentence read: "Even then the shipper in barrels is at some disadvantage, for he must pay freight on barrels as well as oil." To almost tearful pleas of the commission in interviews and letters that the roads were misinterpreting the sentence, the roads would not budge.

The case was heard in 1889, and no decision was handed down until three years later, in 1892, when the ICC ordered the rails to make barreled and tank rates equal. The rails ignored the order. In 1894 the ICC ordered the rails to pay reparations to the injured refiners, which the rails ignored. The refiners brought suit in the courts, and the case dragged on for eleven long years before some compromise was reached.

The New York State Senate held hearings in early 1888, the beginning of a new fusillade of attacks. After some difficulty in locating Rockefeller, he took the stand under the tutelage of the leading lawyer of the day, Joseph Choate. Rockefeller was as benign and self-effacing as usual, with a profusion of deferences: "You are very good" or "I beg with all respect." From his testimony, as the New York *Herald* said, it appeared the trust was "the greatest philanthropy of the age, a sort of missionary society engaged in spreading the evangelical light of kerosene oil over the dark places in a naughty world." The *World* attacked his testimony, saying he was as "candid as a confidence man before a police court."

At one point he astounded his hearers. Asked if Standard Oil ever got cheaper rates than others, he replied: "No, sir. No, we have had no better rates than our neighbors, but, if I may be allowed, we have found repeated instances where other parties had secured lower rates than we had."

Counsel could not believe his ears, so he returned to the subject in the afternoon:

Q. Has not some company or companies embraced within this trust enjoyed from railroads more favorable rates than those rates accorded to refineries not in the trust?

A. I do not recall anything of the kind.

Q. You have heard of such things?

A. I have heard much in the papers about it.

Counsel had heard rumors that Standard Oil had made life uncomfortable for competitors:

A. They have not; no, sir, they have not.

Q. And they have lived on good terms with their competitors?

A. They have, and have today very pleasant relations with those gentlemen.

The stream of blandness and soft soap flowed on, as the New York *World* said, "as smoothly along as if gliding through one of his own oil pipes."

In March, the United States House Committee on Manufactures conducted its own investigation, much more extensive than the New York inquiry, which was confined to Standard executives. Again Rockefeller was benign: "We think our American petroleum is a very cheap light. It is our pleasure to make it so." The trust instrument had been produced in the New York hearings, and Rockefeller was ignorant of any further details, which provoked a congressman to remark that "there is a very great shortness of memory in not knowing this or that or the other, and yet the testimony goes to show you are doing an immense business, and there seems to be nobody that knows anything positively about it."

John Archbold admitted in his salty way that Standard might have got better railroad rates than competitors:

Q. You got the very best terms you could out of the railroads?

A. Yes, sir.

Q. No matter what other people got?

A. I was not attending to business for other people.

Q. But you were at all times willing to do the best you could for yourself?

A. To make the best arrangement I could for the concern for which I was dealing.

Q. Irrespective of any considerations as to whether the obligations of the railroads as common carriers authorized them to do so or not?

A. That was a matter for them to consider and not me.

Q. You did not intend to keep their consciences?

A. I would have had a hard job, I am afraid.

F. D. Carley, now retired, indiscreetly admitted that it had been his policy to "cut to kill."

A. . . . . I thought it was cheaper in the long run to make the price cheap and be done with it than to fritter away the time with a competitor in a little competition. I put the price down to the bone.

Q. You put it down so as to kill him outright.

A. I did not look at him.

On the whole, the Standard officials conducted themselves on the stand in accordance with the advice of one of its executives, Paul Babcock, who wrote to Rockefeller about these 1888 inquiries, "I think that this anti-trust fever is a craze which we should meet in a very dignified way, and parry every question with answers which while perfectly truthful are evasive of bottom facts."

The antitrust fever was not a "craze" and did not pass. The people were up in arms about trusts. The platforms of both major parties had inveighed against trusts in 1888, and even that staunch conservative President Harrison in 1889 had asked that "earnest attention should be given to" the trust problem.

Yet, despite the near unanimity in Congress there was widespread skepticism that the bill sponsored by Senator John Sherman would accomplish much. Senator O. H. Platt of Connecticut said, "The question of whether the bill will be operative, of how it will operate, has been whistled down the wind in the Senate as idle talk and the whole effort has been to get some bill headed 'A Bill to Punish the Trusts' with which to go to the country."

Senator John T. Morgan of Alabama rose in the Senate to say, "All the big fish will escape. The little fish are the men who will have the trouble."

Fears were expressed that the Federal Government was overstepping its constitutional limitations. Senator George F. Edmunds of Vermont said, "The Constitution of the United States intended to leave and did leave to the states of the Union the right of local self-government in every respect except those named that were granted to the National Government. . . . I think it is better to endure a present evil of even the most grinding and most stupendous of monopolies than to step by one inch or attempt to step by one inch over the clear boundary line that has been established." Senator Frank Hiscock of New York said, "Inquisitorial power is given to the officers of the General Government to reach into the management of every industry of the United States. . . . If this bill shall be carried into effect I shall expect the Senator from Ohio [Sherman] to present here next year an amendment that manufacturers are to be licensed and their business carried on under the restrictions of that license and under the inquisitorial power of the Attorney General, the district attorneys, and other officials."

On the final vote the Sherman Antitrust Act was passed by an overwhelming vote in June 1890. In the Senate only the New Jersey Senator with the formidable name of Rufus Blodgett voted against it.

Said Mr. Dooley, "What looks like a stone wall to the layman is a triumphal arch to a corporation lawyer." The early administration of the Act confirmed that expectation. The only success scored under President Harrison was against some Nashville coal dealers. In a case against lumber dealers in Minnesota, the case was dismissed because the agreement "operated [only] among themselves," thus not restraining others, an interpretation that would have killed the Act altogether.

None the less, with the statute on the books Rockefeller was aware that his trust was ever in jeopardy. Moreover, the tempo of the campaign was increasing as states were passing their own antitrust laws; Kansas was the first, in 1889, followed closely by North Carolina, Tennessee, and Michigan. By 1891 fifteen states had such laws.

There was an agonizing reappraisal on the part of Standard Oil of its policy of silence in the face of the diapason of demands for action against trusts. Besides Rockefeller's ingrained belief that silence was the best strategy to minimize attacks against those whom Archbold called "the howlers," there is no doubt that Rockefeller felt that any extensive defense would call for prying into the private dealings of the company. It was a considerable concession for him to grant an interview, his first, to his bitter critic, the New York *World*, published on March 29, 1890. In this interview he defended the trust: "I know that our efforts both in building up this vast oil trade abroad and at home and in cheapening this important product could not have been done except by a combination of persons and capital." In this he echoed in less florid tones the opinion of his counsel, Samuel C. T. Dodd, who in 1888, in his book *Combinations*, wrote, "By combination capital is obtained, enterprises of magnitude conducted, great results accomplished. Without it our railroads would be eaten by rust. Our ships would rot in their harbors. Our warehouses would decay, Mankind would become segregated as savages, each acting for himself alone and endeavouring to destroy others."

From an entirely unexpected quarter the attack by government began. In 1889 a young attorney general of Ohio, David K. Watson, was running for reelection after a two-year term. One afternoon he strolled across the street from the State House in Columbus to a bookstore where he browsed among the books. He came across a book, *Trusts,* in which he found printed the full text of the Standard Oil trust agreement. A thought struck him. If the text was correct (he later checked and found it correct), the Standard Oil of Ohio had violated the state corporation laws by putting the direction of the company into the hands of nonresident trustees.

In May 1890 Watson started quo warranto proceedings in the supreme court of the state, charging that the company had acted *ultra vires* and that its corporate charter should be forfeited and dissolved.

In November of that year, just after the congressional elections, Watson received an amazing letter from Mark Hanna, who had just been frustrated in his attempt to secure the reelection of his friend William McKinley to the House of Representatives. The exact text of this letter is in doubt. It was destroyed; but, as later reconstructed by Watson and persons who saw it, it read this way in the text made public. After saying that he had heard of the suit, Hanna purportedly said:

> . . . While I am not personally interested in the Standard Oil Company, many of my closest friends are and I have no doubt that many of the business associations with which I am connected are equally open to attack. . . . *There is no greater mistake for a man in or out of public office to make than to assume that he owes any duty to the public* [*underlining* supplied] or can in any manner advance his own position or interests by attacking the organizations under which experience has

taught business can be best done. From a party standpoint, interested in the success of the Republican Party and regarding you in the line of political promotion, I must say that the identification of your office with litigation of this character is a great mistake. There is no public demand for a raid on organized capital. For years the business of manufacturing oil has been done with great success at Cleveland, competition has been open and free and the public has been greatly benefited. The Standard Oil Company is officered and managed by some of the best and strongest men in the country. They are pretty much all Republicans and have been most liberal in their contributions to the party, as I personally know, Mr. Rockefeller always quietly doing his share. . . .

The tone of the letter is extraordinary, but the controversy revolves around the *underlined* portion, which is nothing less than a blockbuster. The biographer of Hanna, Herbert Croly, says with a good deal of logic that it is not authentic and was inserted: "Why, even had he believed it, should he be so cynical and incoherent enough to throw in a remark that a public official owes no duty to the public? The supposition is incredible. The folly becomes more inexplicable when it is remembered that the recommendation is addressed to a man with whom Mr. Hanna was slightly acquainted and who would have good ground to be aggrieved by the letter."

The logic of this argument is further buttressed by the reply of Watson. If the offending sentence had been in Hanna's letter, certainly he would have addressed himself to that proposition and his theme would have been that of public duty. Instead, Watson's theme was that he was aware of the need for concentration of capital and he had no intent to wage a campaign against "organized capital."

In March 1892 the Supreme Court of Ohio made its decision on the pleadings. It is said that the Statute of Limitations prevented the forfeiture of the charter but Standard Oil of Ohio was ordered to withdraw from the trust. To claims that the trust had been benevolent, beneficent, and what-not, the Court said: "It is the policy of the Law to regard not what may but what usually happens. Experience shows that it is not wise to trust human cupidity where it has the opportunity to aggrandize itself at the expense of others."

What ensued was to be years of opéra bouffe. The decision was rendered on March 2. Trust certificates had been outstanding for ten years and were in the hands of God knows who. Therefore Standard asked the Court for a period of grace in which to wind up the trust, and the Court said that, as long as the severance of Ohio Standard was being honestly carried on, it would not give a time ultimatum. Then on March 11 a Standard Oil stockholders' meeting was advertised to take place on the 21st. Full steam ahead on a liquidation that was to be bogged down forever. In lachrymose words at the meeting, Solicitor Dodd spoke of the necessity of dissolving the trust. An exchange plan was set in motion—each holder of a trust certificate would get proportionate shares of the constituent companies.

Rockefeller held 256,785 of 972,500 shares, and obtained proportionate shares in the twenty constituent companies. The other trustees did likewise. Financial journals predicted that the liquidation would take four months, but there was no motion beyond the initial one. At the end of the first year there were 477,881 shares uncanceled; at the end of the second year the same amount, and at the end of the third and fourth years exactly the same. The small stockholders felt that there would be no market ripe for the shares of the constituent companies, and refused to turn in their certificates for exchange. The company claimed that it had no way to compel them to do so.

The trustees in liquidation performed the same function in distributing dividends as at the time when they were active trustees. Rockefeller became president of Standard of Ohio, William Rockefeller of Standard of New York, Flagler of Standard of New Jersey, and James Moffett of Standard of Indiana. The presidents did not move to their respective states but all remained in 26 Broadway. Because the majority ownership of the stock of each company was in the hands of the same men, the board of directors of each company was identical. Committees were abolished, but experts in manufacturing, sales, and other functions communicated with their counterparts in other companies through their presidents. They were all located at 26 Broadway. In substance nothing had changed. It was an exercise in flimflam.

Rockefeller in 1892 was only fifty-three years of age, but he was battered and battle weary. In that year he suffered an acute digestive ailment that incapacitated him for a time. The burdens he had been carrying for years, and the ceaseless attacks, were finally taking a toll on his fine constitution. He always had appeared imperturbable and free from worry, but it was only self-discipline that gave him his outward icy composure.

Though he had recovered by 1893, his diet and eating habits had to be watched from that time on. It was found that he was allergic to some foods, including cucumbers, tomatoes, and heavy sweets. From that time, too, he drew away from active participation in the business, and by 1896 he was visiting 26 Broadway only on rare occasions. No news of this leaked to the outside world, which assumed that he was at his desk every day. He was, however, by no means out of the ring. He not only retained his official position but kept his hand on the wheel by telephonic communication. Though he had freed himself from minutiae, he plunged back in when the situation demanded. Though he fended off J. P. Morgan on the sale of his ore interests, saying he was retired, he dropped the pretense when he negotiated with Henry Frick.

Archbold, bold, blustery, and full of fire, was Rockefeller's choice to run the day-to-day affairs of the trust. The magnetic and commanding Rogers ranked next to him. The kindly and substantial William Rockefeller was close to the top of the hierarchy. Henry Flagler was now primarily interested in making the east coast of Florida a new *Côte d'azur*. By 1896 a Flagler railroad had reached into the swamps, which were Miami. Flagler built many hotels along the route, and had donated schools, churches, and hospitals. To finance this great undertaking he had sold a great deal of his stock to Rockefeller. A man of great virility, he gave adequate proof of this when he was a corespondent in a divorce suit at the age of seventy-one and married the young lady thereafter, the Florida legislature having passed a special law to enable him to divorce his wife.

Rogers was an audacious speculator in Wall Street. He would boast: "I am a gambler. Every now and then John W. Gates [known as Bet-a-Million Gates] will come to me and say, 'Henry,

don't you think it's time we had a little fun in the market?' We
made lots of killings and had plenty of fun. I must have action."

Wall Street heard more of what it called the "Standard Oil
crowd," which consisted only of Rogers and William Rockefeller,
who made millions in market manipulations. Standard Oil in the
early 1890's was paying dividends of $11,000,000 a year, and ten
years later the dividends had quadrupled. Rogers and William
Rockefeller, leaving their dividends in the company, paid for
their stock speculations with Standard Oil checks, so that it was
erroneously assumed by many that Standard was playing and
rigging the market, a mistaken notion, since John D. Rockefeller
frowned on stock gambling.

Totally aside from speculations, Standard Oil by investments
was becoming a formidable "money power" throughout industry,
and James Stillman, who became president of the City Bank in
1891, played a conspicuous role in this development. He forged a
fateful friendship with William Rockefeller when both were directors of the Chicago, Milwaukee and St. Paul railroads. William, in charge of the finances of Standard, deposited more and
more of its funds with City Bank. In 1897, when Edward Harriman and Kuhn, Loeb and Company agreed upon the reorgani-
zation of the Union Pacific Railroad, they financed it through the
City Bank, and thus Standard Oil became heavily involved in
Union Pacific.

The City Bank, now the National City, which had deposits of
only $12,000,000 in 1891, soared to over $100,000,000, thanks
mostly to Standard Oil. It was the traditional bank of metal merchants, and through these connections Rogers formed the Amalgamated Copper Company, which got control of Anaconda Copper. Known to be supported by Rockefeller money, the stock was
the favorite speculation of the day. Rockefeller money, under the
aegis of National City, now flowed into public utilities, and after
getting control of the Consolidated Gas Company in New York,
merged it spectacularly with the Edison Illuminating Company,
putting all lighting companies in New York under the control of
National City and the Rockefeller interests. The alliance between
National City and Standard was further cemented when two of
William Rockefeller's sons married Stillman's daughters.

Henry Clews, a long-time broker, wrote with rapt admiration

of the methods of the Standard clique: "Their resources are so great that they need only to concentrate on a given property to do with it what they please. They are the greatest operators the world has ever seen, and the beauty of their method is the quiet and lack of ostentation, no gallery plays, no scare heads in the paper, no wild scramble or excitement. With them the process is gradual, thorough and steady, with never a waver or break."

Turning back to the fortunes of Standard Oil—the nineties saw the company sink further into public obloquy. Standard Oil had to contend with the "yellow journalism" of Pulitzer and Hearst, which found Rockefeller an inviting target. The *World* under Pulitzer was especially vitriolic toward Standard Oil. Every time a Standard executive made an investment, it was represented as a company investment. Climatically, in 1897 the *World* headlined, "Standard Oil to Swallow All." In a feature article it once said, "From hounding and driving prosperous businessmen to beggary and suicide, to holding up and plundering widows and orphans, the little dealer in the country and the crippled pedlar on the highway—all this has entered into the exploits of this organized band of commercial cutthroats."

The publication of *Wealth Against Commonwealth* by Henry Demarest Lloyd in 1894 fused truth and allegations into the stereotype of villainy that was to be the public image of Rockefeller from that time till the dissolution of the trust in 1911. It came at a strategic time, after the Panic of 1893, two years after the bloody Homestead strike, and in the same year as the march of Coxey's Army on Washington and the Pullman strike in Chicago, which necessitated the sending of troops by President Cleveland. Populism was sweeping the Midwest. Passions were running high when Lloyd's bitter attack on the Standard Oil monopoly was published.

Lloyd was talented—and complex. He had graduated from Columbia University, where he studied law and later turned to journalism. He seems to have been endowed with a sense of mission and also a touch of megalomania. In a convention of liberal Republicans in 1872, fighting the nomination of Horace Greeley, a reporter described the twenty-five-year-old Lloyd as "laboring under the delusion that he was carrying the nation on his young shoulders." In Caro Lloyd's biography of her brother, she reveals that in a letter explaining why he had adopted journalism and not law as a profession, Lloyd wrote, "I want power, I must have power, I could not live if I did not think that I was in some way to be lifted above and upon the insensate masses who flood the stage of life in their passage to oblivion. . . ." This psychological motivation certainly has great relevance in understanding the man who undertook to destroy the Standard Oil Goliath with a book.

Lloyd went to the Midwest where he became an editorial writer for the Chicago *Tribune*. In line with the policy of the paper, he crusaded against monopolies and industrial profiteering. He also acquired financial success by a short-cut method—he married Jennie Bross, the daughter of the wealthy part-owner, William Bross. This was important insofar as Lloyd's influence was concerned, since his wife's wealth enabled Lloyd to retire in 1885 to luxury and devote himself to his antiwealth writings with all the research help that money could buy.

Lloyd made his first attack on Standard Oil in March 1881, in the lead article for the *Atlantic Monthly*, "The Story of a Great Monopoly," which attracted such worldwide interest that the issue went through seven printings. The article abounded in errors, but with Rockefeller's fundamental article of faith, that it was best contemptuously to ignore attacks, there was no reply. Ten years later Lloyd boasted, "My article of 1881 remains unanswered to this day," and no doubt Lloyd felt that he was on such firm ground that no answer was possible. In the succeeding years Lloyd became more radically inclined. In 1886 he defended in print the anarchists, convicted in the Haymarket Square bombing, which led to an estrangement with his father-in-law. In 1890 he published a book, *The Strike of Millionaires Against Miners*, and in 1896 and 1900 he voted the Socialist ticket, though in 1895 he had disavowed any sympathy with that party.

Wealth Against Commonwealth is one of the great polemics of all time. Standard Oil is never mentioned by name, nor is Rockefeller, though the allusions are clear. Standard is the "combination" and Rockefeller is the "head of the combination," or more often "the President of the Light of the World." Possibly this was done because of the fear of libel. Harper and Brothers published the book after four publishers had rejected it, and only after the book had been carefully documented. The attack is delivered with masterful satire so wrapped in invective that the book is an adventure in reading. The pungency is illustrated by some of the chapter titles, "You Are Not to Refine," "No," "Song of the Barrel," and "Crime Cheaper than Competition." Literary allusions enliven the narrative with considerable humor. Thus, calling for the outlawry of the rebate as a "wicked projectile," Lloyd recalls that "The Chevalier Bayard declared proudly as he lay on his death-bed that he had never given quarter to anyone so degraded and unknightly as to use gunpowder."

There are many points that can be chalked up to the credit of Lloyd. The book is a monumental piece of research. Professor Chester McArthur Destler, a student of the period, checked 420 of Lloyd's references to source material and found only ten inaccuracies, and those not important. It was the first history of Standard Oil, and a seminal work, since it was the first case history of an alleged social abuse buttressed by facts. Lloyd accurately put his finger on the essence of the monopoly control exerted by Standard Oil, its control of transportation. Lloyd used Standard Oil as a convincing example to prove that Adam Smith's theories about the beneficent workings of the free market were inapplicable to a situation where a monopoly force destroyed competition.

On the other side, there are many demerits. While the basic facts are correct, Lloyd takes liberties with the facts for dramatic effects, and his interpretations of the facts are often grossly distorted. In telling a Victorian "horror story," Lloyd paints the villain too black, while the opponents of Rockefeller are all in shiny white, though it is apparent that they were as eager to use the same tactics and play the same game. Any and every step taken by Standard Oil merely in the interests of simple survival as a business entity is branded as black iniquity. From the beginning Rockefeller beats his competitors to the ground, but in the next chapter he has to do it all over again, so that one reads with astonishment in Chapter XI that in 1883 rival refiners had been able to "maintain and increase" their business, and so on to the end.

Lloyd does not tell a coherent story, but selects the best nuggets, such as the way Rockefeller swindled the Widow Backus by giving a pittance for her refinery, or how a Standard refinery undertook to get rid of a competitor in Buffalo by blowing it up. In all these cases Lloyd wrote his account on the basis of facts supplied by the aggrieved parties but did not bother with the Standard side of the story. He was intemperate in his feelings about Standard. In his correspondence he said that its officials "ought to be in the penitentiary." To George Rice, a professional litigant against Standard, he wrote about its claim to have lowered prices, "This the public—dear fools—believe, and it entirely reconciles them, knavish fools—to the piracies, treason and murders [sic] by which the fabled cheapness has been brought to them." This from one who claimed to be an objective scholar and a spokesman for the public.

The book had a profound effect, but mainly among the intellectuals. Reviews, like that of Wendell Phillips Garrison in *The Nation* (he was the son of the great abolitionist), that it was "five hundred pages of the wildest rant" were in the minority. William Dean Howells said of the "monstrous iniquity" that it was "so astounding, so infuriating that I have to stop from chapter to chapter to take breath," and Edward Everett Hale said that it was "as much an epoch-making book as *Uncle Tom's Cabin*." A dyed-in-the-wool enemy of Rockefeller, Dr. Washington Gladden, said he was surprised the book "had not caused more excitement; it surprises me that it does not cause an insurrection." Lloyd himself was surprised that the effect was not explosive. The message, *écrasez l'infâme*, could not have been delivered in a more inflammatory fashion by a French Revolutionist. But Lloyd wrought better than he believed at the time.

In the first place, the book gave a terrific impetus to what has been called the "muckraking era." "Muckraking" got its name from a speech by President Roosevelt in 1906 in which he lifted a term from Bunyan's *Pilgrim's Progress* to describe those who were thrashing out in public print the abuses practiced by those in the seats of power. It was characteristic of Roosevelt's ambivalence on all issues that while on the one hand he attacked "malefactors of great wealth," with the other he slapped down those who were trying to eradicate evils by bringing them to light. In his speech in 1906, dedicating the new House of Representatives Office Building, Roosevelt spoke of the Man with the Muck-Rake "who was offered a celestial crown for his muck-rake, but who would neither look up nor regard the crown he was offered, but continued to rake to himself the filth of the floor." In his biography of S. S. McClure, Peter Lyon points out that Roosevelt had fouled the meaning of the parable: ". . . muck is a symbol of money and the Man with the Muck-Rake symbolizes those most criticized by the literature of exposure, whom Roosevelt himself would later call the 'malefactors of great wealth.'"

In the second place, *Wealth Against Commonwealth* had its most profound effect because it influenced a writer who was to be much more successful in reaching the masses. This was Ida Minerva Tarbell, who was given a copy of *Wealth Against Commonwealth* by the English writer Wickham Steed, while she was in Paris studying historical research at the Sorbonne. She was deeply moved, and later was to carry the torch passed on to her by Lloyd.

With the election of McKinley in 1896, Standard Oil had little to fear from the Federal Government. Rockefeller had contributed liberally to the war chest to defeat Bryan; his friend Mark Hanna was in the saddle; and the Administration, subservient to Big Business, had scrapped antitrust prosecutions. The revolt in Cuba occurred, and the drift to war. With larger issues in the news, Standard Oil was forgotten by many.

There were some who did not forget Standard Oil, and one was the avenger, George Rice; another was David K. Watson, who was convinced that Standard Oil had been flouting the dissolution decree of the Ohio courts. At his instance, Frank Monnett, the new attorney general of the state, filed an information with the courts of Ohio in November 1897, alleging that Standard Oil should be declared in contempt for not obeying the court's decree. From 1892 to 1897, the number of shares uncanceled and unexchanged remained at 477,881. Then the figure dropped by *all of one share*, to 477,880. What had happened? George Rice had managed to buy one share, and demanded to have it exchanged for shares of the constituent companies. In one company he recieved 50/9725ths of a share. In order to have received a full share in each of the constituent companies, he would at current market prices have had to spend $66,000.

The trust had maintained for years that it was helpless to compel the small certificate holders to exchange their shares, yet

Monnett learned that, within three months of the filing of his information with the court, 100,583 shares were offered for cancellation. Did this not prove that Standard Oil had been thumbing its nose at the court for several years in contumacy?

Monnett was dissatisfied with the answers Rockefeller gave to written inquiries, and asked that a special master be appointed to take oral testimony in New York. On October 11 and 12, 1898, Rockefeller gave his testimony, but, as the *World* said, "The art of forgetting is possessed by Mr. Rockefeller in its highest degree." If he could not be helpful, Rockefeller could be courtly, as always. When, toward the close, opposing counsel said, "Never mind, Mr. Rockefeller, I am almost through bothering you," he replied, "Now I almost regret that. This is very pleasant."

Monnett suspected that, far from being dissevered, Standard Oil of Ohio was continuing to pay dividends from its profits to the other members of the trust family. This was denied. Monnett wanted to examine the books of the company, but the secretary of Ohio Standard said that information from them might be used in pending state antitrust suits against Ohio Oil, Buckeye Pipeline and Solar Refining. Monnett put witnesses on the stand to prove that books, documents, and journals had been burned by Standard Oil in November 1898; however, the evidence was in conflict.

In March 1899 the hearings resumed, and Archbold on the stand gave a volcanic performance, spurting lava in all directions. He shouted at Rice, "There is nothing to you but wind and weight." In an exchange with an assistant of Monnett, he shouted at him, "You dog, you miserable whelp!" and later, "You are a dirty, stinking liar!" The substance of his testimony, apart from his outbursts, was that Standard could have taken no course than what it had done, since it had foremost in mind the welfare of widows and orphans.

Monnett was frustrated at every turn. The Supreme Court of Ohio split 3 to 3 on the contempt charge he had brought, which was later dropped. Monnett claimed that Standard Oil had offered him a bribe of a half-million but could not prove it. Monnett was left with the antitrust suits against the Ohio companies, which were finally dismissed.

It had become apparent to Rockefeller and his associates that the trust instrument of 1882 had outlived its usefulness. Some other legal device would have to be used to keep the trust together. New Jersey, at that time becoming a haven for trusts, afforded the answer. While other states were harrying trusts, New Jersey was opening its gates wide to them, and became known as "the mother of trusts." It was the subject of some merriment. A favorite cartoon pictured small boys, labeled "trusts," being chased and calling "Help," and a full-bosomed matron representing New Jersey stretching out her arms, "Come to Mother."

In 1889 New Jersey passed a law that authorized holding corporations, and in 1896 broadened it to read "Any corporation may purchase . . . the shares or any bonds . . . of any corporation or corporations of this or any other state." Only one member of the board of directors had to be a resident of the state; there was no limit on the capital stock and no annual report was required. Standard Oil had a physical existence in New Jersey, but under the liberal laws of the state that would have been unnecessary for establishing domicile—it would have been sufficient to display a sign with the name of the corporation on the building of a trust company. It was no wonder that under this New Jersey law, in the years 1898 to 1900, 183 holding corporations were organized with a capitalization of over four billion dollars.

One of these was the new holding corporation, Standard Oil of New Jersey, formed in June 1899. All the constituent companies were dumped into it, the capitalization of the New Jersey company being raised from $10 million to $110 million. The trust certificates were exchanged by holders for shares of stock.

The Supreme Court in the Knight Case in 1895 had upheld the legality of the American Sugar Refining Company, although it had 87 percent of the trade, since there was no direct proof of an intention to put a restraint on commerce. ". . . the fact that trade or commerce might be indirectly affected was not enough to entitle the complainants to a decree," said the Court. Standard Oil now seemed to be safely anchored in a snug harbor. Let the storms rage outside.

CHAPTER 18 *Pure Oil*

S TARTING IN 1887, there was another uprising of the oil regions
against Rockefeller. It was to eventuate in the birth and
continued existence of the first real rival to Standard Oil, the Pure
Oil Company.

Between 1877 and 1887, the price of crude had fallen from
$4.00 a barrel to a mere $0.60. Production was so great that over
31 million barrels were being carried in storage, over a year's
production. On this carryover, Standard Oil, as owner of the
pipelines in the oil fields, was collecting huge storage charges,
and thus in the eyes of the producers feasting on their misery;
they also blamed Rockefeller for the low price of crude. Then
there rose a haunting fear that Lima crude from the new field
would soon undercut the position of Pennsylvania crude in the
market.

In 1887 the producers pushed a bill in the Pennsylvania state
legislature, the Billingsley bill, which cut the rates for storing oil
and other services performed by Standard's National Transit
Company. The punitive nature of this proposed legislation was
advertised openly in the preamble of the bill, "An Act to Punish
Corporations, etc.," engaged in transporting and storing of oil.
The charges would be cut in some instances below cost, and Ida
Tarbell in her discussion of the bill admitted that "it was as bad
as it could be." Amid hysterical enthusiasm, the bill was pushed
through the House, but to the chagrin of the Regions was de-
feated in the state Senate. To accomplish this result it is admitted
even by apologists for Standard Oil that many palms were generously greased in an honest and worthy cause.

Infuriated by the defeat of the bill, the producers formed a
new association in June 1887, spearheaded by Lewis Emery, Jr.,
an inveterate foe of Rockefeller, and who as a member of the state
Senate had become a prominent foe of the monopoly. Over 2,000
members bound themselves together to handle their own oil from
well to consumer—a project that surely would not sit well with

Mr. Rockefeller. The first decision of the producers was to get rid of the huge carryover by cutting oil production. But if the producers did so, and the price went up, Rockefeller would be a prime beneficiary because he owned ten million barrels aboveground.

Rockefeller, as usual, was ready with a conciliatory gesture toward the producers. If they would cut production to 17,500 barrels a day, he would sell to the producers, that is, carry for them, 5 million barrels at $0.62 a barrel. If the price went up, the producers would divide the increase in accordance with each producer's cut in production.

The shutdown, beginning in November 1887, was initially successful, but refusals of some to join, who hoped for a free ride, and subsequent defections made a long-time project of the matter. The shutdown lasted until 1889, when the carryover was reduced to 9 million barrels. In June, Rockefeller bought a large quantity for $0.92 a barrel that had cost the Association $0.62, thus netting the producers a substantial profit. Rockefeller had made a real gesture of friendship, as Thomas Phillips, president of the Producers' Association, conceded, saying that he thought Standard Oil was as much disappointed in the modest profit as were the producers. Rockefeller's interest, in truth, was not basically antagonistic to higher prices for crude, since he feared that low prices would ultimately choke off the incentive for exploration.

Now the Association turned to its original project, the cooperative transport and marketing of oil. H. L. Taylor, whom we have seen years before trying to take over Tidewater by a coup with John Satterfield (conjecturally in behalf of Standard), was now appointed chairman of a committee to study the problems. Then came a shock, another reminder of the obstacles to be met in fighting the riches of Standard. Rockefeller had bought out Taylor's oil company and three other oil producers. Overnight Rockefeller had become a big producer. Taylor and his partners, the McKinney brothers, were thereupon kicked out of the Producers' Association. Another blow followed when it was learned that the Association president himself, Tom Phillips, had sold Standard Oil 7,500 acres of oil property for $75,000. Rockefeller had always been adept at "burrowing from within."

In January 1891 a general assembly at Warren set up the Producers' Oil Company. It started out in earnest, buying fifty tank cars and getting the use of an oil terminal at Bayonne from an independent oil refiner, the Columbia Refining Company. In the Regions, Emery lined up more independent refineries that had been hard hit by the recent rail increase for barrel shipments but that now could use the tank cars. In spite of progress, there was considerable skepticism and foot-dragging in the Regions, which had been disillusioned by the earlier Tidewater capitulation and the numerous sellouts. As *The Oil, Paint and Drug Reporter* stated, "Producers no longer clasp hands, shed tears of sympathy and draw on bank accounts to assist in schemes to sell out to Standard. They have been too often betrayed."

Because the Region refineries collectively could use only a small amount of crude, it was necessary to reach the independent refineries on the seaboard. Emery decided to build two pipelines, one for crude and one for refined, which hitherto had not been carried by pipeline. Emery negotiated with the Reading Railroad, hoping to pipe the oil from Bradford to Williamsport, but the Reading declined: "If we give you this contract, it will disturb our relations with Standard Oil. We cannot do it."

Instead Emery and his newly formed United States Pipe Line Company decided to reach Hancock, New York, on the New York, Western and Ontario Railroad, which welcomed the new traffic and could carry the oil to the Hudson River. Standard once more swung into action. "Once more unto the breach, dear friends." It bought land to block the right of way and bought mortgages to put pressure on farmers not to sell permission. It called on the railroads to protect its interest, as it always did.

When Emery's line came close to Hancock, New York, a force of seventy-five men, sent by the Erie, prevented a linkage of the pipe across the Erie's line. The men of Erie and Emery's men glowered at each other for three weeks. Meanwhile, Emery executed a flanking movement from one hundred miles back and secured a right of way to Wilkes-Barre, where he linked with the Jersey Central.

The pipeline was complete.

The demonstration was eagerly awaited at Wilkes-Barre. Could refined oil be successfully piped? The answer proved to be Yes—

and more than that, the agitation of the oil in the pipes seemed to have raised the flash point so that it became safer for use. With scorn, Emery testified before the Industrial Commission: "They [Standard] said it couldn't be done, although they are the infiniteness of everything and the benefactors of the world."

In his fight against the new rival, Rockefeller now turned to the price weapon. Between January and December 1893, the price of crude rose from $0.53 a barrel to $0.78, but the movement of refined was in the opposite direction, from 5.33 cents a gallon down to 5.15 cents. In 1894 crude fluctuated between $0.80 and $0.91, but refined curled up around 5.20 cents. Standard Oil claimed that it had no hand in the amazing phenomenon of the divergent movements of crude and refined, blaming the worldwide depression and the competition with Russian oil; but it was the widely held viewpoint in trade circles that the downturn in refined was managed by Standard, the New York *World* saying that Standard's action was "one of the most daring and unprincipled in the history of American commerce."

In the export market Standard was dumping its oil at such low prices that for twenty months the Emery group lost on every barrel that it sold. In fact, a barrel of refined for export sometimes sold below the price for a barrel of crude. Yet the market for export oil had to be maintained by the new independent, since almost 50 percent of the oil was low-test, suitable only for export.

In the face of these losses, desertions became more common. In the Regions three medium-sized refiners threw in the towel. Rockefeller took their oil stocks and dismantled their plants. Outside the Regions the Elizabethport Refining Works sold a large interest to Standard Oil and shortly thereafter took its place in the Standard empire.

A committee from the new company went to Standard and asked: "Is there no hope of a better market? Is there any chance for us?" None whatever, they were told, except to sell out to Standard. Many, perhaps the majority, of the new group wanted to give up; but at a meeting one of the leaders, J. W. Lee, made an impassioned plea rallying the embattled forces, pointing out that ultimately the higher price for crude would pull up the price of refined, no matter how hard the monopoly fought to resist economic law. Underselling had already been stopped by the

German Government. To the refiners he pleaded: "Do not give in. We will go to the producers, lay your plight before them, and raise money to continue the struggle for independence."

In January 1895 a meeting was held at Butler to which special trains were run. A resolution was passed for the establishment of the Pure Oil Company. The sum of $75,000 was pledged at the meeting and in a few days $200,000. In view of Standard's well-known penchant for infiltration, the prospectus had an interesting clause. The voting power of one-half the stock would be placed in the hands of "five champions of this right of independence," who would be bound "to vote only for such men and measures as shall forever make this company INDEPENDENT. . . ."

Incidentally, the name Pure Oil was chosen because it might have competitive value. "Pure" oil might be more appealing to consumers than "standard" oil. Previous companies had chosen names like "Anti-Trust Oil" and "Independent Oil." (Standard Oil agents joked with customers that really there was no company more "independent" than Standard Oil.)

Then came 1895 and one of the greatest booms in oil history. Crude shot from $0.95 a barrel in January to over $2.00 in the week of April 6. Standard by now was a big producer, and the rise of $0.70 a barrel in Lima crude added millions to the Standard coffers. Refined oil finally rose to 9.12 cents a gallon in April.

Pure Oil had to continue to struggle to keep alive. Its agent in Germany, Herr Poth, inexplicably deserted Pure Oil, which claimed that he had been fed false information by Standard agents that Pure Oil had sold out. Emery rushed to Europe and had to start from scratch in Central Europe, rebuilding a marketing system with depots and bulk stations.

The familiar attempts at subversion occurred. Colonel John J. Carter held 300 shares of Producers' Oil Company (the producing end of the new combine). He was elected to membership, a requirement under the Pennsylvania law governing limited partnerships, which thus made him eligible to vote. First, he tried to get control of the company by voting not only his 300 shares but 13,013 that were lent to him by Standard, but he lacked a majority. Indignation ran high when it came to light that 60 percent of the stock in the Carter Oil Company was owned by Standard. In 1896 Carter bought at a knockdown price from Standard 29,764 shares, or more than enough to take control of the company. But when Carter sought to have the stock transferred on the books, he was met with a stout refusal, and in a court case the management was upheld. Under the Pennsylvania law, a limited partner could vote only the shares to which he had been elected, in the case of Carter, only 300 shares. "A queer law," said Archbold ruefully on the witness stand before the Industrial Commission.

There was more success in penetrating the United States Pipe Line Company. In August 1895 J. C. McDowell was stopped from entering a meeting of the company on the ground that he was a Standard Oil spy. The courts reversed that decision and, to the chagrin of the independents, a Standard representative was admitted to the meetings. Archbold testified frankly, "It placed Standard Oil in the way of knowing what was being done."

The pipeline then was extended from Wilkes-Barre to Bayonne. Again conflict arose with the railroads, who allegedly were always ready to do Standard's bidding, or at least to prove their loyalty. Crossing the tracks of the Delaware, Lackawanna and Western at Washington, New Jersey, the pipeline was torn up by the railroad. Emery led a party of 50 men at night to a culvert he meant to cross, laid pipes four feet underground and then piled rocks on them, anchored them with chains, and then established a camp, prepared for war. He got it. Railroad men armed with picks and bars invaded the camp, and the next day two wrecking cars with 250 men were routed by Emery's troops. A decision was made to take the matter to court. Emery described what came next to the Industrial Commission:

So we arrested their men and they arrested our men and they wanted to know if we would go up and have the trial. We went off to the hotel, as I supposed, when a man came rushing up on horseback and said "They are in a fight down at the crossing." I jumped into the first buggy I found and rode there as quickly as possible. I found the traitors who had promised me that they would put this thing into court there with two locomotives standing on top of the track and they were running hot water and hot steam down into this pit on my men. And they went to the fire box [here Emery broke down and wept] and threw hot coals down on them. I ordered every man out of the pit. We barricaded ourselves and the G. A. R. gave us 48 muskets and I sent to New York and got 18 Springfield rifles . . . and we stayed there for seven months holding possession until the courts decided we had a right to stay there.

A free-pipeline bill was introduced in the New Jersey legislature. Handbills allegedly paid for by Standard were distributed to farmers. One read, "These people are endeavouring to pass a law that will destroy the springs on your farm, it will blow up your houses, it will create havoc in the fields when a pipe bursts killing all the grass." There were rumors that Standard Oil money was at work, and when the bill came to a vote, the senator who had introduced it went somewhere out west. Construction of the pipeline was then shifted to make it pass through Pennsylvania, which had a free-pipeline law. Finally, in 1901, after eleven years of struggle, the pipeline was complete, reaching a terminal at Marcus Hook on the Delaware.

In 1900 the capitalization of Pure Oil was enlarged to $10,000,-000, taking over the Producers' Oil Company and the United States Pipe Line. By 1904 the company was allied with fourteen refineries, handled a daily production of 8,000 barrels of crude, and among other properties had a tank steamer, the *Pennoil*.

In the antitrust suit Standard Oil pointed with pride to the existence of this competitor, proving that the monopoly was not so cruel or oppressive after all.

CHAPTER 19   *The Archbold Letters*

IN THE PRESIDENTIAL ELECTION OF 1908, the publisher William Randolph Hearst, disaffected with his Democratic party and its candidate, William Jennings Bryan, was supporting an independent candidate, Thomas L. Hisgen. On September 17, in a speech at Columbus, Ohio, Hearst sprang a surprise. In discussing corruption in public life he said, "I am not here with empty assertions but with legal evidence and documentary proof." He would read letters written by John D. Archbold, vice-president of Standard Oil, who was actively running it. "These letters have been given me by a gentleman who has intimate association with this giant of corruption, the Standard Oil, but whose name I may not divulge lest he be subjected to the persecution of this monopoly." (Later he said that the letters had been given to him that very afternoon in a hotel room by one who was a stranger to him. That was a lie. Hearst had had the letters for four years and had bided his time for the most advantageous moment to release them.)

Then Hearst read the first two of the sensational Archbold letters, both sent to Senator Joseph B. Foraker of Ohio, one in March 1900 and the second in April. Each told of remittances of $15,000 from Standard Oil to Senator Foraker. Two others, one of February 1900 and the other of March, told of legislation to which Standard was opposed. The February 16 letter said:

MY DEAR SENATOR: Here is still another very objectionable bill. It is so outrageous as to be ridiculous, but it needs to be looked after, and I hope there is no difficulty in killing it."

The letter of April 17 read:

"MY DEAR SENATOR: I enclose your certificate of deposit to your favor for $15,000. . . . I need scarcely again express our great gratification over the favorable outcome of affairs."

Before discussing the Archbold letters, which were revealed piecemeal by Hearst over the next four years, let us review some background on corruption of public officials and the participation of Standard Oil in this pastime. We have previously noted that the loose code of morality prevalent those days seemed also to have embraced servants of government. The new potentates of industry, if they felt it incumbent on themselves to justify their bribes, would have echoed the words of Collis Huntingdon, "If you have to pay money to have the right thing done, it is only just and fair to do it."

Of the United States Senate, William Allen White wrote, "One senator represented the Union Pacific, another the New York Central—coal and iron owned a coterie, cotton had half a dozen senators. And so it went." The difference between one state legislature and another was often the difference between Sodom and

Gomorrah. "Strike" bills were notorious for decades, that is, bills which hurt a particular corporation and which had enough nuisance value to be worth a payoff to have the legislator withdraw it. Samuel Dodd in his memoirs said that it was impossible for Standard to do business with the New York State legislature without doing business with a group called "the Black Horse Cavalry."

Prior to the Archbold letters exposé, the record of Standard Oil in its political activities was relatively a good one. Undoubtedly a major factor was that Standard, unlike other industries, wanted no favors of the government and did not seek to feed at the public trough. It did not seek tariff favors that had enriched so many industries; it did not want subsidies; it did not want for itself part of the public domain. As Ida Tarbell wrote, "All John D. Rockefeller asked of the world by the year 1887 was to be let alone." Samuel Dodd wrote in his memoirs: "I know of no instance of the Standard Oil Company desiring legislation in its favor. It was often opposed to proposed legislation but so far as I know used legitimate means in its opposition."

This statement may be acceptable if the word "legitimate" has an elastic interpretation meaning that what was good for Standard Oil was good for the country. As we have narrated, it is undisputed that Pennsylvania legislators were persuaded with Standard Oil cash to vote against the Billingsley bill. Partisans of Rockefeller exonerate him of responsibility for the Archbold letters, saying that he had retired at the time, though he appeared in public as the head of the company. It is doubtful that Rockefeller was unaware of Archbold's activities. The Rockefeller papers show that when he was active in the company Rockefeller was trafficking in favors or aware of them. In 1882 Camden wrote to Rockefeller, "I have arranged to kill two bills in the Maryland legislature at comparatively small expense." In 1880 Warden wrote to Rockefeller that he had "lent" one Quay (apparently Matthew Quay) $5,000 but that Quay wanted $10,000 more. "I feel that Mr. Quay might be of great use to use in the state [Pennsylvania], but he is fearfully expensive."

A *cause célèbre* in which Standard Oil money was alleged to have been used to achieve political ends was the election of Henry B. Payne to the United States from Ohio in 1884. The distinguished and aristocratic Payne, who had long served in the House, was the father of Colonel Oliver H. Payne of Standard Oil. The elder Payne was a stockholder in Standard Oil, besides being the father of one of its leading executives, and had shown some interest in protecting Standard Oil. We have noted that in 1876, when a motion was made for an investigation of the railroads by a special committee, it was blocked by Payne, who forced the investigation to be made by the friendly Commerce Committee where J. N. Camden of Standard sat as special adviser to the chairman.

At the time, United States senators were elected by the state legislatures. In the election of the Ohio legislature in November 1883, Payne's name was not even mentioned as a Senate possibility. Aspirants for the legislature were either for George Pendleton or for Durbin Ward. No sooner, however, was the legislature convened than a big Payne boom sprang into being, managed by his son. Among the allegations were these: Payne money flowed like water; one of the Payne managers carried $65,000 next to his skin; in the "conversion room" briefcases were scattered around with greenbacks sticking out of them; many legislators who were poor suddenly became rich. The caucus of the Democrats (then in majority in the legislature) was held, contrary to past practice, just before the election of the senator; and, also contrary to practice, the ballot was secret. Payne was elected. One newspaper in Ohio commented, "The whole Democratic legislature was made rotten by the money that was used to buy and sell the members like so many sheep."

Payne spent two years in the Senate, and then came the explosion. A new legislature, a Republican one, was elected in Ohio, and investigated the election, hearing fifty witnesses. No decision was rendered, but the matter was referred to the United States Senate with the statement that Payne's election was "remarkable" and required further investigation. The Senate Committee on Elections considered it. Congress was Republican. There was the normal pressure to make vacant a seat to which a Republican could be elected; but of the five Republican members only two voted against Payne, the others joining the three Democrats in reporting that there were no grounds for an inquiry. The Senate upheld the majority report by an overwhelming majority.

Yet the charge did not die. In 1887 Senator Payne's vote was one of the few cast against the bill setting up the Interstate Commerce Commission. In 1888 Payne rose in the Senate when Standard Oil was under attack to say: "The Standard Oil Company is a very remarkable and wonderful institution. It has accomplished in the last twenty years of commercial enterprise what no other company or association of modern times has accomplished." Senator George F. Hoar responded, "A Senator who . . . failed to rise in his place and ask for an investigation which would have put an end to the charges, sheltering himself behind the technicalities . . . I should think forever after would hold his peace."

This charge that Standard connived to buy an election was given wide circulation by Lloyd and Ida Tarbell. Lloyd's account is a typical example of his method of sticking to basic truth but by judicious selection of the facts conveying an erroneous impression. He thus underlines the fact that the manager of Payne's election was the treasurer of Standard Oil but omits to mention that that person happened to be Henry Payne's son. It is quite possible that Oliver Payne, who was a millionaire many times over, was willing to and did buy out of his own funds a final honor for his father, who was in the twilight of his career. At any rate, the charges that were aired were innuendo and gossip, signified by the overwhelming rejection by the Senate, another fact Lloyd did not mention. Senator Payne can hardly be censured for failing to demand an investigation of himself. This writer cannot recall a case where any man has asked to be investigated, since it is difficult to rebut in the public mind the impression of accusations no matter how irresponsible they are.

In later years Rockefeller was vehement in affirming Senator Payne's claim that Standard had nothing to do with his election. He said to Inglis: "This was true. I repeat it unqualifiedly . . . not one farthing of the money of the Standard Oil Company went to his election." His contention that Standard stayed aloof from senatorial elections is confirmed in the Rockefeller papers with reference to the election of John Sherman in 1885. Mark Hanna wrote to Rockefeller to ask for money, saying that control of the Senate might depend on Sherman's reelection. Rockefeller referred the matter to the Executive Committee of Standard. Flagler wrote that "it is not only unwise but it would be an act of injustice to our Democratic associates" to help Sherman, and no money was contributed by the company.

Certainly the attitude toward political involvement changed under Archbold's stewardship, but Standard by then was in hot water, and more desperate measures were necessary.

How did William Randolph Hearst obtain the very private correspondence of John D. Archbold? Archbold had hired a ne'er-do-well stepson of his Negro butler as his office boy. This boy, Willie Winfield, and a nineteen-year old porter, Charles Stump, had conceived the idea, quite correctly, that the correspondence of their boss, Mr. Archbold, had exchange value to newspapers then roasting Standard Oil. They showed some telegrams to a representative of the New York *World* who turned them down, but at the New York *American* they struck it rich, and were directed particularly to find copies of letters to senators and congressmen. During 1904 and 1905 they brought correspondence of Archbold's to the Hearst paper at night; there the juiciest letters were photographed and then returned to Archbold's files. The thieves collected about $15,000 each for their work. The New York *American* editor conveyed to the thieves a message from Hearst that they were "performing a great public duty." Archbold finally became aware of the thefts, and fired both of them.

Though the letters were genuine, the perfectionist Hearst could not forbear from going on from the letters he had by inventing others. Norman Hapgood, editor of *Collier's Weekly*, in 1912 commissioned the writer Arthur H. Gleason to investigate some of the latest letters Hearst had published. Gleason found that five letters written from 1898 to 1904 had been written on a typewriter with élite type that had not been manufactured by L. C. Smith & Brothers until 1906; obviously, they were forgeries. Testifying before the Clapp Committee of the United States Congress in 1912, Hearst tried to explain away Gleason's findings, saying that because the texts of some letters were too poorly typed or too faded to permit photographic reproduction, he had had them retyped, superimposing the letterhead.

The Archbold letters pulled apart the curtains on a lamentable story. It appeared that some very distinguished names were hirelings of Standard Oil at generous pay for what appeared to be slight favors to the company.

Mark Hanna was a constant suitor for funds. In pleading for funds in 1903, while he was engaged in a fight for the Senate with Tom Johnson, he wrote, "Should Johnson carry the legislature, the corporations will catch it, as I am their representative so-called."

Senator Matthew Quay was on the payroll. "Not because I think we should," wrote Archbold to him, "but because of your enticing ways, I enclose your certificate of deposit for $10,000." Apparently Quay's voracious appetite nettled Archbold, since he wrote to Quay, "Please ask for it in instalments as needed from time to time and not all at once."

Senator Quay's colleague from Pennsylvania, Boies Penrose, was also on the payroll, and apparently came dear, judging from a certificate of deposit in October 1904 for $25,000. From the correspondence we have knowledge of some favors done by Penrose.

Congress had set up the Industrial Commission in 1898 to investigate the trusts. Early in its life, Archbold became concerned with the attitude of a member, Congressman John J. Gardner of New Jersey, and wrote to Senator William Joyce Sewell of that state to set up a meeting with him: "We understand that for some reason his feelings towards us are not friendly. We would greatly like to have him set right. . . ."

In January 1900 Penrose sent an advance copy of the report to Archbold, who objected to a proposal that information about stockholders and receipts, expenditures, profits and losses should be required of corporations. Information about stockholders, wrote Archbold to Penrose, "is an unjust and unnecessary inquisition," and all the public should know was assets and liabilities of corporations. A month later Archbold got a revision. "We think the report is so fair that we will not undertake to suggest any change," he wrote to Penrose.

When the chairman, Senator James H. Kyle, died, Archbold made a "strong personal request" to Penrose that he should assume the chairmanship. "Your name as Chairman would give the report exceptional assurance of integrity [sic] and intelligence." Because Penrose declined the honor, Archbold supported Senator

Albert Clarke, who got the post. Later, Archbold got queasy about some further subversive thinking about trusts, and wrote to Penrose, "If Sen. Baird can be counted on for sensible action, an effort should be made to have him present at the meetings."

Congressman Joseph Sibley of Pennsylvania was the worst jackal and toady of them all. He was elected on the Democratic ticket as a reformer, and blared so much about reform that he got a considerable vote for vice-president in the Democratic Convention of 1896, which nominated Bryan. He was an eager seller of his person. To Archbold, "If you think of anything for me to do, let me know." Again, "If at any time my long scribbles annoy you, chuck them into the wastebasket." Again, "A Republican United States Senator came to me today to make a loan of $1,000. I told him I did not have it but would try to get it for him in a day or two. Do you want to make the investment?"

Sibley told President Roosevelt "that no man should win or deserve to win who depended upon the rabble rather than upon the conservative men of affairs." Reporting to Archbold this free advice, he was the first to recommend to Standard the establishment of a public relations bureau. "An efficient literary bureau is needed not for a day or a crisis but a permanent and healthy control of Associated Press and kindred avenues."

Sibley, as official procurer, brought the glamorous and distinguished Joseph Bailey of Texas into the fold. In 1899, when Bailey was Democratic Leader of the House, Sibley introduced him to former Senator Frances of Missouri, who introduced him to Henry Clay Pierce, head of the Standard distributing organization which had just been ejected from Texas. Pierce needed help to get back into Texas, but Bailey would not help Standard Oil. "I would rather go back to the tallow candle." Pierce lied, saying that his organization was no longer connected with Standard Oil, and Bailey agreed to help out. How much did he want? Drawing himself up haughtily, Bailey said: "There will be no fee. I sell my legal knowledge but not my influence."

Bailey intervened with state officials to get the company reinstated in Texas, and by April 1900 he had hit Pierce for $3,300, the start of a paying relationship. Secretary Gruet of Waters-Pierce testified before a legislative committee, "It was along in 1899 that Mr. Pierce told me of taking Sen. Bailey by the hand

John D. Rockefeller Jr. . . . a strict upbringing

Father and son

and leading him over to 26 Broadway and that the Senator immediately put his feet in the trough and has kept them there ever since."

During the elections of 1900, Bailey was an announced candidate for the Senate, and at Waco, on August 9, he said: "Now, fellow-citizens, do we Democrats of Texas believe that we have fallen so low as to elect a Senator who sells his services to the corporations? I do not believe that the time will ever come when Texas will make that mistake." Texas made that mistake soon afterward, and Bailey went to the Senate.

The word that Standard money was available led senators to Archbold's door. Senator John L. McLaurin of South Carolina wrote to Archbold in May 1902, "I can beat Tillman if properly and generously supplied. There is no time to lose, however."

Bailey was not the most eminent personage to lose his political career as a result of the revelations. That honor belongs to Senator Joseph B. Foraker, who was so eminent that he might have been Ohio's gift to the Presidency had he not had the misfortune to be a contemporary of three other of Ohio's gifts to the highest office, Benjamin Harrison, William McKinley, and William Howard Taft. As it was, all his hopes were brought to an end in 1908. Roosevelt had a long-standing dislike for Foraker, exacerbated by Foraker's criticism of him for disciplining a Negro regiment in Brownsville, Texas, and by Foraker's lone vote cast against the Hepburn rate bill of 1904. Known as a railroad senator, Foraker made 87 speeches against the bill. Roosevelt informed Taft, running for the Presidency, that Foraker had been "purchased," and advised him to shun Foraker's company in the campaign and not appear on the same platform. After the election Roosevelt was quoted as saying that it would be "treason" to the party to vote for Foraker, and he was retired from the Senate. It is interesting that one of the few strong supporters that Foraker had left in Ohio was Warren Gamaliel Harding of Marion.

Foraker stoutly maintained for the rest of his days that he had been paid by Standard only for legal services rendered, and it is true that Foraker did perform some legal services. Foraker, moreover, said that $50,000 of the $100,000 paid him was for purchase of an Ohio newspaper and that it was returned when the deal fell through. However, the evidence indicates generous payment for services of partisanship beyond those of a professional nature. Of the payments of $44,500 in 1900, $29,500 followed close on the heels of requests by Archbold in connection with legislation. Some of Archbold's letters seemed framed like specific orders: "Perhaps it might be better to make a demonstration against the whole bill but certainly the ninth clause should be stricken out." It is questionable whether legal services covered Foraker's advice to Attorney General Monnett of Ohio that he would be driven out of politics if he continued to hound Standard Oil, or Foraker's intervention with the governor of Ohio to quash a bill objectionable to Standard in the state Senate.

Both Foraker and his wife, Julia, later wrote autobiographies including a defense. Mrs. Foraker's book states that when the Hearst charge came out: "Foraker met the accusation like a whirlwind. The afternoon papers of the same day carried his clear and complete setting forth of the association with Standard Oil. . . . I was very proud of my husband, indeed. Had he not succeeded Mr. Choate as advisory counsel to one of the most powerful industries of the world? The only thing secret about it was my personal thrill that my husband had formed a brilliant connection which every lawyer coveted."

Strangely enough, when Foraker was asked in 1898 about the rumor that he had been employed by Standard Oil, he did not inflate with pride over the brilliant connection: "It is impertinent. You might as well ask me how much money I have in my pocket. The report is untrue."

The publication of the Archbold letters was a serious blow, possibly the *coup de grâce*, to Standard Oil in its struggle to keep its life as a combination. In the minds of the public it confirmed all that Ida Tarbell had written about the infamous practices of the trust. About the only public figure to defend Archbold was Edward Day, Chancellor of Syracuse University, who said the letters "shocked only the hypocrites." Day was a faithful friend of Archbold, and he had said of Roosevelt's attack on Standard Oil that it was "the ravings of a disordered mind." It happened by pure coincidence that Archbold was a great patron of Syracuse University and that students there sang:

We have a Standard Oil pipe running up to John Crouse Hall
And a gusher in the stadium will be blowing full next Fall.
We need the money, Mr. Archbold,
We need it right away;
It's the biggest ad we've had
Since the bulldog ran away.

"How little you know the age you live in if you fancy that
honey is sweeter than money in hand," said Ovid of the pursuit of
gold in the Augustan Age. Said William Randolph Hearst who
spoke with authority since his family wealth gained him power:
"Today the only right is the right of dollars. The only law is the
law of dollars." More remarkable than the willingness of Standard Oil to debauch our nation's legislators was their uninhibited
eagerness to sell their virtue. John Flynn refers to Archbold as a
"corruptionist," but to "corrupt" is to seduce from the path of
virtue, and certainly these bought men had left their virtue by the
wayside long before.

Archbold did not play a lone hand in disbursing Standard Oil
funds. He was seconded by the next in command, Henry Rogers,
who said, "We will see Standard Oil in hell before we will let any
set of men tell us how to run our business." Rockefeller, though in
semiretirement, was masterminding the defense of the company.
While Archbold was in charge of day-to-day administration of
the company, Rockefeller as president decided basic policies, and
certainly corrupting the national lawmaking body was a basic
policy. Rockefeller, who took credit for company actions such as
the institution of the pension system in 1903 and who openly
announced in 1907 that he owed it to the Supreme Being to
remain in control of Standard Oil, can hardly be cleared of guilt
in matters of bribery.

If anything can be said in mitigation for Standard Oil, it is that
the favors asked, except for the manipulation of judicial appointments, were the normal ones that constituents ask for even today
and that many corporations were also in a position to ask the
same favors as Standard Oil. In those days, when corporations
were able to contribute unlimited amounts to campaigns, it was
expected that lawmakers would repay such "kindnesses"; therefore many corporations used a normal avenue of bribery through

campaign contributions. That even presidential candidates were expected to be thus beholden is evident from Henry Frick's remark about the heavy corporation contributions to the 1904 campaign: "We bought the son of a bitch but he didn't stay bought." He was referring to the man most important for Standard Oil's future, Theodore Roosevelt.

CHAPTER 20 *Beaten with the Big Stick*

"**D**ARKEST ABYSSINIA never saw anything like the course of treatment which we experienced at the hands of the Administration."

So said John Archbold, in later years, of the furious attacks that beset Standard Oil in the new century, culminating in the greatest antitrust suit in the nation's history and the subsequent dissolution of the Standard Oil combination.

The dawn of the twentieth century did not portend the indignities of darkest Abyssinia for Standard Oil. The friend of big business, William McKinley, had been voted back to the White House, and his faithful companion Mark Hanna was almost a guardian angel for the interests of Standard. Besides Archbold's paid hirelings in Congress, Standard Oil had a corps of unpaid friends, like Senator Nelson Aldrich of Rhode Island who became the father-in-law of John D. Rockefeller, Jr., in 1901 and who was so conservative that he opposed Pure Food and Drug legislation as being socialistic. The Supreme Court seemed to have insulated the holding company in the Knight Case from legal attack. The report of the Industrial Commission was moderate, indeed— trusts should not be exterminated but regulated, and the emphasis was put on the use of publicity to prevent abuses. God was in Heaven and all was right in the capitalist world.

A voice from the cellar could be ignored, that of the Vice-President, Theodore Roosevelt. In the summer of 1901, at the

Minnesota State Fair, in discussing the trusts he used the words "Speak softly but carry a big stick," and said, "More and more it is evident that the states and if necessary the nation has got to have the right of supervision and control as regards the great corporations which are its creatures."

Then, on September 14, eight days after the shooting, the bullet of Leon Czolgosz put an end to McKinley and an era. "The damn cowboy," as Mark Hanna called him, an unpredictable bundle of energy and mavericism, was at the helm. On hearing the news, J. P. Morgan was said to have "wheeled like a man stricken . . . cursed and staggered to his desk while his face flamed red and then turned ashen."

Senator Mark Hanna advised the new President to "go slow," do not "upset confidence." It seemed at first that Roosevelt would heed the advice and that there would be no change in the direction of the Ship of State. In his first message to Congress in 1901, Roosevelt spoke of the "crimes of cunning" in the business world and of "abuses connected with the accumulation of great fortunes"; but at the same time he said, "Publicity is the only sure remedy we can now invoke."

The first thunderbolt loosed by this restless Ajax came in connection with the Northern Securities Corporation, a holding company formed by J. P. Morgan in May 1901 to hold the stocks and amalgamate the holdings of the Great Northern Railroad, the Northern Pacific, and the Chicago, Burlington and Quincy, and thus settle a long struggle for rail control in the Northwest between James Hill and Edward Harriman. In February 1902 Roosevelt ordered his Attorney General, Philander Knox, erstwhile counsel to Carnegie Steel, to sue under the Sherman Act for dissolution of the holding company. Morgan was confounded. Why a nasty court suit? He sent word to the President, "Send your man [Knox] to my man and they can fix it up." When Roosevelt said that no compromise was possible on this issue, Morgan sought reassurance that Roosevelt did not contemplate action against "my other interests," meaning the newly formed United States Steel Corporation, and was given that reassurance.

In view of the Knight decision, there was grave doubt that Roosevelt would succeed in the courts. Two years later, in March 1904, the dissolution of the Northern Securities Corporation was upheld by a five-to-four vote, Holmes dissenting, and the door was now opened for more trustbusting.

After interruption by the excitement of our Spanish-American War and adjustments to "Manifest Destiny," the press returned more shrilly than ever to the exposure of social and economic evils that we know today as "muckraking." This phenomenon did not develop by accident, but was a response to a widespread feeling that reform was imperative. Although strongest in the Midwest, the home of Populism, William Jennings Bryan, and Eugene V. Debs, the tide of popular opinion was nationwide— alarm about the fantastic growth of the new industrial Molochs, the trusts, and their heedlessness in many instances of the public good, fears about the survival prospects of the small man, resentment at the abuses of the railroads, anger at abject poverty in the midst of plenty, and at unchecked graft and corruption.

Pulitzer, Hearst, *Life, Collier's,* and *Harper's* were carrying on the crusade, idealism paying off in heightened circulation and profits. The most successful purveyor of "muckraking" was S. S. McClure, who had a fine stable of writers at his comand, among them Lincoln Steffens, Ray Stannard Baker, and Samuel Hopkins Adams. One of McClure's writers who had been associated with him since 1892 was Ida M. Tarbell, who had already written for *McClure's Magazine* a highly successful series on Napoleon and another on Lincoln. After the turn of the century she was regularly employed by McClure as managing editor. In 1901 McClure, looking for a sensational subject, decided that the trust was the thing, and proposed to Miss Tarbell that she write a series on the steel trust. She mulled it over and discarded the idea. In September 1901 she sailed to Europe to talk with Mc-Clure in Switzerland, where he was taking a rest cure, about three or four articles on the gigantic trust that had been a model for all the others, Standard Oil. McClure enthusiastically agreed. This series grew like Topsy, eventually running to nineteen articles during 1902 and 1903 and coming out in book form in 1904 as *The History of the Standard Oil Company.*

It was strange destiny that Miss Tarbell should have been with *McClure's* at this time, on tap to write *The History.* Her childhood had been spent in Pithole and Titusville, and she had attended Allegheny College in the Regions. In her family life she had been steeped in the struggle against Standard Oil. Her father had joined in the boycott of Rockefeller in the great Oil War of 1872 revolving around the South Improvement Plan, and had refused offers of premium prices to furnish oil to Rockefeller. Her brother, William Tarbell, was treasurer of Pure Oil Company, the first great rival refiner to Standard, and was a prominent witness in the antitrust suit to dissolve Standard Oil Company. Miss Tarbell was hardly likely to see anything Rockefeller's way.

The Tarbell book was somewhat different from Lloyd's book, although it covered the same subject, and the differences were all in favor of Miss Tarbell's. Instead of extracting nuggets, her book was a coherent, chronological account, covering ten more years since the Lloyd book. Unlike Lloyd, she named names, identifying Standard Oil with the man, Rockefeller, and citing Emerson that "an institution is the lengthened shadow of a man." Like Lloyd, she quarried industriously the two main sources, the inquiry conducted by the New York State Assembly in 1879, the Hepburn Probe, and by the New York State Senate in 1888, but she had also for use the hearings of the United States Industrial Commission set up in 1898. While Lloyd's book was as strident as a fire-engine siren in the night, Miss Tarbell's was a softly voiced plea to a jury, acquiring its greatest persuasiveness by its seeming detachment. While Lloyd conceded nothing good to Rockefeller, Miss Tarbell conceded that Rockefeller as a field general was excelled only by Napoleon, and her last chapter was, surprisingly, "The Legitimate Greatness of the Company." While Lloyd had the sketchiest knowledge of the economics of the oil industry, Miss Tarbell had made some effort in that direction. Her book was far more accurate and more sophisticated than that of Lloyd. In fact, only one slight error was found after painstaking dissection, though there are inconsistencies and contradictions in abundance.

Whatever the merits of the Tarbell book, it owed its success in greatest measure to the fact that its thesis happened to be in the mainstream of popular thinking at the time; certainly from that standpoint the target for attack could not have been better chosen. It was a worldwide sensation, and continued to be for some time (as evidenced by the edition in this author's possession, published in 1912 by William Heinemann in London). Mc-

Clure wrote to Miss Tarbell: "You are today the most generally famous woman in America. You have achieved a fine distinction. People universally speak of you with such reverence that I am getting sort of afraid of you."

Standard Oil was not unaware that the Tarbell book was in preparation in 1902. S. S. McClure acquainted Mark Twain with the news, who passed it on in turn to his beloved friend Henry Rogers. Miss Tarbell got an invitation to visit Rogers at 26 Broadway. "Can anything be done to stop this?" asked Rogers. "Nothing in the world," replied Miss Tarbell. Then Rogers told her that he was greatly concerned lest his children believe that he was in any way connected guiltily with the Buffalo explosion attempt of 1880 (see page 192), and talked to her about the case. In her book she gracefully exonerated Rogers from any imputation of blame. Solicitor Dodd read some of her chapters for accuracy. For a time Miss Tarbell had a desk in the Standard Oil building —which she lost when the articles began appearing in print.

Rockefeller was taken aback by the impact of the book on public opinion. "Not a word about that misguided woman," he said with accustomed benignity when her name came up. But when Miss Tarbell, deserting scholarship, wrote a vitriolic personal attack on Rockefeller in *McClure's* the following year, Rockefeller shed a little of his sangfroid and referred to her among his friends as "Miss Tarbarrel."

Rockefeller had an attack of a nervous disease, generalized alopecia, which resulted in a loss of all his hair, including even his eyebrows and eyelashes. This must have occurred sometime between 1901 and 1904, since photographs of him at the decennial celebration of the University of Chicago in June 1901 show him moustached, with a full head of hair, and spare of stature. Photographs of him in 1904 show a totally bald man with no moustache, and quite stout. It is hard to believe that they are the same person. For a time Rockefeller wore a skullcap to conceal bony protuberances on his scalp, and then donned the white-haired wig he was to wear for the rest of his days.

In her 1905 article in *McClure's*, Miss Tarbell had the bad taste to analyze Rockefeller's physiognomy after his recent illness. In his face she found "craftiness, cruelty, and something indefinably repulsive." About his eyes, she wrote: "Ever small and intent and steady, they are as expressionless as a wall—a blank eye; looking through and through things and telling nothing of what they find in the way." As for his mouth, she said that it was tragic for him that his illness cost him his moustache: "It is at once the cruelest feature of his face and the most pathetic." The cheeks "puff, bulging unpleasantly under the eyes and the skin which covers them has a curiously unhealthy pallor. It is the puffiness of this unclean flesh which repels as the thin slit of a mouth terrifies."

The only explanation for the favorable reception of this billingsgate is that the public was indulging in some kind of pathological hate orgy against Rockefeller.

In the same year that the Tarbell book was published, *Everybody's Magazine* began serial publication of a book by Thomas Lawson, *Frenzied Finance*, the story of the manipulations in Wall Street of Amalgamated Copper stock. Without going into details, it can be summed up that the substance of the manipulation was moneymaking by promoters, without any investment, by using the proceeds of stock flotations to pay for properties bought on credit. This has been done time and again in Wall Street up to the present day. The parties participating were Henry Rogers, William Rockefeller, and James Stillman, but by loosely flinging around the name of Standard Oil the reader got the impression that John D. Rockefeller was a main party to the so-called swindles that, Lawson said from his personal knowledge, caused thirty suicides. Lawson invested the whole story with the sinister aura of Standard Oil. Here, for example, is how the innocent-looking building at 26 Broadway appears in the book: "Solid as a prison, towering as a steeple, its cold and forbidding façade seems to rebuke the heedless levity of the passing crowd." Although John D. Rockefeller was not involved in the story, Lawson wrote of him, "John D. Rockefeller can be fully described as a man made in the image of an ideal money-maker. . . . An ideal money-maker is a machine the details of which are diagrammed on the asbestos blueprints which paper the walls of hell."

Newspapers excoriated Rockefeller—that was what the public wanted. The "tainted money" episode discussed in the opening of this book showed the unreasonable bounds to which this passion could be carried. However, while there was invective there was also a good deal of pungent American humor. In early 1907 there was an announcement that Rockefeller had given $32,000,000 to the General Education Board. One paper said he planned to get it back since it was "a vast scheme to promote the burning of midnight oil." Another paper said it was a plot to protect his descendants: "All the other inhabitants will be so finely educated that they will be unable to earn money." Another thanked him for his graciousness in telling us "what *he* is doing with *our* money."

Cartoonists delighted in poking fun at Rockefeller's piety. One in the Indianapolis *Star* showed Rockefeller in his skull cap, patting the head of a little boy, the Public, and saying: "Once upon a time a Christian young man started in the oil business. Other men did the same but they were not good men and did not know how to run their business for the benefit of their fellowmen. So the good young man put them out of business. He did not hurt them—no, he would not hurt a fly. He just kicked them in the stomach and twisted their necks. And so he kept on and on working and praying and finally etc. etc."

John D. Rockefeller, Jr., got pelted with some brickbats, too. In 1902 he returned to his alma mater, Brown University, and made a speech to the local Y.M.C.A. chapter in which he discussed trusts. A reporter on an off-chance attended and took shorthand notes. Rockefeller, Jr., said, "The American Beauty Rose can be produced in its splendor and fragrance only by sacrificing the early buds which grow up around it." The simile is a wonderful example of social Darwinism, but the reasoning did not impress editorial writers, who did not regard Standard Oil as splendid or fragrant.

President Theodore Roosevelt had a glint in his eye for Standard Oil. He was a big-game hunter, and Standard Oil was big game. In a speech he said that the nation had to grapple with the problem of big fortunes. "Of course, no amount of charities in spending such fortunes can compensate for the misconduct in acquiring them." Every hearer knew whom he meant.

In February 1903 his bill to establish a Department of Commerce with a Bureau of Corporations to put the spotlight on business was encountering rough going in Congress. He told the press that several senators had received wires from Rockefeller saying: "We are opposed to any Anti-trust legislation. Our counsel will see you. It must be stopped." The news helped to propel the legislation to passage, but the President's version was grossly inaccurate. Rockefeller, Jr., and not his father, had wired to four senators, asking for appointments for Archbold and his counsel: "Our people are opposed to all the proposed trust legislation except the Elkins Anti-Discrimination Bill. Mr. Archbold with our counsel goes to Washington this afternoon. Am very anxious they should see you at once and shall much appreciate any assistance you can render them."

This was all quite different from the way Roosevelt had put it. One recalls the words of a nonadmirer, H. L. Mencken: "No man facing Roosevelt in the heat of controversy ever actually got a square deal. He took extravagant advantages; he played to the worst idiocies of the mob; he hit below the belt almost habitually. . . . One always thinks of him as a glorified longshoreman engaged eternally in cleaning out bar-rooms—and not too proud to gouge when the inspiration came to him, or to bite in the clinches. . . ."

The conservatives in the Republican party wanted to dump Roosevelt in the presidential contest of 1904 in favor of a reliable man like Senator Hanna, who angled for the nomination. Roosevelt edged a little closer to Standard Oil, and the toady Congressman Sibley reported to Archbold that Roosevelt told him that he welcomed news of Standard's more friendly attitude to him and that "He urged strongly that you come over to meet him." Soon it became unnecessary for Roosevelt to woo anybody, since Hanna died and all roadblocks to the nomination were removed.

Roosevelt was gloomy about his chances of election. Repeatedly he sent messages to big-business elements that he was their man and that they need have no fear about him. In 1903 he confided, "I'm finished, I have no machine, no faction, no money." When he was reminded of the big crowds that turned out to see him, he replied, "They came to see the President much as they would have come to see a circus."

The Democrats nominated a gold Democrat, Judge Alton B. Parker, who was too ultraconservative to win any following in the North. The conservative New York *Sun*, which had often gagged at Roosevelt, none the less came out for him with the shortest endorsing editorial on record: "Theodore—with all thy faults."

However, afflicted with a basic insecurity, Roosevelt continued to be nervous about the outcome. About six weeks before the voting, Roosevelt appealed to Henry Frick for financial aid, and Frick raised a "big money" war chest, including $150,000 from J. P. Morgan and $50,000 from Edward Harriman. A congressional inquiry in 1912 found that 72 percent of the fund of over $2,000,000 came from big corporations and trusts. That was what Frick meant when he said, "We bought the son of a bitch."

Rockefeller had always been a generous contributor to the G.O.P. His $250,000 contribution to beat Bryan in 1896 was the largest from any corporation. In 1900 he gave a like amount; after the campaign, Hanna remitted $50,000 as unused. This is probably the only case on record of a refund of a campaign contribution, but then Hanna was not the normal political boss— he regarded himself rather as a seller of protection to business.

Now, in 1904, the Standard Oil Company made a contribution of $125,000 to the war chest. In a letter of October 26, Roosevelt directed Republican Chairman Cortelyou ". . . if true, I must ask you to direct that the money be returned to them forthwith." This exhibition of chastity in politics was more Roosevelt buncombe, since the money was never returned; in fact, the party asked for another $100,000. One version is that Roosevelt wrote the letter for the record if later queried about the contribution; the other is that he was mollified by an explanation that the gift was a personal one from Henry Rogers. (The $125,000 with which it parted was the worst investment Standard Oil ever made.)

In the election, Roosevelt carried all the states in the Union except for the Solid South, the Republicans winning the border state of Missouri for the first time. Now Roosevelt regarded himself as a free agent dependent on no one. "I am no longer a political accident," he said to his wife and to Secretary of State John Hay. "I shall come into office in my own right. Then watch out for me." The troubles of Standard Oil began in his second term.

Beginning in 1903, the great midcontinent oil field of Kansas and Oklahoma was discovered and exploited—by 1908 this field turned out more oil than the whole United States did in any year before 1902. Standard Oil, as a testimony to its vast financial resources, threw in $100 million of cash, without borrowing, to develop these fields, pushing pipelines southeast 550 miles to the new fields and another 500 miles to Baton Rouge, building large new refineries at North Alton, just above St. Louis, and another at Baton Rouge.

It was in Kansas that the troubles of Standard Oil began. Production increased from 932,000 barrels in 1903 to 4,250,000 barrels in 1904 from 4,000 wells. In 1904 Kansas learned to its chagrin that the Standard that gathered the oil in its pipelines was the only buyer—and the company, owing to the tremendous outflow, had cut the price from $1.38 a barrel to $0.80. Standard, which had never been distinguished for its prudence in dealing with public opinion, chose this time to infuriate the public by refusing to pipe from producers who had supplied an independent refiner at Humboldt. The state was seething with Populism, and anybody and everybody who had money held stock in an oil producer. The state legislature in 1905 aimed a swift kick at Standard, authorizing a state refinery at Peru to compete with the Standard refinery at Neodesha, which was the only one in the state. Anti-Standard feeling in the state was now rampant, and Ida Tarbell toured the state making speeches. When Prairie Oil and Gas, the Standard subsidiary, halted construction of pipelines in retaliation, the legislature passed laws declaring pipelines common carriers and regulating their rates. Finally the attorney general of the state filed quo warranto proceedings designed to throw Prairie Oil and Gas out of the state.

The turmoil in Kansas came to the attention of the President, who requested the head of the Bureau of Corporations to make an investigation and report on Standard Oil. This was the first gun fired by Roosevelt, the Fort Sumter of the war.

Standard's Waters-Pierce Company had been ousted from Texas under its antitrust laws—but under a false affidavit and with Senator Bailey's help had been reinstated. Now Waters-Pierce was in hot water in its home state of Missouri. There was another open Standard company operating in the state, Standard Oil of Indiana. And there was a third company. Scofield, Shurmer and Teagle had sold out to Republic Oil Company, supposedly an independent but in reality a blind for Standard Oil. Its mailing address in New York was not 26 Broadway but the back door of the building, 7 New Street.

On investigation it appeared to Attorney General Herbert S. Hadley of Missouri that there were three Standard units operating in the state, dividing territories and careful not to undercut each other. Thus Standard of Indiana did not sell in Kansas City, and Waters-Pierce did not sell in St. Louis. In March 1906 he filed a quo warranto suit against the three companies.

Armed with subpoenas Hadley came to New York to question the heads of the trust. Where was Rockefeller? He had supposedly fled his estate near Tarrytown, New York, and was reported in a dozen places; actually, after crossing the Hudson he had backtrailed to his estate. He finally came to New York City and answered questions. The idea that Standard companies had limited territories was ridiculous. As for Standard of Ohio: "Its field is the world. That is its mission, to light the world with the cheapest and the best." Henry Rogers on the stand was defiant. When asked if he was familiar with Standard Oil of Indiana, he replied, "I know it's in the oil business but I am not familiar with the details. . . . I am familiar with dividends when they are declared."

However, after court orders backing up Hadley, the atmosphere changed, and Standard freely conceded that all the companies in contention lived under its roof. The New York *Times* on March 25, 1906, reported: "The trust lawyers breathed soft words instead of exceptions, they wore winning smiles and vied with each other in finding out just what Mr. Hadley wanted. From the witness stand H. H. Rogers beamed approval."

Armed with these admissions, Hadley presented the facts to the Missouri courts, which ousted Standard Oil of Indiana and Republic Oil from the state and forced Waters-Pierce to sever its connection with Standard. As a penalty for its brazen perjury that it had no connection with Standard Oil, Waters-Pierce was ousted from the State of Texas, and heavily fined.

The incubus of the attacks lay heavily on Rockefeller as he sailed for Europe in the spring of 1906, accompanied by his daughter, Alta, who was Mrs. Parmalee Prentice, and his physician, Dr. Biggar. His daughter, Bessie, Mrs. Charles Strong, lay ill in Europe, reportedly of a malady in which she feared that she would die in poverty. (She died late in the year.) Almost simultaneous with his departure, the Hepburn bill became law, strengthening control over railroads and subjecting oil pipelines to federal control. Rockefeller relaxed for some time in Compiègne, France, and ruminated with reporter William Hoster about the reasons why he had been selected as the target for the slings and arrows of outrageous slander.

According to Hoster's high-flown prose (since Rockefeller spoke simply), he said: "Is it not patent that I have been made into a frightful ogre to slay which has become a favorite resource of men seeking public favor? It is not from the body of the people whence I sprung that these denunciations come but from the self-seekers who would be leaders. What advantages had I that every other poor boy did not possess? No one could have begun life with less than I had. But it is a fact that all of this criticism comes from or is inspired by men who have been my business competitors—men who would have bested me, if I had not bested them—and from public officials, agitators and demagogues."

A very incomplete explanation.

What peace of mind he had left was further marred by news that he had been indicted in Ohio for violation of the state's antitrust laws and that a sheriff would be on the dock to greet him on his return and arrest him. This encounter was averted by Rockefeller's pledge that he would go voluntarily to Ohio to meet the charge.

On his return in late summer, Rockefeller was much more conciliatory in his attitude toward the public—even forgiving: "Sometimes things that are said of me are cruel and they hurt but I am never a pessimist. I believe in man and the brotherhood of man." As the main figure in the antitrust furor, Rockefeller was the cynosure for all eyes, and continually harried by cranks. One Sunday, on his way to church, he was waylaid by a woman from Louisville who claimed that she had been run over by one of Standard's tank wagons, and was moving in with him with all her baggage until settlement.

In May 1907 the first report of the Bureau of Corporations was issued, and it discussed mostly the heart and core of Standard's historic domination, its advantages in transportation by secret rates, rebates, and discriminations. In truth, the report that Standard continued to enjoy freight advantages seemed well grounded. In the Missouri investigation it had been brought out that when kerosene was shipped by rail from Kansas City to St. Louis it cost $0.17 a barrel, but when shipped from St. Louis to Kansas City it cost $0.23. Was it only coincidence that there was a Standard Oil refinery at Kansas City and an independent at St. Louis? Another example—the rate on commodities was usually cheaper from Cleveland to southeastern cities than from Chicago. Thus from Chicago to Atlanta it cost two cents per hundred pounds more to ship flour. But on oil the situation was reversed, and it was three cents cheaper to ship from Chicago. This was attributed to the fact that Standard had its big plant near Chicago at Whiting. The rails covered up the low rate by quoting a rate from an obscure point named Dolton close to Whiting to an obscure point in Tennessee named Grand Junction. Another example—if a commodity was shipped from the West into New England, the uniform rate quoted to any point was the rate to Boston. But in the case of oil there was no "through" rate quoted; the shipper had to pay the rate to Boston and then to the point of destination. Was this due to the fact that Standard Oil used Long Island Sound and the Atlantic for shipment of refined oil?

Standard officers from Archbold down had by now abandoned the policy of silence. In retorting to the report that the rates it got were cheaper, the company said that it located refineries to take advantage of cheaper rates. Archbold and Rogers took a direct poke at Roosevelt: "He [Roosevelt] has given us of his advice most generously upon every subject from the size of our families to the mistakes of the Federal judges and some error is inevitable now and then to the most conservative man under such circumstances." The company sent a special report to its stockholders, and the *World's* headlines said: "Standard Oil Whimpers—Says It Is Victim."

The Director of the Bureau of Corporations, James R. Garfield (son of the former President), pointed with satisfaction to the fact that soon after his Report the railroads made adjustments to wipe out the inequities against the independents. However, by virtue of its control of the pipelines, Standard Oil continued to play with loaded dice throughout the life of the trust. Through its trunkline from Lima, Ohio, to Philadelphia, Standard charged a tariff to independents of 53.5 cents a barrel, while its actual service cost was only 9.8 cents. Moreover, Standard could at its will tear up the pipe to wells supplying independents. It could cut down the amount of oil reaching independents. In 1903 a group of independent refiners who told the National Transit Company that they wanted an increased flow, twice as much as they were getting, finally had to settle for 80 percent of what they were receiving before they had the temerity to ask for more. The alternative would have been protracted litigation. If a refinery built its own pipeline, it could be sure that Standard would bid up the price of oil in the area and that the refinery would have to pay premium prices.

The Hepburn bill of 1906 subjected the pipelines to control as common carriers; but on the advice of Standard's counsel, John Milburn, this control was fended off by Standard Oil. It made the interstate pipelines intrastate, and thus immune to federal regulation. It was done in this way: The National Transit Company, which ran the pipeline from Pennsylvania fields to the refinery at Olean, New York, sold to the New York Transit Company the line from the Pennsylvania border to Olean. Receiving stations were built directly on the border. On the Pennsylvania side the oil poured in, and on the New York side it was pumped out into the pipeline. The result was that pipelines no longer crossed state lines, and Standard declared that the pipelines were purely intrastate property. Not until 1914, in the Pipeline cases, did the Supreme Court uphold the constitutionality of federal regulation of pipelines.

Now the embattled giant was raked with gunfire from bow to stern. By the end of 1906 there were twenty-one state suits pending, eight in Ohio and the rest in nine other states. In November, Standard Oil of Indiana was indicted by a federal grand jury for allegedly accepting rebates in violation of the Elkins Act. Then, on November 15, 1906, came the major suit, a bill of equity in Federal Court in St. Louis, filed by Attorney General Bonaparte, asking for a dissolution under the Sherman Act.

The case revolving around the alleged rebates paid by the Chicago and Alton Railroad to Standard was a spectacular one because the presiding federal judge, Kenesaw Mountain Landis, was a theatrical personality who later left the bench to become Baseball Commissioner after the Black Sox scandals following World War I. His reputation for rugged honesty acquired in this Standard Oil case was the reason for his selection as commissioner. In later years President Taft said of Landis, "I have no criticism to make of Judge Landis except . . . that he is too much of an actor and too much occupied with how he appears to the public to be a good judge." From beginning to end he played to the grandstand in this case. The government asked him not to call Rockefeller to the stand, which might interfere with the Sherman Act suit by giving him some claim of immunity, but Landis refused.

The Rockefeller appearance on July 7, 1907, though a smash hit in terms of the public turnout, was a dud insofar as testimony was concerned. Actually, his place as president of the company was only honorary. He had not even been to the office in eight years. He was no longer even sure what Standard Oil did when he was queried by government counsel:

Q. What is your general impression as to what the business of the Standard Oil of New Jersey is?

A. They have a refinery and they refine oil. That was the —yes—it would be impossible for me to give—to make an answer to that question intelligently without a study of the case.

The case against Standard Oil was a weak one. It was alleged that the railroad charged six cents a hundredweight from Whiting to East St. Louis instead of the rate of eighteen cents on the rate sheet filed with the Interstate Commerce Commission. Standard claimed that while the class rate was eighteen cents, the commodity rate was only six cents, which was the properly filed rate of another road, the Chicago and Eastern Illinois, over which it could have shipped all its oil. It also offered to prove that because no one else shipped over the route, no competitor was hurt, evidence that Landis excluded.

If Landis had aimed to use the case as a springboard to celebrity, he won. In a castigating opinion, after a jury verdict of guilty, Landis assessed the unheard-of fine of $29,240,000— $10,000 for every carload of oil. Standard Oil, according to him, was no better than counterfeiters and letter-thieves, and he would impanel a grand jury to put the lot of them in jail. As for the evidence offered by the company that no one was hurt, "It is novel indeed for a convicted defendant to urge the complete triumph of a dishonest course as a reason why such course should go unpunished."

Rockefeller commented to friends, "Landis will be dead a long time before the fine is paid." It was so obviously confiscatory that President Roosevelt considered asking for a reduction of the fine.

Would the fine ever be paid? It was a prominent subject for discussion with the public. Rockefeller could peel off 29,000,000 dollar bills if he wanted to, said Mr. Dooley. He refuses to pay only as a matter of principle, since he doesn't need the money:

> He don't care f'r money in th' passionate way that you an' me do, Hinnissy. Th' likes iv us are as cracy about a dollar as a man is about his child whin he has only wan. Th' chances are we'll spoil it. But John D., havin' a large an' growin' family iv dollars, takes on'y a kind iv gin'ral interest in thim. He's issued a statement sayin' that he's a custojeen iv money appinted by himself. He looks afther his own money an' th' money iv other people. He takes it an' puts it where it won't hurt thim an' they won't spoil it. He's a kind iv a society f'r th' previntion iv croolty to money.
>
> If he finds a man misusin' his money, he takes it away fr'm him an' adopts it. Ivry Saturdah night he lets th' man see it f'r a few hours. An' he says he's surprised to find that whin, with th' purest intintions in th' wurrld, he is found thryin' to coax our little money to his home, where it'll find conjanial sur-roundin's an' have other money to play with, th' people thry to lynch him an' th polis arrest him f'r abduction.

On appeal to the Circuit Court of Appeals, the case was re-versed, Judge Grosscup speaking for the Court that there was inadequate proof of a fixed rail rate that Standard Oil circum-vented. Roosevelt was infuriated. In a public announcement he said, "There is absolutely no question as to the guilt of the de-fendant nor of the exceptionally grave character of the offense . . . the President would consider it a grave miscarriage of justice if through any technicality of any kind the defendant escapes punishment which would unquestionably have been meted out to any weaker defendant." Privately he inveighed against the judges. They had "hurt the cause of civilization. . . . There is altogether too much power in the bench."

On retrial before a judge other than Landis, the trial judge threw out the government's case. However, the great antitrust case was well in progress. There were twenty-five industries prosecuted under the antitrust laws during the Administration of Theodore Roosevelt, but the Standard Oil case was by far the most formidable. The case lasted four and a half years. The government hired as special counsel Frank B. Kellogg of St. Paul, who won fame from this case. (In later years he became Secretary of State and gave his name to a peace pact that was a genuine "scrap of paper.") The Standard Oil's legal staff was headed by its counsel, John G. Milburn. There were so many lawyers hired on both sides that it was said that the legal profession had at last struck oil.

Hearings began before Examiner Franklin Ferriss in September 1907. Four hundred witnesses testified, and twelve thousand pages of testimony filled twelve volumes. Rockefeller appeared for three days of testimony, starting on November 17, 1908. Under direct examination by Milburn, Rockefeller was sharp as he described in detail the history of the company up to 1879 when he revealed that the first trust agreement was framed. This was news, since it had been generally believed that the 1882 agreement had been the first and original trust. Aside from that, the only newsworthy feature was the impression conveyed by Rockefeller that the rebates received by Standard were all the fault of the railroads. This led the *World* to publish the Rockefeller definition of a rebate: "A voluntary compensation paid by the railroads for ample services rendered at a great disadvantage to the beneficiary of the rebate."

When it came Kellogg's turn to cross-examine, a strange thing happened—Rockefeller's memory faded out completely. As the New York *Sun* said, his sharp recollections of as long ago as forty-two years "had faded until the details were scarcely to be traced in the perimetric shadows. Even recorded facts had lost their power to convince." Amid his dull reiteration that he recalled nothing, there was one moment of levity. Asked about the dividends Standard had paid the previous year, Rockefeller answered that they were $40 million. Kellogg corrected him, saying that they were $39 million. Rockefeller shrugged and sighed, "One more million for poor old Standard." Amid the gale of laughter, Rockefeller sat poker-faced.

Now the election of 1908 was on hand, and Roosevelt's choice, William Howard Taft, was opposing William Jennings Bryan. On October 29 Rockefeller announced quite innocently that as a lifelong Republican he would vote for Taft. He would do so in spite of the fact that the Republican Administration was waging a court struggle to dissolve the oil trust. "I feel the more impelled to answer this question because it cannot be said that the present administration has in any way whatever favored the interest to which my life has been devoted."

Curses! What a blow to be endorsed by that arch-criminal! President Roosevelt, who was pulling out all the stops for Taft, said that this was a "perfectly palpable and obvious trick" to ensure the election of Bryan. Candidate Taft said, "If the Standard Oil were anxious to bring about my election, the last thing they would have done would have been to advertise their support of me." Republican Senator Henry Cabot Lodge said he had "absolute proof" that Standard Oil had instructed its 60,000 employees to vote for Bryan.

Taft survived this underhand trick and was elected. Roosevelt left on a big-game hunt. When J. P. Morgan heard of the safari, he muttered, "Let's hope the first lion he meets does his duty."

Theodore Roosevelt, as fascinating a personality as we have had in the Presidency, had left the White House, though he was to make another try for it in 1912. He had built a reputation as a trustbuster and an apostle of reform, though he really did not have much heart for it. At one time he said to Chauncey Depew, "How I wish I wasn't a reformer, oh, Senator. But I suppose I must live up to my part, like the Negro minstrel who blacked himself all over."

He was an aristocrat by background. Reformers might have radical tendencies, and thus his emotional attacks on "muckrakers" and "the lunatic fringe." Of "sentimental humanitarians," he said that they had "an influence for bad hardly surpassed by that of the professional criminal classes." He had a pathological fear of the mob, and in 1896 feared that the Bryan movement smacked of the Paris commune.

Yet he did resurrect the Sherman Act and start a wave of antitrust prosecutions, most prominently against the Standard Oil Company. It was in part a political response to what he conceived to be popular demand. It was also related to some inward fear of mobocracy—if capital would behave, if privilege did not take undue advantage from its position of power, then it would fear no threat of being overturned by the mob. Business greed could imperil the foundations of society. In that sense he was the wisest of the conservatives, while the rich who did not agree with him were suffering from "dull, purblind folly."

It was all, as he himself put it, a question of simple morality. After listening to one of his discourses in that vein, former Speaker Tom Reed said, "You know, Theodore, the one thing I most admire about you is your original discovery of the Ten Commandments."

In his attack on the Lords of Industry one cannot overlook another of his foibles, his addiction to the brummagem, as when he shook his fist under J. P. Morgan's nose at a Gridiron Club dinner and shouted, "If you don't let us do this, those who will come after will rise and bring you to ruin!" He had, in his makeup, a goodly dose of ham.

CHAPTER 21   *Dissolution*

THE IDA TARBELL BOOK, followed by the "tainted money" affair in 1905, finally convinced Rockefeller that the policy of silence, followed by himself and Standard Oil, would have to be abandoned. It was too dangerous to lie supine in the face of the increasing attacks. Moreover, counterpropaganda would have to be undertaken if Standard Oil were to survive, and the reaction to the Tarbell book made it clear as early as 1905 that the continued existence of the trust was in jeopardy. Rockefeller had always fanatically believed that his property was his and only his, but he had gradually awakened to the realization that there was a mighty imponderable, called public opinion, that affected his property, and that the way to command it was to fight for it. Earlier, there had been no reply at all to the Lloyd book beyond the statement of John D. Archbold that it was "cunning fiction, made up entirely of one-sided testimony dressed for sale." This new onslaught called for full-scale action. The next few years were to witness a counterattack by the printed word.

The new policy was soon evident. Archbold and Henry Rogers, leading company executives, broke into print in popular magazines. Rockefeller's talks to Bible classes were published. Then, in 1906, Standard Oil hired its first public relations man, Joseph Ignatius Constantine Clarke, a playwright who had worked for the New York *Herald*. He took over the public relations office in being, which consisted of an office boy who pasted clippings. Not knowing how to classify this new genus, Standard made him part of the legal division. Clarke was only the second public relations man in big business, Ivy L. Lee having gone to work for the Pennsylvania Railroad in the previous year.

Standard Oil had not been totally oblivious to public opinion, but its previous efforts had been haphazard, not centrally directed, and concerned mostly with shutting off adverse publicity. Subsidies to win newspaper goodwill had been commonplace since the United States Bank had paid them in the days of Andrew Jackson. The New York *World* had been tossed between Tom Scott of the Pennsylvania Railroad and the banker Jay Cooke. Standard, so plentifully supplied with the sinews of war, knew that money could buy goodwill. As early as 1880, Standard books carried a loan of $10,000 to the Cleveland *Herald*. Newspapers in the Pennsylvania oil regions were always fouling the atmosphere, and so the Bradford *Era* and the Titusville *Herald* passed into Standard control. The Oil City *Derrick* had been famous for its leadership in attacks on Rockefeller; in 1881 the books of the Standard carried an item, "Special investment at Oil City," signifying that it had bought up that pesky organ. From 1885, under the editorship of Patrick Boyle, it became a leading Standard mouthpiece. A picturesque, voluble personality, Boyle was not exactly a shrinking violet in letting the public know what he thought of an opponent, as witness this description of a rival newspaper editor: "that aged, acidulous, addlepated, monkey-eyed, monkey-browed monogram of sarcasm and spider-shanked, pigeon-witted public scold, Major Bilgewater Bickham and his backbiting, blackmailing, patent medicine directory, the Journal, etc. etc."

Conforming to the general attitude of industrial kings, Rockefeller was content to let his paid scribblers scribble—he hoped along soundest lines. However, in the 1890's a new twist in publicity appeared. During that decade Standard Oil had, as we have seen, an ordeal in Ohio, owing to the state's crusading attorney generals. To get its point of view across and to develop better feeling for the company, Standard hired the Malcolm Jennings News Bureau and Advertising Agency, which made contracts with 150 newspapers in Ohio and Indiana. The agency made contracts for advertising that appeared as paid advertising, but it also contracted for news items and even editorial comment, for which the Jennings Agency paid three cents a line but which were not labeled as advertising and which the reader could not know emanated from Standard Oil. Thus the Xenia, Ohio, *Herald* carried a typical paid-for comment: "Whether the Standard Oil Company is in a trust or outside a trust is for the courts to decide, but whether the consumers of oil are getting a better grade at less cost and greater safety is a question for the people to decide."

Incidentally, for the benefit of those who feel a revulsion against the use of money to influence the Fourth Estate, let it be noted that the records of Standard Oil show that there was a flood of requests from publications of all kinds, newspapers and newspapermen, to be corrupted with Standard Oil funds.

The Archbold letters revealed that Archbold had sent $3,000 for a subscription to the enlightened *Manufacturers' Record,* praising it for its "most admirable" work, and $1,250 in like admiration to the *Southern Farm Magazine.* These subscriptions at the then current rates were for the next 3,000 and 2,500 years respectively. Archbold also sent an "additional" $5,000 contribution to Professor George Gunton, editor of *Gunton's Magazine,* praising him for "your excellent work." Gunton is worth examining further.

When Lloyd's book appeared, Professor Gunton attacked Lloyd in the *Social Economist,* quoting the English economist John Hobson. Lloyd claimed that in reply to his own letter, Hobson wrote that he had written to Gunton the exact opposite of what Gunton claimed that he had said. Gunton established *Gunton's Magazine* and built for himself a reputation as an economic thinker and also as a friend of the workingman, espousing the cause of unionism. However, in his magazine, Gunton always saw things the same way as Standard Oil, which won his unstinting praise. When Miss Tarbell's book came out, Gunton walloped it, saying that the ideas were borrowed from Lloyd. He also attacked journalists for "feeding the popular prejudice against large corporations." He said, "It is bad indeed for businessmen to get rich by questionable methods but it is much worse for publishers to get rich by poisoning the public mind against the institutions of society through misrepresentation."

This paladin of virtue was later revealed to have been a hireling of Standard Oil for years at $15,000 a year, losing his stipend in 1904 when he got into a divorce scrape. The intellectual who hires his reputation to industry or any other buyer infested the woods then as he does now.

The public relations department under Joseph Ignatius Clarke was a novel attempt systematically to manufacture news slants, create an "image," and infect neutral or even hostile newspapers with the gospel. Clarke had some success. His circle of friendships in the newspaper fraternity was wide, and soon friendly references appeared, even in Pulitzer's *World* and the Hearst press. (It would have been interesting to examine Clarke's expense account.) Magazines carried sweet stories like "How the World's Richest Man Spends Christmas." (Taking time off from his philanthropies, he celebrated it like everyone else.) Some news stories were not happily inspired. In 1907 Frederick Gates stated that Rockefeller's fortune was less than $300,000,000. This was evidently intended to rebut rumors that Rockefeller had a billion dollars, but it led to gibes like, "How does the poor man survive if he doesn't have even $300,000,000?"

The obvious move on the part of Standard Oil was to have a book written to counter Miss Tarbell's. This was long a high-priority matter; in the end nothing came of it, because Rockefeller was unenthusiastic about disclosing company affairs and also because no defense could be made without also making damaging admissions. A twenty-two-year-old graduate student at Harvard, Gilbert Montague, published in Harvard's *Quarterly Journal of Economics* two articles about Standard Oil that pleased its executives no end—first because the *Journal* had the right aura of academic dignity and second because Montague could see nothing censurable in the conduct of the company. Its success was merely an involuntary reflex to the economics of the times, mostly transportation economics. Standard Oil had these articles put together in book form, *The Rise and Progress of the Standard Oil Company,* a discussion that unfortunately was far above the layman's head.

Who could write a history of Standard Oil that would carry weight? In 1906 a minister, Leonard Woolsey Bacon, was selected for the assignment as author. Rockefeller was enthusiastic, and wrote, "The best [talent] that can be secured is not too good for this important writing." Henry Flagler, who had abandoned his role in the company for his work in building eastern Florida into an American Riviera, was scheduled to make an important contribution. Bacon became ill in 1907, and the project died.

The selection of a minister to compose a business history brings up an interesting feature of the times. Somehow ministers and priests, perhaps rabbis, were supposed to be gifted with business expertise, and they had no hesitancy in offering themselves as arbiters in the contest of business with the public. Members of the cloth delivered sermons based on the Lloyd and Tarbell books, and the Montague book was sent by Standard to a host of church leaders. Rockefeller himself seems to have felt that ministers had authority in this field. When the Lloyd book came out, a Reverend B. Gay Mills of Fort Edward, New York, conferred with Frederick Gates and Solicitor Samuel C. T. Dodd of Standard Oil, and was persuaded that the book was erroneous. Then the Reverend Mr. Mills, at Rockefeller's suggestion, invited Lloyd, more ministers, and two leading economists, John R. Commons and Richard T. Ely, to come to Standard's headquarters in New York to investigate the charges. Lloyd said it was "opéra bouffe," and Ely's refusal to join put a quietus on the matter. We have mentioned the role of Dr. Washington Gladden as a Rockefeller opponent. Gladden, who has been called the Father of the Social Gospel, took over the pastorate of the First Congregational Church of Columbus, Ohio, in 1882, and saw at first hand the bitter Hocking Valley Coal strike of 1884–1885. Reversing an earlier bias, he became thereafter a foe of the theory of the iron law of wages, and from that time on preached and wrote in behalf of a greater share of the wealth for labor. Preachers today are more apt to stay apart from these secular activities, but the self-interposition of Father Charles E. Coughlin as an authority on business and government in the time of Franklin D. Roosevelt was not without precedent.

The preeminence of Standard in wealth, and approval or hope of approval from gold-rimmed Mount Olympus, would be enough to command support in publications. Syracuse University, as we have seen, was the pet philanthropy of Standard's John D. Archbold; and the Chancellor of Syracuse, James R. Day, took up the cudgels in a book published in 1907, *The Raid on Prosperity*, the raid being the attack on big business. Two chapters were devoted to an ardent defense of Standard Oil. Who were those who attacked it? "Vindictive competitors, socialists and anarchists, frenzied magazines, slanderous yellow journals." Elbert Hubbard, popular writer and aphorist, obviously subsidized by Standard Oil, went on the attack against Miss Tarbell. "She shot from cover and she shot to kill. Such literary bushwackers should be answered shot for shot." Her book was "over-the-fence gossip raised to fortissimo." If we destroy faith in business, "we are taking the roofs from homes, snatching food from children and pushing bodies naked into the storm." A novel was published that painted Standard Oil as good and its opponents as evil. It was *Oil Wells in the Woods* by John Christopher O'Day, a doctor who might have been related to the Standard Pipe-line executive Daniel O'Day. The villain, Weatherbee, tries to get into the combination "with the tactics of a snake." By underhand methods Weatherbee tries to induce a "declining politician" to introduce a bill harmful to Standard, and so forth.

The publisher, F. N. Doubleday, had made a good deal of money out of the Tarbell book, sharing its publication with S. S. McClure. He wanted to get the other side of the story, and became friends with Rockefeller, introducing Rockefeller, Sr.,

Rockefeller, Jr., and Henry Rogers to a group of publishers at a luncheon. He wrote warmly of Rockefeller in an article in *World's Work*, edited by the liberal Walter Hines Page.

Rockefeller was persuaded by Doubleday to write his memoirs; they first appeared serially in *World's Work* in 1908 and were published by Doubleday and Page in 1909, and entitled *Random Reminiscences of Men and Events*.

The world waited expectantly for the Rockefeller disclosures. Advertisements heralding the publication said in effect, "Now it can be told." But great was the disappointment when they appeared in print—the book was all Rockefeller. Although he had literary assistance from his aide, attorney Starr J. Murphy, the style was Rockefeller's, not that of a ghost writer. It was written with his characteristic economy and precision of expression, and his literalness of thought. The ideas were all Rockefeller, too— syrup and soft soap: The success of Standard Oil was built entirely on the fact that it produced the best products at the lowest cost. The organization was made up of happy people whose dearest wish was to make the rest of the world as happy. Rockefeller defended the company against charges that had never been made, that it did not pay bills promptly or that its stock was "watered." Rockefeller was meticulous in his use of words, and every sentence showed it: "We did not ruthlessly go after the trade of our competitors and attempt to ruin it by cutting prices or setting up a spy system." What is "ruthlessly"? "It was never our purpose to interfere with a dealer who adequately cultivated his field of operations." What is "adequately"? "The profits of the Standard Oil Company did not come from advantages given by railroads." Technically correct, since special rates only enabled it to knock out competitors, and all profits did not stem from this advantage. "The railroads rather were the ones who profited by the traffic of Standard Oil." This was a favorite rhetorical device of Rockefeller, *Tu quoque*. "It's you, not me."

All this made not a dent in public opinion. In the battle of the printed word, Standard Oil was a bad loser to Miss Ida Minerva Tarbell.

President Taft pushed the antitrust suit against Standard hard. His Attorney General, George Wickersham, advised him that this, was really a total monopoly; whatever competition existed lived only by sufferance of Standard, which tolerated it as a stage prop to keep alive a fiction. In November 1909 the Circuit Court of Appeals decided in favor of the government, and the case went immediately to the Supreme Court. There the case dragged on, since it had to be reargued because of the death of an Associate Justice. President Taft prodded the Court to act.

Politically the case was important for Taft, and it is amusing to see what precautions he took to avoid any hint of contamination by Standard Oil. In the letters of Archie Butt, his military aide, we find that on August 11, 1910, Butt wrote to his sister-in-law Clara that the President consented to see former Senator Aldrich but not his son-in-law John D. Rockefeller, Jr. On April 20, 1911, Butt wrote to Clara as follows:

At three there was to be a reception of the Children of the Revolution. I had already directed one of the junior aides to be there to present them to the President, when I got a message from him that he wanted me and no one else. I was somewhat mystified until I learned that ex-Senator Aldrich, with his daughter and her husband, Mr. Rockefeller, were to be at lunch and that nothing was to be said about them being there. It is strange how men in public office shudder at the names of Aldrich and Rockefeller.

All guests for luncheon enter the White House by the main entrance, but the President gave the tip that he wanted them to come in unobserved, so the usher telephoned Mr. Aldrich to drive to the East entrance where he would meet them and take their wraps. Of course, the Senator understood. The President said he wanted no note of the fact that they were there entered on any of the books or made known even at his office.

Isn't it funny what politics will do to a man? There is no one in all the world so little prone to fear appearances as the President and yet there he is entertaining Aldrich and his son-in-law at a simple family luncheon with the secretiveness which might mark the clandestine meeting of anarchists.

Finally, on May 15, 1911, the unanimous decision ordering the dissolution of Standard Oil was read, standing up, by Chief Justice White to a packed courtroom. In this decision the Chief

Justice introduced the Rule of Reason, saying that the restraint must be "undue" or "unreasonable," a clear piece of judicial legislation, as Justice Harlan separately pointed out. The loophole altered the course of our industrial history by allowing many industrial combinations, such as United States Steel, to survive.

The Court gave six months for the dissolution to be accomplished, beginning June 21. The alacrity with which the company moved showed that its response in 1892 to the order of the Ohio courts to dissolve had been nothing but a charade. On July 28 Standard announced that the separation of the companies would take place as of September 1. On that date stockholders received their due proportion of the stock in each of thirty-two constituent companies. The distribution was completed by December 1 except for Anglo-American shares, for which permission was granted for a brief extension.

Out of the breakup Jersey Standard emerged as the most powerful unit. At the end of 1911 the net value of all the properties was estimated at $660,000,000. Of this amount in the combination, Jersey and its affiliates were first in assets with $285,532,000, New York Standard second with $60,024,000, and Ohio Standard third with $44,052,000.

Of the 983,383 shares in the holding company, Rockefeller's holdings were 244,385 shares, making his holdings of the company worth over $160,000,000 at the time of dissolution. The Harkness family came next with 93,670 shares, then Oliver H. Payne with 48,000, the Pratt family with 58,250, Flagler (who had retired from the company) with 36,700 shares, the Rogers family (he had died in 1909) with 20,190, and William Rockefeller with 6,000 shares. There were 6,006 stockholders in 1910, double the number of ten years ago. The stock was not listed on the New York Stock Exchange, but an active over-the-counter market had developed.

A weird division of shares took place. For each share of Standard Oil the holder received a fraction of a share of each company, the denominator being 983,383 and the numerator being the proportion the assets of the particular company bore to the assets of the whole. Thus for each share the stockholder received one 994/983,383 of Swan and Finch Company with a face value of 10 cents and one 1,995/983,383 of Borne-Scrysmer Company with a face value of 20 cents. When companies issued dividends they were often for a few cents each. Galena-Signal Oil Company mailed 600 dividend checks for three cents or less in 1912.

Within a week after the distribution, brokerage houses specializing in Standard stocks sprang up in Wall Street. The stocks skyrocketed, and in three months $200,000,000 was added to the market value of the stocks in the wildest bull market in any one stock up to that time. It was the envy of stockholders in trusts the government had let alone. The rise has been attributed to the fact that for the first time the public learned of the true values in the companies, and the prices rose to reflect these values. Between January and October 1912, Standard of New York rose from 260 to 580; this was less than the rise in Standard of Indiana, which rose from 3,500 to 9,500, adjusted for a 29 for 1 stock split. Rockefeller's wealth zoomed with this upward surge in prices.

Taking as long a view of history as we can, let us consider some questions in connection with the dissolution decree. First, had the trust served the public interest badly by grabbing too high a profit? In 1907 Commissioner Herbert Knox Smith of the Bureau of Corporations (succeeding Garfield) issued a report in which he said, "The profits of the Standard Oil Company particularly on domestic business are altogether excessive." Between 1891 and 1899 earnings increased from $27,367,000 to $64,457,000; in 1907 and 1908 they were $131,291,000 and $116,460,000 respectively. Rockefeller contended that the profits were not excessive and not "larger than those from many other large businesses with less risk." He pointed out that the population was growing, the price level was advancing, the pipeline business was booming as distant fields were being tapped, and gasoline was coming into demand for motors. There was also what he called a "ramification of profits" as the company engaged in different lines of activity, such as real estate, insurance, brokerage, banking and foreign exchange.

Whether the profits were excessive could be endlessly argued, but there is no doubt that the increase was spectacular. This merges into another question, whether prices were excessive and whether the public was gouged, as Commissioner Smith claimed. While Rockefeller claimed that the public was treated fairly, statements made by other officials did not help to strengthen that impression. Before the Industrial Commission in 1899, Henry Rogers was asked why pipeline charges had not gone down in twenty years despite the increase in efficiency. He replied, "We are not in business for our health but are out for dollars."

Ida Tarbell's major argument that consumers were overcharged by the profit-mad Standard ignored a basic inconsistency—if prices were set very high by Standard, that fact would enable competitors to live and make a profit, and it was a major thesis of Miss Tarbell that Standard's primary aim was to kill off competitors. Yet Miss Tarbell wanted to be believed both ways. The price policy of Standard accorded with the advice of Benjamin Brewster to Rockefeller years earlier: "Make prices at which the outside interests may keep moving but not derive sufficient comfort to induce increased consumption."

In his report Commissioner Smith's own view was that "Standard has superior efficiency in running its own business; it has an equal efficiency in destroying the business of its competitors. It keeps for itself the profits of the first and adds to them the monopoly profits secured by the second."

Smith claimed that the margin between crude and prices for illuminating oil increased from 5.3 cents to 7.1 cents between 1898 and 1903, and the margins rose for other products—gasoline from 5.2 to 9.2 cents, and lubricating oils from 10.7 to 13.7 cents.

It does seem that in its later years profit margins could have been cut to pass on to consumers the benefit of increases of efficiency. Actually, 41.6 percent of the company's profits came from transportation. In the segment of domestic marketing where Standard made only 16 percent of its profits, some sacrifice of profit margins could have been made, if only for better public relations. Since Archbold was running the company, apologists for Rockefeller have tried to exonerate him by putting the blame on Archbold. But Rockefeller could hardly have overlooked so fundamental a policy as prices and profits.

Dividends of almost $40,000,000 a year compared with a wage bill of about $65,000,000, estimating the average pay at $1,000 a year for 65,000 employees. This seems a very high reward for capital compared to labor. The Standard Oil of New Jersey in 1963 had a wage and salary bill of $1,011,278,000 compared to

Right, Rockefeller Jr. (left) inspecting the mines in 1915, a year after the Ludlow Massacre; *below*, with his five sons in 1937. Left to right, David, Nelson, Winthrop, Laurence, and John

John D. Rockefeller Sr. at Pocantico with Mr and Mrs Rockefeller Jr. and
four of their children

cash dividends of $592,499,000—not too wide a change in the
ratio, but the oil industry today is perhaps the most automated;
and in most other industries the ratio in favor of labor is much
higher. Thus for General Motors dividends in 1963 amounted to
$1,148,737,000, compared to wages and salaries of $4,312,752,000,
and for United States Steel dividends were less than 10 percent
of the labor bill—$133,450,000, compared to $1,416,800,000.

Did some salutary changes come for Standard as a result of the
dissolution? Undoubtedly.

A fresh wind blew through the company, since the decree was
a signal for the withdrawal of many old personalities and the
coming to the fore of a host of young faces, given their chance
years before they expected it. Then, too, there was far too much
centralization in the old company—every authorization for more
than $5,000 had to be approved by New York. After 1910, Dr.
William Burton at Whiting made successful experiments in
"cracking" gasoline, greatly increasing the yield. He later said,
"We would never have made the rapid progress we did in cracking oil if we'd had to go to New York for every dollar we spent."

Another change for the better was the demise of the Rocke-
feller-Archbold practice of secrecy in corporate affairs and the
exclusive reliance on plowing back of profits for capital needs.
This was unsuited to the needs of an oil industry in the modern
age, which would grow to a $50 billion industry largely by infu-
sion of capital from the public. From this standpoint the interests
of the nation and of the Standard units were well served.

Was the competition within the industry increased and the
position of the independent operator enhanced as a result of the
dissolution? Hardly.

In the beginning the change was not substantial. "How in hell
is any court going to compel a man to compete with himself?"
growled J. P. Morgan. There was logic in this rhetorical question.
Bonds of friendship continued, and by tacit understandings the
different companies preserved and respected spheres of influence
where one or the other company continued to dominate. Each of
the Standard units had been set up with specific functions, and
they continued to do business in the same way. Thus the pipes of
Prairie Oil & Gas continued to serve Standard of Indiana, and
Standard of New Jersey continued to sell refined products to

Standard of New York. In recent times Standard companies have had scant respect for one another's territory, but such practices were long acoming. Meanwhile, the share of refining of Standard companies has dropped sharply, down to 50 percent by 1925 and 20 percent today, while their share of production has climbed from 11 percent to 25 percent.

However, the Standard companies continue to be the industry price leaders—Socony-Mobil in New England and Esso in New Jersey and New York. Price competition is only sporadic, even less than in the trust days with its frequent price wars. Because of technological developments that have made small-scale operations impracticable, the share of refining held by the majors has increased from 53 percent in 1920 to over 85 percent today. The trust is long since dead, but for the consumer and the small refiner it has been pretty much *Plus ça change, plus c'est la même chose.*

BOOK FOUR

THE AGE OF PHILANTHROPY

Your fortune is rolling up, rolling up like an avalanche. You must distribute it faster than it grows.

—FREDERICK T. GATES TO JOHN D. ROCKEFELLER

Is this great fortune to be handed down to posterity as other great fortunes have been handed down by their possessors with scandalous results to their descendants and powerful tendencies to social disintegration?

FROM THE PRIVATE PAPERS OF FREDERICK T. GATES

CHAPTER 22 *"God Gave Me My Money"*

IN 1889 Andrew Carnegie wrote an article in the *North American Review* in which he said, "The man who dies rich dies disgraced," and, "The day is not far distant when the man who dies leaving behind him millions of available wealth which was free for him to administer during life will pass away unwept, unhonored and unsung."

Rockefeller wrote to Carnegie after reading the article, "I would that more men of wealth were doing as you are doing with your money, but be assured your example will bear fruit."

Gift-giving to the less fortunate had been ingrained in Rockefeller, and he had practiced it from his earliest working days, beginning at sixteen years of age, as his Ledger A gives testimony. The curve of gift-giving slowly ascends through the years. By 1872 his gifts amounted. to $7,000 a year. By 1882 they amounted to $65,000 a year; and ten years later they had reached the rate of $1,500,000 a year.

Philanthropy was intimately associated with religious feeling. He was indoctrinated in childhood with the idea that the practice of good works was part of being a Christian. His worldly success linked his thoughts to heavenly Providence and his obligations to his fellowman. In 1896, at the University of Chicago on the occasion of its fifth anniversary, when the university had already received $10,000,000 from him, he said in a speech, "The good Lord gave me the money and how could I withhold it from Chicago?" The thought that the Lord was keeping a special watch for one who was then regarded by most as an industrial pirate did not sit well with all the Chicago newspapers. He repeated the thought in an interview with the *Woman's Home Companion* in 1905: "God gave me my money."

He did not enlarge on the thought. What he meant was clarified to some extent by what he had to say to reporter William Hoster in 1906:

I believe the power to make money is a gift from God—just as are the instincts for art, music, literature, the doctor's talent, yours—to be developed and used to the best of our ability for the good of mankind. Having been endowed with the gift I possess, I believe it is my duty to make money and still more money and to use the money I make for the good of my fellowman according to the dictates of my conscience.

He was in his own mind a steward of God's will. He was endowed with this talent and assisted with favorable circumstances because he had the wisdom to handle it best. Fortifying further Rockefeller's belief that his whole life had been destined for helping his fellowman was the belief, stated in his *Reminiscences,* that the greatest philanthropy was to give employment to the most people at the highest wages and to develop all our resources, human and physical. Had his daily vocation therefore not been one of philanthropy, and had it not also resulted in the furnishing of cheap light to the world?

The methodology of giving that Rockefeller applied is stated in his *Reminiscences,* and owes much to Frederick Gates, but it seems to have been inchoate in Rockefeller's mind from the inception of his giving long before he met Gates. It encompassed these principles:

First, the effort should be to build for strength and not for weakness. The important objective is to build people or institutions to a point where they can help themselves.

Second, the best philanthropy is in search of the finalities—a search for cause, an attempt to cure evils at their source. To help the investigator who is searching for the causes of sickness and distress does not have the same heart balm to the kindhearted as does direct gifts of help to the sick and distressed, but it accomplishes far more in the long run.

Third, money should be given insofar as possible for work already organized and of proved worth. It should be of a continuing character that will not be in danger of disappearing. For this end, gifts should be conditional on the gifts of others, because "we wish in this way to root the institution in the affections of as many people as possible who as contributors become personally concerned and thereafter may be counted on to give to the institution their watchful interest and cooperation."

The first great Rockefeller philanthropy was the University of Chicago, of which he was officially declared Founder. It was in the course of this that Frederick Gates's association with him began. Rockefeller at times may have been drawn into this philanthropy further and faster than he wished, and Gates believed that his hand and pen had been rudely forced to the checkbook. Yet Rockefeller acquiesced so gracefully that it can be assumed that the external pressures were congruent with his own impulses.

For years, Rockefeller gifts had gone to every college of the Baptist denomination, and beyond that to Barnard and to Vassar, a college his daughter Bessie attended. He had been much impressed by the purposive giving of his Standard Oil associate, Charles Pratt, who was very much interested in engineering as a profession and had given $4,000,000 to establish Pratt Institute in Brooklyn. Rockefeller had come to believe that in the search for finalities it was important to widen the boundaries of human knowledge by research, and he made it evident that he would consider wide-scale donations to higher education.

A University of Chicago had been established in 1856, in which Senator Stephen A. Douglas had had a hand, but it had atrophied, and by 1886 the mortgage had been foreclosed. This placed in jeopardy the Morgan Park Seminary, a Baptist institution to which Rockefeller had given financial aid. He was dismayed when its chief biblical scholar, young William Rainey Harper, left the seminary to take the post of Biblical Professor at Yale University.

Observing Rockefeller's interest, Dr. Thomas Goodspeed, president of the seminary, seized the occasion to broach to Rockefeller the idea of reviving the university on a great scale. "Chicago is the place of all others in the world to build a great Baptist University," he wrote to Rockefeller, who hung back both because it was his custom to ponder long before making any important step and because he failed to see any great interest from others. For the next two years Rockefeller was besieged with letters from Goodspeed and from another educator, Dr. Augustus Strong, head of the Rochester Theological Seminary, the leading training ground for the Baptist clergy. Strong's argument was twofold. First, there was no great Baptist school of higher learning in the country. Brown, the leading one, had only three hundred students. Second, there was in this country no great university like

Oxford and Heidelberg; even Harvard was primarily an under-graduate rather than a graduate school. Thus Rockefeller would have the double honor of founding the first American super university and a Baptist seat of learning of which to be proud. Though Dr. Strong accompanied Rockefeller on a European trip in 1887, he was not able to put it over. His proposal was that Rockefeller should donate $20,000,000 for the university, which would rise on Morningside Heights in New York where Columbia University now stands.

In 1888 the American Baptist Education Society was formed, with Gates as the executive secretary, whose first task was to make a study of the state of Baptist educational facilities, which was admittedly feeble. Gates became convinced that the need for an institution of higher learning was most acute, not in the East, as Strong proposed, but in the West. Half the Baptists lived west of Pennsylvania and east of the Rockies, but the eleven Baptist schools in that whole area had less than a million dollars in property and endowments.

The report made a great impression on Rockefeller, and to a large extent he was swayed not only by the facts and logic but by the recommendation of Gates, whom he had learned to trust. Rockefeller still delayed, showing the same cold calculation that he would give to entering into a business scheme. He wanted the right man to head it, and met with William Rainey Harper at Yale and at Vassar, quizzing him about himself, and testing the idea of a great university in the West, probably Chicago. He also tested the idea with President James Taylor of Vassar, and with other educators.

The ambitions of Dr. Strong died hard. He knew Rockefeller well, his son, Charles, having married Rockefeller's firstborn, Bessie, in 1889, and he tries all the gambits that might have an appeal. First, he tried to push, almost bully, Rockefeller into accepting his plan. It was the voice of God. Impatiently: "I feel as if I could hardly go through the strain of meditating and praying about this for another year. I would almost rather leave my testimony and die." A plea that Rockefeller would get joy out of attending to the details of the founding followed: "Would it not make the noblest work as well as the noblest recreation of your life if not neglecting other and distant interests you should devote yourself mainly to the travels and investigations . . . ?" Rockefeller must have been horrified at the suggestion that his moneymaking activities should take a back seat. Then a practical plea that the gift he suggested would "stem the tide of aspersion." He wrote, "Very many people do not understand you and they unjustly accuse you. Your friends love and admire you but very many are not your friends." There is no evidence that Rockefeller was ever prevailed on to make a gift by the hope of winning popular favor. Even before *Wealth Against Commonwealth* appeared in 1894, he was giving away a million and a half a year. Then a Parthian shot, an attack on Harper, who was designated to head the university in the West, on the ground that he was not a Fundamentalist—Strong had gathered from his daughter's lecture notes that he rejected the supernatural in the fulfillment of the biblical prophecies. This had more effect on Rockefeller than other arguments, since the last thing he wanted or felt equipped to do was to get in the middle of a theological dispute, but in the end this was settled to Rockefeller's satisfaction.

The negotiations had dragged on for three years. The first proposal by Dr. Goodspeed was for $100,000; "enough for a high school," Dr. Strong had belittled it. The next jump, however, was an impressive one. Rockefeller was to give $3,000,000 in installments, with others to give the remainder of a million. In November 1888, after a talk with Rockefeller at Yale, Harper wrote to Goodspeed, "I am sure that is the way it will come out." The initial amount turned out to be much less. Some months later Rockefeller and Gates walked together in front of his West Fifty-fourth Street house. As they reached Fifth Avenue, Rockefeller turned to Gates and said that he would give $600,000 if others would give $400,000. Gates almost shouted for joy. "Never shall I forget the thrill of that moment . . . no gift of his has ever thrilled me as did the first great gift of $600,000 on that May morning after those months of anxious suspense."

At a convention of the Baptist Education Society on May 18, 1888, the gift was announced amid scenes of delirious joy and chants: "The man who has given us this gift is a Godly man" and "A man to lead. It is God's doing." Sermons in Baptist churches throughout the nation rang out on the theme "A man of God." There was universal expectation that Rockefeller, having made the first benefaction, would not shrink from further gifts to make the project a success. The follow-up requests were not long in coming.

Within a matter of months the $400,000 matching fund was raised, plus a ten-acre tract of land donated by Marshall Field. Then came the problem of persuading Harper to leave the salubrious climate of Yale for the wilderness of the new, untried university. He finally consented, but only if Rockefeller would give another million dollars. A pedagogical holdup! Rockefeller consented. Then Harper had qualms of conscience as to whether he really was Fundamentalist enough for the new university. Rockefeller, losing patience, had to remind him that a contract was a contract.

There was discouragement for Rockefeller in the way things were going. Chicagoans were not pitching in as he had expected, and he might conceivably have to carry the entire load. Operating expense budgets drawn up showed that deficits might have to be met, and that meant only Rockefeller. There was difficulty in attracting the best men for a faculty. Having just recovered from his digestive illness in February 1893, Rockefeller gave another million for the endowment. "I make this gift as a special thank-offering to Almighty God for returning health."

The joy in Chicago was mixed with some merriment about the widening wedge in the Rockefeller bankroll. From the *Reminiscences,* one gathers that Rockefeller was a bit tickled with a cartoon that shows him working peacefully in his office clipping coupons. Dr. Harper is announced. He jumps out of the window. Next, Rockefeller is seen fleeing across a river, hopping from one cake of ice to another with Dr. Harper in pursuit; next he is seen on a country road, delaying Dr. Harper in Russian-troika style by dropping million-dollar bills for Harper to pick up. Rockefeller wrote that the cartoon pained Harper, since he had never personally asked Rockefeller for money, but Harper apparently did not have any hesitancy in asking Gates, who was now in Rockefeller's employ, and he could build up circumstances that made a further gift mandatory. In December, Harper, ruminating blackly that "the work is too much for me," made it clear that another million was needed. Rockefeller came forward with a Christmas gift of a million, and within nine months he gave another half-million.

Under Gates's tutelage the university was learning that if it were more modest in its demands, it would fare better. As Gates wrote, "What I wanted to do was by whittling down the requests of the University to give to Mr. Rockefeller an opportunity of seeming to do voluntarily more than was asked, to seem to act freely and without compulsion." On October 30, 1895, this policy bore best fruit when Rockefeller supplied an endowment of three more millions.

In time, Rockefeller became increasingly irritated with Harper's administration of finances. No matter how large Rockefeller made the endowment, the deficits continued year after year, and Rockefeller had to make them good. Dr. Goodspeed wrote, "It sometimes seemed as though Dr. Harper was deliberately forcing the Founder's hand and had adopted this as a thoroughly considered and permanent policy." Gates had the same idea, and in 1897 forced Harper to modify his spendthrift policy.

Rockefeller visited the campus for the first time in 1896. The student sang to the tune of "Daisy Bell":

> John D. Rockefeller,
> Wonderful man is he,
> Gives all his spare change
> To the U. of C.
> He keeps the ball a-rolling
> In our great varsity;
> He pays Dr. Harper
> To help us grow sharper
> For the glory of the U. of C.

Dr. Harper in his opening address pointed out that for lack of a suitable building the convocation was being held in a tent, the while looking at Rockefeller knowingly, who nodded and smiled knowingly. In his speech Rockefeller began, "This is only the beginning," and there was a joyous roar. Then Rockefeller set his hearers straight: "You have the privilege of completing it." No one needed to fear. It was only the beginning of the Rockefeller benefactions, which were to total, in all, $40,000,000.

In this great philanthropy Rockefeller demonstrated what was to be his customary self-effacement. The university was not named for him, and originally there was not a trace of his name on the campus. (In later years there was the beautiful Rockefeller Chapel.) At the insistence of the trustees he was named as Founder, and the early stationery bore his name as such. As in all his future philanthropies he did not interfere with the administration in any way, and once, when he was asked for his opinion, Gates wrote back, "No management can gain skill unless it exercises its functions independently." The only instance of a demurrer on his part was a question he raised as to the propriety of having an actor, Joseph Jefferson, address the students after chapel.

Though Rockefeller did not express assent or dissent with the views of any member of the faculty, of course everyone was aware of the orientation of the founder. The *Journal of Political Economy,* established in 1892, did not contain a single article on trusts for ten years, even though it was the subject on everyone's mind in the economic world. Then there was the case of Professor Edward Bemis, who had the temerity to criticize the railroad presidents after the Pullman strike of 1894. President Harper wrote to him: "It is hardly safe for me to venture into any of the Chicago clubs. I am pounced on from all sides." Bemis, who later became an outstanding expert on public utility regulation, was released so that he could be happier elsewhere. Professor Oscar L. Triggs, of the English Department, did not make the same mistake—he proclaimed George M. Pullman and Rockefeller "superior in creative genius to Shakespeare, Homer and Dante."

By applying the same type of money muscle in the academic world as did Standard Oil, paying unheard-of salaries up to $7,000 for department heads, President Harper garnered a fine faculty, including Jacques Loeb, Albert Michelson, and Lloyd Morgan. An obscure economics instructor asked for a small salary raise, and was refused by Harper on the grounds that he did not advertise the university. Thorstein Veblen shortly thereafter published *The Theory of the Leisure Class.*

Frederick Gates not only became Rockefeller's chief almoner but, projecting what he termed his "pregnant ideas," he became the architect of the imaginative, trail-blazing philanthropies that followed those of the University of Chicago.

When he met Gates, Rockefeller was engaged more or less in piecemeal giving. The demands on his time were staggering, plaintiffs pursuing him from his home, riding with him downtown and uptown on the elevated train, besieging him in his office. It became impossible for him to investigate the petitions, since Standard Oil had priority on his time. When he asked Gates to become his assistant in 1891, he said, "Either I must shift part of the burden or I must give up giving." When he undertook his work, Gates was astonished at the number of entreaties. After the public announcement of one gift, Rockefeller received 50,000 letters, one steamer from Europe bringing 5,000 letters. Gates found that Rockefeller was conducting a miniature Baptist foreign mission society. Returning missionaries, each ignorant of all fields but his own, filling his office, his home, and his table. Gates cut off these appeals, sending each applicant back to the missionary executives in the Boston office for screening. This mission experience convinced Gates that there must be overall concepts and organization to manage the philanthropies.

Throughout his life Rockefeller enjoyed association with outgoing personalities in contrast to himself, and he found in Gates a person temperamentally at the opposite pole from himself, verbose, fiery, overwhelming. Gates. described himself this way in 1891, "eager, impetuous, insistent and often exacting and irritable." Powerful in exhortation, he would preach to Rockefeller in evangelistic, even bombastic, fashion—and apparently Rockefeller liked it, or did not mind.

"Your fortune is rolling up, rolling up like an avalanche. You must distribute it faster than it grows. If you do not, it will crush you and your children and your children's children."

Again, he lectured Rockefeller:

"If any man's happiness in doing good depends on human gratitude or praise, if his satisfaction is sought from any source except the silent approval of conscience, that man's sun will go down to the end amid the clouds of a disappointed and embittered life."

Rockefeller answered, "I know that."

Gates wrote a memorandum of his thoughts that was found among his papers: "Is this great fortune to be handed down to posterity as other great fortunes have been handed down by their possessors with scandalous result to their decendants and powerful tendencies to social disintegration?"*

Gates pondered the problem. He was not in search of small ideas, which he termed "retail business." Out of his mind sprang the majestic conceptions that were to characterize the Rockefeller philanthropies.

In 1897 Gates read, for pure enjoyment, William Osler's *Principles and Practice of Medicine*. Gates had been curious about progress in the medical profession, since a doctor in Minneapolis had told him that only in one case out of a hundred was a doctor able to perfect a cure; in other cases of recovery the cure was effected by Mother Nature. Homeopathy, which was widely practiced in the city, was looked into by Gates, who decided it was humbug. Osler's book showed that while there were ample diagnoses of many diseases, there were cures for only half a dozen. Out of this haphazard reading, an idea was born in Gates's mind. Why should the United States not have an institute like the Koch Institute in Berlin or the Pasteur Institute in Paris? The Pasteur experiments in the cure for anthrax had saved France more money than its entire cost of the Franco-Prussian War. "Even if the proposed Institute should fail to discover anything, the mere fact that he, Mr. Rockefeller, had established such an institute of research would result in institutes of similar kind or at least other funds for research being established, until research in this country would be conducted on a great scale, and out of the multitudes of workers we might be sure in the end of abundant rewards."

Rockefeller, Jr., undertook to sell the idea to his father, and his mother was a valuable go-between, since Rockefeller, Jr., sent her memoranda to read to his father when he was in a receptive mood. Rockefeller, Jr., canvassed the idea with Dr. William H. Welch, of Johns Hopkins; Dr. T. Mitchell Prudden, of the College of Physicians and Surgeons in New York; and L. Emmett Holt, a well-known New York City practitioner. The recent development of diphtheria antitoxin after years of patient laboratory work by Emil von Behring and Pierre Roux increased the enthusiasm of the doctors for an institute here.

* Such a case would be that of the granddaughter of Henry Rogers, Millicent Rogers, whose marital problems filled the tabloids in the twenties.

The Institute was incorporated on June 14, 1901. Originally Rockefeller gave $20,000 a year for ten years, and the Institute distributed scholarships and fellowships over the United States and made grants to laboratories. According to Gates, the meager beginnings were due to the fact that the medical group could not see the project on the same grandiose scale as he could. The conception grew. In 1902 Rockefeller gave a million to establish a research laboratory of which Dr. Simon Flexner became the first director. Then Rockefeller bought a tract of land for a building of its own on the East River between Sixty-fourth and Sixty-seventh streets in New York. Rockefeller never stinted. His representative would always say, "If you had more money, what would you do with it?" Millions in gifts followed. Rockefeller's attitude toward the scientists was as Dr. Flexner described it: "Don't hurry and don't worry. We have faith that you will make good and if you don't the next fellow will."

There is a remarkable feature to this philanthropy. Rockefeller would have nothing to do with the discoveries of the Institute as far as his own health was concerned. He believed in homeopathic medicine, and his personal physician for years, Dr. H. F. Biggar, was a homeopathic doctor. Dr. Biggar attacked the Institute, and Gates blasted back to Rockefeller that Biggar was "living in the twilight of two or three generations ago," and Rockefeller continued his support of the Institute.

John D. Rockefeller, Jr., was to take an equally active role in the initiation of the General Education Board. The Rockefeller family, with its keen interest in the Negro, had long been deeply interested in Negro education. In 1901 Robert C. Ogden, a Philadelphia merchant, chartered a special train to visit educational facilities for the Negro in the South. Among fifty prominent guests were Rockefeller, Jr., Walter Hines Page, George Foster Peabody, and Albert Shaw. At a meeting on the train, Henry St. George Tucker, president of Washington and Lee University, voiced a sentiment that was accepted by the group. "If it is your idea to educate the Negro, you must have the whites of the South with you. If the poor white sees the son of a Negro neighbor enjoying, through your munificence, benefits denied to his boy, it raises in him a feeling that will render futile all your work."

Out of meetings at the younger Rockefeller's home in which

Gates took a leading role, there emerged in 1902 the General Education Board in which Wallace Buttrick, chairman of the Baptist Home Mission Society, who was intimately acquainted with southern education problems, was a leader. Another of the remarkable men who were involved in the Rockefeller philanthropies in their germination, Buttrick had been a brakeman and postal clerk on a railroad in northern New York for five years before entering Rochester Theological Seminary in his late twenties. Federal incorporation was obtained for the new organization by Act of Congress in 1902, the bill being sponsored by Senator Nelson Aldrich, and Rockefeller immediately gave it a million dollars, the first of many gifts.

The first task undertaken by the board was to raise the level of education, and it was decided that the best means was to raise the quality of teaching. A professor of higher education for each state university was paid out of the funds of the board. His function was to travel to localities throughout the state and set up meetings leading to the establishment of high schools. By this missionary work, it was estimated that, by 1922, 1,600 new high schools were set up in the South.

The problem was deeper, since the chief cause of ignorance was poverty. The average income of the farmer of the South was $150 a year, and this was due to ignorance of good farming methods. The boll weevil was the chief menace. Dr. Seaman Knapp, a scientific farmer, had shown on a demonstration farm how he could raise more cotton by scientific methods on a weevil-infested farm than could be raised on an uninfested farm without his methods. This demonstration work was phenomenally successful. Originally it was not believed that federal authority was such as to enable expenditures to be made for this type of education within a state, but by 1905 the federal government was sharing the work with the board, and later took it over.

The story of the fight on hookworm reaches back to the long years in which Dr. Charles Wardell Stiles of the United States Public Health Service studied hookworm abroad and became convinced that "chronic anemia" and "continuous malaria," known widely in the South and associated with dirt eating (geophagy), was the same disease. In 1908 Stiles was appointed as a member of the President's Commission on Country Life, the other two members being Henry Wallace, editor of *Wallace's Farmer*, and Walter Hines Page, editor of *World's Work*. Stiles pointed out a man on a train platform while traveling through the South. The man is thus described by Mark Sullivan:

> . . . a miserable figure, a type hardly to be recognized as human, misshapen, his dwarfish body small in proportion to his apparently elongated limbs and fingers and unnaturally swollen joints; shoulders hunched and pointed, neck attenuated like that of a very old man, his dropsically protuberant stomach forming a hideous contrast with his pathetically emaciated, unnourished frame; skin, the greenish yellow tint of tallow, shrivelled and parchment-like, eyes like a fragment of faded rag, nose almost transparent, mouth sagging; his attitude that of a three-fourths empty sack supported by contact with the wall.

Stiles said to Page, "That man is a 'dirt eater.' His condition is due to hookworm infection. He can be cured at a cost of about fifty cents in drugs, and in a few weeks' time he can be turned into a useful man." Page replied, "You can make a healthy man of that wreck? Good God, Stiles! Are you in earnest?"

Stiles explained that the hookworm, half as long as a pin, lodges itself by hundreds on the mucous walls of the small intestine, sucks the blood of the victim, and discharges poisons into the system. Its eggs are ejected in human wastes and hatch in the soil, where they attach themselves to a bare foot, then bore through, and another human being becomes almost inert. The cure was simple—a few doses of thymol to make the hookworm relax its grasp on the intestine, and then Epsom salts to eject them.

Page introduced Stiles to Wallace Buttrick, and they talked through the night. Buttrick rushed up to New York to see Gates, who listened and then said, "This is the biggest proposition ever put up to the Rockefeller office." In November 1908 it was announced that Rockefeller would give a million dollars to combat hookworm. Thus the Rockefeller Sanitary Commission began.

Initially it was greeted with jeers, as a slur on the South and as Yankee interference. Irvin S. Cobb joined in the jeering with a satire, "Kid Rockefeller versus Battling Hookworm, winner to take all." The Macon, Georgia, *Telegraph* voiced the Confederate feeling still strong in the South: "Where was this hookworm or lazy disease, when it took five Yankee soldiers to whip one Southerner?" Skepticism disappeared later, with the sensational success of the commission.

Gates wrote in 1911, "Is there not something within us, an instinct of humanity which cannot be fenced in by the boundaries of a merely national patriotism, a sympathy which finds complete expression only when it identifies us with all humanity?"

As early as 1905, Gates had broached a far-flung conception of the Rockefeller Foundation, a plan that, Gates advised Rockefeller, would "befit the vastness of your fortune and the universality of its sources." In June 1909 Rockefeller handed over $50 million in securities in a plan "to promote the well-being and to advance the civilization" of people of the world.

In 1910 a federal charter was sought for the Rockefeller Foundation. This type of federal charter was not unusual. The General Education Board, heavily endowed by Rockefeller, had been granted such a charter in 1902. Between 1887 and 1907 a total of thirty-four organizations had been chartered by Congress, including the Carnegie Institution of Washington and the American Historical Association. Though a federal charter would have more prestige than a state charter, it would not increase the privileges of Rockefeller to give away his own money, while it would allow for restrictions.

None the less, when the bill was reported favorably from the District of Columbia Committee, a hue and cry erupted, all too familiar when the name of Rockefeller was uttered. The bill was called a "Trojan Horse" and "the kiss of Judas Iscariot." Many saw it as a plot. *Hampton's Magazine* said, "if the Standard Oil Company is a monster, the Rockefeller Foundation might easily become a whole platoon of Frankensteins." It was a plan "which will prevent the dissolution of Standard Oil and allow it to remain intact as a solid financial unit." Attorney General Wickersham advised President Taft that there had never been presented to a legislative body "such an indefinite scheme for perpetuating vast wealth" and that it was inconsistent for the Federal Government on the one hand to be seeking to break up Rockefeller's creation of wealth and at the same time creating in his name an institution to hold and administer it. There was more of this tendentious reasoning in Wickersham's memorandum, which seems absurd in retrospect. But President Taft swallowed it whole. To Wickersham he replied, "I agree with your . . . characterization of the proposed act to incorporate Mr. Rockefeller," which Taft, as a good lawyer, knew was a grossly inaccurate description of the bill.

There were some reasonable objections against the bill, and it was withdrawn and revised. When presented in the concluding congressional session of the Taft Administration, the foundation was hemmed in with all types of safeguards. But Congress adjourned in 1913 without approving the charter. Application was then made to the New York State Legislature, which promptly gave its approval to a charter without restrictions, so the outcome for the launching of this great philanthropy was just as auspicious as far as the future development of the foundation was concerned.

There were many who felt that the hate campaign was being pursued too far. In 1911 the Chicago *Inter-Ocean* said that there are statesmen "who only wait for Rockefeller to come out in favor of the Ten Commandments to ask that they be recorded against the whole iniquitous proceeding . . . if he should ask Congress to sanction his retirement to a monastery or a trip to the Holy Land or a gift of several millions to the famine sufferers of China, such attempts to subvert the very foundations of Republican Government would never deceive the statesmen of America."

The charter without restrictions was granted on May 14, 1913. The purpose in the charter merely read, "To promote the wellbeing of mankind throughout the world." The original gift had been revoked by Rockefeller, but now he gave $34,430,000 in 1913 and $65,670,000 the next year. Rockefeller, Jr., was elected president and Jerome Greene secretary. Greene later commented, "There was a brief time in my little room in 26 Broadway when one secretary with a four-drawer file constituted the staff and equipment of the Rockefeller Foundation." In October 1914 Greene presented to the trustees the first statement of principles, that the Foundation would avoid local enterprises and individual

charities in favor of objects "which go to the root of individual or
social well-being, ill-being or misery."

The first grant was to set up an International Health Commission to extend the attack on hookworm to other lands. Then
came the plans for the China Medical Board and the Peking
Union Medical College, which Dr. Flexner called the Johns Hopkins of China.

The college was completed in 1921 at a cost of $8,200,000. It
consisted of 59 buildings on 21 acres of land. The project was a
rare case of catering to Rockefeller's interest, since reports of
returning missionaries had made him concerned with the needs of
the Chinese for better doctors.

In October 1914, W. L. Mackenzie King, former Minister of
Labor in Canada, was engaged to head a department of industrial relations. Since this study was set up against the backdrop of
the Rockefeller involvement in the strike of Colorado Fuel and
Iron, it subjected the Foundation to a great deal of criticism.
The report of a Federal Commission on Industrial Relations
that studied the strike and took testimony was critical of
foundations in general: "The funds of these foundations are
largely invested in securities of corporations dominant in American industry. . . . The policies of these foundations must inevitably be colored if not controlled to conform to the policies of
such corporations." Thereafter the Foundation decided to make its
grants for studies to outside agencies except for noncontroversial
fields like agriculture, public health, and medicine.

The impassioned dedication that Gates tried to maintain in the
work of the Foundation can be judged from this excerpt from his
speech in 1923 when he resigned as trustee:

> When you die and come to approach the judgment of Al-
> mighty God, what do you think he will demand of you? Do
> you for an instant presume to believe that He will inquire into
> your petty failures or your trivial virtues? No. He will ask just
> one question. WHAT DID YOU DO AS A TRUSTEE OF THE ROCKFEL-
> LER FOUNDATION?

CHAPTER 23 *Recessional for John D.*

WHEN THE TRUST was dissolved in 1911, Rockefeller was seventy-two years of age. He was to live another quarter of a century. After the fret and fever of his business career, he was to have rest and peace for the remainder of his days, applying his mind to the task of planned enjoyment as he had applied it to the task of making money.

Of his public battles and those of Standard Oil he had no more to say. The *Reminiscences* is the closest he came to an *apologia pro vita sua.* He spoke with feeling to William Inglis in defense of himself, but none of this broke into print. His freedom from misgiving as to his own business career is evidenced by his statement in 1916 that if the Apostle Paul were then alive, he would be a captain of industry, a thought that drew not a little ribbing from the press.

In March 1915 his life partner, Laura Celestia Spelman died. At this tragic moment the complications of his fortune obtruded themselves upon his life in a disagreeable fashion. The month before, Rockefeller had received notice that for purposes of taxation in Ohio he must list all his property. He refused to do so, claiming that he was a resident of New York, and thereupon was sent a bill on property valued at $311,000,000. If he had returned to bury his wife in the family vault in Forest Hill, he would have been met by process servers. Therefore the body was kept in the Archbold mausoleum at Tarrytown until August, when the case was decided in Rockefeller's favor. Services were then held in Cleveland for final interment.

In his *Reminiscences* in 1909, Rockefeller wrote that he had counted sixty of his associates who had passed away. The number grew into an army. Henry Flagler lived to see the Florida East Coast Railroad completed to Key West in 1912, and then passed away in 1913. Three years later came Archbold's death. The death of William Rockefeller in 1922 was a heavy blow. During Rockefeller's long life span he saw not only the Old Guard but the New Guard disappear, among whom in 1929 was Frederick Gates, who had joined him as a young man. At each new departure Rockefeller said, "Let us close ranks and move ahead," and so the ranks closed and closed to fill the gaps, until at last there were no ranks left to close, and Rockefeller stood as the lone relic of the past.

His family, his close spiritual relationship to his son, his grandchildren, the successive additions of his great-grandchildren— these were his chief joy. After his family, the interests that absorbed him were his investments and his golf. Rockefeller took up golf about 1898, when it was first being introduced into this country. In time, applying to it his characteristic perseverance, he became fairly proficient. His best score for nine holes was 38. One of his problems was the choice of golfing companions, since he found more often than not that a new golfing partner by the seventh hole thought that he had built a sufficient foundation to broach a business proposition. He took pride in the fact that, good or bad, he never fudged on a golf score, which was more than he could say for some high church dignitaries with whom he had played.

After his philanthropies had been launched, Rockefeller took little active interest in them, apparently on the theory that the administration was in better hands than his own. In 1909 he said, "I have not had the hardihood even to suggest how people so much more experienced and wise in these things than I, should work out the details even of those plans with which I have had the honor to be associated."

At the time he wrote he had not met with the General Education Board for five years. He did not see the building housing the Medical Institute for some years, until his son inveigled him into a taxicab ride to view the exterior. In 1915 Jerome Greene mentioned the name of Rockefeller often in the hearings of the United States Commission on Industrial Relations, but when asked specifically how often he had seen him he had to admit only twice, once at a ten-minute meeting and again at a social dinner when he was seated ten chairs away.

Until near the end of his days, Rockefeller gave a good deal of time to his investments. He bought a seat on the New York Stock Exchange and did his own buying and selling. While he made all final decisions, he had a small group working on his investment strategy, including, besides his son and Gates, Henry Cooper and Bertram Cutler. His holdings in oil stocks were gradually reduced, and heavy investments were made in other companies. At one time or another Rockefeller had a controlling interest in American Linseed Oil, Colorado Fuel and Iron, Equitable Trust, and American Shipbuilding. He was persuaded by George Gould, Jay Gould's son, to make heavy investments in railroads, including the Missouri Pacific and Western Pacific, which were disappointingly laggard in his portfolio.

For a long time it was a favorite indoor sport for outsiders to figure out how much Rockefeller was worth. On September 29, 1916, the New York *Times* in a front-page story estimated that his oil holdings alone were worth $500,000,000 and that he was America's first billionaire. The increase in oil-stock prices on that day alone, September 29, had increased his wealth by $8,000,000.

When a man's wealth increases effortlessly in one day by $8,000,000 despite the fact that his whole conditioning in life has been to save on every dollar of expenditure—well, then it is hard to keep values in balance. We have referred before to the difficulty Rockefeller must have had in maintaining the dichotomy between scrimping in business and lavishing money on philanthropies. An excellent example occurred in 1918, during which, as in every year, he gave millions to philanthropy. In that war year, when it was patriotic to save coal, he had an excess at his Pocantico Hills estate. Part he sent back to the mines, and part he sold to residents of Ossining at $8.75 a ton, a price which the official assessor of Ossining decided was exorbitant and reduced to $7.43. To Rockefeller, apparently, while philanthropy was philanthropy, business was still business, and old habits prevailed.

From the time Rockefeller retired from Standard Oil in 1911, and could no longer siphon dollars from the American pocketbook or corrupt our incorruptible citizenry, a thaw developed in the glacial attitude of the public toward the man. In 1914 an event of great symbolic significance occurred—Alonzo Barton Hepburn became a trustee of the Rockefeller Foundation. The wheel of time had made a full revolution, since it was Hepburn who as a young member of the New York State Legislature had

headed the first exposé of Standard Oil, the Hepburn investigation of 1879.

During the First World War large purchases of Liberty Bonds
by Rockefeller were accompanied by generous gifts to the Red
Cross and Belgian Relief, largely by the Rockefeller Foundation,
and the reputation of Rockefeller brightened. After the war,
Cardinal Mercier and King Albert of Belgium called on Rockefeller to give their thanks. Ivy L. Lee had become a publicity adviser to Rockefeller in 1915 in the midst of a labor dispute in a
Rockefeller company in Colorado, when Lee was dubbed by the
union group "Poison Ivy" Lee. His ministrations undoubtedly
had something to do with the better press. Yet the impression,
which has become current, that Lee staged a mammoth buildup of
Rockefeller is belied by the paucity of news items about Rockefeller, which is apparent on checking news indexes since 1915. The
buildup was rather of Ivy Ledbetter Lee, who, while he received
a moderate stipend from Rockefeller, had a stable of corporate
clients.

After the war Rockefeller became revered. America was proud
of the oil industry that helped to make us a world power, and
propelled the automobile, the airplane, and the locomotive, and
drove the pistons in our factories. Obviously the industry could
not have developed if it had consisted of a host of small refineries
engaged in cutthroat competition. Combination was no longer a
cussword. Much as the average American cherished the Jeffer-
sonian ideal of small farms and businesses, he could see the savings
in largeness, and wanted standard goods with nationwide brands.
Hysterical journalism, which had delighted in making an auto-
da-fé of business leaders, went out of fashion. The fact that newspapers realized that profits came from advertising from big business rather than from mass circulation should not be ignored. In
the bull market, the stock of business leaders rose too. (In the
halcyon twenties, transmutation from even base metal was possible—the ex-Kaiser, the "Woodcutter of Doorn," became a
mildly sympathetic figure.) In Rockefeller's case there were special circumstances bringing him reward. There was recognition of
his great philanthropies. Another factor was the good works of
John D. Rockefeller, Jr., who had abandoned all business interests to devote his life to humanity.

The years rolled by. The last time Rockefeller addressed the public was in October 1929, when the stock market collapsed. Announcing his opinion in a terse statement that fundamentally conditions were healthy, he said, "My son and I are buying sound common stocks." It was a cardinal principle of Rockefeller's market operations to buy during periods of market distress and to sell at bull market peaks. It was a point of pride, too, with Rockefeller that he always lent a hand during periods of panic. In the panic of 1893 he had not only carried many friends but had contributed to a fund raised by Morgan when the government needed $50 million in gold. In 1907, when the Knickerbocker Trust closed its doors, and the market crashed, again Rockefeller contributed the sum of $10 million to a fund raised by Morgan to extend credit to Wall Street houses. Rockefeller once recounted, "They always come to Uncle John when there is trouble." Uncle John lent his hand in 1929 again, but this time even he could not pour oil upon the waters.

In the same year, 1929, he was greatly disturbed when someone bought his birthplace at Richford and proposed to cart it to Coney Island for exhibition. To have the multitude gawking through his first home was, he thought, a gross indignity. The home was already on rollers when a permit for transport was withdrawn.

John Winkler visited his Pocantico estate and spent a day with Rockefeller when he was in his ninetieth year. The routine was as follows. He rose at seven after eight hours' sleep. Breakfast was at eight with his cousin, Mrs. Fannie Evans, who became his hostess after the death of his wife. Favorite guests were officials of the Rockefeller charities, and ministers, including members of the Catholic clergy. Rockefeller, now less than a hundred pounds in weight, sampled everything: a drop of coffee, a spoonful of cereal, a forkful of egg, and bit of chop the size of a pea. (Contrary to popular belief, he did not live on bread and milk.) Then came a reading of the Bible and an inspirational message for the day. The first of five rest periods of the day followed. After that came the reading of the paper and odds and ends of business matters. Six holes of golf came next, though Rockefeller felt strong enough to play eighteen, he said. His score averaged 30 for the six holes. (Even at this age, his drives were over 150 yards.)

Lunch at one-thirty consisted of three spoonfuls of a favorite soup and a dip into several vegetables. After rest and business came a motor trip of two hours. Then rest again, and dinner in formal clothes at seven-thirty. This was followed by several games of Numerica, which Rockefeller had played for thirty years. There was no reading and there were no discussions that might be termed intellectual, only gossip and topics of the day.

His Pocantico Hills estate, in which the children of John D. Rockefeller, Jr., have their homes today (with the exception of Winthrop) was perhaps the costliest on earth. Estimates of its size have varied up to 7,500 acres. When opened to the press for the first time in 1959, at the time of the marriage of Governor Nelson Rockefeller's son Steven, it was stated that it was 4,180 acres in size. There were seventy-five buildings occupied by the Rockefellers and their attendants in 1929, a hundred families living on the estate. The main building, home for the aged patriarch, was called Kijkuit, a Dutch name for Lookout, because the home commands a magnificent view of the Hudson River and Saw Mill Valley. A broad avenue built of native rock leads up to the house. "Centered amid a royal setting of excellent gardens, with many transplanted trees of gigantic size, with monuments, Renaissance portals, stone terraces, bulwarks and balustrades of stone, it is the focal point of a wonderland."

Reaching from North Tarrytown almost to Ossining, it was reported that the value of the land alone in 1930 was $50 million. No expense was spared by Rockefeller to remove anything that might mar this pastoral paradise. He gave the New York Central $700,000 to move its tracks, and $1,500,000 to a small college, St. Joseph's Normal School, to relocate elsewhere. It had seventy miles of private roads, orchards, groves, private lakes and streams, vegetable gardens, and four great flower gardens with statuary, fountains, cascades and water falls.

Yet, despite the panoramic beauty of this barony, it was deserted by Rockefeller in 1932 in favor of his other homes, which he decided were better for his health. At Lakewood, New Jersey, he lived the life of a country gentleman in the Golf House, surrounded by flocks of grazing sheep, the source of his lamb dishes. In his Florida home at Ormond Beach, the relatively modest The

Casements, he was happiest as Neighbor John to his fellow residents.

In his later years he had become more outgoing, interested in meeting new faces in all walks of life (barring intellectuals). Occasionally he would take girl employees at the Ormond Beach Hotel for an afternoon ride. Throughout his life he knew nothing of caste and "society." In 1907 he had said, "I respect every man who has to work and is trying to get along," and that was his credo. He became much more accessible to the world. As he said to Curt Engelbrecht, who became his unofficial photographer by sending him a photo and asking to see him, "I am a little weary of playing the fox before the hounds."

At Ormond Beach he chatted freely with the residents after church service at the Ormond Union Church. He was described by a reporter who attended a service with him when he was eighty-eight. After the service he chatted and shook hands with everyone, saying: "This early feeling about handshaking has stayed with me. All my life I have enjoyed this thing that says 'I am your friend.' It means more to a man than a sermon. See how I've enjoyed myself today. [Then he winked at a woman.] Why, I've shaken hands with some of you three times."

He passed around nickels and then graduated to shiny new dimes, treasured by many as good-luck pieces. It might have been a stunt dreamed up by Ivy Lee, but at any rate it was effective in creating a good-humored link between donor and recipient, and saved him useless chatter. Sloan Wilson, author of *The Man in the Gray Flannel Suit*, when a boy lived close to the Rockefeller home in Ormond Beach. He has told how when he was in his early teens he passed the Rockefeller home and heard him call in front of his home, "Look, no money, no money." To Wilson's embarrassment, at Rockefeller's request, the boy had to search through all the old man's pockets, and indeed there was not a sou in any of them. It apparently tickled the aged Croesus to be found penniless.

He delighted, as always, in singing the old church hymns. At the age of ninety-one, a sound film showed him on the golf links singing "God will take care of you" in a resonant and resolute baritone. When the operatic diva, Mary Garden, visited him he said, "I am glad to meet you. You know, we both sing." At Christmas time The Casements was completely panoplied inside and out with greens and tinsels of the season, electric candles in all the windows, and the exterior illuminated with floodlights. It was quite a sight to see. Neighbor John officiated at a Christmas party for invited residents, mostly children, and Santa Claus by his side gave small gifts.

Will Rogers was a favored guest at The Casements; his banter delighted Rockefeller, and his column, published every day, was the first thing Rockefeller read. He developed a taste for simple jokes. One he delighted to tell owlishly was of an old Negro, arraigned in court on a charge of vagrancy, who gave his name as John D. Rockefeller. Scratching his head in perplexity at the outburst of laughter, the old darky said, "Yassah, dat's mah real name, and it's been a trial to me all mah life."

However intricate his mind in ways of money, his viewpoint on the rest of life was simplicity itself. This is reflected in a poem he supposedly wrote on his birthday in 1925, which he had printed and distributed:

> I was early taught to work as well as play,
> My life has been one long, happy holiday;
> Full of work as well as play—
> I dropped the worry on the way—
> And God has been good to me every day.

His mind, eyesight, and hearing remained unimpaired to the end. From the time he reached ninety-five, his physical strength faded, and he no longer appeared in public.

Rockefeller faced death calmly, feeling that he had led the good life for himself and for others. None the less, the last two years saw every effort made to protract his days. There were complete hospitals at each of his homes, in Lakewood, New Jersey, and Ormond Beach, each with fluoroscope and machines to test his basal metabolism. Oxygen tanks accompanied him wherever he traveled. He was wheeled or carried everywhere to save his energy. He died suddenly on May 23, 1937, only two months short of ninety-eight. He left an estate of $26,410,837, all the rest having been distributed. He had in his possession only one oil share, of Standard Oil of California, the first issued, which he kept for sentimental reasons.

In the late twenties, shortly before his own death, Frederick Gates wrote this in his private papers:

> Of a great fortune he was the creator. Of his colossal fortune he is the victim. Who could envy his lot? He cannot give away more than he is doing without high probability of doing more harm than good. He cannot spend his wealth. His reward is just his board and clothes and really little else. Out of it [his fortune] he will have had a life of great care, of very simple living, the daily pleasure that comes to him who takes pains, and let us presume, the consciousness that he has added to the permanent resources of the country.

His life, compared to the lot of his fellow mortals, was not as piteous as all that. Yet, from the time he reached sixty, Rockefeller often reflected that the happiness that great wealth brings is greatly overrated in this world. In his *Reminiscences* he says so, explaining that the rich cannot gratify the pleasures of the palate beyond very moderate bounds, cannot lavish too much money on fine clothes without inviting ridicule, and cannot go much beyond the comforts of the less wealthy in their homes without involving themselves more in pain than in pleasure.

Surely the world's richest man must have mused on the impossibility, despite all his wealth, of staying time's wingèd chariot and the ravage it brings in its train to all mortals, "battering days when rocks impregnable are not so stout, nor gates of steel so strong, but Time decays"? Once, when he was having a body massage, he heard the crackling of his bones. Sadly he said, "All the oil in the country, they say, but not enough to oil my own joints."

CHAPTER 24 *John D. Rockefeller, Jr.*

DUTY.

That was the prevailing motif in the life of John D. Rockefeller, Jr. He once said of his early life, "My mother and father raised but one question, Is it right, is it duty?" Just before Frederick Gates died, he wrote a note about Rockefeller, Jr., and left it in his private papers: "I have known no man who entered life more absolutely dominated by his sense of duty. . . ."

Duty was Christian duty. From his earliest childhood he was saturated with lessons of Christian duty. Rockefeller, Sr., was indoctrinated with Christian duty only by his mother—Rockefeller, Jr., got it in massive doses from four persons, Grandmother Rockefeller, his father, his mother, and his Aunt Lucy Spelman. Of the four, his mother exerted the most powerful influence, and he later recalled, "Our attitude was due to mother who talked to us constantly about duty and displeasing the Lord. She instilled a personal consciousness of right and wrong."

His biographer, Raymond B. Fosdick wrote, "It would appear from the evidence that John's childhood was too full of religion and responsibility to be highly enjoyable." Each morning at seven-thirty there was a Bible lesson that might last an hour. The "society" life that surrounded him in childhood was church life; the home entertainment was the entertainment of church people. The Forest Hill home in Cleveland was "almost an asylum for superannuated Baptist ministers." The Fifty-fourth Street home in New York was the scene of constant missionary meetings, church socials, and temperance meetings. Recreation was always mixed with prayer. When the family traveled to Yellowstone Park in a private car in 1887, Rockefeller, Jr., recorded in his diary, "It was our custom every morning when possible to have a Bible lesson of about an hour and we took the Beatitudes, each morning the doctor [Judson] would take one verse and explain it."

His father did not neglect his training in handling money—spending it and earning it. Rockefeller, Jr., always recalled a trip to Europe when he was a boy during which his father checked item by item every bill. "What are poulets, John? Bougies, bougies—what in the world is a bougie?" Like his father, the son had his own Ledger A with a list of his expenditures. His notebooks show his earnings for small chores—2 cents each for killing flies, 2 cents for sharpening pencils, and $1 for mending a vase. He was twelve at the time. Later he was given responsibilities such as handling the Forest Hill payroll and taking charge of the making of maple syrup.

On the wooded Forest Hill grounds he picked wild strawberries in the spring, went chestnutting in the fall, swam in the lake his father had built by damming a brook, and rode on the half-mile riding course. This developed, as he said, his "passionate awareness of the outside world," and led to his conservation interest in later years. The house, the "Homestead," burned in 1917, and he gave the remaining 266 acres as a public park in 1938.

After education in private schools, he entered Brown College, the leading Baptist school in the East, at the age of nineteen. His mother's reminders of Christian duty followed him there. On his twenty-first birthday she wrote to him, "You can celebrate your birthday in no better way than by such earnest work as I know you are giving for God and the saving of the souls of your fellow students." Again she wrote to him that she wished she could be with him "to help you decide matters." Grandmother Rockefeller wrote to him that he should enter manhood "with the Bible in your hands." The distaff side of the family was somewhat concerned about him because he had recently taken up dancing, and liked it.

He seems to have been popular with his fellow students, though the Rockefeller habits set him apart. A classmate recalled: "On the subject of money he was incredible, entering every cent of expenditure in the little book he carried. It used to be a great joke." However, he was generous to friends, and regularly gave 10 percent of his allowance to charitable organizations. In his senior year the most exciting activity was his managership of the football team. His tightness with money became a legend. When the team went to Boston to play Harvard, he had the men eat at a hotel lunch counter rather than in the dining room to save money. At the end of his senior year he was elected to Phi

Beta Kappa. (Grades were not the only determinant for election at Brown.) All in all he was grateful to Brown for a fruitful college career, and Brown received a greater bounty from him in later years than any other school, over $8,000,000.

After graduation he joined his father's financial staff at 26 Broadway under the guidance of Frederick Gates. At first he attended to minor matters, such as repairs for the family home and transferring a granite shaft for the family cemetery, but soon graduated in responsibility. Always he was plagued by doubts as to himself. Throughout his life he seemed to have borne around his neck the albatross of guilt that he had not proved himself like his father and that wealth had been showered on him with no struggle on his part. Was he worth his salt? Female secretaries in the office who earned their own way had an advantage over him. "I envy anybody who can do that," he said to Raymond Fosdick. "I never had that kind of reassuring experience." He turned to a friend, Henry Cooper, who had graduated from Brown two years earlier and who wrote him a long letter convincing him that he really had talents to contribute and was not a burden to his father.

Then came a humiliating experience. He was caught in the toils by David Lamar, the Wolf of Wall Street, and lost a million in a speculation on United States Leather, a million he did not have. He made a full confession of the débâcle to his father, who listened and said only: "Don't worry, John. I'll see you through." The forbearance of his father filled him further with mortification, and in a letter to him he told of his grief. Wanting only to help his father even to blackening his shoes, "To realize now that instead of doing that I have been partially and largely instrumental in adding to your burdens is bitter and humiliating." Another disagreeable fact that he was learning, besides the fact that he could be the victim of sharpsters, was that his entire life was to be spent in a goldfish bowl. Newspapers reported that he spent thirty cents for lunch, and told what he bought. It was hard, too, to distinguish friends who cultivated him for himself from those who cultivated him for his money, if only to bask in the aura of his wealth.

In 1901, when Rockefeller, Jr., was twenty-seven, he married Abby Aldrich, the daughter of Senator Nelson Aldrich of Rhode

Island, who was as conservative as Rockefeller was rich, and equally unpopular. Rockefeller, Jr., had met Abby while at Brown and had had dancing dates with her. He thereafter had courted her, but diffidently, fearing that she had other suitors. It was characteristic of his mother's influence on him that it was his mother who told him that he was in love with Abby. "Why don't you go at once and tell her you love her?" He spoke to the senator first, as a good suitor should, and proceeded to tell of his financial future. The senator, with a wave of his hand, brushed the trifle aside. "I am only interested in what will make my daughter happy." The senator had an inkling of the finances of his future son-in-law.

The marriage was a great affair, with a thousand guests, a special pavilion being built in the senator's home at Warwick. Despite the wishes of the groom, champagne was served. The couple moved into a home on West Fifty-fourth Street adjoining that of his father, and they raised six children, a daughter and five sons. Abby was a gayer person than John, and a tonic to her more rigid and severe mate. John tried to interest her in keeping an expense book as he did, but she said No, and that was the end of the matter.

With the overpowering interest in John D. Rockefeller, Sr., it has been quite natural to overlook the inheritance genetically from Nelson Aldrich, who was quite a distinguished personality in his own right. A descendant from Roger Williams, Aldrich was born on a farm near Foster, Rhode Island, in 1841. His education was modest, as befitted his means. He entered the wholesale grocery business and became a millionaire before he was thirty-five. He had married Abby Chapman, who was herself wealthy, and he had become something of an art connoisseur. Public service beckoned, and he was elected to the United States House of Representatives, where he served two terms, and was elected to the Senate in 1881. The high quality of his mind soon was apparent to his colleagues, and he was designated an expert on the tariff—in later years he was co-author of the Payne-Aldrich Tariff Law.

By the time that Theodore Roosevelt became President, Aldrich was the dominant Republican figure in the Senate. Though he often jousted with Roosevelt, the latter had a high regard for him, writing to Senator Henry Cabot Lodge, "My intercourse with Aldrich gave me a steadily higher opinion of him." The powerful, rich, conservative senator was the object of attack in the muckraking press. Lincoln Steffens, in an article in *McClure's*, asserted that Aldrich wangled tariff favors for the sugar trust and then was paid off in campaign contributions which he used to buy votes in Rhode Island elections, paying as high as thirty-five dollars a head.

Aldrich retired from the Senate in 1907, and then devoted his interest to monetary reform. He became Chairman of the National Monetary Commission established under the Aldrich-Vreeland Act of 1908. He advocated a flexible currency that would expand and contract in accord with the exigencies of business, and to that end favored an emergency currency based on rediscounting of commercial paper and creation of a national reserve association. The Aldrich Plan was taken over bodily by the Democrats when they came to power in 1913, and the Federal Reserve Act was passed, for which little credit was given to Aldrich.

Within a few years of his marriage, the young Rockefeller occupied a commanding place in the administration of his father's philanthropies, and a good deal of credit must be given to him for the inception of the Rockefeller Institute and the General Education Board. Though he was elected a director of seventeen companies, having little interest in them he shuffled them off. As for Standard Oil, John Archbold thought it would be a good idea to use the handsome youth as a showpiece to offset the image of his now cadaverous-looking father. Rockefeller, Jr., declined the role. Except for his remarks at Brown about the American Beauty rose, he was not involved in the public wars of his father. Nor did the hostile press embroil him, except for one incident. In December 1908 the New York *American* published a story that he was responsible for a peonage system at the Corn Products Refining Company in Chicago. Rockefeller, Jr., went to District Attorney William Travers Jerome and successfully had Hearst's printing company prosecuted for criminal libel, though the damages awarded were nominal.

As time went on, Rockefeller leaned more and more heavily on his son. "Mr. John is a wonderful man," he would say over and over again. His recommendation on a philanthropy would automatically mean its approval. In 1918 the father wrote to his son, "What a Providence that your life should have been spared to take over the responsibilities as I lay them down." In 1929, when he was ninety, he wrote to him, "What could we have done without you?" And again, after a visit, "I felt like crying like a baby after you had gone."

For his part, young Rockefeller's attitude toward his father was one of veneration. During and after his father's lifetime he spoke of himself as only his father's viceroy. When his father was ninety-four the son wrote to him: "I have tried to do what you would have me do. I have striven to follow in your footsteps. In all these years of striving your own life and example have been to me the most powerful and stimulating influence." In his passionate loyalty, he could not abide hearing any slighting remark about his father. Once, when James Stillman dropped in on him at 26 Broadway and made such a remark, Rockefeller, Jr., jumped up and said, "Mr. Stillman, you can say those things to the father but not to the son. Good day."

In some characteristics of the father, the son exceeded him. In the desire to be a perfectionist he slaved over letters very much like his father. He became a detail person early in life, and formed the habit of keeping a four-foot rule with him for measurements. His devotion to detail was such that it provoked remonstrances from his father. "Let the world wag," Rockefeller, Sr., advised; don't take it all so seriously, delegate. But the son was too conscientious for that. Rockefeller, Sr., had a standard method of tipping—holding a fistful of change into which the person tipped could dip at will. Rockefeller, Jr., for years did not tip at all; when he gave his barber a nickel tip, the barber framed it. Of a gardener who went overboard in buying rosebushes, the son wrote his father: "He had not learned our ways. He seems to feel that because we have money it is not necessary to economize." He seemed to feel that modern baths and toilets at Spelman College might be a luxury. "Are we justified in spending $2,000 for what seems to me not an imperative need?" He was old-fashioned in many tastes. For some time he sent his children to school in horse and buggy. While his father had a garage with twenty cars, for a long while the son had only one battered Pierce-Arrow.

Rockefeller, Jr., was far from a throwback to an earlier age. He was alive to the lively arts of art, music, and books, though he was by no means an intellectual. He enjoyed the Radio City Music Hall Rockettes and light musical comedies. He found dancing such good relaxation that he had dancing teachers come to his home to teach him the latest steps.

His thinking was more liberal than that of his father. In 1904 Rockefeller, Sr., said he would make no further gifts to Johns Hopkins unless it recognized homeopathy, to which the son replied that it makes no difference how the sick are cured so long as they are cured. "As it seems to me of increasingly less importance how a man is saved, whether through the Baptist, Methodist or Presbyterian or any other church, so long as he is really and truly saved."

Throughout his life, in his attitudes and philanthropies, Rockefeller, Jr., was to display broadmindedness, practicality, and an astonishing catholicity of tastes and freedom from dogma. In 1900 he became leader of the Fifth Avenue Baptist Church Bible class, succeeding Charles Evans Hughes, and remained leader for eight years. Perhaps owing to newspaper publicity, the class grew in size from fifty to two hundred members. Rockefeller, Jr., did not talk much about theology, but, even more so than his father had in his Sunday-school class, he tried to relate religion to problems of practical living, asking questions such as "Is a lie ever justified?" Out of the thinking generated by this class, he came more and more to the idea that religion was made for man rather than man for religion.

He and Gates agreed that sectarianism in the Protestant Church was wasteful (like competition in the oil industry, perhaps). It was stupid to have competing churches starving in the same small town. After the First World War Rockefeller threw himself into the Interchurch Movement to unite the Protestant churches of the country. It was a failure. Several studies that were in process on the relationship of the church to the community were completed with Rockefeller funds, one of which became the famous study by the Lynds, *Middletown*.

He was long concerned about the effectiveness of foreign missions, and in January 1930 organized a commission that sailed in September 1931 for a year's investigation in China, Japan, and India. Out of this study the book *Rethinking Missions* was published, putting emphasis on the need for personal contact rather than on evangelistic teaching. Pearl Buck hailed the book, saying that we had been sending ignorant people abroad to teach superstition. In 1935 Rockefeller, Jr., decided that the Northern Baptist Convention was not heeding the findings of this study, and with regret notified his father that he had discontinued further gifts to them in favor of gifts to other denominations.

This same broadmindedness and flexibility were evidenced in his attitude toward the Prohibition experiment. With the ardent temperance background of the Spelmans, it was inevitable that he should be an ardent champion of the Eighteenth Amendment. Between 1900 and 1919 he contributed $350,000 to the Anti-Saloon League, and small sums thereafter. In 1926, when it became evident that Prohibition was not meeting with popular acceptance, he stopped all contributions. On June 7, 1932, after several conferences, he issued a public statement that Prohibition was a failure, that the speakeasy had replaced the saloon threefold. This announcement was front-page news all over the nation, and was a major factor in turning the trend in thinking in favor of repeal into a tidal wave.

When did the elder Rockefeller transmit to his son his great fortune? It was, the evidence shows, some time between 1915 and 1923. In 1913 Rockefeller, Jr., began his collection of Chinese porcelains that became a passion with him. In 1915 he had an opportunity to buy the J. P. Morgan collection of Chinese porcelains which Joseph Duveen had acquired after Morgan's death. He needed a million dollars, and did not have it. He asked his father for the money but was turned down. He then addressed his father again, "I have never squandered money on horses, yachts, automobiles or other foolish extravagances. A fondness for these porcelains is my only hobby—the only thing on which I cared to spend money." As a clincher, he told his father that even on a forced sale he could recover within 10 percent of the cost and that in time the market price would appreciate. He got the money.

By 1923 he did not have to entreat for money, since it was

almost all his. In 1924 the government released income-tax figures for 1923 that revealed that the younger Rockefeller's tax was the greatest in the nation, with $7,435,169, and Rockefeller, Sr., with only $124,266. (Next after Rockefeller, Jr., was Henry Ford with a payment of $2,467,000 and Edsel Ford with $1,984,000.) The steep drop in the senior Rockefeller's philanthropies after 1921 indicates that 1921 was the year of the transfer. From that date, the great gifts of Rockefeller, Jr., begin.

The best format for presentation of the wide range of the gifts of John D. Rockefeller, Jr., is by way of a Baedeker since they are associated with places. We shall first tour New York City and then sites in this country and then abroad.

Riverside Church. This beautiful Gothic Church, which rose on Morningside Heights in 1930, is an interdenominational church, fathered by Rockefeller, Jr., as an experiment in Christian unity. More than thirty denominations are represented in its membership.

United Nations. On December 11, 1946, Rockefeller, Jr., donated six Manhattan blocks along the East River, costing $8,500,000, as the site for the United Nations. The United Nations had been meeting for the first two years of its existence at Hunter College and Lake Success. A decision on the final site was to be made on December 11, and there was a possibility that a recommendation might be made for a European home. The day before, Nelson Rockefeller discussed the problem with his father, and suggested giving the family Pocantico estate at Tarrytown to the United Nations but said that New York City was preferred by the organization. Rockefeller, Jr., brought up the subject of the Zeckendorf property on the East River, and said, "Why shouldn't I give this site to the United Nations?" Nelson's reaction according to an onlooker was a breathless, "Why, Pa!" And it was bought that night, Zeckendorf being traced to a nightclub, where he agreed to it.

Rockefeller Center came about through the accident of a thwarted philanthropy. The site originally belonged to a prominent physician, Dr. David Hosack (who attended Alexander Hamilton after he was shot in the duel with Aaron Burr). He sold it to New York State. Columbia University had lost lands in Gloucester County when Vermont was admitted to the Union, and asked for compensation; the legislature granted it the Hosack site in 1814. Botanic gardens were on the site for years, and one of the arguments for locating St. Patrick's Cathedral where it is today was that it would permanently overlook gardens. As the city moved uptown, however, by 1928 the site was occupied by stores and brownstone residences.

In 1929 there was a move to relocate the Metropolitan Opera there, and Rockefeller, Jr., took a long-term lease on a three-block site from Columbia University, intending to donate part of it as a public square in the opera project. But the Metropolitan backed out, largely due to the fact that the onset of the depression would prevent it from realizing much on a sale of its property at Thirty-eighth Street. Rockefeller, Jr., now had on his hands what appeared to be, during the depression, a white elephant.

None the less, Rockefeller, Jr., decided to develop it for office property and theaters, and the conceptions that were worked out were largely his. The National Broadcasting Company and Radio-Keith-Orpheum (which soon went bankrupt) were persuaded to locate there, and the original name was Radio City. As Nelson Rockefeller, who was a moving spirit in the project and who became president in 1938, said after the demise of the opera project: "The answer was radio. Opera was the great old art, radio the new—the latest thing in this contemporary world of ours, the newest miracle of the scientific age." The proposal to change the name to Rockefeller Center was rejected by Rockefeller, Jr., since he did not want to "plaster the family name all over a piece of real estate," but he acceded to a plea that it would help a shaky commercial gamble.

It was Rockefeller, Jr.,'s idea to give an international flavor to buildings and restaurants. It was also his idea to have murals painted by prominent artists. Matisse and Picasso declined, but Diego Rivera accepted. A well-publicized incident occurred when Rivera painted a head of Lenin and anticapitalist symbols in a mural in the RCA building, which were removed by Rockefeller's orders, amid cries of "cultural vandalism."

At the time of construction, when office space in New York City was a drug on the market, it seemed that the project was a Rockefeller philanthropy for the thousands of workers employed. A skit in the musical *As Thousands Cheer* showed Rockefeller, Jr., trying to force the project on his father as a birthday gift. In the end, however, it turned out to be a stunning commercial success for the Rockefellers. Built at a time of low construction costs, for $125,000,000, Laurance Rockefeller stated to me that it could not be reproduced today for double that amount.

Lincoln Center for the Performing Arts. Later circumstances gave Rockefeller, Jr., his opportunity to make a contribution to the performing arts in Lincoln Center, which was designed to give a new home to the Metropolitan Opera, the New York Philharmonic-Symphony, and other artistic groups. An initial gift of $5 million in 1956 got it rolling, and his total gifts to the Center amounted to $10,805,000. John D. Rockefeller, 3rd, is Chairman of the Board for Lincoln Center.

The Museum of Modern Art, which is located on West Fifty-fourth Street, on the site of the former Rockefeller homes, is a tribute to Rockefeller, Jr.,'s tolerance, since he said that, after many years of exposure, "by and large I do not find beauty in modern art. I find instead a desire for self-expression, as if the artist were saying 'I'm free, bound by no forms and art is what flows out of me.'" It was owing to the enthusiasm of his wife that the museum was founded in 1927 and received gifts from him of $5 million. His son, Nelson, was president for a number of years.

Despite his indifference to modern art, Rockefeller, Jr., had an avid appreciation of other forms, and his 10 West Fifty-fourth Street home bulged with paintings, statuary, tapestries, Oriental rugs and, what was most precious to him, his Chinese porcelains (his collection of K'ang Hsi porcelains was the finest in the world); so that the overflow had to be put in the adjoining 12 West Fifty-fourth Street.

International House on Riverside Drive, close to Columbia University, was the first of four built by Rockefeller funds. The other three are at the University of Chicago, the University of California, and the University of Paris. These are laboratories in human relationships, giving foreign students an opportunity to meet not only one another but also American students, and visit their homes. Potential leaders of the world are enabled to acquire an understanding of other nationals, and tolerance for their point of view.

Memorial Hospital. Rockefeller, Jr.,'s interest in cancer began

in his college days when he was shocked by the death from
cancer of a girl friend, the sister of a Brown classmate. Beginning
in 1927, he contributed from $60,000 to $100,000 a year to the
Memorial Hospital engaged in research on cancer. In 1935 he
gave a block site on Sixty-seventh Street at First Avenue for
construction of a new building to be located near New York
Hospital, and then the General Education Board gave $3 million
for a building. Merged with the Sloan-Kettering Institute, Memorial Hospital today is the leading center in the world for cancer research, and continues to be a prime interest of the Rockefeller family.

The Cloisters. At the northerly end of Manhattan was the old
Revolutionary outpost of Fort Tryon. Rockefeller, Jr., in 1917
bought sixty acres of land and offered it to New York City for a
public park. The offer was not accepted for many years, Fort
Tryon Park opening in 1935. It was there that in 1938 The Cloisters Museum was opened to the public, a towering monastic
building with the atmosphere of the Middle Ages, the dimensions
of its granite blocks patterned after Romanesque buildings.

For years the sculptor George Grey Barnard had been collecting Romanesque and Gothic sculpture and had opened a museum
called The Cloisters. In 1922 Rockefeller, Jr., bought the collection for the Metropolitan Museum of Art but had in mind the
construction of a building to house them in Fort Tryon Park.
When The Cloisters was completed, having been financed by
him, he stocked it with other art treasures such as his own Uni-
corn tapestries, the Nine Heroes tapestries, the Arlanza frescoes,
the Catalan tombs, and the Chalice of Antioch.

Williamsburg was the old colonial capital of Virginia where in
May 1776 the original resolution for independence was passed.
Dr. William A. Goodwin for years had a cherished dream of
restoring the town. After persistent efforts, he finally won Rockefeller, Jr.,'s ear. Since William and Mary College at Williamsburg
is the birthplace of Phi Beta Kappa and since Rockefeller, Jr., was
interested in that organization, Goodwin succeeded in personal
contact there. Goodwin told him, "I am convinced that from a
historical point of view this is the greatest teaching opportunity
which exists in America."

Williamsburg became the most ambitious restoration project

ever undertaken in this country. The original estimate of $5 million rose to almost fifteen times that much. Old foundations of buildings were excavated; scores of tons of artifacts were sifted by archeologists; old deeds were searched; wills, inventories, and court records were studied. A chandelier like the one in the Governor's Palace was found in China; chemical tests of original building materials were made so that eighteenth-century formulas could be reconstructed; bricks were made locally according to handmade methods used by colonial brickmakers. Rockefeller, Jr., became completely engrossed in the details of reconstruction, and for some years spent two months of the year in Williamsburg. He was pleased by the enthusiastic reception accorded the restored town by the unexpectedly large throngs of visitors.

Parks. Rockefeller, Jr., was a nature lover, and even in his eighties a horseman who loved to spend hours riding in the country. When he was still a boy he would take his horse across the Hudson on the ferry and ride around the magnificent cliffs and the escarpments of the Palisades, which lie across from New York City. When the Palisades Park was established soon after 1900, Rockefeller, Sr., gave $500,000 on the advice of his son to save it from the quarrymen blasting it to rubble. In later years Rockefeller, Jr., donated parcels of land, to round out the development, to the amount of $20 millions. Today, it is a forty-mile belt of recaptured wilderness.

This was the first of the many park developments that were the recipients of the Rockefeller philanthropies. Others include Acadia National Park in Maine, Yellowstone and the Grand Tetons with Jackson Hole in Wyoming, the Great Smokies in North Carolina and Tennessee, the sequoias of California through the Save-the-Redwoods Campaign, and the George Washington Birthplace Memorial in Virginia.

Versailles. On a trip to France in 1923, Rockefeller, Jr., was appalled by the decay of the Versailles palace erected by Louis XIV. This once magnificent historical monument was becoming a shambles. He donated $2,166,000 to the reconstruction of Versailles, and additional sums of $114,000 to rebuild the château at Fontainebleau and $570,000 to rebuild the Cathedral of Rheims, which had been almost wrecked by German shells.

Archeological Sites. Rockefeller, Jr., became interested in the studies of Dr. James H. Breasted of the University of Chicago, who felt that the real fountainhead of our civilization was in the Near East rather than in Greece and Rome. He contributed to Breasted funds for excavations in Egypt and Palestine, Breasted receiving, in all, $11 million from Rockefeller, Jr., and the Rockefeller institutions, which financed the construction of the Museum of Oriental Studies at the University of Chicago. Rockefeller, Jr.,'s interest in archeology broadened, and he gave a million to the excavation of the Agora, the public square of Athens. Among the fascinating finds were dozens of ostraka, pottery scraps on which were written the names of citizens condemned to exile, and among the names were those of Aristides the Just and Themistocles.

Two of his notable philanthropies cannot be included in a Baedeker. One was the International Education Board, which was the counterpart of the General Education Board in the international field. Under the leadership of Dr. Wickliffe Rose, it spent $28 million on constructive endeavors within the ten years of its life from 1923. Two of its important grants were to Dr. Niels Bohr for his work in atomic physics at Copenhagen and to the California Institute of Technology for a 200-inch telescope on Mount Palomar in California.

Rockefeller, Jr.,'s work for Negro education was important. A long list of educational institutions received his help, and prominent among them were Negro institutions like Fisk, Hampton, and Tuskegee. He served for many years as chairman of the National Council for the United Negro College Fund, and by his influence and leadership raised large sums for thirty-two Negro institutions.

The gifts of John D. Rockefeller, Jr., ranging over a wide gamut of activities and causes too long to be listed here, showed intelligence and discrimination. Cynics may say that the distribution of money is relatively easy, compared with its acquisition, yet it is easy to see how a much less effective job could have been done with the stewardship of the fortune. A characteristic throughout his life was the ability to perceive a need and then make a vigorous attempt to cure it insofar as a money gift can do so. This is illustrated by an activity he undertook in 1909. He was

designated as foreman of a grand jury impaneled in 1909 to investigate organized prostitution. He accepted the assignment reluctantly, fearing that it would be a "grim, depressing subject,"
but soon found it otherwise. Tammany Hall had set up the grand
jury as a gesture to appease public opinion, not intending that it
would do much, but under Rockefeller, Jr.,'s leadership it sat for
six months instead of the one month planned for it and became a
"runaway grand jury," handing down fifty-four indictments, to
the consternation of Tammany. That was only the beginning for
Rockefeller, Jr. He wanted a permanent attack on the problems
of prostitution, and conferred with over two hundred people who
might offer solutions, such as lawyers, doctors, social workers,
clergymen, and editors. As a result of his efforts, the Bureau of
Social Hygiene was established, which he financed for twenty-five
years at a cost of $5 million. Among its accomplishments it built
the laboratory for social hygiene for the New York State Reform-
atory for Women and established in New York City the diag-
nostic clinic for venereal diseases.

The person who was most ready to downgrade the contribution
of John D. Rockefeller was himself, since one of his salient characteristics was his humility. He declined all honorary degrees
offered him except from his alma mater. He was chary even of
having his portrait painted. In 1927 Paris newspapers featured a
striking incident reflecting his retiring personality. Upon driving
to the gates of Versailles, the reconstruction of which he had
recently financed, Rockefeller was told that the gates were closing, and turned back instead of telling who he was. When Raymond Fosdick told him that he was writing his biography, he was
incredulous. "What on earth would you find to write about?"

But there had been no lack of dramatic events in his career.

CHAPTER 25 *The Ludlow and Stewart Affairs*

O N APRIL 20, 1914, in a remote spot in the mountains of Colorado named Ludlow, a colony of striking workers of the
Colorado Fuel and Iron Company lived in tents, together with
their families. They were living in tents because they had had to
leave the homes belonging to the company when they went on
strike on September 23 of the previous year. The camp was
guarded by a small detachment of state militia that had been
considerably reduced and had been infiltrated by company
guards, hired strikebreakers, and thugs.

A shot was fired, and the militia and strikers engaged in a
bloody battle. By nightfall the militia, under Lieutenant K. E.
Linderfeldt, who had a venomous hatred of the miners, had captured the colony. Linderfeldt killed a strike leader, John Tikas,
with the butt of his gun. Then he ordered the tents to be set
ablaze and a machine gun turned on them. The next day the
bodies of eleven children and two women were found burned to
death in a cave under the tents.

Infuriated by the "Ludlow Massacre," the strikers began an
orgy of looting and burning and killing. On April 29 nine strikers
were killed in an attack on the Forbes mine. Governor E. M.
Ammons appealed to President Wilson, who sent federal troops
into Colorado and restored order.

The news of the massacre shocked the nation. At the time, we
were debating whether to recognize General Huerta as President
of Mexico, and the New York Evening *Post* commented that
"Victoriano Huerta might well prefer to sever relations with a
Government under which it is possible for women and children to
be mowed down by machine guns in a frenzy of civil war."

Massive indignation was directed at John D. Rockefeller, Jr.,
who owned 40 percent of the stock of the company, and controlled
it. Mass meetings in New York addressed by "Mother" Jones, the
labor organizer for the United Mine Workers, who had just spent
four months in Colorado jails, demanded that Rockefeller, Jr., be

prosecuted for murder. Another agitator, Upton Sinclair, wrote later, in his book *The Brass Check:* "I thought I would go to young Mr. Rockefeller's office and watch for him in the hall and give him a horsewhipping. But this would have been hard on me because I am constitutionally opposed to violence and I did not think Mr. Rockefeller worth such a sacrifice of my feelings." Instead he led a small picket line before 26 Broadway, whom he called "mourning pickets" because they had no banners but wore crepe armbands; they were joined by an uninvited woman who carried a white flag with a bleeding heart. Sinclair landed in the Tombs, and there wrote "Marseillaise in the Tombs." He was succeeding in getting wide publicity for the protest movement, which was his primary objective. After his release he delivered a sermon in a church entitled "How to Kill John D. Rockefeller, Jr." His conclusion was that the greater punishment would be to make him a social outcast.

A good deal of sympathy for the strikers was lost when I.W.W. and anarchist forces entered the fray and when Emma Goldman and Alexander Berkman led violent demonstrations near the Pocantico estate. Then an associate of Sinclair's, Arthur Caron, and two others were killed in a Third Avenue tenement while admittedly preparing bombs to be used to blow up the Rockefellers.

The Ludlow tragedy was to be the beginning of the education of John D. Rockefeller, Jr., in labor relations and, with his characteristic flexibility, the inauguration of a more sympathetic attitude toward labor. It is probable that he was telling the truth when he testified before the Federal Commission on Industrial Relations in February 1915 that prior to the bloodshed he knew little of the facts of the dispute. His main interests were in philanthropies. Among the many Rockefeller investments, that of Colorado Fuel and Iron was a bad apple, not having paid a dividend in the fourteen years the Rockefellers owned the stock. As to his philosophy, since he had been exposed to no other, he undoubtedly shared that of his father, who in 1917 said to Inglis: "I have watched and studied the trade unions for many years. Times change, but men change very little. It is hard to understand why men will organize to destroy the very firms or companies that are giving them the chance to live and thrive; but they do it and soon the real object of their organizing shows itself—to do as little as possible for the greatest possible pay." L. M. Bowers, chairman of the board of the company, said later that in talks with the elder Rockefeller, his labor policy had been sanctioned and approved.

Bowers, a nephew of Frederick Gates, was an economic royalist of the eighteenth-century mentality. Those responsible for the strike were "disreputable agitators, socialists and anarchists . . . together with cheap college professors and still cheaper writers in muckraking magazines, supplemented by a lot of milk-and-water preachers. . . ." According to him, the workers should have been content. They lived in a company town, with company stores, company doctor, company preacher, and company police. Union organizers were turned away at the gates of the town, and malcontents were thrown out. Bowers wrote to Rockefeller, Jr., "The word 'satisfaction' could have been put over the entrance of all our mines." The company always maintained that it had granted the eight-hour day, provided a hospital with free treatment, and did not make a penny profit on operations of company stores.

The workers, in striking, had demanded higher pay and shorter hours, and such miscellaneous demands as the right to have their own doctor and to trade in their own stores. It was the closed-shop demand that was the chief snag. Clashes occurred frequently before the April 20 killings, and Rockefeller, Jr., was asked to appear before the Committee on Mines of the House of Representatives at the end of March 1914 to testify on conditions. All he knew was what he had learned from Bowers. He had not attended meetings of the board of directors, which were held in Colorado. In his testimony, however, he spoke dogmatically: "My conscience entirely acquits me. We would rather that the unfortunate conditions should continue and that we would lose all the millions invested than that American workers should be deprived of their rights under the Constitution to work for whom they please."

It was hard for the public to swallow the assumption that he was opposing the closed shop solely in the interests of workers. The statement made less palatable reading to the public after the "Ludlow Massacre."

After the "massacre" Rockefeller was still unyielding. He would not grant the closed shop; he would not submit to arbitration. The only solution was to call off the strike. His father was so pleased that he turned over to him the remainder of his stock in Colorado Fuel and Iron, and his mother applauded his stand as a "bugle call." There never was any attempt to mediate the strike, even though Governor Ammons told President Wilson that such a move was in progress. Finally, the strikers had to surrender, the strike ending in December 1914 with a complete company victory.

Rockefeller, Jr., had second thoughts after the event, because he began to reconsider his attitude on labor rights. His tutor was Mackenzie King (later a famous wartime Prime Minister of Canada), who had been selected to head a division of economic research for the Rockefeller Foundation. King, who had studied labor problems in this country, had been Minister of Labor in the Canadian Cabinet. King evolved a plan for a joint board of worker and employer representatives to discuss and work out grievances and employee problems. Chairman Bowers could not see the light, and Rockefeller, Jr., asked for his resignation. As he put it, "He was not ready to go forward into the new day."

In September 1915 Rockefeller, Jr., personally visited the mines with King, ate and fraternized with the men, went down into a mine, where he wielded a pick and danced with miners' wives at a get-together. On that occasion he launched the joint-representation plan that was overwhelmingly approved by an employee referendum. "We are partners," he said; "that's what we are, and I want to do business with you on that principle."

Over the protests of company officials, Rockefeller, Jr., permitted union organizers to circulate among the workers. He wrote to the company management: "Paternalism is antagonistic to democracy. Neither is perfect. Under either system many must suffer. But on the whole, democracy has far more in its favor than paternalism."

Whether this was delusion by semantics or some of the power of rationalization inherited from his father it is hard to say. The dispensation was almost meaningless, since unions, even though permitted to organize, were not recognized by the company. The operating union was a "company union," which at least by standards of today is considered "paternalistic," and was outlawed by the Wagner Act in 1934.

Yet in a day when employees had no voice in setting labor policy, Rockefeller, Jr., undoubtedly believed that his plan for employee representation was a radical one and that when the workers had asked for bread he had given them cake. Rockefeller, Jr., made this defense of his plan: "Unionism benefits only one class of workers, those who belong to the union. Our plan takes in all men irrespective of whether they join a union or not." The Philadelphia *Public Ledger* commented, "It is obvious that hearty acceptance of the Plan means the slow death of the [UMW] union." The concessions that Rockefeller made in pay and working conditions were generous. If "the Rockefellers recognize that employers are not wise enough or generous enough to govern huge masses of employees with unlimited power, then the women and children of Ludlow had very fruitful deaths."

He used his influence for better labor conditions in other companies in which he owned stock. In fighting the prevalent seven-day week and twelve-hour day, his contribution was a substantial one. Evidencing his strong feelings in 1920, he sold all his stock in United States Steel after Judge Gary ignored his protest against the seven-day week and twelve-hour day then in force in steel plants.

The battle waged by Rockefeller, Jr., to oust Colonel Robert W. Stewart from the chairmanship of the board of Standard Oil of Indiana has historic significance. It was the first time that the leader of a large corporation was called to book and ousted because of a shortcoming in business ethics. It was the first time that such a leader was construed to owe a duty to the public at large to maintain the reputation of the corporation for probity. This was the issue raised by Rockefeller, Jr., with the stockholders, although in fact it appears that Colonel Stewart had practiced a swindle on the stockholders of the company, so that more than purity in the abstract was involved.

This battle for integrity was waged by the scion of a family whose name only two decades earlier had been a symbol of moral turpitude. So swift had been the metamorphosis that, in inspecting the press of the time, I found no rude reference at all to what would have been interesting background information.

The transaction that was the hub of the controversy was not part of the Teapot Dome scandal, but came to light later, in the aftermath of the facts that were dredged up. Some of the bonds that were delivered as the famous bribe to Secretary of the Interior Albert Fall by H. F. Sinclair had been purchased by a company called the Continental Trading Company. No one had ever heard of it. Then, slowly, a congressional committee under the bulldog Senator Thomas Walsh unearthed this mysterious company, which was born in 1921 and died in 1923, a paper company that did no work but left some oil executives much richer for its existence.

It was born in a hotel room in New York in November 1921. A. E. Humphries, owner of the Mexia field just discovered in Texas, met with Colonel Stewart of Standard Oil of Indiana, H. F. Sinclair of Sinclair Oil, James E. O'Neil of Prairie Oil and Gas, and Harry Blackmer of Midwest Refining, a subsidiary of Standard of Indiana. Humphries was under the impression that he was to sell his oil to these companies, but instead found that he was to sell it to a company unknown to him, the Continental Trading Company, at $1.50 a barrel. Because the heads of the oil companies guaranteed that Continental Trading would perform the contract, he had no further cause for worry.

Continental was a phantom company, a familiar device for bilking stockholders. It turned around and resold the oil at $1.75 a barrel to Prairie Oil and the Sinclair Crude Oil Purchasing Company, which was under the joint ownership of Sinclair and Standard of Indiana. In the year and a half after January 1922, the profit to Continental amounted to over $3,000,000, made without capital, risk, or effort.

The trail was getting hot, and in May 1923 the company ended its life and its books were destroyed. O'Neil and Blackmer took off for Europe and exile. When the government instituted suit at Cheyenne in 1925 to cancel the Teapot Dome leases, Stewart was not to be found either. Rockefeller, Jr., reacting to the criticism being made of Stewart, which reflected on the Rockefellers, who were known to be large shareholders, directed that a cable be sent to Stewart, wherever he was, asking him to return. After the Cheyenne trial was over, Stewart returned, saying that he had been incommunicado in South America all the time, and was ignorant of the uproar. He assured Rockefeller, Jr., that the transaction in question was completely honest and that Standard of Indiana had been fortunate to be able to buy the oil for $1.75 a barrel.

Up to this point, Rockefeller, Jr., had no cause to feel that Colonel Stewart had been in a crooked deal. A bad odor, however, emanated from the sudden liquidation of Continental and the assignment for $400,000 to the oil companies of the privilege of buying the oil at $1.50 a barrel, a privilege that was worth many millions. And Colonel Stewart was one of the men who had guaranteed the company to Humphries.

In February 1928 the United States Senate authorized an investigation of the Continental Trading Company. Rockefeller, Jr., was insistent that Colonel Stewart voluntarily offer to appear, cabling him in Havana that "your own high sense of honor and duty will prompt you to act immediately upon this suggestion." Stewart acquiesced.

On the witness stand at the hearing, however, Stewart was very vague:

SEN. WALSH: My question is how it came about that the Continental Trading Company was able to get it at $1.50 and you were not.

COL. STEWART: I suppose without knowing anything about it, I suppose there were some propositions there; that somebody was getting a brokerage out of that thing and I was perfectly satisfied that they should.

SEN. WALSH: Who would you imagine was getting the brokerage?

COL. STEWART: It does not make any difference who I imagined. I am not here to give you my imagination. You would not expect me to testify what I imagined.

Colonel Stewart's attitude was arrogant and overbearing. At one point he blurted out to Senator Nye, "Why, you're crazy!" The colonel's title derived from his being the head of the state militia of South Dakota, but his naturally autocratic and domineering instincts would have made his proper calling that of a tribal chieftain.

His attitude had been evasive throughout, although he said

repeatedly, "I personally did not make a dollar out of this trans-action." Rockefeller, Jr.,'s patience was being sorely tried. Rocke-feller, Sr., although close to ninety at the time, followed the case, and felt that the stigma attached to the company had to be re-moved. When he testified before the Senate committee, Rocke-feller, Jr., said of Stewart, "I am bitterly disappointed that he did not answer all the questions asked of him."

Now the case broke wide open. The chairman of the Prairie Oil and Gas Company testified that James O'Neil, the fugitive presi-dent, on a secret trip to Canada had delivered $800,000 in Liberty Bonds, his ill-gotten gains in the transaction, to be turned over to the Prairie Company. O'Neil was dying, and wanted to clear his conscience. A year later Harry Blackmer also came back in secret to Canada to put his $750,000 in Liberty Bonds in the hands of his attorney, pending determination of their rightful ownership.

The Liberty Bonds bought by Continental Trading had always been wrapped in four packages. The recipients of two of these were now known, and Sinclair's would make three. The fourth was exposed when an examiner, searching a Stewart account in a Chicago bank, found that in 1922 and 1923 Stewart had depos-ited $750,000 in Liberty Bonds of the same issue as that bought by Continental. He had clipped the coupons only for 1923, ap-parently hesitating after that time.

Stewart owned that he had received the bonds from Conti-nental. Then, asking his hearers to accompany him on a gorgeous flight of fancy, he said he had been holding them for Standard of Indiana all those years and that he had a trust agreement to that effect in his safe-deposit box. It was written out in pencil. Why? He didn't want anyone to know about it.

This was too much for Rockefeller, Jr. He demanded publicly on May 9, 1928, that Stewart resign, and in a private confronta-tion with Stewart was adamant. Stewart previously had told Rockefeller, Jr., that he would resign at his request, but now he changed his mind. As far as he was concerned, he said, Rockefel-ler, Jr., was only a single stockholder, and Stewart defied him to do his worst.

The issue was joined. The Rockefellers were by far the largest single interest, but not a majority. Rockefeller, Jr., had 4.5 per-cent of the stock, his sisters 5 percent in a trust fund, and the

Rockefeller Foundation another 5 percent. The only recourse was to wage a proxy campaign, with the distinguished Charles Evans Hughes as counsel, to get from among the 58,000 stockholders votes over 35 percent of the shares in order to oust Colonel Stewart.

Stewart put up a hard fight, and at first it seemed that he would win. Tried for contempt of the Senate, he was acquitted. Tried for perjury, he was acquitted. He claimed that he was therefore vindicated, ignoring the fact that the perjury case fell on the technicality that a majority of the Senate committee was not present when he allegedly lied. On Stewart's recommendation the board of directors voted a dividend of $116,000,000 to stockholders while the proxy solicitation was going on, which undoubtedly helped to sway votes for Stewart.

The proxies came to the annual meeting at Whiting on March 7, 1929, under armed guard. Rockefeller, Jr., had won when the votes were counted, having 5,519,000 of the 8,446,000 shares that were represented at the meeting. The ousted Colonel Stewart had the consolation of a $50,000-a-year pension voted by a grateful board.

It was a famous victory, and there were superlatives of praise from the press, although a few felt that Rockefeller, Jr., had waited too long before acting. The St. Paul *Pioneer Press* said that Rockefeller had furnished the government "with almost the first whole-hearted cooperation it has received from the oil industry since it started to clean up the Teapot Dome scandal."

The Louisville *Courier-Journal* said, "No material benefits the Rockefeller fortune has conferred on humanity can surpass this timely intervention on the side of law." This is somewhat extravagant, yet the victory was notable in its implications. It is a lasting reminder to corporate management which does not own the company that it cannot count on the complications and expense of using the proxy machinery to exonerate it from answerability for its actions to the stockholders. Moreover, with their large constituency of stockholders, and serving the public at large, our major corporations have a semipublic character. Their officers, like public officers, have a duty so to comport themselves as to uphold the reputation of the company.

CHAPTER 26 *The Philanthropies*

THE VALUE of the securities given by John D. Rockefeller to his five main philanthropies as of the date of gift are listed below. They include one not previously mentioned, the Laura Spelman Rockefeller Memorial, established in 1918 to honor the memory of Mrs. Rockefeller, a philanthropy that under Beardsley Ruml specialized in the social sciences, and was merged with the Rockefeller Foundation, in 1928, as the Foundation's Division of Social Sciences.

Rockefeller Institute for Medical Research	$ 60,673,409.45
General Education Board	129,209,167.10
Rockefeller Foundation	182,851,480.90
Laura Spelman Rockefeller Memorial	73,985,313.77
University of Chicago	40,000,000.00
TOTAL	$486,719,371.22

While these were the central philanthropies, there was a long list of other beneficiaries, including many universities and of course churches and foreign missions. The grand total was $531 million. The total of gifts by John D. Rockefeller, Jr., was $473 million; the philanthropies of father and son were over the billion-dollar mark.

At the time of the initiation of the Rockefeller Institute and the General Education Board, their far-flung scope was not yet contemplated by John D. Rockefeller. On June 3, 1905, after consultations with Rockefeller, Jr., Frederick Gates addressed a letter to Rockefeller, Sr., urging the cosmic conception that these philanthropies and the Foundation were later to assume. Unless this were done, he said, "at the close of a few lives now in being, it [this great fortune] must simply pass into the unknown like some other great fortunes with unmeasured and perhaps sinister possibilities." Gates urged: "These funds should be so large that to become a trustee of one of them would be to make a man at once a public character. They should be so large that their administration would be as much a matter of public concern, public inquiry and public criticism as any of the functions of the Government are now."

The letter had such an immediate impact on Rockefeller that within two weeks he gave $10 million to the General Education Board, and the fountainhead had been primed to gush forth ever larger amounts. Incidentally, it is interesting to note that Gates's prediction as to the shining repute that association with the Rockefeller philanthrophies would bring has been borne out—two of our most recent Secretaries of State were previously with the Rockefeller Foundation, John Foster Dulles having been Chairman of the Board of Trustees, and Dean Rusk having been President.

These philanthropies on the large scale to which they were finally committed were pioneering expeditions to fight the ills of mankind, and they had few, if any, precedents and guideposts. The roots of foundations go back to the fourteenth century when merchants were urged to gain remission for their sins by leaving perpetuities to "repair hospitals, mend bad roads, put scholars to school, help maidens marry or make them nuns." By the beginning of this century, the accomplishments of humanitarian ventures endowed by the rich had been so meager that the record was practically a *tabula rasa* on which the trustees of the Rockefeller philanthropies could write their own program with the assurance that their experimentation was as solid as available experience.

The goals of the philanthropies were dictated by the needs of the times. To the trustees of the Rockefeller Foundation in its early life, "disease is the supreme ill of life . . . and the main source of almost all human ills." Dysentery, typhoid, smallpox, malaria, and hookworm infected millions. Life expectancy in the United States was 52 years in 1913 compared to 70 today, and 1 out of 10 infants died in the first year of life compared to 1 out of 40 today. Ignorance was the second major problem. In 1913, only a half-century ago, the illiteracy rate was 7 percent. Only 9 percent of the population finished high school, compared to 60 percent today, and only 5 percent went to college, compared to 30 percent today.

In making a brief survey of the accomplishments of the Rockefeller philanthropies, they may be considered together, since their goals have been coordinated. In 1926 Rockefeller, Sr., wrote to his son that if he had it to do over again there would have been only one organization. Afterward some thought was given to amalgamating all of them, but the only action taken was to absorb the Laura Spelman Rockefeller Memorial Foundation into the Rockefeller Foundation in 1928. Later, the General Education Board became a subsidiary part of the foundation.

The Rockefeller Sanitary Commission under Dr. Wickliffe Rose (a philosopher, incidentally, and not a physician) launched an attack on hookworm, with traveling dispensaries in 653 out of 1,142 counties in 11 southern states. A monetary contribution was required from the local governing body, and as the Rockefeller contribution diminished in time it resulted in the gradual setting up of local public health offices. At first local resistance was considerable. Thus Josephus Daniels wrote in his Raleigh *News and Observer*, "Let us not canonize Standard Oil Rockefeller by putting laurels on his head because he seeks to buy the appreciation of the people whom he has been robbing for a quarter of a century." But a few months later Daniels was writing columns of praise for the work.

During 1913 a half-million people in the South were treated. After patients were cured by Epsom-salt purges, they were taught the importance of wearing shoes if they did not wish to become infected again. The sanitation methods introduced in the fight on hookworm prevented other diseases in the South: typhoid, infant diarrhea, dysentery, and tropical diseases. The public health offices established throughout the South were equipped to fight other diseases also.

Within fifteen years hookworm in the United States became as extinct as the dodo, the end of a fearful disease that had crippled the capacities of the South. This attack on hookworm was extended into a worldwide attack by the International Health Board under Dr. Rose, beginning in the West Indies and Latin America and eventually extending to 52 countries and 29 islands. The disease has been eradicated or brought under control in all areas where the fight against it has been carried on.

Malaria and yellow fever were also under combat on a worldwide basis. After five years of experimentation, the Foundation spread knowledge of malaria-control measures through demonstration and education to foreign countries, beginning with Nicaragua and Brazil in 1921. Such measures included specially designed mosquito nets and the use of certain types of fish.

Yellow fever at one time was termed "the terror of the Western Hemisphere." As an example of this terror, in the Civil War a rumor that the Confederates were sending rags infected with yellow fever across the Niagara River caused a wholesale evacuation of the city of Buffalo. General William C. Gorgas had made the Panama Canal construction possible by destroying the beds of mosquitoes that were identified as the carriers of the disease. The Foundation established the Yellow Fever Commission in 1916, and General Gorgas was made chairman. After an expedition sent to Lagos, Nigeria, in 1925, four members of the commission gave their lives, the famous Japanese bacteriologist Dr. Hideyo Noguchi, Dr. Adrian Stokes, Dr. William Alexander Young, and Dr. Theodore Hayes.

It was believed that the culprit was the *Aëdes aegypti* mosquito, and the commission attacked and cleaned out the centers where they bred, such as the one in Guayaquil in Ecuador. More study and experience showed that yellow fever was primarily a disease of jungle animals and was carried by jungle mosquitoes. After extensive research in its laboratories, the Foundation developed the Sawyer vaccine. By the end of 1938 over a million people in South America had been vaccinated. During World War II the Armed Forces of the United States, Great Britain, and other Allies were vaccinated with this Sawyer vaccine. In 1943, at the height of the Mideastern conflict, there was an outbreak of yellow fever in Egypt, and King Farouk called on the Rockefeller Foundation for assistance in stamping it out. After the war the Foundation, in conjunction with UNRRA and ECA, conducted a campaign to rid Sardinia of mosquito beds; with an army of 33,000 Sardinians covering every foot of the island, it saved Sardinia from becoming a permanent liability.

Prior to World War I, more died in wars from the dread disease of typhus than died on the battlefield. Typhus was carried by the louse, and a laboratory for a study of this pest was built by the Foundation on New York's East Side, using lice from denizens of the Bowery. A powder was successfully developed for killing the vermin. As one example of its use, when the Allies took

Naples in 1943 there was danger of typhus, and in one month 1,300,000 residents went to delousing stations to have the powder swooshed through their clothes.

Though the Foundation has conducted medical research on its own, the chief medical research has been done by the Rockefeller Institute, and many discoveries have been made there. The first one found by Dr. Simon Flexner was a serum for epidemic meningitis. Dr. Noguchi identified organisms causing paresis, enabling him to devise a better test for the disease. Dr. Alexis Carrel found methods of suturing arteries and veins that enabled organs to be transplanted, and made contributions to heart surgery. The Carrel-Dakin solution for treatment of wounds was useful in World War I. Dr. Carrel's experiments together with Colonel Charles Lindbergh on a mechanical heart in 1937 caused worldwide interest. Peyton Rous discovered that certain cancerous tumors in fowls and small mammals are caused by viruses and this was an important step toward the present-day focus on viruses in the attempt to find a cancer cure. Rufus Cole found that the germ pneumococcus, causing pneumonia, could be divided into many immunological types, and developed serum for a highly fatal type.

The list is a long one. The Institute has developed a better smallpox vaccine, new serums for diphtheria, typhoid, Rocky Mountain spotted fever, and trachoma. It made a significant contribution to the development of penicillin. It has made studies of amino acids, vitamins, venereal diseases, influenza, tuberculosis, rabies, yaws, hormones, blood components, and senescences. In 1963 the Institute was making headway in chromosome analysis, which may enable prediction of the likelihood of inheritance of diseases, and may pave the way for prevention of hereditary diseases. The battle to discover the cure for cancer is a relentless one, and from time to time some new clue is uncovered.

The Institute (which has now dropped the words "for Medical Research" from its title) has since 1954 become a graduate university giving the advanced degrees of Doctor of Philosophy and Doctor of Medical Science. Under its president, Dr. Detlev Wulf Bronk, who lives in the $600,000 president's residence, the Institute is a community of research scholars that is most unusual, since there are 97 students and 291 faculty members, a ratio of 1 to 3 in favor of teachers. There are only ten students, or "research fellows," that are awarded degrees each year.

Surely the greatest boon to medical treatment for Americans was the work of the Foundation and of the General Education Board in lifting the standards of medical education in this country. In 1910 Dr. Abraham Flexner, the brother of Simon Flexner, published his *Medical Education in the United States and Canada* under a grant from the Carnegie Foundation. His findings were appalling. Of the 155 medical schools studied, only a half-dozen had any kind of decent education. Eighty-nine required only a common school education. In one leading school the two-year course was a four-month series of lectures repeated the next year. Of one typical school laboratory, Flexner said it was ". . . dirty and disordered beyond description. Its outfit in anatomy consists of a small box of bones and the dried-up filthy fragments of a single cadaver."

In World War I it appeared that this nation lacked the medical talent even to staff its base hospitals. Before the war the General Education Board was beginning to make gifts to reform and uplift educational facilities in medicine. The first, in 1913 to Johns Hopkins, was of $1,500,000 to enable it to have a full-time teaching staff instead of the occasional services of local doctors, which was the then prevailing custom at medical schools. "Full time" became a rather sticky point in dealing with the medical faculty. In many schools the full principle was achieved, and in others the Harvard plan of "geographical full time," in which the faculty may practice close to the school, was an expedient compromise.

In all, the General Education Board gave $100,000,000 for medical education and training. Together with the Foundation it gave $2,000,000 for a medical center in conjunction with the University of Chicago, $2,000,000 for the one in New York carried on by Columbia University and Presbyterian Hospital, $2,500,000 for the one in Iowa City, and $5,500,000 to Vanderbilt University to build a fine medical center in the South. Negro medical schools received generous amounts. (In all, Negro education has received over $66 million from the General Education Board and the Foundation up to today.) While Howard University Medical School received only $600,000 from the General Education Board, since it is the primary charge of the federal government, Meharry Medical School in Nashville received a total of $8,673,000.

The grants of the General Education Board were not confined, of course, to medical schools, but were made to a wide cross-section of schools and universities. There was no lack in number of self-styled "colleges," since local areas and church denominations competed with each other in establishing colleges. At the beginning of the century, Ohio had forty colleges, or twice as many as in the whole of Germany, but the quality of most of them was no better than that of secondary schools. The Board tried in its grants to single out the most promising schools from the standpoint of academic worth, growth potential, and support from others. Its contributions to endowments ranged from as little as 5 percent, in the case of Harvard, to 75 percent for small schools. No denomination was slighted if other standards were met; thus an Episcopal school, Hobart; a Quaker school, Swarthmore; a Lutheran school, St. Olaf; and a Catholic school, Fordham, shared in the largesse. One of the most striking gifts in the cause of higher education from John D. Rockefeller was made at Christmas of 1919. The nation was then in the riptide of postwar inflation, which was particularly oppressive to college teachers struggling on small fixed salaries. Rockefeller gave $50 million in securities to the Board, the principal and interest to be used to help colleges and universities to enable them to raise teachers' salaries. A few months later, Rockefeller struck away all conditions, restrictions, and limitations that had been attached to gifts to educational institutions, enabling them to spend the money they had received with complete freedom of purpose.

One of the most interesting of the many grants by the General Education Board was that of $6,000,000 for establishing the Lincoln School at Columbia University in 1917. This revolutionary school for primary and secondary education discarded the theory of education known as "formal discipline," that is, the idea that subjects such as Latin and algebra teach children how to think logically about all problems. Instead the school concentrated on utilitarianism, that is, the teaching of practical methods of living and the encouragement of individual creativity. This controversial school has been a beacon light in progressive education. Mrs. Rockefeller, Jr., was so enthusiastic about the school that she sent four of her five sons there. The boys (all except John D., 3rd) mingled with Negro children and poor children on scholarships. There were other grants to colleges for experimental teaching projects, including those to Sarah Lawrence, Bennington, and Swarthmore.

An important phase of activity has been financial assistance, through fellowships and grants, to promising scientists and scholars. More than 16,000 have been the recipients of such aid both here and abroad. Rockefeller fellowships trained our leaders in atomic research—J. Robert Oppenheimer, Enrico Fermi, Arthur Compton, and Henry Smyth.

Such grants have run a wide gamut. One enabled the drug prontosil to be developed at the Queen Charlotte's Maternity Hospital in London; over $1,350,000 has gone to a team, headed by Dr. Elton Mayo, at the Harvard Business School for experiments in a "clinical approach to human relations in industry"; a grant to Dr. Alfred Kinsey, Professor of Zoology at Indiana University, promoted the study that so titillated the public a few years ago, *Sexual Behavior in the Human Male;* the outpouring of knowledge today from microbiology, genetics, and other biochemical and biophysical sciences is largely due to the aid they received from the Foundation in their early development.

The Foundation has financed the 184-inch cyclotron at the University of California, studies of the aurora borealis in Alaska, the building and equipping of an oceanographic institute in Massachusetts, and the development of data on prehistoric man by radiation tests on discovered fragments of the Peking Man.

Grants to aid in the advancement of the social sciences were continued by the Foundation after it absorbed the Laura Spelman Rockefeller Memorial Foundation. Among the organizations it has substantially helped (some of which it brought into being) are the Social Science Research Council, the Council on Foreign Relations, the National Bureau of Economic Research, the Russian Institute at Columbia, the Public Administration Clearing House in Chicago, the Brookings Institution, and the Institute of Pacific Relations.

In philanthropy, as in all other human affairs, the old order changeth, yielding place to new. In the last half-century the cause of education has become the concern of all; state boards of education that were then nonexistent are now functioning in every state; states and the federal government pour out money for education, recognizing it as a prime public concern. Medical education with facilities for medical research has been increasingly able to tap public and private funds. Many more private foundations have entered the field in recent years, spurred on by the sharp rise in federal taxes. Medical discoveries and better sanitation have wiped out diseases that were epidemic in former years.

Certainly a major factor in the winds of change has been the growth in the concept of the welfare state. With the federal government appropriating over $20 billion a year for health, education, and welfare programs, a sum of $30 million spent by the Rockefeller Foundation shrinks into insignificance. What, then, can be the role of a private foundation in this country? J. George Harrar, president of the Rockefeller Foundation, said recently that their function is to identify key problems and demonstrate means of their solution. "Since they are free to act without the restraints of either profit-making or official policy, they can assume the risks and controversy involved in working on the growing edge of things."

The Rockefeller Foundation has been in concept an international agency; and certainly throughout the world the problems of disease, hunger, malnutrition, and illiteracy survive as cliff-high barriers to progress, particularly in the underdeveloped nations of Africa and Asia. The work of the Rockefeller Foundation has undoubtedly forged the way for our Point Four program and even for the Peace Corps. The operations of the Agency for International Development and the instrumentalities of the United Nations may raise some question as to the need for a private Foundation abroad, but at the present time the unfilled need is so vast and urgent that the problem of competition seems remote.

"Disease is the supreme ill of life." That still remains true of large areas of the world. The work of the International Health Division was terminated in the 1950's, but the Foundation is still engaged in research on the anthropoid-borne (arbo) viruses. These insect-transmitted viruses are thought to be the cause of many little-understood diseases that are often broadly categorized as "tropical fevers." Staff units were located in areas all over the world, and in the years since 1950 about 150 hitherto unknown arboviruses have been collected and classified as a first step toward the identification of the diseases and control, in conjunction with the Department of Epidemiology and Public Health of Yale University.

In the well-developed nations a ratio of one doctor to every 1,200 people is considered essential. In Africa the gravity of the problem is indicated by the fact that the World Health Organization has set a goal of one doctor to every 10,000 people to be achieved within the next decade, and only a handful of African and Asian nations have a chance of reaching this goal. In order to increase the supply of physicians and other professional help, such as nurses, sanitary engineers, and laboratory technicians, the Foundation has built and endowed many schools of public health to train public health physicians, nurses, and technicians.

To assure permanence, a basic policy of the Foundation has been to make foreign governments responsible participants in medical and scientific projects.

On September 24, 1963, in its fiftieth anniversary year, the trustees of the Foundation announced that for the foreseeable future they would concentrate on five pressing areas. In large part this plan for the future reaffirmed its most recent activities.

I. Toward the Conquest of Hunger

Millions upon millions in the world are denied a diet adequate to support requirements for normal existence. The Foundation has engaged in cooperative efforts to increase food supply. Its major program stems from a casual remark made in 1941 by the then Vice-President of the United States and a distinguished biologist in his own right, Henry A. Wallace, to Raymond Fosdick, then president of the Foundation, that if anyone could devise a way of increasing the yield per acre of corn and beans in Mexico, that would be the greatest boon that could be conferred on that country. Yields of corn were as low as ten bushels to an acre. This chance comment sparked a program that was initiated in conjunction with the Mexican Government in 1943, beginning with major crops like corn and wheat, and expanding to others—potatoes, beans, feed and forage crops—and to animal husbandry. In the twenty years since 1943, Mexican deficits in basic foods have been corrected, and the country can now satisfy its own requirements for corn, wheat, beans, and potatoes. This program was so successful that a unit was established in Colombia in 1950, in Chile in 1955, and in India in 1956. In Mexico, seven hundred young Mexican graduates have obtained in-service training experience, and are accepting responsibility for the agricultural development of the nation.

Two international institutes have been established to carry on basic and applied research on food problems of major importance for relevant areas, and others are in propsect. One is the International Rice Institute, a cooperative venture of the Philippine Government and the Ford and Rockefeller foundations. The second is the International Center for Corn and Wheat Improvement, at Chapingo, in central Mexico, a venture of the Mexican Government and the Rockefeller Foundation. The present president, J. George Harrar, was a plant pathologist who was engaged at the initiation of the Mexican project. His selection indicates the heavy emphasis that is placed today upon this activity.

II. The Population Problem

Heretofore population has been kept in check by great catastrophes, such as wars, epidemics, famines, and floods. Now, with our bright, sanitary new world, a million are added each week to the top-heavy world population of 3.5 billion, putting a tremendous burden on available food supply and essential services. Precisely what the Foundation is going to do about the problem is not explicitly stated in its last report, but the use of the term "family planning" indicates that it will disseminate information about birth-control methodology.

III. Strengthening Emerging Centers of Learning

One way of offering educational opportunities to individuals from underdeveloped nations is by way of scholarships and grants. In 1963 there were 709 Rockefeller fellows and scholars from 52 countries. In addition the Foundation is helping emerging institutions with contributions of qualified personnel or by

training personnel, and by grants for various purposes, such
as for new construction or for teachers' salaries. The University of
Valle in Latin America has received support for a decade. Others
now receiving help are the University of the Philippines, the
University of East Africa, which consists of constituent colleges in
Kenya, Uganda, and Tanganyika, and the University of Ibadan in
Nigeria. Thus, in 1963, the Foundation aided the establishment
in the last-named university of a Department of Psychiatry,
Neurosurgery and Neurology, the first in Africa to train students
in this field.

IV. *Toward Equal Opportunity for All*

This objective is truly in accord with the Rockefeller tradition,
since it means primarily help for the Negro, particularly in the
realm of higher education. A substantial contribution was made
to the United Negro College Fund, which will strengthen faculty
and plant of thirty-two predominantly Negro member colleges. A
major problem for the predominantly white colleges is that there
are so few Negro students qualified for admission. The Foundation made grants to Princeton University, Oberlin College, and
Dartmouth College to conduct on-campus summer sessions over a
three-year period to prepare promising students, white and
Negro, from secondary schools. Though Duke, Emory, Tulane,
and Vanderbilt, which are all southern schools, have opened their
doors wide to Negroes, they have found that by and large Negroes
cannot compete on equal terms with white students for scholarship aid. To fill the gap, the Foundation has appropriated funds
to these institutions for a six-year period for grants to qualified
undergraduates.

V. *Aiding Our Cultural Development*

Man does not live by bread alone, and in a so-called "affluent
society" where there is more leisure and where incomes are above
subsistence requirements, the Foundation has embarked on a
more extensive humanities program "out of the conviction that
every society has needs for self-realization and creative fulfill-

ment." In 1962 a grant was given to Station WNDT, the first educational television project in the New York City area. In 1963 a grant was made to the Actors Studio in New York to develop new plays in the hope of introducing more experimental works of merit into the general theatrical repertoire. A grant was made to the University of Minnesota to assist the University, which has established close working relationships with the new Tyrone Guthrie Theatre, and to develop the talent of playwrights by affording them more freedom. In 1963 the Foundation also supported a unique plan of the School of Music at the University of Southern California to educate and train six to eight music critics a year. Its help to local community cultural centers is illustrated by its grant of $1 million to the John F. Kennedy Center for the Performing Arts in Washington, D.C., which will be the cultural center for the nation's capital. The Foundation has made grants to the symphony orchestras of Dallas, St. Louis, Salt Lake City, Buffalo, and New Orleans so that in the summer of 1965 they can go to neighboring universities to perform new symphonic works by young composers.

In the roundness of time John D. Rockefeller is assuming the role that he rejected in life, that of a patron of the arts, a Maecenas or Lorenzo de'Medici, which was the historic role of the rich in bygone days.

Through the balance sheet of the Foundation, the spirit of John D. still stalks, since of the $658,000,000 of stocks held at the close of 1963, no less than $351,092,000 is invested in Standard Oil of New Jersey, so that the health and prosperity of the Foundation for years to come is linked to that of the parent oil company of John D.'s empire.

CHAPTER 27   *The Third Generation*

JOHN D. ROCKEFELLER JR. died in Tucson, Arizona, in May 1960, at eighty-six years of age. At his bedside was his wife, the former Martha Baird Allen, the widow of a Brown classmate, whom he had married in 1951, three years after the death of Abby Rockefeller. A musician, his second wife had made his last years gay with music, since she was accomplished in light as well as in serious music.

Surviving him was his eldest child, Abby, now Mrs. Jean Mauzé, and his five sons—John D., 3rd, born in 1906; Nelson Aldrich, born in 1908 (in Bar Harbor, Maine, the only child not born in New York City); Laurance Spelman, born in 1910; Winthrop, born in 1912; and David, born in 1915. Winthrop was originally Winthrop Aldrich, the name of his mother's brother, but when it was pointed out to his peace-loving mother that the initials spell WAR she immediately disassociated him from Mars by clipping off his cognomen.

The training of the children was designed to preserve a continuity in attitudes toward life and feelings of responsibility. Just as their grandfather had kept his Ledger A and their father had followed suit, the boys kept their accounts with allowances on one side of the ledger and expenditures on the other, their books being periodically reviewed by their father. Like their father, they were paid for small chores, and were encouraged to give a tithe for charity. In the family tradition were a prayer session before breakfast and regular churchgoing. (As an example of the carryover to the next generation, Nelson taught a Sunday-school class while at Dartmouth, and maintained the prayer sessions for his own family.) Their father taught them to swim and skate as Rockefeller, Sr., had taught him; he worked with the boys on landscaping and building roads and took them on trips to Yellowstone and national parks, thus indoctrinating them with the love of the outdoors. It is interesting that they were even taught the game of Numerica, the strange numbers game that so fascinated

Rockefeller, Sr., for years, the lure of which baffled outsiders who visited him.

In their childhood, Rockefeller, Sr., was already in his declining years, being sixty-seven at the time John D., 3rd, was born, "a car coasting downhill," as he said to them. The boys all recall him as a storyteller who relished the role greatly. As they grew older, they became aware that this kindly, shrunken man was once a giant on the earth, and a man about whom storms had swirled. A piquant incident is the thesis that Nelson wrote for Economics honors work at Dartmouth, taking up the cudgels for the honor of Standard Oil and his grandfather. Its tenor can be judged from this excerpt: "Those [competitors] who did not wish to come in could go on just as before. They were not forced to sell out under threats of being crushed out nor were any of them coerced into selling. As Mr. Rockefeller himself says 'We left them to the mercy of time.'" One can almost feel the shudder of Miss Tarbell's spirit.

It was the figure of their father (whom they all called "Pa") that loomed large in their minds as they grew up, as he looms large today in their memories. "It is example, not precept," says Laurance, "which is the important influence in molding character of the young." It was not by lecturing to them but by his example that they absorbed the thought that their wealth was not only a means of gratifying their wishes but also a sober obligation to help others.

Stories were published in the past that the children were shielded from the knowledge that they were the scions of the nation's richest family and that they believed they were only second-class rich. Later it was admitted that this was a fairy tale. A boy brought up in the magnificence of Pocantico Hills, with its $500,000 playhouse, surrounded by governesses and tutors in early years, and in the nine-story town house, stocked with art treasures, on West Fifty-fourth Street could hardly fail to grasp the awful truth. Yet steps were taken to democratize the boys, to give them a sense of belonging with others, and to teach them to mingle with children of a lower social and economic stratum. The most important step in that direction was to send all of them, with the exception of John D., 3rd, to the Lincoln School of Teachers College, which was coeducational and attended by foreign-born and poorer children, including Negroes, who were there on scholarships.

The influence of the Lincoln School, which, as a progressive school, encouraged students to explore their own interests and taught them to live in society, has been a dominant one in their lives. It is notable that John D., 3rd, who did not attend, is a retiring person in contrast to the more or less extroverted other sons. He and Nelson are at opposite ends of the spectrum. John is reputed to be so deliberate that he will spend two weeks writing a two-minute introduction. Laurance states that the Lincoln School experience whetted his interest in gadgetry, and thus led to his investments in the new technology, and that it trained him as well as Nelson in "person to person contact." David, too, shows the influence of being encouraged to follow his own bent, since he developed an early interest in insects and has one of the finest collections of beetles in the world, numbering 40,000.

Yet Laurance gives startling confirmation as to "Why Johnnie Can't Read." He says that the Lincoln School did not teach him to read and write as he wishes he now could. Nelson, today, admits that reading for him is a "slow and tortuous process" that he does not enjoy doing but compels himself to do. This is significant evidence in the debate that has raged about modern educational techniques.

After secondary school the boys went to different colleges, and their lives diverged so that their careers today are markedly asymmetrical. Nevertheless, early bonds persist in a union of sentiments and sympathies and also in common business relationships. They have operated as a team in dividing up the activities of John D., Jr., which are being maintained in this generation, and have assumed others. Nelson, because of his overriding duties as Governor of New York State, has stepped out, but here are how the others carve up these family responsibilities:

John D., 3rd—Rockefeller Foundation, United Negro Fund, Lincoln Center.

David—Chase Manhattan Bank, Rockefeller Institute, International House, Museum of Modern Art.

Winthrop—Winrock Farms, Arkansas Arts Center, Colonial Williamsburg, National Urban League.

Laurance—Rockefeller Brothers, Inc.; Rockefeller Brothers
Fund, Inc.; Rockefeller Center, Inc.; Memorial Sloan-Kettering
Cancer Center, and all conservation activities.

Although Laurance is president of Rockefeller Brothers Fund,
they all take part in its decisions. It is today the ninth largest
private foundation, with assets of about $105,000,000. (The
Rockefeller Foundation is second in size after the Ford Foundation.) It was set up partly by a gift of Rockefeller, Jr., in his lifetime, and supplemented by a gift of about half the $150,000,000
he left at his death, the other half having been left to his widow.
In 1962 its gifts amounted to $7,450,000, and in 1963, $8,012,000,
mostly to standard charities and projects in the public interest.
Among the recipients were the Red Cross, the Community Blood
Council, the Museum of Modern Art, the Lincoln Center for the
Performing Arts, the Negro rights movement, the National Urban
League for a listing of skills of Negro workers, and $500,000 to
modernize rural schools in Chile.

This is by no means the end of giving, since each brother and
Mrs. Mauzé make gifts to suit individual predilection and interest. Laurance gives away a minimum of 30 percent of his income
each year, the maximum allowed under the tax laws for deduc-
tion for gifts to charities and to eligible churches, hospitals, and
schools. The business of giving, he says, is no easy matter, and he
cites a statement of Julius Rosenwald that it is easier to make a
million that it is to do a good job of giving it away.

Another joint activity, though Laurance is chairman, is Rockefeller Brothers, Inc., which, contrary to some reports, is not a
holding company for Rockefeller investments. Most of the fortune is in trust funds that were set up by Rockefeller, Jr., in his
lifetime. Thus, the brothers and Mrs. Mauzé can handle only the
funds not in trust, and income above gifts and living requirements. Rockefeller Brothers, Inc., is primarily a holding company
for ideas, a service agency that provides research and management. Its security analysts make recommendations upon which
each Rockefeller may act differently, or possibly they may act in
concert. Such a recommendation that was adopted by them was
the investment in Chrysler in the spring of 1962, when it was
selling for a fraction of its present market value. The cumulative

investment was large enough to enable them to put the president of Rockefeller Brothers, Inc., J. Richardson Dilworth, on the board of directors of Chrysler. "It was a phenomenally successful recommendation," says Laurance, "but possibly misleading to the public, since most of the investments made as a result of the recommendations are not that happy and require a good deal of patience."

Will there be room in the future for private philanthropy with the strides being made in the development of the welfare state? Laurance replies "Yes. The help of the government is palliative in character. A search must still continue to find the fundamental causes of distress, and private philanthropy must continue to point out to the government where it must step in with massive aid. The difference is between government spending, which is quantitative, and ours, which is qualitative."

What is the pyschology of one born to vast riches who works hard on various jobs and whose brothers seek political elective office? We can guess as to what makes Sammy run, but what makes a Rockefeller run? I asked Laurance if the underlying motive is to prove one's worth entirely apart from the station in life that being a Rockefeller brings. "The motivation and the goal are the same as in the case of all, that is, to fulfill one's own capacities and potential to the maximum. Of course, I must be candid that my situation is quite different from most since it is noncompetitive with others. I set standards and try to bring others to the level I require, rather than having to bring myself to the level of others or exceed them."

The oldest, John 3rd, matriculated at Princeton. A classmate of his, the columnist Holmes Alexander, tells me that he was unusually diffident and retiring, giving the impression to his classmates that he was supremely self-conscious about being John D. Rockefeller. An amusing episode in his college career was his attempt to cash a check in a store at Princeton—the storekeeper was convinced that the signature was some sort of college gag. The boys, incidentally, did not have unlimited funds while at college—an allowance of $1,800 a year, which sometimes let them run very low.

Even while an undergraduate, his interest developed in international affairs, and he spent a summer as a clerk at Geneva for the League of Nations. Soon after graduation he made his first trip to the Far East, and it has been his passion since then. In the years after 1951, he has visited the Orient two or three times a year. He accompanied the Dulles peace mission to Japan. He took the leadership in founding the International House in Japan, founded Japan Society, Inc., which tries to bring the peoples of Japan and the United States together, and heads the Asia Society, which emphasizes cultural ties and brings performing artists to this country. His son, John D. Rockefeller, 4th, continues this Asian interest, serving on the Indonesian desk of the State Department.

In the Far East John 3rd is among the best-known Americans, and holds numerous decorations such as, from Laos, L'Ordre des Millions d'Eléphants et du Parasol Blanc, and, from Thailand, that of The Most Excellent Order of the White Elephant. Can one hope for anything more in this life?

In 1952, John 3rd established the Rockefeller Public Service Awards, administered by Princeton University. Under this program, meritorious government servants in the career category with long years of service are rewarded with cash awards of approximately $10,000.

John's main job is that of Chairman of the Board of the Rockefeller Foundation, succeeding John Foster Dulles in that post. The domination of the Foundation by the Rockefeller family was a matter of some criticism in its early days. Rockefeller, Jr., once explained that it was only natural for the family to look after it in its growing stages: "However, as rapidly as capable and interested men were found they were added to the Board in which members of the 'official family' gradually and properly became a minority." Today, although John D., 3rd, holds the highest post, he is only one member of the board, and can be outvoted on any question of policy.

In a family that is not notable for being intellectual, although all have some appreciation for the arts, the youngest son, David, is perhaps the most intellectual. After undergraduate work at Harvard, he attended the London School of Economics and got a

Doctor's degree from the University of Chicago. Presently he is president of the Chase Manhattan Bank, the second largest in the country, of which his uncle, Winthrop Aldrich, was once president. The job is in the family tradition, since his grandfather, Nelson Aldrich, as we have noted, was a foremost authority on money and banking.

Prior to military service, in which David enlisted as a private and emerged as a captain, he had an exciting experience as a secretary to Mayor La Guardia. In the Chase, he manifested his brother Nelson's interest in Latin America, supervising the bank's business there as vice-president. In 1950 he started a Chase publication that came to be highly regarded, *Latin American Highlights*. His chief family responsibility has been the presidency of the Rockefeller Institute, which he regards as a serious job, filling his every Saturday, and not as an honorific post. Extracurricularly, his most interesting undertaking has been the chairmanship of the Downtown-Lower Manhattan Redevelopment Association, which has drafted and presented a plan to Mayor Wagner for the remodeling of the lower part of Manhattan, including a new site and building for the New York Stock Exchange and a gigantic World Trade Center.

Laurance is the helmsman, the business manager for the Rockefeller fortune. He buys and sells the stocks for the family. He is at the head of the Fund, Rockefeller Brothers, Inc., and Rockefeller Center.

There are strange quirks in the Rockefellers, and one is that Laurance majored in philosophy at Princeton, and believes today that his decision to major in that subject, rather than in economics or business, was the proper one. Philosophy, he says, enables him to understand things broadly, makes him aware of interrelationships, and thus enables him to arrive at a better value judgment. His thesis at Princeton was "The Concept of Value in Relation to Ethics," which sounds deep indeed.

Laurance has become a significant factor in the financing of new ventures that are important in aeronautical, space-age, and advanced technologies. The authoritative financial organ, *Barron's*, states, "Possibly the biggest and probably the wealthiest individual investor in speculative scientific ventures is Laurance S. Rockefeller."

Aeronautics had hardly been in the family line, since neither John D., Sr., nor Jr. had ever been up in a plane. Laurance liked speed and from commuting down the Hudson by speedboat every day from Tarrytown (as John Archbold used to do years before) he graduated to planes. In 1938 he, together with Winthrop, established Air Youth of America to get the young airminded. His first money venture in the field was to enable Captain Eddie Rickenbacker to buy the part of General Motors that became Eastern Air Lines. It was a successful venture financially. In early 1964 the company, through competitive conditions, was foundering and on the way to bankruptcy, and Laurance, along with others, lent it large sums to tide it over, a fact not publicized.

His next venture was a $10,000 loan to an aircraft designer from St. Louis who came to him for help, J. S. McDonnell, who had a small experimental shop and ideas for a new pursuit plane. Later advances followed, from Laurance and from his brothers, totaling $400,000. McDonnell has become a huge aircraft company, and since the Rockefellers took 20 percent of the stock (they sold it by 1955), it was also a phenomenal investment for them. The company built the first Phantom jets and Banshee fighters, and today supplies most of the fighters for the United States Navy and Air Force. It also builds the Mercury and Gemini space capsules.

During the war, Laurance served in the Production Division of the Navy Bureau of Aeronautics, which stimulated his attachment to this field. On his return to civilian life, he nurtured many companies in the growth stage. One was Reaction Motors, now a Division of Thiokol, which was developing liquid rockets but encountered grave financial difficulties. Later, with help supplied by him, it turned out the Viking Rocket and rocket engines for the Bell XS1, which achieved supersonic speeds for the first time. Others he helped to launch are Marquardt Aircraft, Piasecki Helicopter, which was the warhorse during Korea (now Vertol, a division of Boeing); and Nuclear Development Corp., now a part of United Nuclear Corp.

Laurance seeks to get into companies in the gestation stage and put them on a three-legged basis of ownership, one-third for management, one-third for private investors, and one-third for himself. The period before the investment bears fruit is expected to be a long one, from five to fifteen years. His batting average of success has been .900, a most unusual one in view of the frightfully high mortality among new enterprises.

Here are company investments most prominent in his portfolio at the present time:

Itek: Electronic handling and retrieval of printed information.

Scientific-Atlanta: Makes two-thirds of all recorders, receivers, and equipment used in antenna testing, as well as underground sound and telemetry instrumentation equipment.

National Astro Laboratories: Furnishes calibration and repair services to manufacturers who need precise machinery and instrument settings to meet tolerances demanded by the National Bureau of Standards.

Cryonetics Corp.: Provides research on low-temperature phenomena; thus it is working on a refrigerator for research on materials at temperatures within one degree of absolute zero.

Thermokinetic Fibers, Inc.: Makes available metallic whiskers, which are three-quarters of an inch in length and down to one-tenth the diameter of a human hair. They exhibit phenomenal strength, and command extraordinary magnetic and optical qualities.

Geophysics Corp. of America: Engages in research, development, and manufacturing programs based on sciences relating to the Earth and its environments.

New England Nuclear Corp.: Produces radioactive chemicals for use by medical institutions, industry, and government agencies.

The Rockefellers claim to be less interested in making money than in making a contribution to social and economic progress. These new ideas, if they prove feasible, will push forward the frontiers of science. "If it were merely the making of money," says Laurance, "I would be content to leave my money in oil stocks and I would be more confident about the outcome in money terms." A few years ago the Rockefellers invested $1.5 million in Island Packers, Inc., a scheme for using Fiji Island natives to catch tuna that would be processed in an American packing plant in Samoa, and thereby help an underdeveloped area of the world. They lost their money because tuna was not there in sufficient quantities. Whatever the social objective of the investment, Laurance believes that if there is a need, it will ultimately be self-sustaining—or else there was no real need.

Laurance maintains the conservation activities that were so dear to his father's heart. He is president of the Jackson Hole Preserve, Inc., which was established by his father in 1940. With funds contributed by him, the Preserve bought 5,000 acres on the Virgin Islands that were then donated to the federal government and became the basis for the Virgin Islands National Park. He is Chairman of the New York State Council of Parks, President of the American Conservation Association, and was appointed by President Eisenhower as Chairman of the Outdoor Recreation Resources Review Commission established by the Eighty-fifth Congress.

Interest in the outdoors has led tangentially to making him an owner and builder of resort hotels, which he believes will eventually, by attracting tourists, aid in the economic development of the areas in which they are located. They include the Dorado Beach Hotel on 1,500 acres in Puerto Rico, twenty miles west of San Juan; Estate Good Hope on St. Croix in the Virgin Islands, and a $10 million resort to be opened in 1965 as the Mauna Kea Beach Hotel on the Knoa coast of Hawaii.

There is another by-product from his coeducational experience at the Lincoln School. He is an ardent advocate of coeducation, and believes that it is unrealistic to segregate women in training for life. He has made study grants to review theories of segregated leadership training; he has worked with his wife to bring the YMCA's and YWCA's into closer union; he helped to endow the Abby Rockefeller Mauzé Professorship for a woman at the Massachusetts Institute of Technology to dramatize the acceptance of a woman in science; and he has made career-guidance grants to Vassar and Wellesley to bring more women into careers monopolized by men.

Drive and determination are hallmarks of the Rockefellers. The "human touch" is marked in two of them, Winthrop and Nelson, which predestined them for the cockpit of politics. Winthrop in his youth was little interested in books but very much in human beings. He left Yale in his junior year in order to meet life sooner. Brawny, and six foot three, he began work in the Texas oil fields as a "roughneck" laborer with a crew, digging eleven-foot-square holes in the ground, which is a preliminary to sinking a well. For months he wielded pick and shovel while living in a $4.50-a-week room and eating at chili stands. He then returned to New York to work for Socony-Vacuum, and served as Executive Vice-Chairman of the Greater New York Fund in 1938, which in that year was a pioneer effort in unifying the fund-raising for four-hundred charities, a practice followed in the years since.

He enlisted in the Armed Forces as a private ten months before Pearl Harbor, and graduated from Officers Candidate School as a second lieutenant a month after that event. As a major he was in active combat with the 77th Division in assault landings on Guam, Leyte, and Okinawa. On April 2, 1945, a Japanese kami-kaze carrying two 500-pound bombs hit the troop transport *Henrico* off Okinawa, killing seventy-five men; Major Rockefeller was the senior officer left in command. He had suffered flash burns, and was hospitalized for six weeks. Leaving the service as a lieu-tenant colonel, he was awarded the bronze star with oak leaf clusters and the Purple Heart.

He went back to Socony-Vacuum, where he was in charge of the industrial relations division for foreign production. In his so-cial life he was a fun-loving playboy who once won a dance contest with Mary Martin. In 1949 he married Mrs. Barbara "Bobo" Sears, a member of Café Society, who, whatever her humble beginnings, which were blazoned in the tabloids, was at the time far removed from them. The marriage broke up soon after the birth of their son, Winthrop Paul, and in 1953 they were divorced, with a settlement on her of $5,500,000. He had estab-lished a close army relationship with Frank Newell of Little Rock, and decided to go there for his divorce. He stayed.

"We thought he had come down here to sit on his tail," said Harry Ashmore, famous journalist of the Arkansas *Gazette*, "but we soon found out differently."

The first step Winthrop took was the purchase of a 927-acre tract atop Petit Jean Mountain, about fifty miles northwest of

Little Rock. At first he planned it for a weekend retreat, but gradually his enthusiasm mounted. Worn-out land was cleared, graded, and planted. A complete irrigation system was set up, and a 10-inch pipeline was installed to carry water 850 feet up the mountain from a pumping station on the Petit Jean River. Six artificial lakes were built, the one closest to his home being named Lake Abby for his mother. A mile-long airstrip was constructed, where today he operates his three planes, including a million-dollar Sabreliner jet. He has five pilots in his employ. He has donated this airstrip for the use of the public; and since it is high enough not to be fogbound, it has often been used by commercial airliners for emergency landings.

Winrock Farms has today become a spectacular agricultural operation and scientific farm attracting 125,000 visitors a year. Headquarters is 1,000 acres at the original site but there are now, in all, five divisions operating a total of 34,000 acres—17,000 acres devoted to cattle and 17,000 to the production of rice and small grains.

Winrock is something of a feudal barony, having its own flag, its own color on all its vehicles (Winrock Green), its own short-wave radio network, auxiliary power system, and private fire engine. But Winrock is more than a baron's plaything. It is today a primary source for stock for Santa Gertrudis cattle, the first true American breed of cattle, originating at the King Ranch in Texas. In 1953 Winthrop bought at auction at King Ranch a bull he named Rock, for $31,500, to sire this breed, the highest price ever paid for this type of bull. The Santa Gertrudis are big in size, cherry-red in color, and combine the best features of the Brahman and Shorthorn. They have a high tolerance for hot weather and insects, can flourish on grass alone, and can take a lot of drought punishment. Winrock has over 2,500 head of these cattle, and on the second Saturday of May every year buyers from all over the world, about two hundred in number, come to Winrock for the Santa Gertrudis Production Sale.

In the breeding of the cattle the newest techniques of artificial insemination are used in 60 percent of the cases. A healthy two-year-old bull can inseminate an average of 25 cows, and at his prime of four to six years, 50 to 60 cows a year. According to Winrock's manager, G. W. Adkisson, Jr., by artificial insemination the farm is able to inseminate many more than this number, and is able to start the insemination process at an earlier age. In order to obtain the best results, the farm uses an IBM computer system for matching characteristics of bull and cow to produce the desired calf. The characteristics of the first progeny of both are recorded on cards, and then the computer is able to predict the best mates on the basis of that information for the calves with the characteristics wanted.

In March 1955, Governor Orval Faubus asked Winthrop to be chairman of the newly established Arkansas Industrial Development Commission. Arkansas had been on the downgrade since the war, with a declining population and an emigration of industry as well. The legislature had granted an annual appropriation of $127,500; believing this inadequate, Winthrop immediately organized a committee to raise the sum of $200,000 through donations, which was done. He asked towns and cities to submit lists of plant sites, empty buildings, and prospects. He launched a $100,000 advertising campaign to let outside business know of cheap labor and plant sites in Arkansas. Many industries were won over by his personal solicitation, such as Mohawk Rubber of Akron. When he resigned in April 1956, he could claim credit for bringing 600 new industrial plants into the state, with 90,000 new jobs.

One of the objections raised by outside business to moving into Arkansas was the cultural and educational backwardness of a "hillbilly" state. Winthrop has tried to advance the state culturally. With his second wife, Jeanette, he has taken a leading role in the founding of the Arkansas Art Center, which opened in Little Rock's MacArthur Park in 1962. In 1956 he established the Arkansas Opportunity Fund to award college scholarships to promising high school seniors. He persuaded the legislature to establish the Graduate Institute of Technology, whose graduates can serve industry in the state. He provided the equipment and three-year financial support for a pilot project, a rural health clinic in Perry County. He donated a model elementary school to the Morriltown School District close to his farm, and a five-year grant to increase teachers' salaries.

The Rockefellers, like their grandfather, accept all people, regardless of class or race, and Winthrop in his personal life has been most democratic. He has been active in the National Urban League, and his gifts in Arkansas have crossed race lines. Undoubtedly his enlightened viewpoint was a handicap in his race for Governor of Arkansas, though he tried to soft-pedal his views in the campaign, opposing the federal Civil Rights bill then in Congress, for example.

The drive of Nelson can best be described as kinetic. His confidence and cocksureness are best illustrated by the first thing he did when he arrived as a freshman at Dartmouth—he dropped in on the president to announce "I am here." He resembles his paternal grandfather in his superabundant energy that he must work off by physical exertion, in his stubbornness in pursuing his goals, and an absorption in his jobs so intense that his social friends are mostly his business associates—he is most unlike his grandfather in having a cast-iron stomach that can be a receptacle for endless blintzes and pizzas when on the campaign trail. His political proclivities may be an atavism of genes from his maternal grandfather, Nelson Aldrich, a born politician and political boss.

Prior to entering politics and public service, Nelson was chairman of the board of Rockefeller Center, wherein he acquired a reputation as a tough-fisted renting agent whom other landlords accused of enticing away their best lessees. Another activity was the presidency of the Museum of Modern Art, which he thoroughly enjoyed, since he had acquired, principally from his mother, a lively art appreciation, and his Fifth Avenue apartment today is stocked with a magnificent collection of art treasures.

We shall not discuss here the public career of Nelson Rockefeller, which has been well discussed elsewhere, but we shall note a very interesting venture in business and international relations that may be meaningful for the future. After several trips for Creole Oil, he became very much interested in Latin America before the war, and learned Spanish in order to familiarize himself better with their problems. Viewing the poverty so evident in many countries, he conceived the idea that the private-enterprise system could do much to ameliorate conditions of want and poverty, and could do it at a profit. As he said: "In the last century capital went where it could make the greatest profit. In this century it must go where it can render the greatest service."

The war, during which he served as Coordinator of Inter-American Affairs and Assistant Secretary of State for Latin America, interrupted his plans, but after the war he returned to them. He formed two organizations of which he became president. The first was the American International Association for Economic and Social Development (known as AIA). It is a nonprofit philanthropic agency, operating in what we call the public sector of the economy, to better the standard of living of people in Latin America by advancing education, health, farm training, roads, and the like. The Rockefellers have made contributions in the millions; oil companies have discharged in this way their social responsibility, and the countries concerned have also contributed.

The second entity was the International Basic Economy Corp. (known as IBEC), which was formed in 1947 with a capital of $2 million and today has assets of over $110,000,000. It can be regarded as an experiment to test the theory that good business can be done in the developing nations by providing food and housing at higher quality and lower cost than normally obtainable. As examples it has introduced supermarkets in Peru and Argentina, and no less than twenty-one of them in Venezuela. IBEC Housing has already built 9,000 middle-income houses in Puerto Rico by the "IBEC method," which involves a mechanized, poured-in-place building. IBEC sponsors and manages mutual funds so that local residents can invest in the growing industries of their countries; Fundo Crescinco of Brazil had the equivalent of $26.5 million invested at the end of 1963.

In books about Nelson Rockefeller many pages have been devoted to praise of these two undertakings, and indeed they have been noble experiments; but on closer examination their success looks very dubious. AIA, for all the work it has done, has spent only an average of $1 million a year, which is hardly anything for a vast continent. (The Alliance for Progress is doing this work today, or supposed to be doing it, on a large scale.) IBEC had a profit of over $1 million in 1963, a good deal less than in 1962, but in examining the annual report it seems that IBEC has now gone far afield from its original concept. The major income producers for IBEC are two manufacturing establishments it has acquired in Ohio, U.S.A. It is also operating now in western Europe, and in 1963 bought a leading poultry breeding concern in Glastonbury, Connecticut. Because there has been a high percentage of failures in Latin America and because currency depreciation has hobbled the projects, the original theory has not apparently worked out too well.

What is the size of the Rockefeller fortune remaining today after all the philanthropies? However academic the dollar figure, it has always been an absorbing question for speculation. The authoritative figure we have is that given to Professor Allan Nevins by John D. Rockefeller, Jr., that a year-end inventory soon after the dissolution of the trust showed that it totaled $815,647,796.89, and that at the peak of the stock market in 1913 it totaled about $900,000,000. It was clear during World War I, from income tax figures released at that time, that Rockefeller, Sr., had become America's first billionaire.

Since that time everything is guesswork. One would have to have a catalogue of the investments, as well as a timetable of giving, since a gift of securities when the market is low takes a greater percentage of the fortune than when the market is high. Disparate estimates point out all the imponderables that must be made subjective valuations. Thus in 1921 a financial analyst, H. H. Klein, estimated the fortune at $2½ billions, and in the same year B. C. Forbes put the figure at $1.2 billions. In 1927 Stuart Chase, in an article in the *New York Times* (February 13) claimed that the Rockefeller fortune was reduced by gifts to $600,000,-000. This is the lowest estimate ever made, but then Chase was featuring a news angle that the Fords were now the nation's richest (although income tax figures for 1923 showed that Rockefeller, Jr., paid about a 50 percent higher tax than Henry and Edsel Ford combined).

All estimates of the fortune must take into account (a fact often overlooked) that the fortune has been considerably chopped up. It is not all in the hands of the descendants of John D. Rockefeller, Jr. There were three daughters of John D. Rockefeller, Sr., each with children, who received generous amounts from their father—Bessie, who married Charles A. Strong; Alta, who married E. Parmalee Prentice; and Edith, who married Harold F. McCormick; and so the wealth of their descendants must be considered, too, in any total. At the time of the proxy contest to oust Colonel Stewart as head of Indiana Standard, the holdings of stock in the company by the families of the three daughters was actually greater than that held by Rockefeller, Jr., which is an indication as to how much they were left. Then, too, the $75,000,000 that Rockefeller, Jr., left to his widow on his death must be made part of the total.

However conjectural, it is this author's opinion that estimates that have been tossed about for some time of $2 to $2.5 billion for the fortune, or $200 million in the hands of each brother and Mrs. Mauzé, are gross undervaluations, and do not take into account the sensational rise in security prices. An X factor would be the amount of tax-exempt state and municipal securities in the portfolio in order to escape the impact of the 90 percent federal surtax. Tax-exempts would have the effect of keeping the capital value constant, but tax-exempt holdings are small. Thus, allowing for a moderate amount in United States Government bonds purchased during the two wars, the fortune is by and large invested in securities with a view to capital appreciation.

The best method of valuation, albeit a rough one, is that of projection or extrapolation from the $900,000,000 figure at the peak of the 1913 stock market. Here are some relevant facts:

1. Since that time industrial stock prices as measured by the Dow-Jones Industrial Average have leaped from about 90 to 890.

2. The bulk of the fortune undoubtedly remains in oil stocks for the same reasons that the balance sheet of the Rockefeller Foundation shows that most of its assets are in oil stocks. On January 9, 1935, the Securities and Exchange Commission published a report that showed that on November 30, 1934, John D. Rockefeller, Jr., owned 10,181,000 shares in three oil companies, Standard Oil of New Jersey, Standard Oil of California, and Socony-Vacuum, with a market value of $245,000,000. This stupendous sum in only three companies at a time when

the stock market was almost at the depression nadir shows how ridiculously low was the estimate of Stuart Chase.

3. As an example of the heights to which oil stocks have soared, the New York *Times* on August 7, 1955, published a table showing how the original $50,000,000 which John D. Rockefeller, Sr., gave in oil stocks in 1909 to the Rockefeller Foundation, and later withdrew when Congress did not grant the charter, would have grown. The capital value by that date in 1955 (when the Dow-Jones Average was about 500) would have been $743,130,388.12, and that excludes $225,000,000 in cash dividends.

4. I have worked out with stock dividends and stock splits the rise in value of Standard Oil of New Jersey and Standard Oil of Indiana, two prominent stocks in the Rockefeller portfolio, since the peak of 1913, and find that the former has risen 24 times in price and the latter 18 times in price. Standard Oil of New Jersey is by far the heaviest investment that the Rockefellers hold.

5. Totally aside from oil stocks, we know of fantastic appreciation in other securities. Rockefeller, Sr., bought General Motors and International Harvester at their formation. In the modern age the investments in Chrysler and McDonnell Aircraft have been equally fabulous. Rockefeller Center, worth at least $300,000,000, and Pocantico Hills, worth tens of millions, must be added.

With such clues, one can grope in the dark with more assurance than by the use of any other approach, and it would seem that even with gifts and estate taxes and healthy amounts given by the present generation for philanthropic causes the total fortune today must be a minimum of $4 billions.

As great as is the fortune, the controlling force it exerts in American industry today is very small. Of course, the Chase Manhattan is a Rockefeller-controlled bank, (although the Rockefellers own less than 5 percent of the stock), and Laurance Rockefeller controls a handful of growth companies by his rifleshot investments. The fortune today, however, is not concentrated, but is diversified and diffused over many companies and industries. In 1929 John D. Rockefeller, Jr., was able to topple the

management of Indiana Standard, but barely, on a great moral
issue, and the decisive factor was that he was able to mobilize the
stock of old associates of Rockefeller, Sr. Today, those ties have
grown dim. Today, it is highly doubtful that the Rockefellers
could step in to control any of the companies that made up the
famous Rockefeller oil empire, on the basis of existing stockownership.

CHAPTER 28 *Conclusion*

AMONG THE INDUSTRIAL KINGS of the nineteenth century, John
D. Rockefeller holds a preeminent place. The Standard Oil
Company, welded from a conglomeration of small refineries in a
chaotic, cutthroat industry, was a towering achievement. It was
due largely to the drive, determination, and foresight of this one
man who, a hundred years ago, decided that oil was here to stay
as an article of human use and began to build a permanent
.edifice on that basis, while others were sure that he was building
on quicksand.

It was a fabulously profitable company. We have focused only
on the Rockefeller fortune, but there was a Flagler fortune, a
Harkness fortune, a Rogers fortune, a Pratt fortune, a Payne
fortune, and so on. At the same time, besides the individual rewards, even its sternest critics have conceded that the company
by its commercial enterprise and its constant emphasis on new
technology had brought dividends to the general public by making possible cheap, abundant oil available in a large variety of
forms and uses.

Had there been no John D. Rockefeller, the Lord would have
invented one. It is hard to visualize the oil industry continuing
under the anarchic conditions that plagued the bituminous coal
industry for decades. Because the process of consolidation and
centralization in the oil industry paralleled the march toward

larger units, together with the standardization of products that occurred in many other fields, there may have been a higher determinism at work. None the less, all that history tells us is that Rockefeller, with his strong personality and singlemindedness of purpose, did bring it about.

Rockefeller was a leader and catalyzer in the process of shaping the mold of big business. The Standard Oil trust, the first trust, was the prototype for other trusts, giving big business the legal organizational fiction for surmounting the barriers to growth. With his Puritan detestation of waste and gambling, Rockefeller introduced economy and system into an industry that had been conspicuous for the absence of those characteristics, and promoted cost-consciousness in industries that envied the success of Standard Oil. Although the company occupied an almost complete monopoly position, Rockefeller renounced short-term avarice in favor of long-run goodwill, selling an honest product and catering to consumers in many ways. From the beginning he saw the prime importance of brainpower, and bought his competitors' best brains as well as their oil works; he encouraged his executives to *think* in new ways, *ad maiorem lucrum* of Standard Oil, delegating less strenuous work to others. When asked for the success of Standard Oil, Rockefeller answered without hesitation, "The ability of my associates."

Though specialization had been the vogue, and was considered the alpha and omega of business success, the oil trust developed an amazing diversity of operations, branching into many functions and enterprises, a tactic that put the company on a sounder footing economically. As the operations in oil extended vertically by integration, the trust owned its wells at the source and sold the end product at wholesale and retail, transporting oil through its own pipelines, by its tankers at sea, and by its own tank wagons on the streets of cities, even in foreign countries. It conducted its own banking and brokerage business. Emphasis by the trust on high-level administrative teamwork called for introduction of the committee system into business, now the bane of all bureaucracy. These are some, but not all, of the facets of the new look Standard Oil gave to American industry, pioneering operations in big business that were to be widely studied and copied.

Many of Rockefeller's techniques do not seem profound or

startling. To an uncomplicated mind, they were the simplistic conceptions of the shortest distance between two points, pursued with persistence, which is the formula for success in many fields. The sagacious Dr. Samuel Johnson once remarked, "Trade could not be managed by those who do manage it if it presented much difficulty." And yet in the latter half of the nineteenth century, a period of tumultuous expansion in business, when it seemed impossible to lose, most did lose, including some of Rockefeller's hapless competitors.

In retrospect, it is hard to understand the rancor generated against Rockefeller because of the competitors he ground down in the march toward unification. They were certainly as piratical as he in their ambitions, and many were bought out by him at exorbitant prices. Many, before they fell by the wayside, had milked the public for golden profits; and, since they were less efficient, they were weeded out in a good cause. Today, when we are accustomed to the idea of overriding public necessity and thinking in terms of the highest socio-economic good, hundreds on hundreds of small businesses are uprooted and perish because of an urban renewal project in lower Manhattan or because of the building of a superhighway, and not a tear is shed, nor is any note made of it in the press.

Yet the public's fear of the trust becomes more understandable in retrospect. Big business was a new and unfamiliar phenomenon. The theory that the small manufacturer and artisan were, like the farmer, the bulwark of the country, and the idea that all good to the consumer and the public at large came from free, unrestricted competition were part of embedded popular belief. The trust was the Devil incarnate to such concepts. Moreover, the trust arrived on the scene at an unwelcome time, in a period of deflation when agricultural prices were falling by more than half between 1873 and 1896, and when wages were being ground down because of an influx of millions of immigrants who were willing to work for mere subsistence but who at the same time furnished an increased market for consumer goods, notably illuminating oil. The spectacle of a trust whose main function seemed to be to gouge greater profits by holding up prices, rewarding not only producers but promoters and manipulators, was abhorrent to most Americans. The stories sensationalized by

Lloyd and Miss Tarbell about helpless victims gobbled up by the oil trust channeled public resentment against Rockefeller, making him the butt and whipping boy for a more generalized hostility.

John D. Rockefeller's simplistic conceptions of business were carried over to his philanthropy. He gave because "God gave me my money," and thus he owed a reciprocal obligation. In his practical credo, philanthropy, without undermining individual enterprise, should attack the ills that beset mankind—disease, ignorance, poverty—by enlisting the initiative and enthusiasm of others to enable such projects to become self-sufficient and to grow in scope. Again, as in his business, he put emphasis on the brainpower of those who were to be the administrators. His son recalled that his father once told him, "John, we have the money but it will have value for mankind only as we find able men with ideas, imagination and courage to put it to productive use." The success of the philanthropies has been largely due to the group of able men that were found to administer them.

Philanthropy to Rockefeller was dictated by an inner voice; it was not a response to external pressures. The prevalent belief to the contrary conforms to the pattern of a morality play—man sins, man repents, man gives away money, and seeks forgiveness. Because this old-wives' tale suits the public fancy, it will continue to be believed despite this book or any book; but all the evidence shows it to be false. It would fail on the primary premise alone, since Rockefeller was never aware of any sin or dereliction on his part. He repelled all suggestions to use gifts to win goodwill, which never interested him much anyway. He gave generously long before he was accused of sin, and he gave generously after he had retired from Standard Oil and did not have to give a tinker's damn for public opinion, which had by that time done its damage by destroying the trust he had so laboriously built.

There can be no suspicion of ulterior motivation in the philanthropies carried on by Rockefeller, Jr., since his whole career was one of dedication to the public good. Once when Abby Rockefeller was asked where her husband was, she replied: "I don't know. He's out somewhere trying to save the world." Indeed, that was his mission in life.

Though we have not had in our modern society a concept of *richesse oblige* to match the *noblesse oblige* of the feudalistic society of the Middle Ages, certainly the Rockefeller family has done most to exemplify it. In the third generation the tradition of philanthropy, good works, and a sense of responsibility for riches has been preserved. There has as yet been no case of what Frederick Gates feared, "scandalous results to descendants."

And what of the future? Asked this question, Laurance Rockefeller replied, "The one certainty is that there will be a diffusion of wealth and responsibility"—indeed, upon the horizon is the fourth generation, the twenty grandchildren of John D. Rockefeller, Jr. Whether the same cohesion in family purpose and teamwork will be preserved is problematical. Though the economic power of the individual will be lessened, from the proliferation of the family may spring a greater abundance of ideas, which will result in a richer contribution to American life.

Certainly, the tall, serious-looking boy of sixteen who during the summer of 1855 trudged the hot streets of Cleveland, looking for a job, has bequeathed an invaluable legacy to the nation and to the world.

SI MONUMENTUM REQUIRIS, CIRCUMSPICE

BIBLIOGRAPHY

There are a number of basic sources. The most valuable are the two-volume work by Allan Nevins, *John D. Rockefeller: The Heroic Age of American Enterprise*, Scribner's (1940), and the two-volume work *Study in Power: John D. Rockefeller, Industrialist and Philanthropist*, Scribner's (1953), because they contain the Rockefeller papers, which have been relied on heavily by me for this study. They also contain the results of Rockefeller's extensive conversations with William O. Inglis.

Though it gained a reputation as a polemic, Ida M. Tarbell's *The History of the Standard Oil Company*, McClure, Phillips (1904), is for the most part a factual account of the birth and development of the oil industry, and is therefore an indispensable source for any research in this subject. From the standpoint of scholarship and reliability, it is far superior to *Wealth Against Commonwealth* by Henry Demarest Lloyd, Harper & Brothers (1894). Nonetheless, Lloyd's book is an accurate reflection of what Rockefeller's opponents thought and said about him and about Standard Oil. An interesting debate on the Lloyd bias is found in the *American Historical Review* for October 1944 and April 1955, the disputants being Professor Nevins and Professor Chester McArthur Destler, the discussion incidentally showing the extreme partisanship of Professor Nevins for Rockefeller.

An answer of sorts to the Tarbell book was Rockefeller's *Random Reminiscences of Men and Events*, Doubleday, Page (1909), an excellent source for an understanding of Rockefeller's viewpoints.

The best technical history of the oil industry I have found is *The American Petroleum Industry* by Harold F. Williamson and Arnold R. Daum, Northwestern University Press (1959).

The first comprehensive biography of Rockefeller was *God's Gold* by John T. Flynn, Harcourt, Brace (1932), and is particularly valuable because Flynn did considerable research on Rockefeller's early life and by his own account had the collaboration of W. O. Inglis.

For the later period, the outstanding work is *John D. Rockefeller, Jr.: A Portrait* by Raymond B. Fosdick, Harper (1956), which has also some interesting new material on Rockefeller, Sr.

In 1955 there appeared *Pioneering in Big Business,* an exhaustive history of the Standard Oil Company from its inception until dissolution of the trust in 1911, the authors being Ralph W. and Muriel E. Hidy (Harper). For this painstaking study which emphasized the development of internal technical and managerial know-how the Standard Oil Company opened its archives and records without restrictions.

There were two governmental investigations that are basic sources because they brought to light the vital facts about the development of the Standard Oil monopoly. For the earlier period we have the Hepburn Committee Investigation of 1879, the Special Committee on Railroads appointed under the Resolution of the New York State Assembly on February 28, 1879. For the later period we have the hearings before the Industrial Commission on Trusts and Industrial Combinations authorized by Congress in 1898, which were held in Washington, D.C. Other valuable documents are the proceedings and report of the House Committee on Manufactures, relating to the Standard Oil Trust (1888), and the briefs filed by the government and Standard Oil in United States *vs.* Standard Oil (1909). Other books I have used for this book follow:

Allen, William H. *Rockefeller: Giant, Dwarf, Symbol.* Institute of Public Service, N.Y. (1930).

Bacon, Raymond Foss, and W. A. Hamor. *The American Petroleum Industry.* McGraw-Hill (1916).

Beard, Charles A., and Mary R. *The Rise of American Civilization.* Macmillan (1927).

Bonham, John M. *Railway Secrecy and Trusts.* Putnam (1890).

Brandeis, Louis D. *The Curse of Bigness.* Viking (1934).

Brown, Marcus M. *A Study of John D. Rockefeller.* Published by the author in Cleveland (1905).

Burr, A. R. *Portrait of a Banker: James Stillman.* Duffield (1927).

Butt, Archibald W. *Taft and Roosevelt: Intimate Letters of Archie Butt.* Doubleday, Doran (1930).

Carnegie, Andrew. *Autobiography.* Houghton Mifflin (1920).

Carr, Albert Z. *John D. Rockefeller's Secret Weapon.* McGraw-Hill (1962).

Chamberlain, John. *The Enterprising Americans.* Harper and Row (1963).

Childs, Marquis, and Douglas Cater. *Ethics in a Business Society.* Harper (1954).

Clews, Henry. *Fifty Years in Wall Street.* Irving Publishing (1908).

Cochran, Thomas C. *The Age of Enterprise.* Macmillan (1942).

Crawford, William L. *Crawford on Baileyism—Story of the Alliance Between Standard Oil and Sen. Bailey*. Dallas, Texas, Eclectic News Bureau (1907).

Croffut, W. A. *The Vanderbilts and the Story of Their Fortune*. Belford, Clarke (1886).

Croly, H. A. *Marcus Alonzo Hanna*. Macmillan (1912).

Day, James R. *The Raid on Prosperity*. Appleton (1908).

De Kruif, Paul. *The Seven Iron Men*. Harcourt, Brace (1929).

Desmond, James. *Nelson Rockefeller: A Political Portrait*. Macmillan (1964).

Dodd, Samuel C. T. "Memoirs." Written for his children and friends, mimeographed copy in Library of Congress.

———. *Combinations: Their Uses and Abuses*. Nesbitt (1888).

Dolson, Hildegarde. *The Great Oildorado*. Random (1959).

Dunne, Philip, editor. *Mr. Dooley Remembers: The Informal Memoirs of Finley Peter Dunne*. Atlantic-Little, Brown (1963).

Engelbrecht, Curt E. *Neighbor John: Intimate Glimpses of John D. Rockefeller*. The Telegraphic Press (1936).

Finch, James A., editor. *Bills and Debates in Congress Relating to Trusts*. U.S. Government Printing Office. (1903).

Forbes, B. C. *Men Who Are Making America*. Forbes (1917).

Foraker, Joseph B. *Notes of a Busy Life*. Stewart and Kidd (1916).

Foraker, Julia B. *I Would Live It Again: Memories of a Vivid Life*. Harper (1932).

Fosdick, Raymond B. *The Story of the Rockefeller Foundation*. Harper (1952).

———. *Adventure in Giving: The Story of the General Education Board*. Harper and Row (1962).

Gates, Frederick T. *The Truth About Mr. Rockefeller and the Merritts*. Knickerbocker Press (1897).

Giddens, Paul. *Early Days of Oil*. Princeton (1948).

Goodspeed, Thomas W. *The Story of the University of Chicago, 1890–1925*. University of Chicago (1925).

———. *William Rainey Harper*. University of Chicago (1928).

Hacker, L. M. and B. B. Kendrick. "The United States Since 1865." Crofts (1932).

Hager, Dorsey. *Fundamentals of the Petroleum Industry*. McGraw-Hill (1938).

Harrar, J. George. *The Agricultural Program of the Rockefeller Foundation*. Rockefeller Foundation (1956).

Hendrick, Burton J. *The Age of Big Business*. Yale (1919).

Henry, James Dodd. *History and Romance of the Petroleum Industry.* Bradbury, Agnew, London (1914).

Hobson, J. A. *The Evolution of Modern Capitalism.* Rev. ed. Scribner (1926).

Hofstadter, Richard. *The American Political Tradition and the Men Who Made It.* Knopf (1948).

Josephson, Matthew. *The Robber Barons.* Harcourt, Brace (1934).

Lawson, Thomas W. *Frenzied Finance.* Ridgway-Mayer (1905).

Leonard, Charles C., under name of Crocus. *History of Pithole.* Morton, Longwell (1867).

Lloyd, Caro. *Henry Demarest Lloyd.* Putnam's (1912).

Lorant, Stephen. *The Life and Times of Theodore Roosevelt.* Doubleday (1959).

Lyons, Peter. *Success Story: The Life and Times of S. S. McClure.* Scribner (1963).

MacPherson, Logan G. *Railroad Freight Rates in Relation to the Commerce and Industry of the United States.* Holt (1909).

Manchester, William. *A Rockefeller Family Portrait: From John D. to Nelson.* Little, Brown (1959).

Manning, Thomas G. *The Standard Oil Company: The Rise of a National Monopoly.* Holt, Rinehart and Winston (1962).

Martin, Sidney. *Florida's Flagler.* University of Georgia (1949).

Montague, Gilbert H. *The Rise and Progress of the Standard Oil Company.* Harper (1904).

Moody, John. *Masters of Capital.* Yale (1919).

Morris, Joe Alex. *Nelson Rockefeller: A Political Portrait.* Harper (1960).

———. *Those Rockefeller Brothers.* Harper (1953).

Mowry, George E. *The Era of Theodore Roosevelt: 1900–1912.* Harper (1958).

Myers, Gustavus. *History of the Great American Fortunes.* Kerr (1910).

Newhall, Nancy. *Contribution to the Heritage of Every American: The Conservation Activities of John D. Rockefeller, Jr.* Knopf (1957).

O'Day, John Christopher. *Oil Wells in the Woods.* Deposit, N.Y. Oquaga (1905).

Peto, Sir Samuel Morton. *Resources and Prospects of America.* Strahan and Lippincott (1866).

Pringle, Henry. *Theodore Roosevelt.* Harcourt, Brace (1931).

———. *The Life and Times of William Howard Taft.* Farrar & Rinehart (1939).

Ripley, William Z. *Railway Problems*. Ginn, rev. ed. (1916).

———. *Trusts, Pools and Corporations*. Ginn, rev. ed. (1916).

Rose, William Ganson. *Cleveland: the Making of a City*. World Publishing (1950).

Rostow, Eugene W. *A National Policy for the Oil Industry*. Yale (1948).

Shaplen, Robert. *Toward the Well-Being of Mankind: Fifty Years of the Rockefeller Foundation*. Doubleday (1964).

Sinclair, Upton. *The Brass Check: A Study in American Journalism*. Published by the author (1920).

Stocking, George W. *The Oil Industry and the Competitive System: A Study in Waste*. Houghton Mifflin (1925).

Sullivan, Mark. *Our Times*. Scribner, particularly *America Finding Itself*. (1927) and *Pre-War America*. (1930).

Sumners, Festus. *Johnson Newlon Camden: A Study in Individualism*. Putnam (1937).

Swanberg, W. A. *Citizen Hearst: A Biography of William Randolph Hearst*. Scribner (1961).

Tawney, R. H. *Religion and the Rise of Capitalism*. Harcourt, Brace (1926).

Veblen, Thorstein. *The Theory of Business Enterprise*. Scribner (1904).

———. *Absentee Ownership and Business Enterprise in Recent Times*. Viking (1923).

Washburn, Benjamin C. "As I recall the Hookworm Campaign Initiated by the Rockefeller Sanitary Commission." Rockefeller Foundation (1960).

Winkler, John K. *John D.: A Portrait in Oils*. Vanguard (1929).

———. *Morgan, the Magnificent*. Vanguard (1930).

While it is impossible to list all the newspaper and magazine sources that were used by me, the following articles deserve mention as being the most useful:

Briggs, H. M. "Impressions of Rockefeller." *American Magazine* (Nov. 1910).

Camden, J. N. "The Standard Oil Company." *North American Review* (Oct. 1883).

Cousins, Norman. Review of Nevins' *John D. Rockefeller: The Heroic Age of American Enterprise*. *Saturday Review of Literature* (Oct. 26, 1940).

Destler, Chester McArthur. "The Standard Oil, Child of the Erie Ring." *Mississippi Valley Historical Review* (June 1946).

Doubleday, F. N. "Impressions of Rockefeller." *World's Work* (September 1908).

Du Bois, Peter C. "Unshaken Confidence." An article about the investments of Laurance S. Rockefeller, *Barron's Financial Weekly* (June 24, 1963).

Flynn, John. "Col. Stewart and the Standard Oil of Indiana." *Outlook* Feb. 20, 1929).

Galantière, Louis. "John D., An Academy Portrait." *New Republic* (Dec. 9, 1940).

Gates, Frederick T. "Memoirs." *American Heritage* (April 1955).

Harrar, J. George. "New Ventures for Private Philanthropy." *New York Times Magazine* (June 9,1963).

Mencken, H. L. "John, the Baptist." *American Mercury* (Dec. 1932).

Rogers, G. D. "Recollections of John D." *Saturday Evening Post* (Oct. 21, 1921).

Smith, Richard Austin. "The Rockefeller Brothers, Grandsons of JDR." *Fortune* (Feb., March 1955.)

Tarbell, Ida M. "John D. Rockefeller." *McClure's Magazine* (July-Aug. 1905).

——. "Rockefeller versus Roosevelt." *American Magazine* (Dec. 1907, Jan. 1908).

Trowbridge, J. T. "A Carpetbagger in Pennsylvania." *Atlantic Monthly* (June 1869).

Unwin, T. F. "The Great Oil Octopus." *Truth* (London, 1911).

Wilson, Sloan. "The Octopus." *New Yorker* (June 9, 1946; Sept. 27, 1947).

Winston, Ambrose Parè. "Public Opinion and the Standard Oil." *Bulletin of the Washington University Association* (April 1908).

Woodbury, Charles. "Rockefeller and the Standard Oil Company." *Saturday Evening Post* (Oct. 21, 1911).

INDEX

Rockefeller, Nelson, 300, 312-14, 341
 birth of, 341
 personal characteristics of, 343
 private career of, 354-56
 on Standard Oil, 342
Rockefeller, Steven, 300
Rockefeller, William, 19, 22, 27, 72
 death of, 295
 enters oil industry, 46-47
 in Standard Oil, 64, 140, 149, 219,
 272
 in Wall Street, 221, 251
Rockefeller, William Avery, 19, 20,
 33
 character of, 21-23, 29
 indicted for rape, 23-24
 later life of, 44-45
Rockefeller, Winthrop, 341, 343, 348
 career of, 350-54
Rockefeller, Winthrop Paul, 351
Rockefeller, Andrews & Flagler
 formed, 49
 rebates and rise of, 65-66
 reorganized as Standard Oil, 64
Rockefeller and Andrews, 46
Rockefeller and Company, 47
Rockefeller (William) and Company, 46-47
Rockefeller Brothers, Inc., 344, 347
Rockefeller Brothers Fund, Inc., 344,
 347
Rockefeller Center, 312-14, 347, 354
Rockefeller Foundation, 328-40
 Division of Social Sciences, 328,
 335
 establishment of, 292-94
 present assets of, 340, 344, 357
 recent work of, 335-40
 Rockefeller, Jr., in, 293, 346
 Rockefeller, 3rd, in, 346
Rockefeller Institute, 22, 288-89,
 308, 328, 332
Rockefeller (Laura Spelman) Me-
 morial, 328, 330
Rockefeller Public Service Awards,
 346

Rockefeller Sanitary Commission,
 291-92, 330
Rogers, George D., 44, 167, 171
Rogers, Henry H., 74, 79, 186, 272
 background of, 154
 in Standard Oil, 108, 153-54, 161,
 245, 256
 indicted, 193
 Tarbell and, 250
 in Wall Street, 220-21, 251
Rogers, Will, 302
Roosevelt, Theodore, 211, 243, 263-
 264, 307-8
 antitrust policy of, 246-47, 252-
 53, 261, 264
 "muckraking" and, 225-26
 "war chest" for, 254
Rose, Dr. Wickliffe, 317, 330
Rothschild, Baron Alphonse de, 163
Rouse, Henry, 15
Rouseville, Pa., 15, 131
Rudd, Mary Ann, see Rockefeller,
 Mary Ann
Ruml, Beardsley, 328
Rusk, Dean, 329
Russian oil, 163-65

Sage, Russell, 91-92
Sargent, John Singer, xi
Satterfield, John, 150, 230
Scheide, W. T., 101, 110
Schell, William P., 148
Schwab, Charles, 168
Schofield, Schurmer, and Teagle,
 113-15, 203, 255
Scott, Thomas, 61, 69, 126, 145, 265
 South Improvement Plan and, 71-
 72, 80
 in war against Rockefeller, 121,
 124
Sears, Mrs. Barbara "Bobo," 351
Seneca Oil Company, 9-11
Sewell, William Joyce, 241
Sherman, John, 48, 239-40
Sherman, Roger, 65